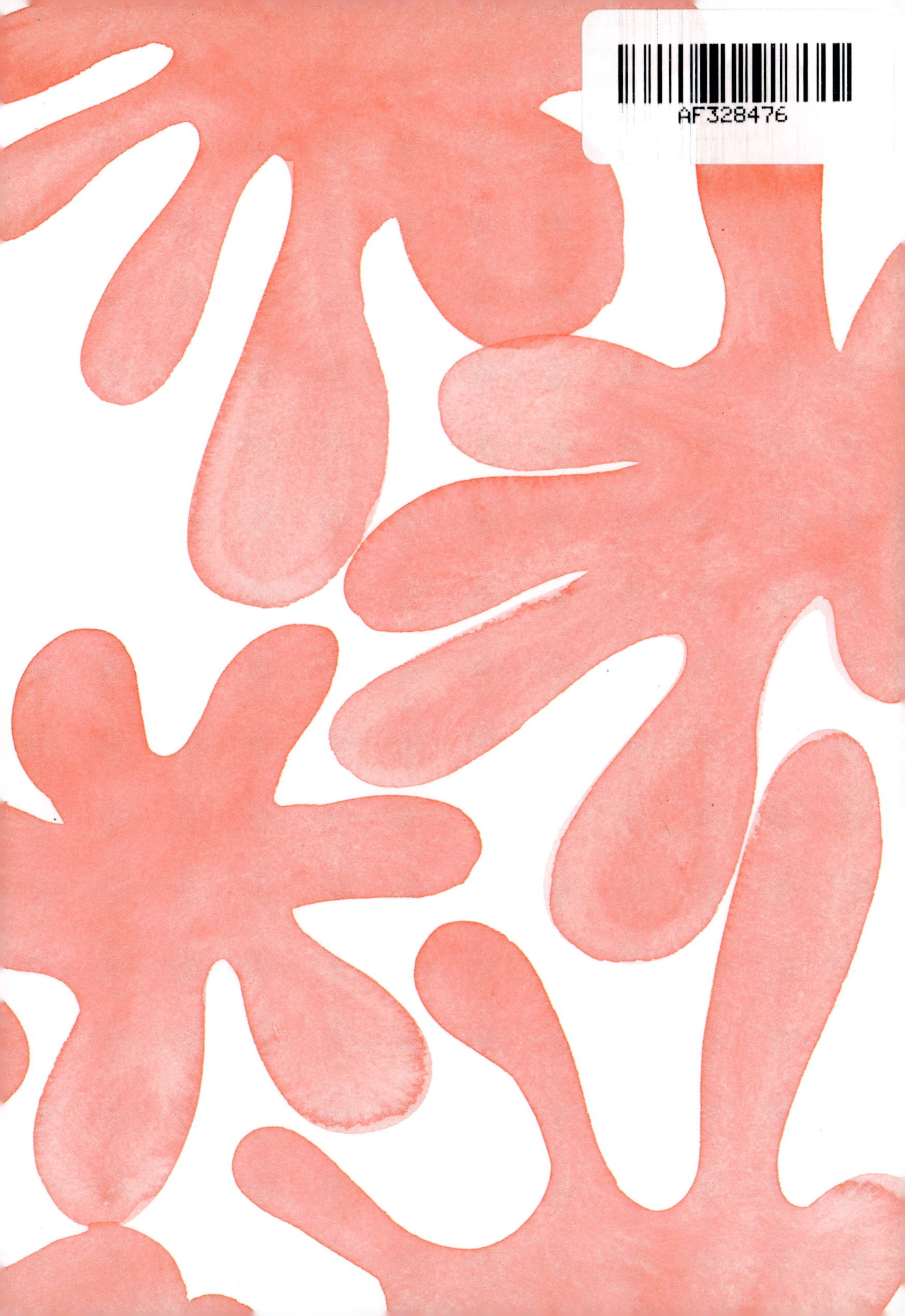
AF328476

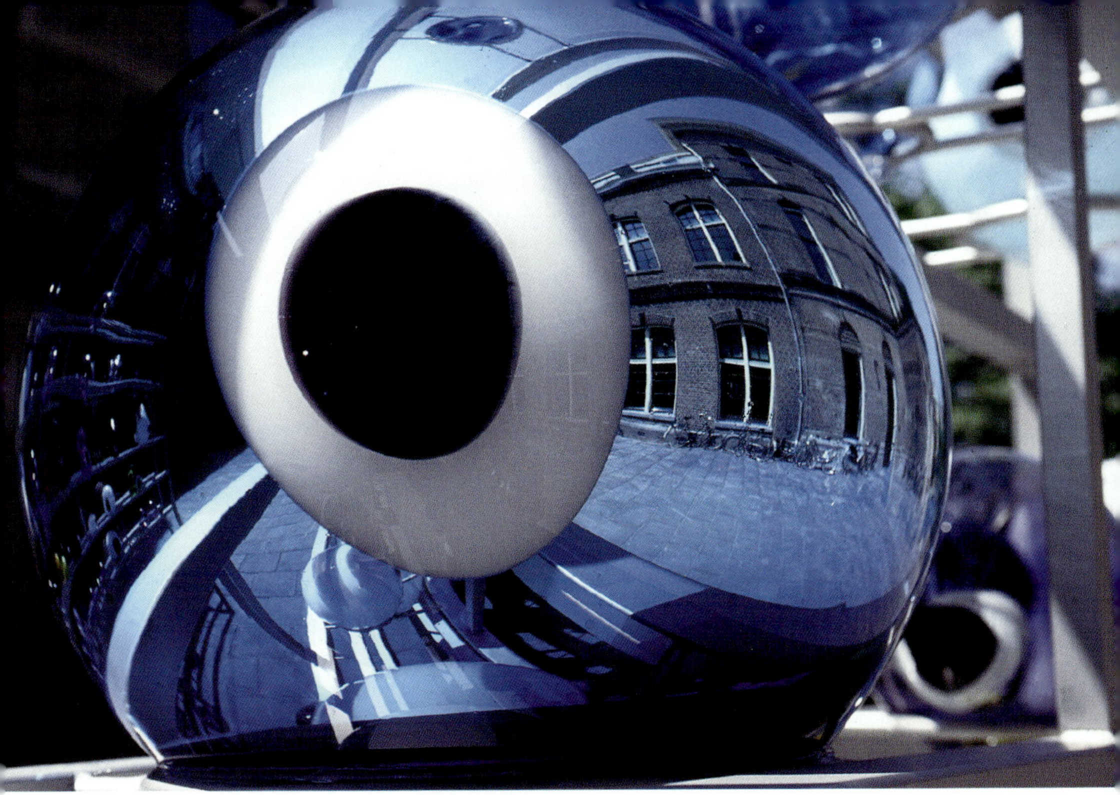

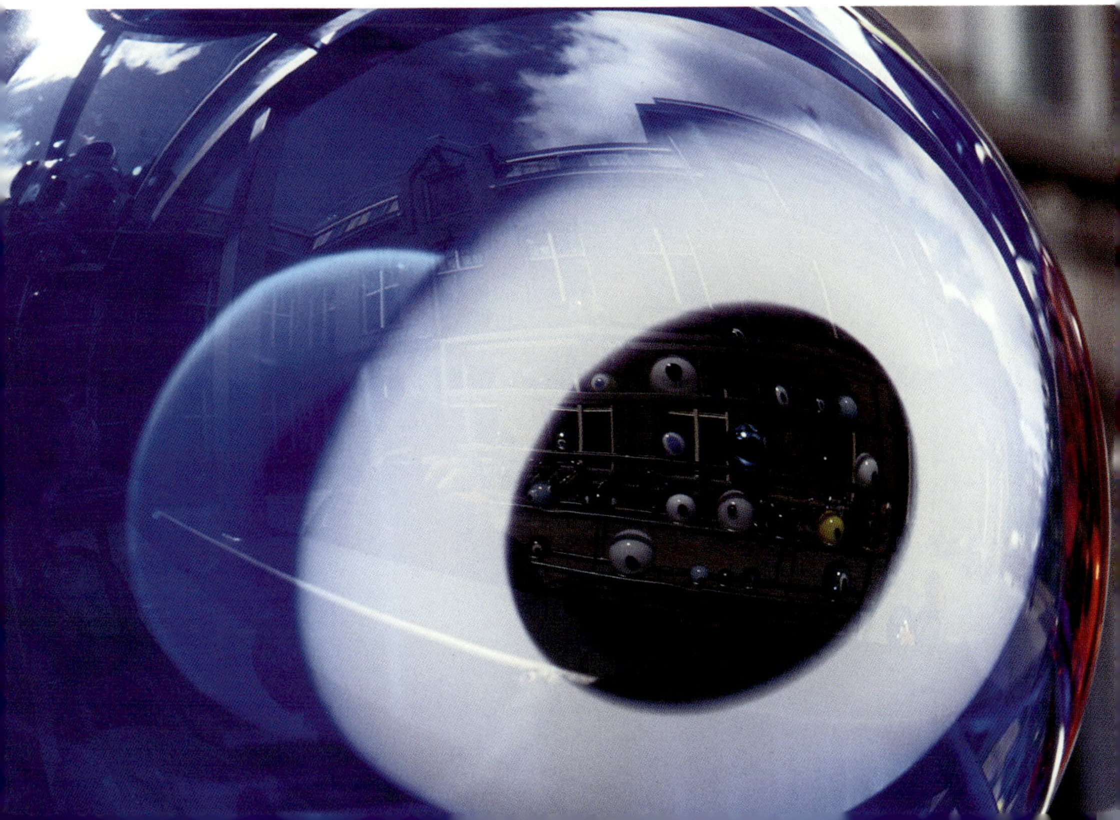

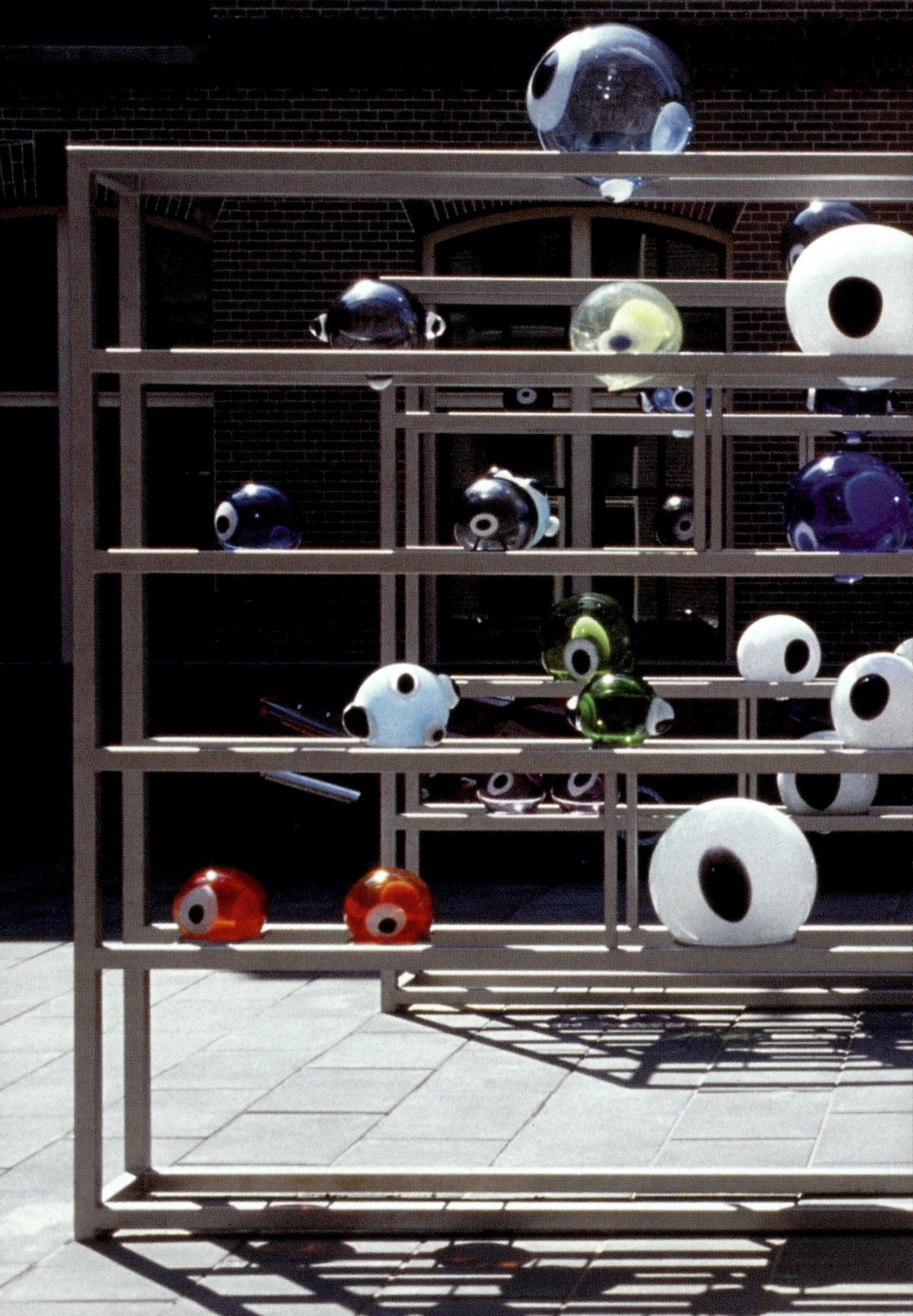

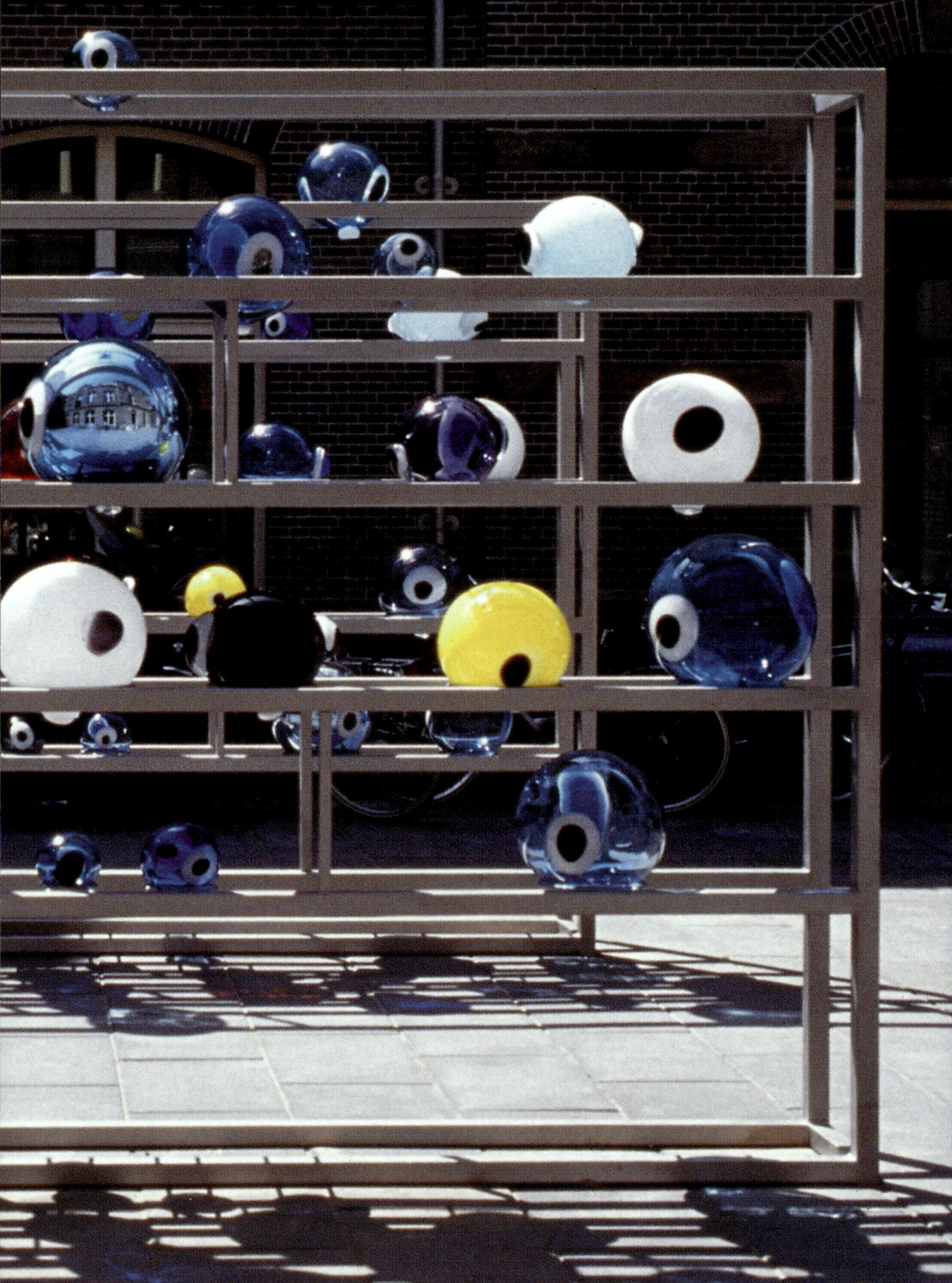

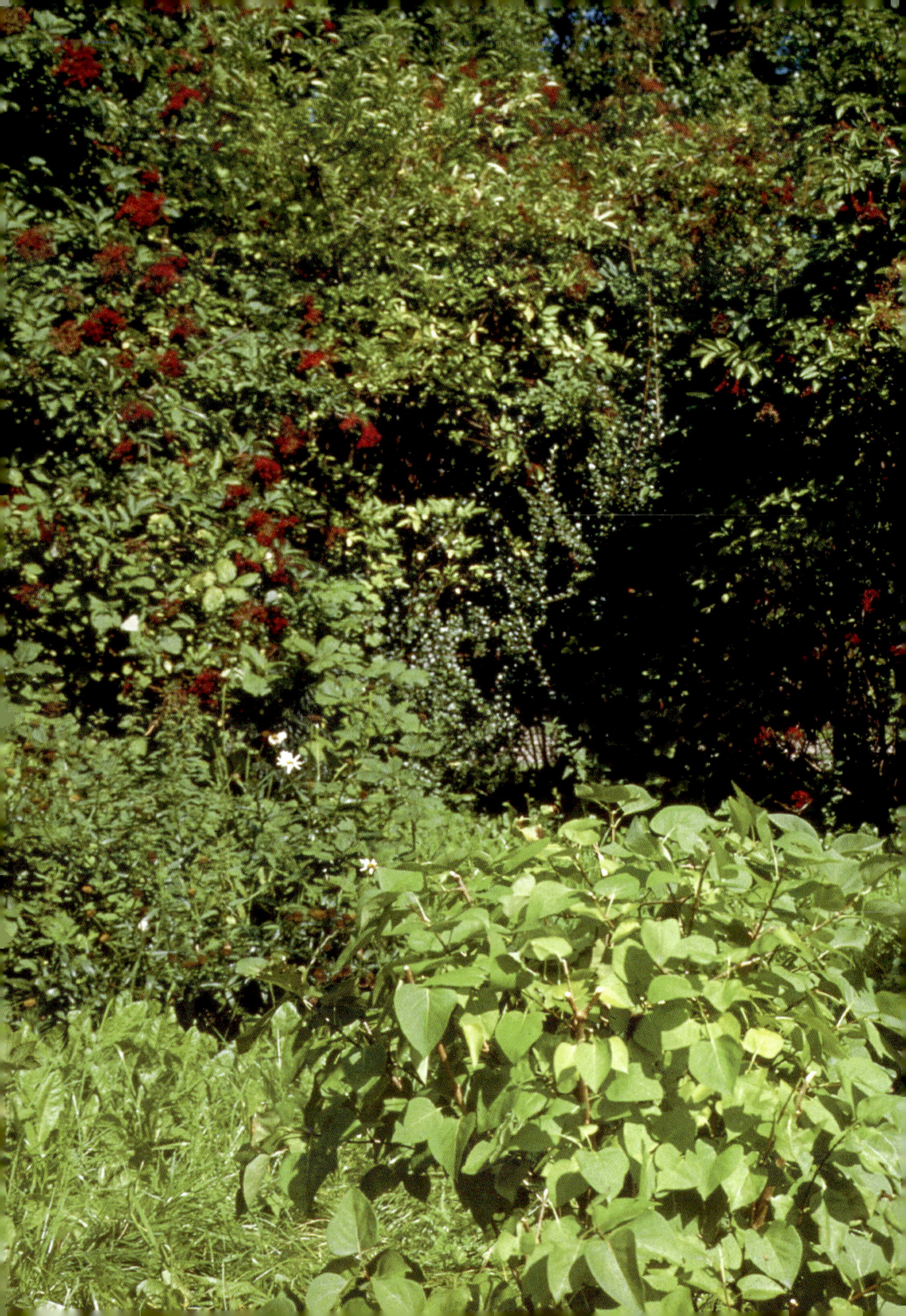

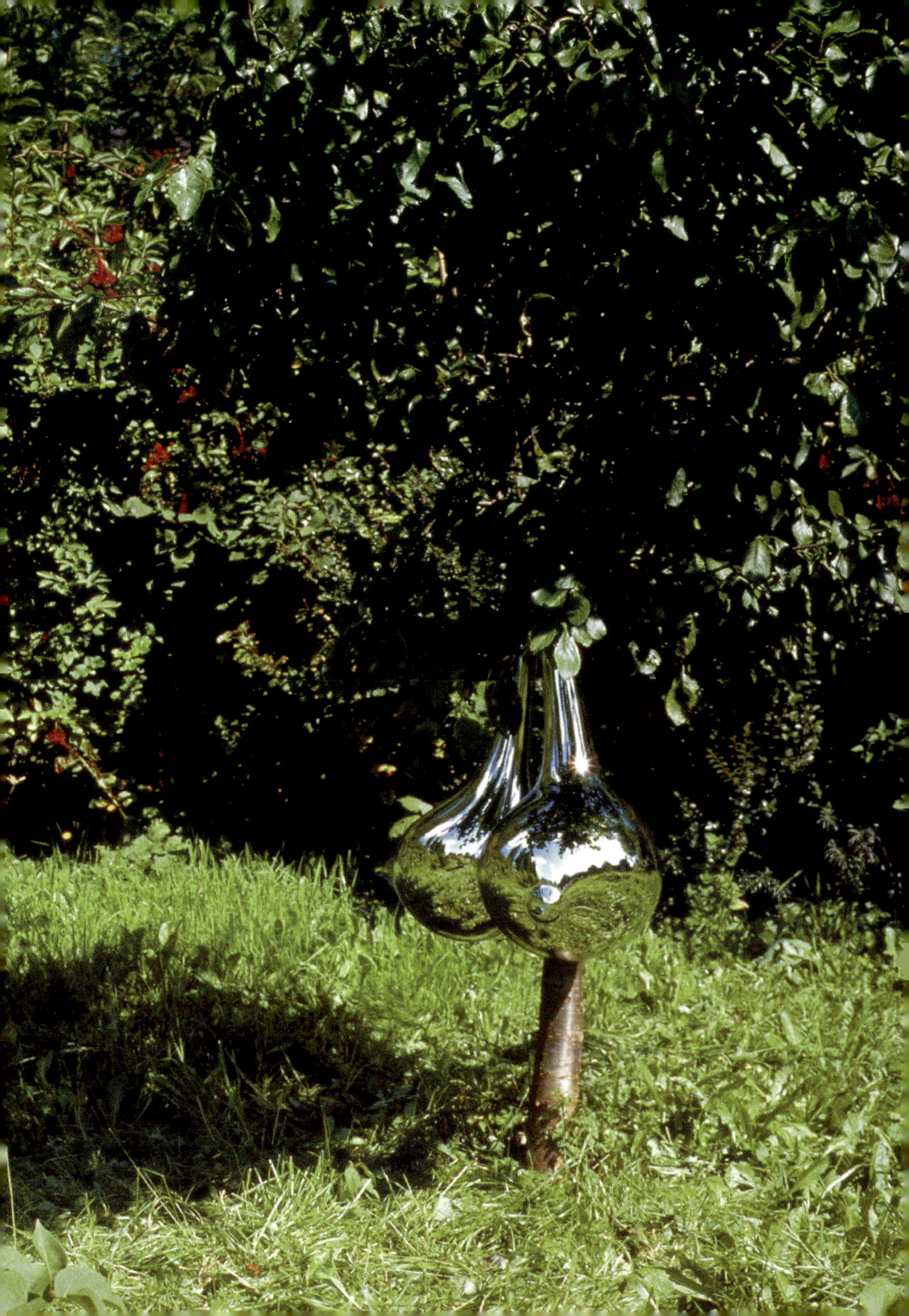

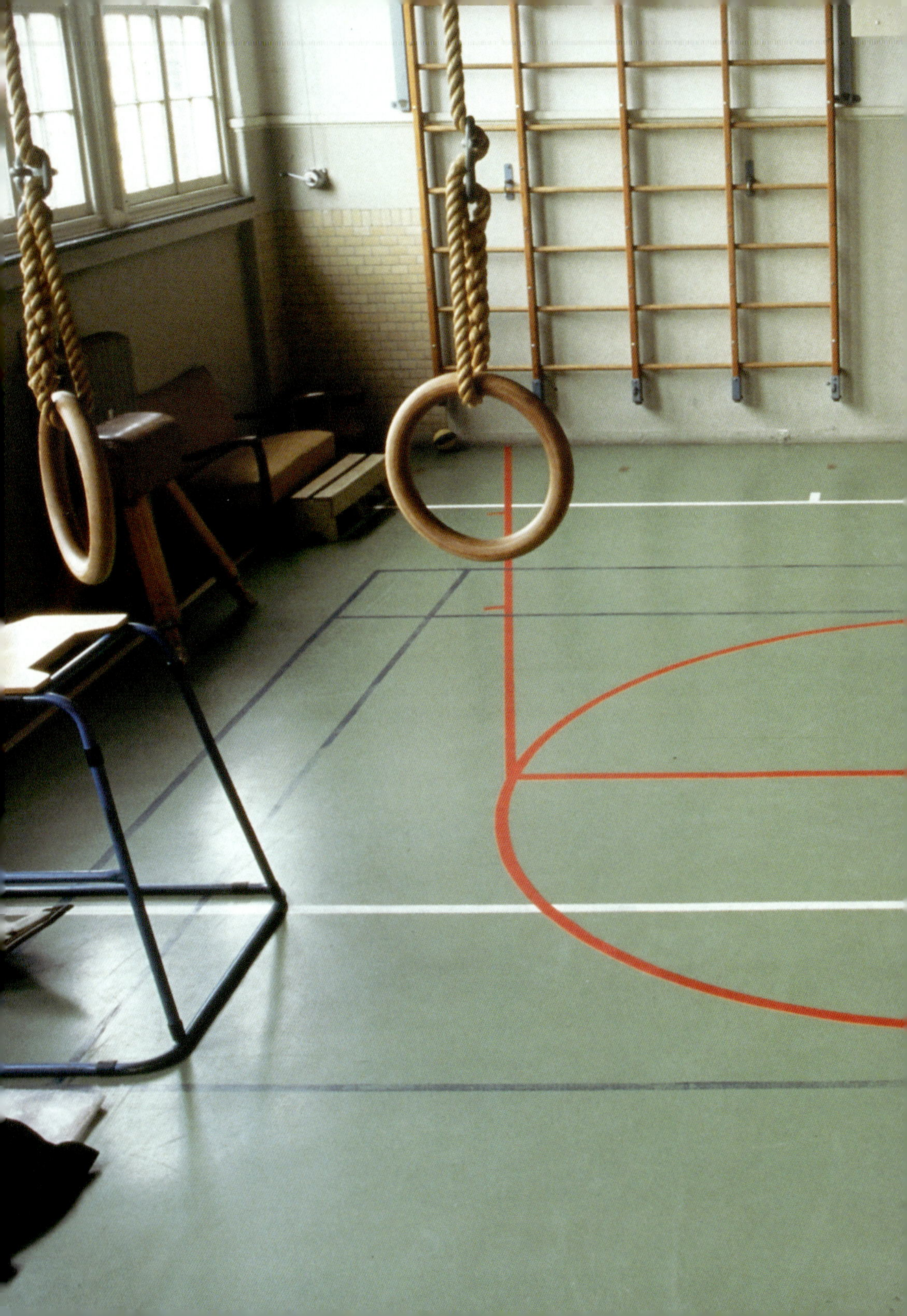

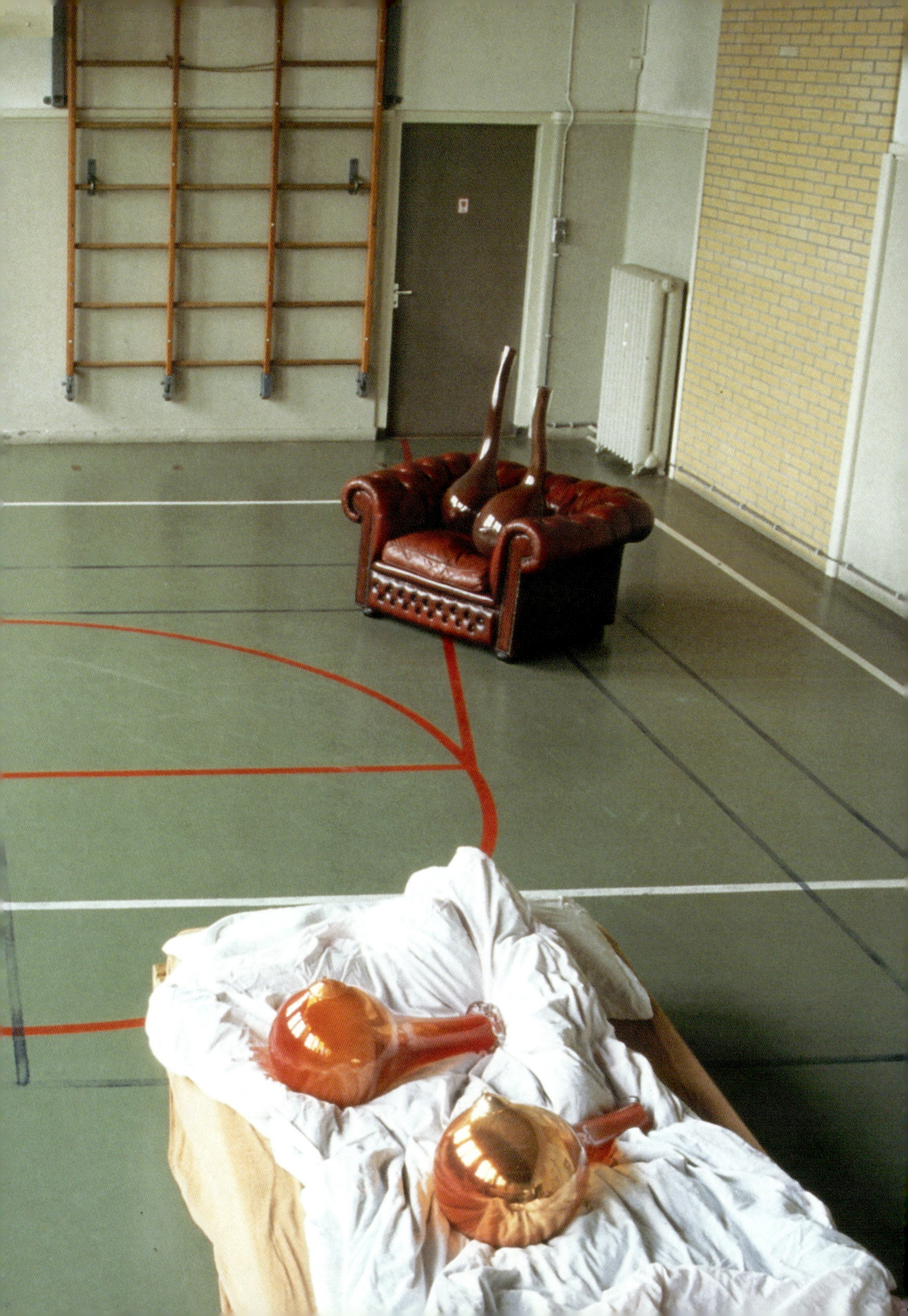

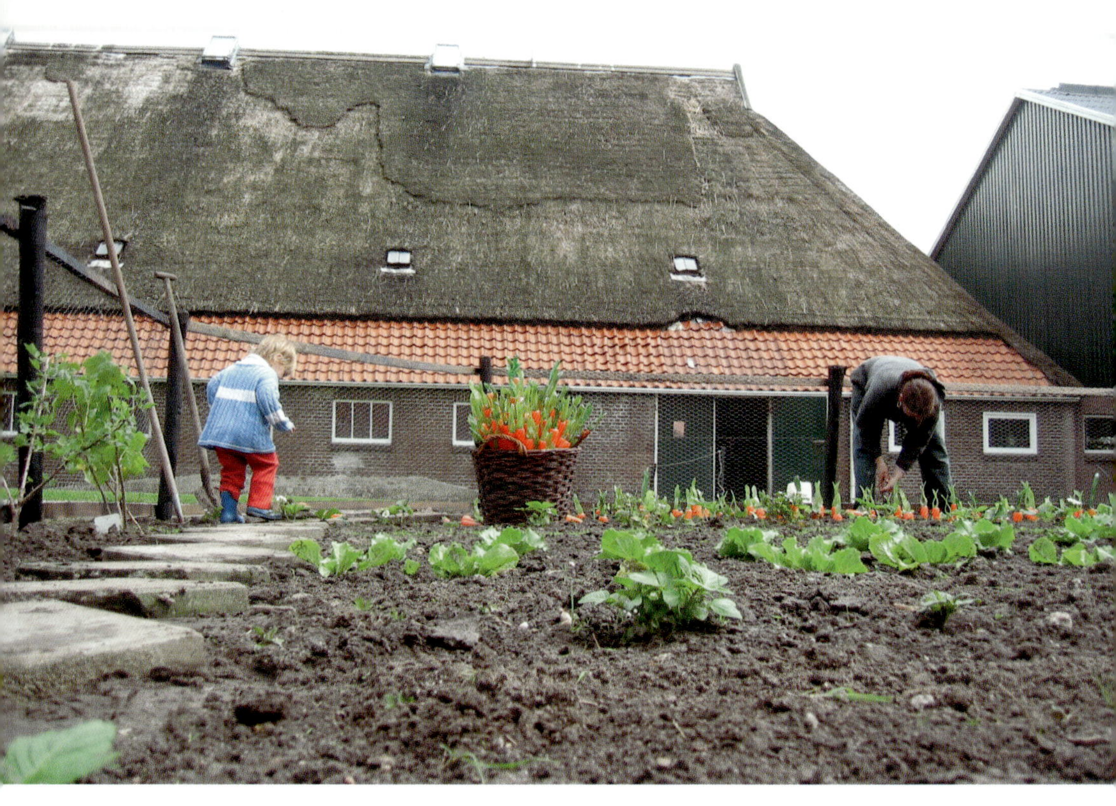

Maria's

Hans den Hartog Jager

It is a cold winter morning at the beginning of March, the day after the heaviest snowstorm in the Netherlands in the last twenty years. The woods around Arnhem have turned into an ice palace; the deep layer of snow reflects so much light that Maria Roosen's studio is bathed in a beautiful heavenly brilliance. Maria lays her arms on the table and leans forwards. 'An old blackberry picker once lived in a cottage deep in the wood', she says. 'He has never seen anybody else in his whole life. Then, one day, a man who has lost his way knocks on his door. The blackberry picker is astonished: "Hey, you look exactly the same as I do!" The man laughs and says: "Do you live here?" "Oh yes", the blackberry picker replies, "it's so beautiful here! I have fields full of pearls, rooms full of mirrors, and very high buildings with columns." The man hurries back to his village and says: "I've met somebody who is so rich that he is surrounded by treasures, but doesn't realise it." The villagers flock en masse to the wood – but the pearls turn out to be dewdrops, the mirrors pools, and the columns trees. They are so enraged with the blackberry picker that they kill him.' She leans back, pensively.

Is it a classic fairy-tale?

'I know it from Godfried Bomans. But I don't know which work it's from.'

Is it a parable about your own work?

'Well, I think it's a pity that there is so little space for imagination in the world. Everything has to be so literal, so one-to-one. You see it in society, in politics, re-enactment is now starting to find its way into art There's no room for people to get lost, there are no places to hide.'

Just as I am about to ask whether her oeuvre is a haven like that, the phone rings. With a gesture which says 'that's exactly what I mean', Roosen walks away – she is waiting for a transport that cannot wait. It is only now that I see that the studio is filled with Roosen's own work, not work in progress, but finished work. On top of a filing cabinet are six glass doves that she has recently had made by a Venetian master blower. Lumps of pink glass lie on the floor. A big salmon-pink milk jug with a glass carrot inside it. Packaged watercolours. And on the ground there is a part of the series of photographs that she has been cutting out of newspapers since 1985: dozens of 'winners', people who express their joy in front of the camera – carefree, happy, euphoric. Sport is well represented (footballers and skaters, Anky van Grunsven), Oscar-winning actors, politicians like Gorbachev and Clinton, but also Henry the Eighth, painted by

9

Hans Holbein, and Matthias Grünewald's crucified Christ. Suddenly I realise that Roosen's studio is actually more of a storage depot than a workshop, more of a showroom than a studio.

When Maria returns, she walks straight to the table with photographs of her work. She picks up a photo of a mother and child in a vegetable garden. The garden looks like any garden, the farm can be seen in the background, but that makes the carrots in the ground all the more striking – their heads shine as though they have been touched by a fairy. 'This is what I mean by imagination', Roosen says. 'A few years ago I was invited to do a project on a farm. I had hundreds of bright orange glass carrots in my studio, which had been used in a play. I thought: I'll plant them in a vegetable garden, that must be a pretty sight. It turned out that the farm did not have a vegetable garden at all, but they had a great time making one. They did it beautifully with lettuce and leeks and a fence to keep the rabbits out – and I planted the carrots in between them.' She smiles. 'It turned out to work very well. Quite a lot of the carrots disappeared – stolen. That's how it works. If you display something beautiful and stimulate the imagination, even glass carrots turn into gold.'

Which brings us to the core of Roosen's work, for that stimulation of the imagination, sometimes gently, sometimes less gently, has been her trade mark for more than fifteen years. Not that you can immediately pin her down to a fixed style or fixed form. In her own words, Roosen is a 'searching' artist who always wants to find the right material, the right form for each idea. In the early 1990s she became known for a series of voluptuous and robust pink glass jugs. They were followed by glass breasts and glass clubs, but in between there were apparently matter-of-course 'independent' projects such as an enormous pair of slippers for the 'giant of Rotterdam', and a wooden baby church that she hung from the St Eusebius church in Arnhem for the 9th edition of the Sonsbeek festival. She also gave the Blankenberge watertower in Belgium a wig of orange ship's rope, and recently had two enormous sunflowers knitted which were draped through her gallery in long strands.

At the moment Roosen is working on a similarly large-scale project, although it hardly stands out among all the works. She has been invited to do something with the local lighthouse for the Yokohama Triennial, so a small model of the lighthouse stands in a corner. For the time being she has wrapped bright pink thread around the top of it. Roosen picks up the model, weighs it in her hands, and pulls on the thread. 'It is nowhere near finished yet, it might turn out as something totally different.'

Have you any idea how they found out about you in Yokohama?

'Oh, it must be connected with the fact that I've already worked on a few big buildings. The St Eusebius church in Arnhem, the Blankenberge watertower, so the organisers soon think: she does things with towers. It is for that very reason that I try not to agree too quickly to such requests. First of all I go to see if it feels right, of if I can do anything with it. If that is OK, I'm prepared to give it a try.'

What was good about Yokohama?

'The first thing that appealed to me was that the curator Tadasi Kawamata is himself an artist. You can see that straight away: he is concerned with the content of the work, and not with the idea of whether it will pull in a large enough audience or not. He showed me some photos, and they led me to take a look for myself. It turned out to be a very tall tower, more than a hundred metres tall, in an old neighbourhood: a sad widow,

8

50-52,
94,120
4-7,96-97
112-113
116-117

3
53-
104
102

but also a typical phallic symbol. So I soon asked myself whether I couldn't feminise it a bit.'

Is that the first thing that comes to mind, the relation between masculine and feminine?

'Well, yes. It is an ingredient.'

What else do you think about?

'My first idea was simply to drape another building over it. You often see that nowadays on scaffolding, that they print fine netting with a photo of the building that it conceals. Of course, you can hang something completely different in front of it too. But I found that too much like advertising. And I also wanted to make use of the view...' She stares at the model. 'I haven't worked it out completely yet. For the time being I enjoy wrapping that enormous tower in pink rope, there's something cheerful and exciting about it. But it's not yet enough.'

If you wonder about the next step, as you do now, do you call in others to help?

'No, it usually works out... (laughs). At most my boy friend, because he is good at making models. But otherwise I have to discover it all by myself, at this stage.'

That does not alter the fact that help is bound to arrive, if only because collaboration has gradually become an essential part of Roosen's way of working. In fact, the process is always the same: Roosen conceives the idea, elaborates the concept, and makes the plans, but she does not wrap rope, blow glass, build churches or knit flowers – at most she is there when it is done, as a supervisor and 'inspirer'. That seems a clear-cut choice, which makes it all the more remarkable that Roosen discovered this 'method' relatively late – when Roosen exhibited her first glass jugs, which made her famous, she was already 34.

Is that how you see it yourself, that you found your form relatively late?

Roosen hesitates. 'Yes, perhaps that's true. There's a whole history behind it, but whether I should tell it now? Well, OK, I trained as a drawing teacher and did the art academy afterwards. I was still searching at the time. Then, when I was 27, my lover died. That created an enormous hole in my life. I was at my wits' end and got stuck in a heavy mourning process which therapy couldn't pull me out of. On the recommendation of my therapist I started to make watercolours. Then I sat at my desk, with paper and paint, and tried to put down how I felt. It was a bit like: "Oh, today I feel blue", and then I painted a blue bubble'. Roosen chuckles. 'Yes, it really was very serious.'

Did it still have anything to do with being a professional artist?

'Well, I soon imposed a demand on myself: I had to do five paintings each time. Exactly five. The first was usually a very literal depiction of my mood. With the second I tried to forget about the aesthetics a bit and to go straight to the heart of my feeling, and so on. Proceeding in that way, I was usually finished by the time I had done four, I had vented my emotions. But I still had a fifth to do. So then I started doing whatever I felt like, emptying my brush, you could say. But the remarkable thing was that it was often precisely in those watercolours that I managed to express what I meant. Apparently I was only able to give it a form once the first emotions were out of the way. That awareness helped me enormously to arrive at an essence. At honesty.'

What was so honest about those watercolours?

'The most striking thing was that things happened on paper which I could never have imagined. I was trained as an artist, and then you're very practised in matters like composition, form and structure. It is not directly connected with expressing emotions. Precisely by abandoning that form, by working more intuitively, I no longer had to focus so obsessively on composition. It worked perfectly.'

Did you soon realise that that way of painting could also be good for your work?

'It went even further: I soon realised that I could solve questions in the studio that I was not always able to tackle in real life. That gave me the courage to go further and further.'

How did you do that? How can you go 'far' in a watercolour?

'In all kinds of ways. At first I just worked in a sketchbook, but sometimes I had done watercolours and thought: I can try them in a larger format or in a different material. Sometimes I took a whole bowl of paint and threw it over a sheet of paper a couple of square metres large. It was very liberating.'

You started to make glass objects fairly soon after that. Where did the idea come from?

'It was an extension of that search for limits. My watercolours were growing larger and larger, and I began to ask myself whether I could catch that fluidity of a watercolour in other materials too. I had worked with glass at the Academy, and I always found it very beautiful. So I enrolled for a course in glass-blowing. You went with a group of people to a glass-blower, where you could see how it worked. At the end you could have an object of your choice blown in glass. Most people asked for the craziest things, in all kinds of colours, but I noticed that I found a transparent sphere the most beautiful of all.'

Why a transparent sphere?

'It's the perfect form, isn't it? If you look into a glass ball, you see the whole world upside down, and at the same time it is such a wonderful symbol. In Venice I once saw a St Christopher with a glass sphere, and there's a beautiful one in a painting by Tintoretto as well – in his day the transparent sphere was the symbol of the entire world. Anyway, the funny thing was that I found those spheres so beautiful, but that the glass-blowers didn't find them interesting at all. For them, such a sphere is the basic form. I got them to blow a series of those spheres at the time and used them as part of an installation in which all those spheres were like bubbles on the edge of a space.'

Didn't you feel the urge at that moment to learn to blow glass yourself?

'No, not at all. I mean, I've tried it, I've worked in the glass studio, opened doors, handed people things. But to learn it properly, really properly, takes years. And that wasn't my aim at all. For me it works just as well, perhaps even better, if I can direct and supervise the blowing process.'

But still, don't you feel that your work lacks a sort of 'signature' as a result? That it is too far removed from you? Or to put the question differently: at that time did you do any other work, besides the watercolours, that you actually carried out yourself?

'Oh yes. When my lover died I spent a lot of time on very labour-intensive work. The first thing I made was a wooden necklace with large wooden beads. I spent months on it, just to get the beads properly round – I discovered that making things round is very consoling. If you roll up your sorrow, you can carry on living, and it rolls along beside you. And the weaving was a way for me to get rid of my aggression. Later I made a ball of brambles, a large ball of rolled up bramble branches. It was incredibly beautiful. I had bought special gloves and knew exactly where the best bramble branches grew. I drove out there to pluck branches, which I put in the boot of my van. When I got home the boot burst open from the pressure, as if a monster had jumped out. I was very proud of those balls, I really was the super-bramble-ball-maker.'

So you found it satisfying to do that yourself?

'Yes, I would never entrust it to someone else, if only because you have to discover for yourself how to do it. There was also something of a calvary in it – I was always covered in scratches at the end of the day. So it worked at the time, perhaps also because I was still looking for something. It was beautiful too, you know. I was in the wood collecting branches. I came across a man who showed me lots of passages in the woods. It turned out that he was digging tunnels and passages there – that was his project. By the way, years later, I ritually set fire to my ball. That was quite a spectacle, with the ball on the ground and six-metre-tall flames above it. It looked as if a meteor had landed.'

But you no longer had the urge to make things yourself when it came to glass?

'No, that's really when contracting work out to third parties started. It may also have been connected with a sort of disengagement. I originally resorted to it because I did not master the technique well enough, but I soon discovered that the process of cooperation, of farming out part of the work, adds a great deal for me.'

You don't find it difficult to lose a part of the control?

'No, because it yields a lot in return.'

And you don't have any difficulty in regarding it as your own work?

'Oh no, because the initial idea is always mine. I determine the starting point and the elaboration.'

But still, when were talking about that tower just now, you stated that making work is a kind of growing process for you, in which you are constantly trying out new ideas. To what extent does collaboration make it easier to take decisions? Or does it make it more difficult?

Roosen hesitates. 'Sometimes it does help, but that is not what counts. Every work of mine starts with an idea, but that idea is not very specific. It is a matter of feeling, making associations, links. Look, a good image, a good work must provoke a kind of translation, just like the digestion of food, more or less. That always has to be present, because if it's too direct, too one-to-one, it doesn't interest me. And that translation takes place precisely because I bring different processes together. My own ideas and those of others combine to form a sort of chemical reaction which is no longer completely under my control. In the end it results in something unique, something that I couldn't have predicted, and that shows me something that I'm curious about, and from which I get something in return.'

Is glass a particularly suitable material for that?

'Well, at any rate is has an attractive ambiguity. Glass is solidified material that is still very close to a fluid. It is very fragile, vulnerable, while a glass object may still be thousands of years old – glass from the Roman era is still being excavated. That's why I call glass solidified energy: it can exist for centuries, but it can also be gone in a flash. I can still remember the first time one of my jugs broke. One jug touched another and suddenly five of them were broken – it was terrible. I learnt straight away that pink glass is very vulnerable. There are considerable differences from one colour to another.'

Do you also make use of that knowledge? Does it make different colours of glass mean different things to you?

'Yes, it certainly plays a part. In this work, for instance' (she picks up a photo of her 'bubble rack', in which 140 differently coloured glass 'test bubbles' hang) 'the shape is determined to a large extent by the properties of the glass. They look like semen or spermatozoa, but red glass, for instance, is very hard so that the bubble stays very small, while a tap is enough to smash the tobacco-coloured one. So that is the longest. And that pink one is broken. I want to show the fact, so I've stuck it together again with tape and hung it up again.'

'Yes, I remember the first time I was at the glass-blower's and said: 'I'm never going to do anything with colours'. But once you know more about it, that it takes on meaning…. That's how it works with me, you know. I was fascinated by that pink first of all, and afterwards I decided to make jugs with it. I don't think that up beforehand, it follows from the colour.'

When you talk about cooperation, how far do you go in demarcating your own ideas, and where do you put yourself in someone else's hands?

'I usually still begin with a watercolour, for instance of a jug with an enormously long spout. Then I take it to Bernard Heesen, the glass-blower. That watercolour is a starting point for him. He starts blowing, but I stay on the spot to watch, to think things through with him, and to direct the process. A lot has changed in that process, by the way. I used to be very involved, interfering and shouting things all the time. Now I've learnt to be more distanced, to discuss the things beforehand, and during the work to make a few remarks at most.'

Does it always proceed like that?

'Well, I am pretty unpredictable. I just said that I don't like literal images, but sometimes that's just what I do want. For instance, recently I thought that I wanted simply to make a glass prick, tits and an arse and then to hang them up together in a net, as a sort of orgy of glass. I didn't do a watercolour of those pricks, I just went to the glass-blower and said: "Lads, we're going to make pricks today". It's hilarious, of course, especially when I say that they can choose what they should look like. It immediately creates the kind of atmosphere that I like, a sort of bonding.

And they turned out to be very good pricks.'

But you haven't hung them up in a net, but very cruelly, from sharp, tight, orange twine.

Roosen grins. 'That net didn't work. The pricks were delivered here in my studio and I put them in the net, but it didn't work. So then I try out things, as I always do with this kind of work. In this case I thought at some point in time: I'll hang one of the pricks up. First I hung it high, then I thought: no, it has to be at groin level. That was already an improvement. Then I thought of the twine, and that worked well, but I wasn't sure if it was right. I discussed the possibility of steel cables with some other people, but no, this worked the best.'

Still, if you describe it like that, to what extent is your current work still connected with channelling emotions, as it was when you started with your therapeutic watercolours?

'It all comes from inside me. But I've come to see what interests me, how I find the right form for things. And above all… (hesitates) I've become better at accepting things that I can't think up for myself.'

Have you transcended yourself in that sense?

Roosen laughs. 'That's not how I would put it.'

Let me phrase it differently: if you were to put your entire oeuvre together, all those objects and vases and jugs and flowers in one big space, is that an adequate reflection of your personality, of who you are? Or is it mere, or less?

Thoughtfully: 'I've thought of calling the book we're talking about *Maria's*.'

Why?

'It's typical Brabant dialect, where they say: "She's of Maria's" – in the plural. And Maria is the woman of all women.'

Is your oeuvre in that respect a reflection of your personality?

'Well, I have the feeling that there are shortcomings.'

So the work is less?
'Yes.'

Is that because a work in your head is always better than the actual work?
'Yes, certainly. But it's also connected with the fact that I always find it difficult to see a lot of my work in one place. For some reason or other I find that my work always comes across better in group exhibitions. Perhaps that's connected with the fact that I like relating to other people or something...'

Could it also be that you recognise too many patterns if you see a lot of your own work?
'Yes.'

What are those patterns, then?
'Repetition, for example. Take the carrots we were talking about, the fact that I make an installation consisting of hundreds of glass carrots In the past I would have found that an admission of weakness. I did it, but mainly with the argument that I wanted to explore the different aspects of a form or theme. It was the carrots which made me realise that repetition also reinforces the individual components. All those carrots combined receive an enormous growing power, and that I find beautiful. Growing power is the greatest force that there is, isn't it?'

Are there other patterns in your work?
'Oh yes. Those grand gestures, for example, those trials of strength, that power-lifting. The wooden church hanging from the St Eusebius church, or four hundred glass balls suspended from the ceiling of the Antoni van Leeuwenhoek hospital. Those kinds of gestures are something of the last few years, I had to overcome something to arrive at them. But it was good for my work, it enabled me to go further, to widen my horizon. And I was a bit tired of all those shoes and jugs. This was a breath of fresh air.'

It may be a strange question, but if we're talking about having ideas and farming work out, is there something that you think you are really good at? A particular skill?
Roosen is silent. 'Well, that's... that's difficult to say about yourself. At any rate, I think that I'm good at observing.'

Is that all?
'I'm also quite accommodating... But then you will of course ask me where I stand myself.'

Is that a typically feminine property? In other words, your work, especially in the past, has often been associated with femininity: breasts, fragility, pink glass. Is that what you want?
'Yes, but I also play with it. I don't at all like my work to be seen as a sort of plea for femininity. That's too easy, too simple for me. What I want is to question the clichés about femininity, to challenge those clichés a bit, by working in a very feminine, or a very fussy, or a very tough way.'

Do the spectators always see that hidden meaning, do you think?
'No, of course not all the time. But that doesn't matter.'

Let me put it differently: Do you consider it important to know what kind of effect your work has on the spectator?
'Jan Hoet once said to me: "Your work is about giving". I found that very beautiful, although I would never dare to say it myself. But that is perhaps because someone once wrote, when I had just become more famous, that I fulfilled a sort of mother role in my work. Caring, giving, offering. I hated it at the time.'

Why?
'Oh, it was probably because I was just beginning to make a name for myself. I became better known, took part in the Biennale, and desperately wanted to be professional. The last thing you want in that situation is to be classified as a sort of

mother of all mothers. Now it doesn't bother me any more. However you look at it, it's still a strength of mine. I can make things exist, make them grow, make them flower. Especially now that I have a daughter myself, I realise that there's nothing wrong with that.'

'No, those winners started out in a very different way. I once saw an exhibition of all kinds of artists' collections. I already cut out photos now and then, but I had never seen it as a collection. At the exhibition all those collections were displayed side by side, shoes and miniature buildings, which made them look just like sculptures. I was so impressed that I thought that I could turn my winners into a collection too.'

'Yes, well, the first criterion for choosing them is that they are good photos. Good images, say. And they must evoke something in me, so they are often connected with what I'm working on at that moment, with my fascinations. In that sense it is almost a diary. Since people know that I have this collection, they sometimes send me winners, but that never really works. They don't do anything for me.'

'Well, I see it more as being about the fact that time seems to stand still for those people. At such an important moment, everything is centred on them, there is nothing else – and time stands still. I find that beautiful, precisely because it reminds you of what you are doing it all for. I have the same thing in my work. Sometimes it goes very slowly, I'm not in the mood, I'm full of doubt, but if it goes smoothly I forget the difficult times. You are rewarded with those moments of victory, which transcend time, just as happens with major events like birth and death.'

'That's why it includes Grünewald's Christ as well. Of course, it is in the first place a masterpiece, but I am also very fond of the remark by the sculptor Brancusi, who once said "that a good sculpture must be able to heal". Later I read that psychiatric patients from the neighbourhood of Colmar are sometimes confronted with Grünewald's painting because it has a calming effect on them. I can imagine that, it is such a detailed painting, if you are a bit confused you can see an awful lot in it, and it can give you an awful lot.'

'You know, you asked me just now what I'm really good at, what my specific skill is. I think I know the answer: I make things grow. I sow the seed and then call others in to help to cultivate the plant. I direct the process, supervise it – in fact, I'm the artist with the green fingers. Isn't that beautiful?'

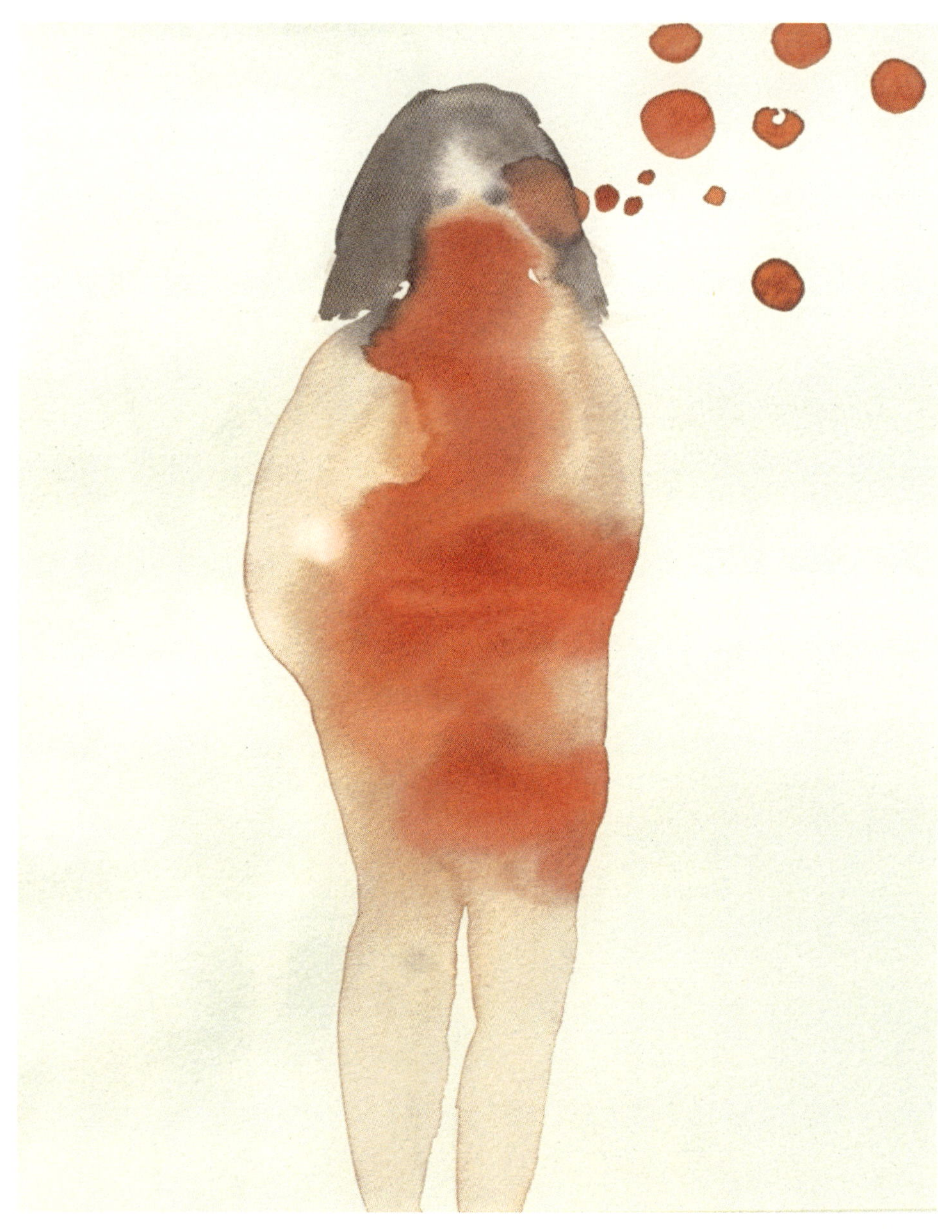

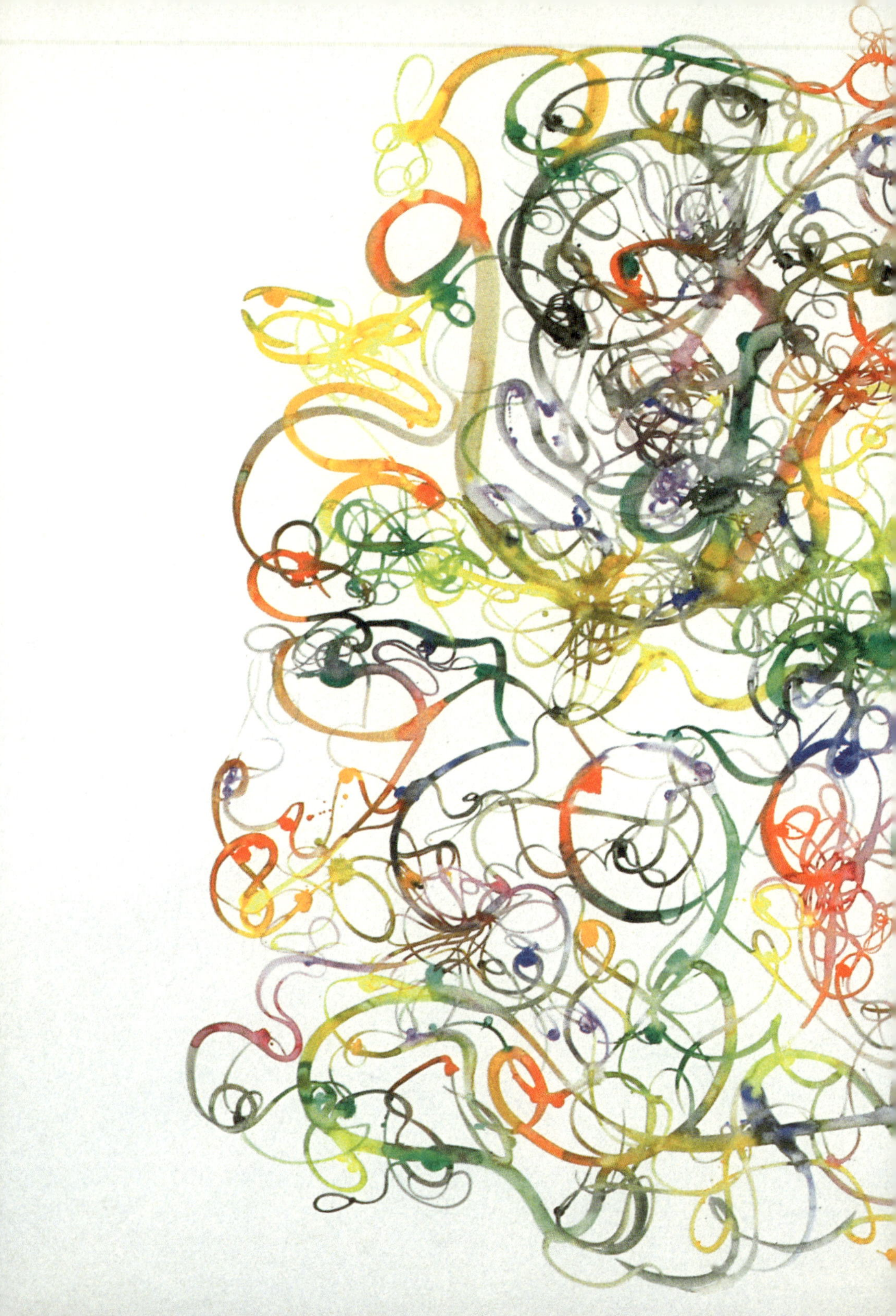

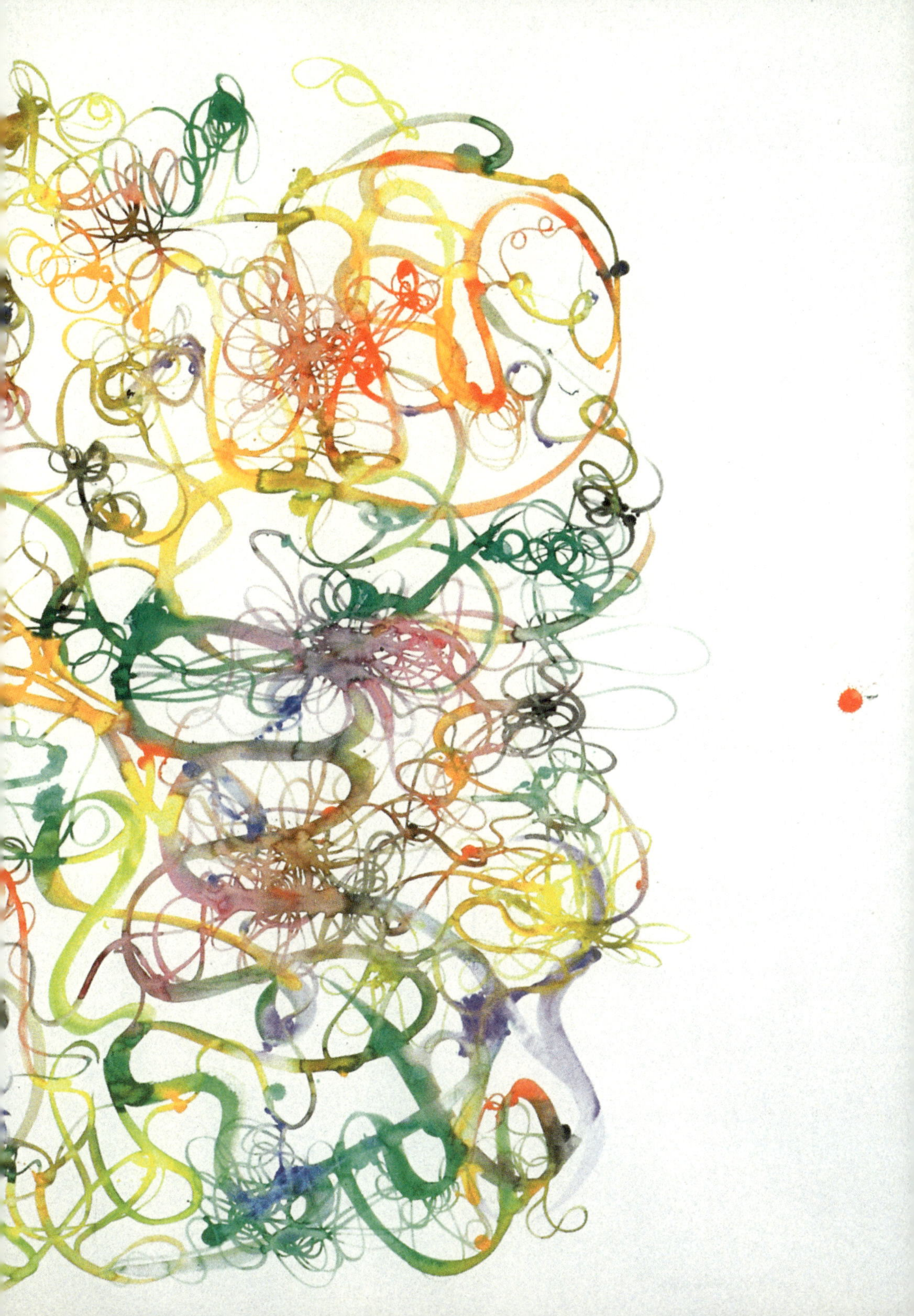

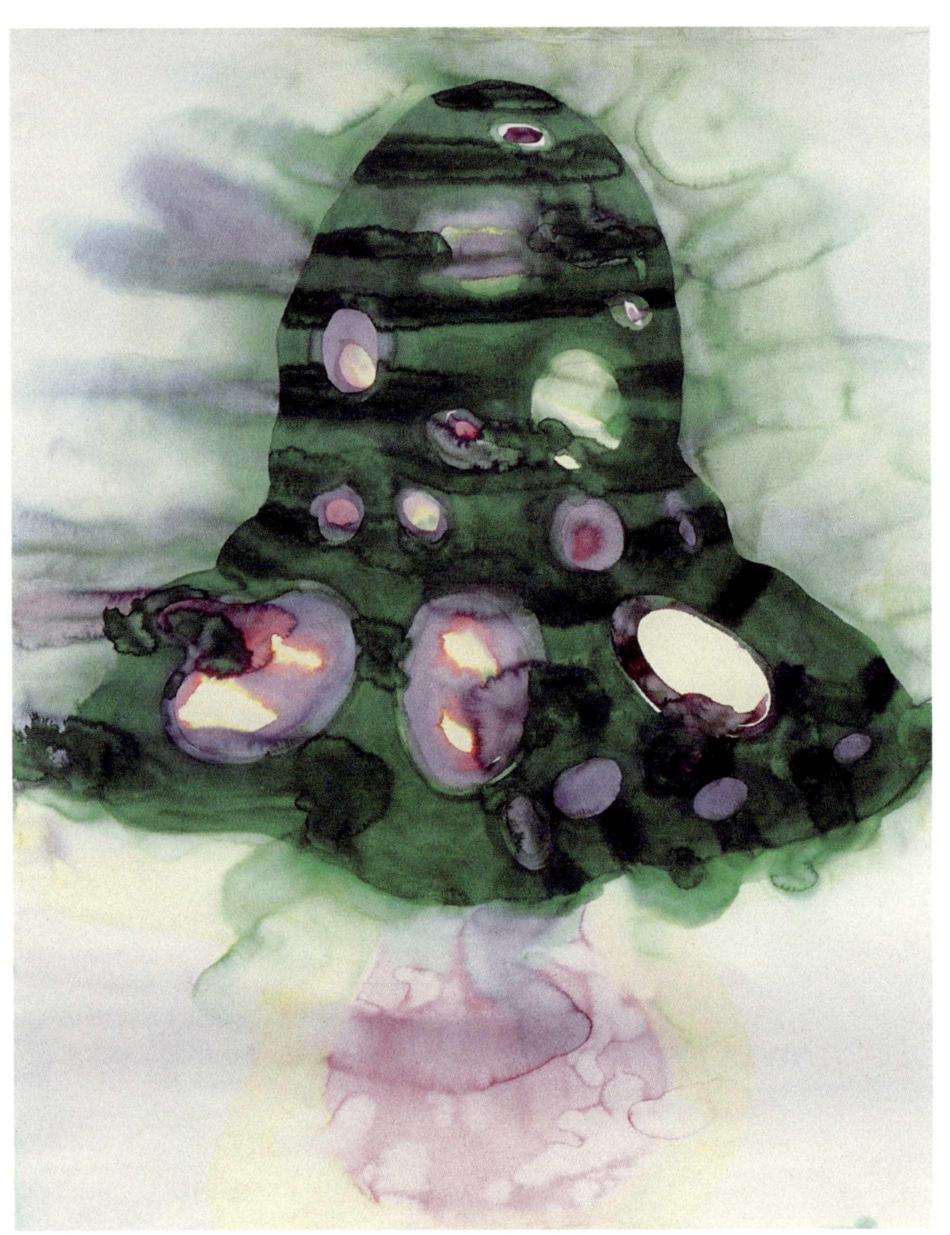

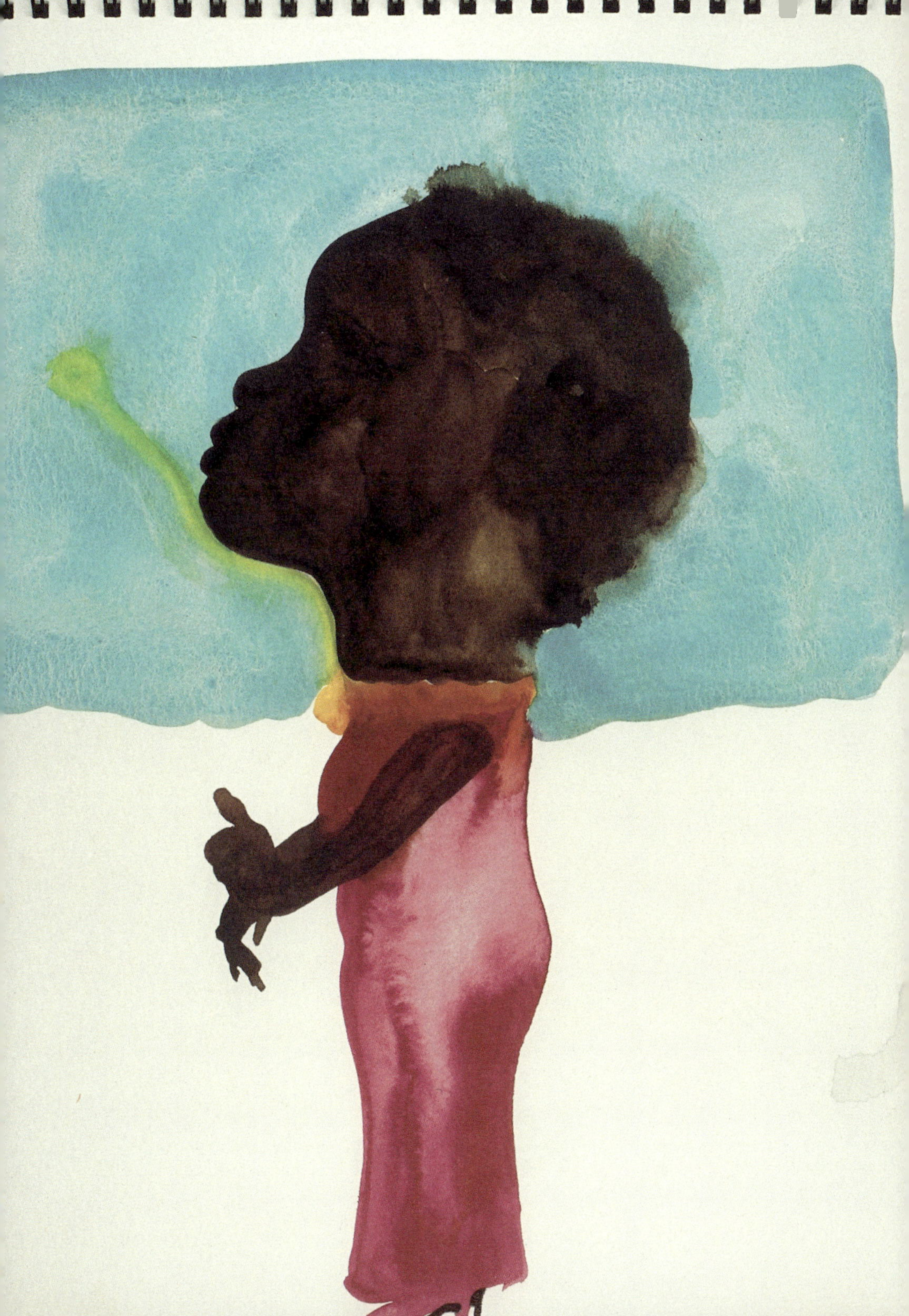

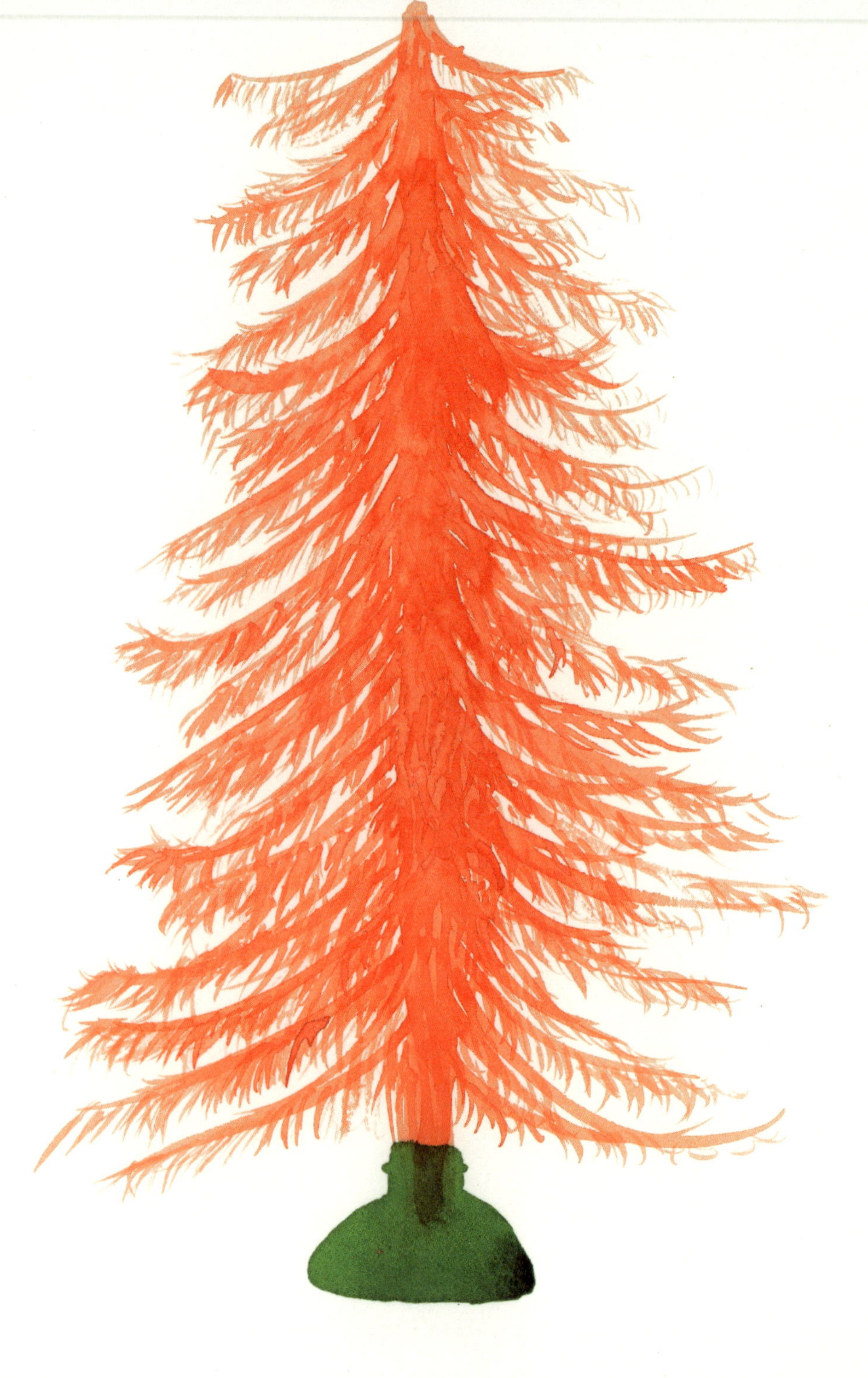

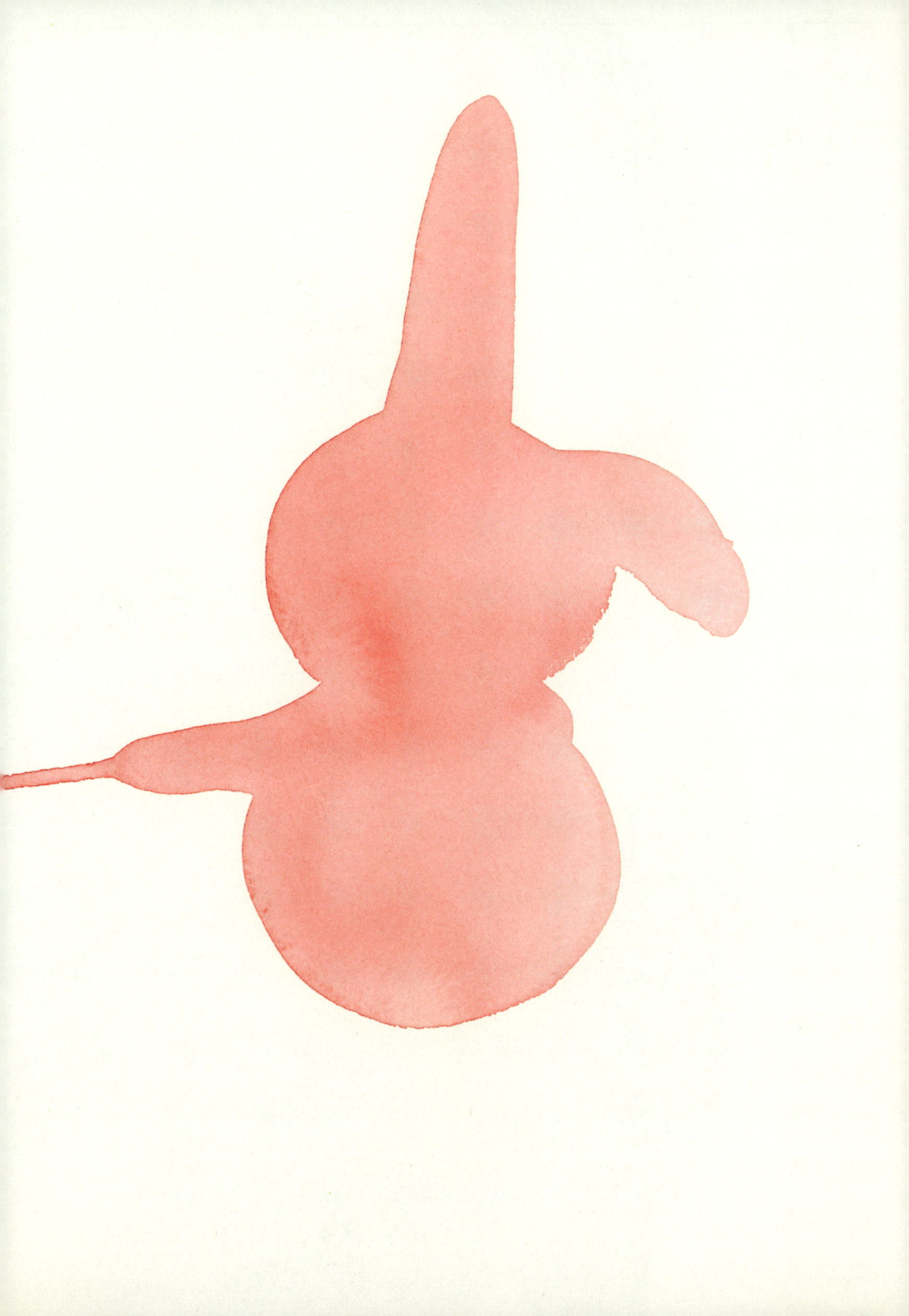

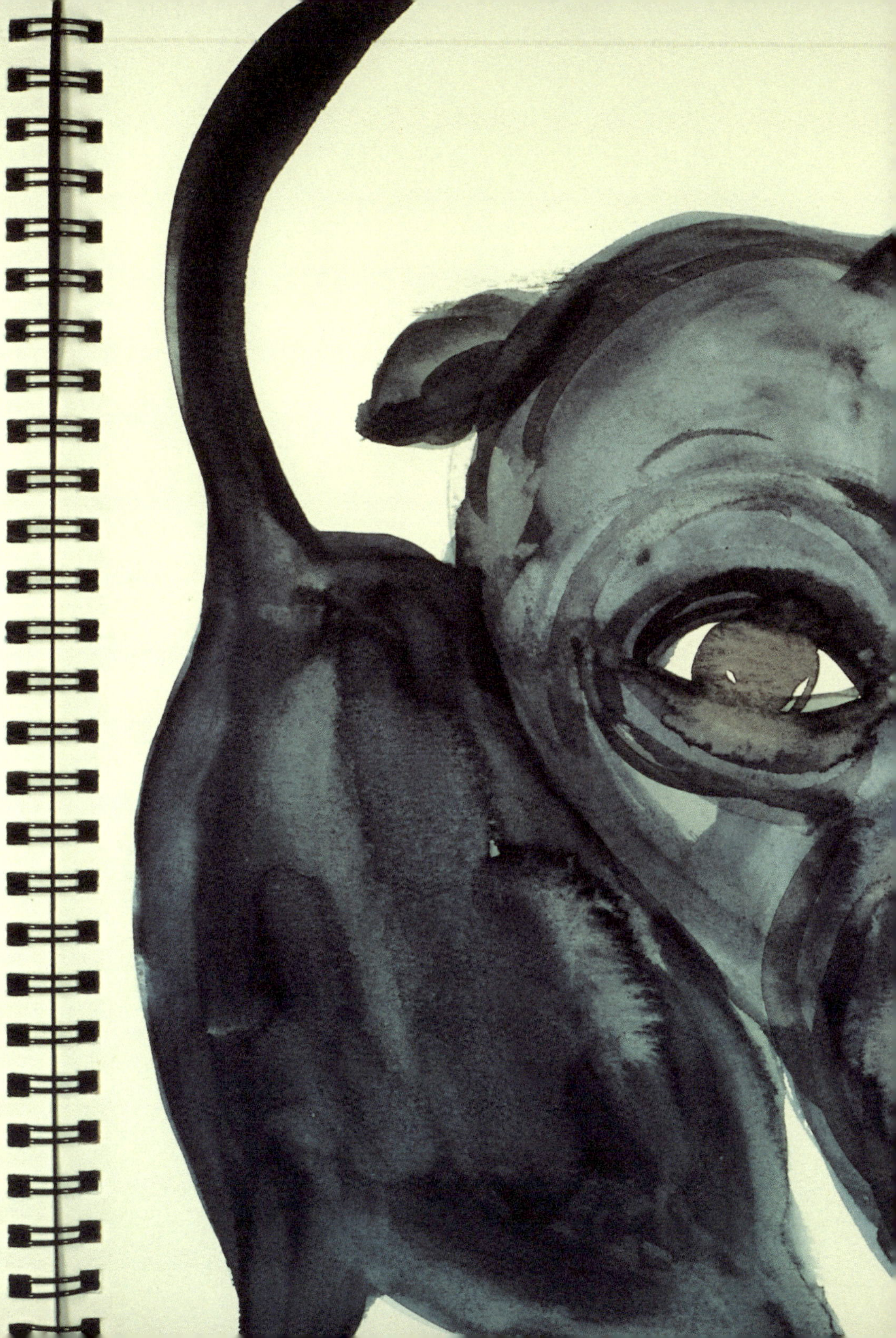

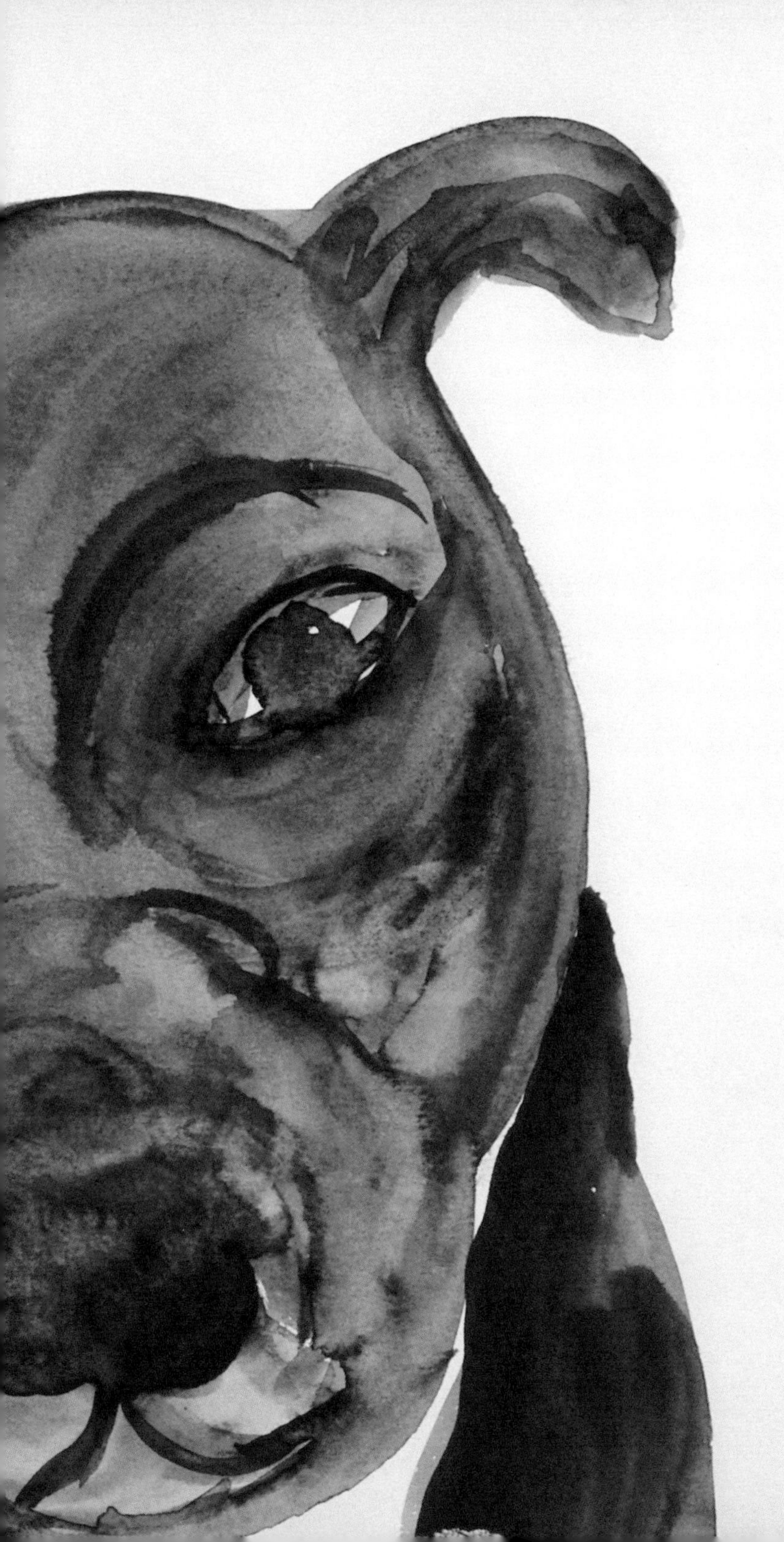

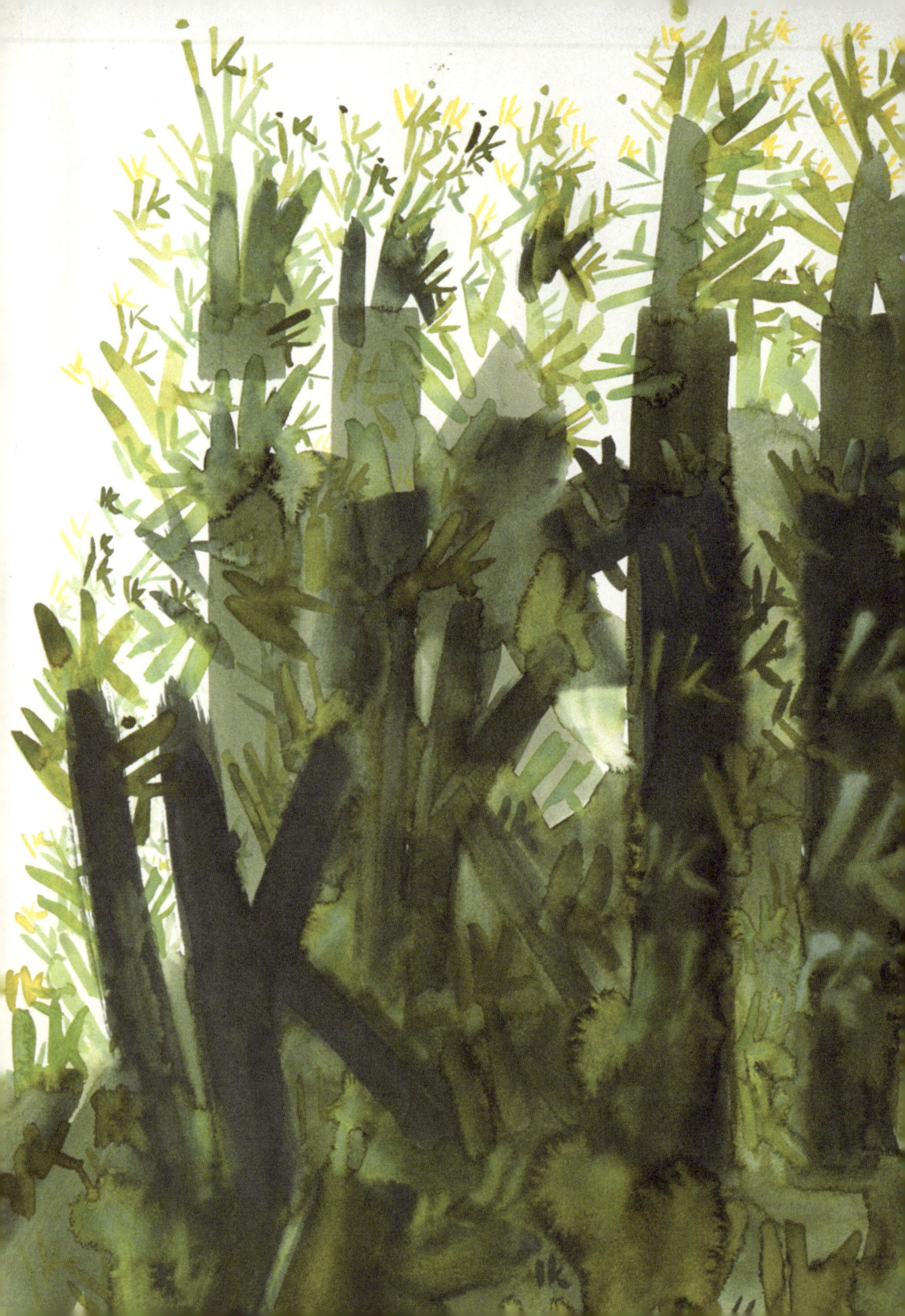

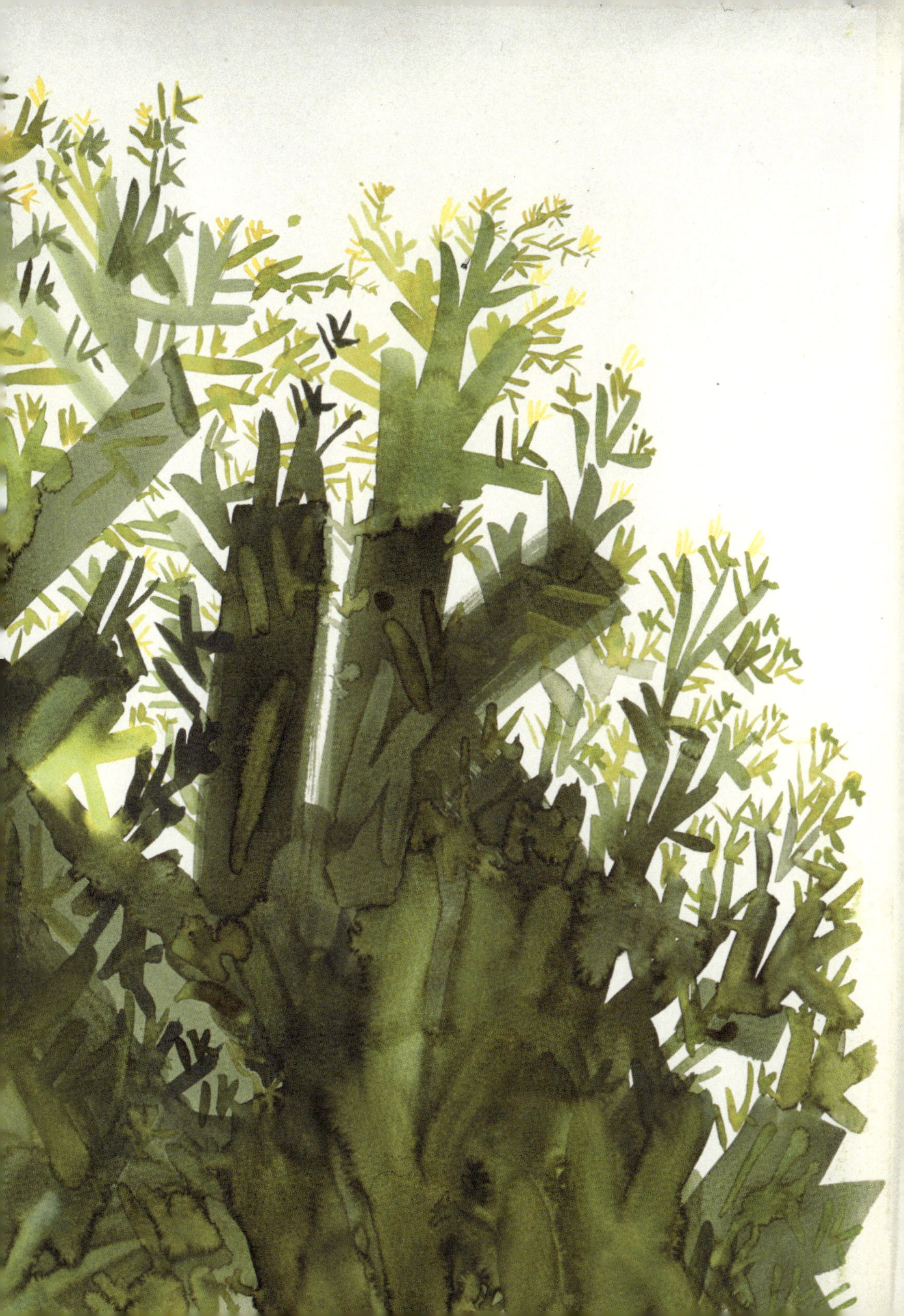

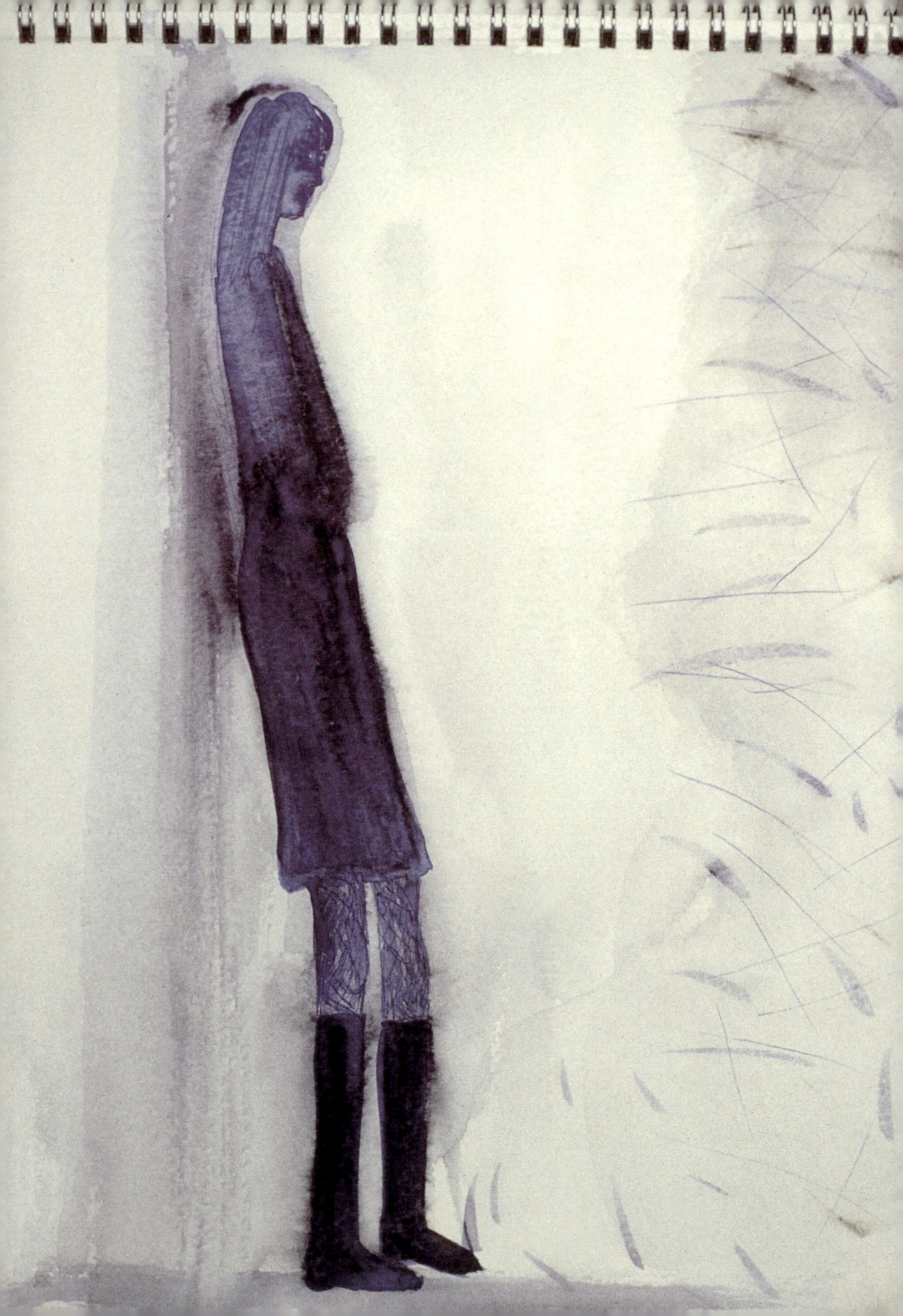

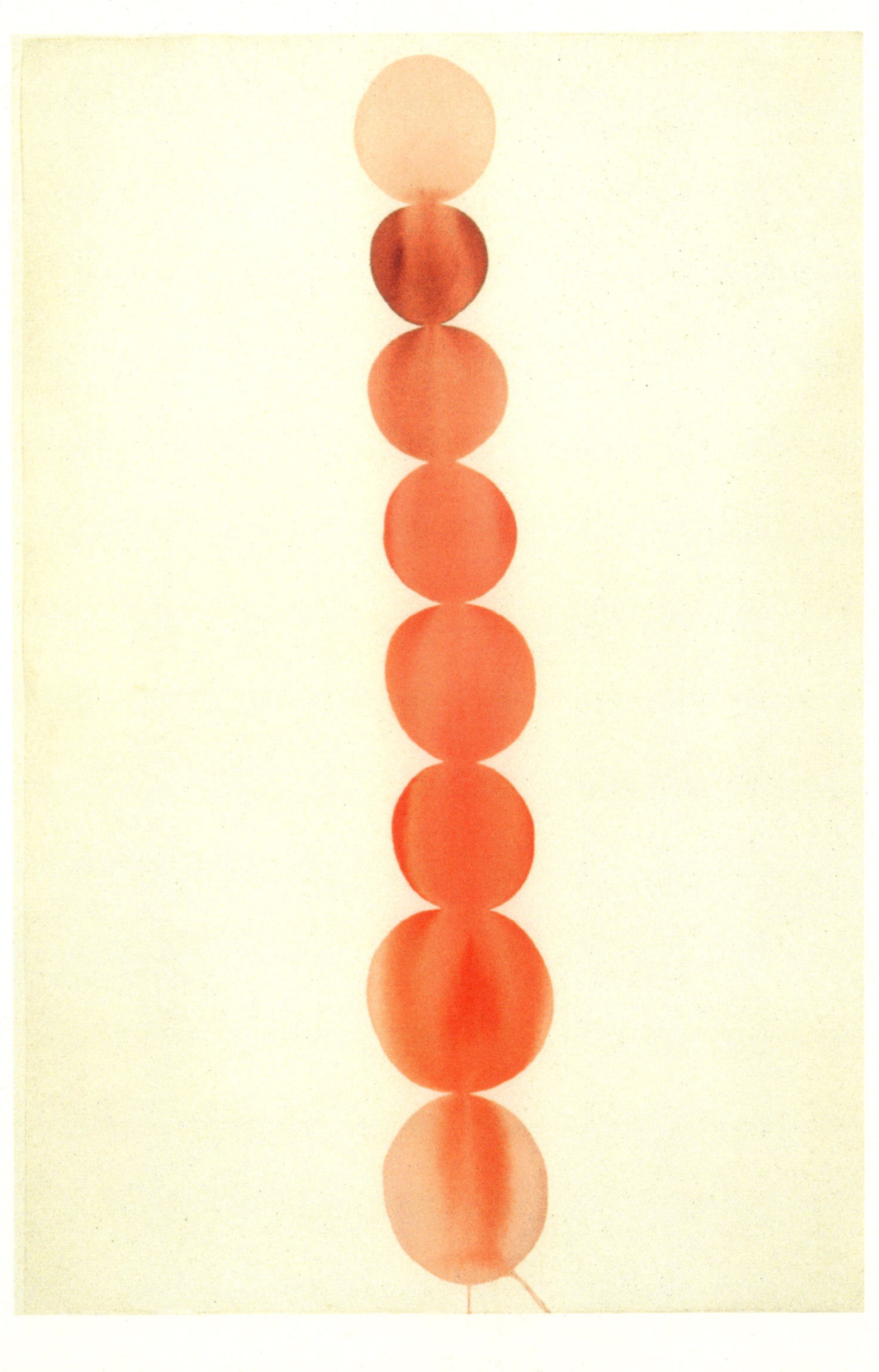

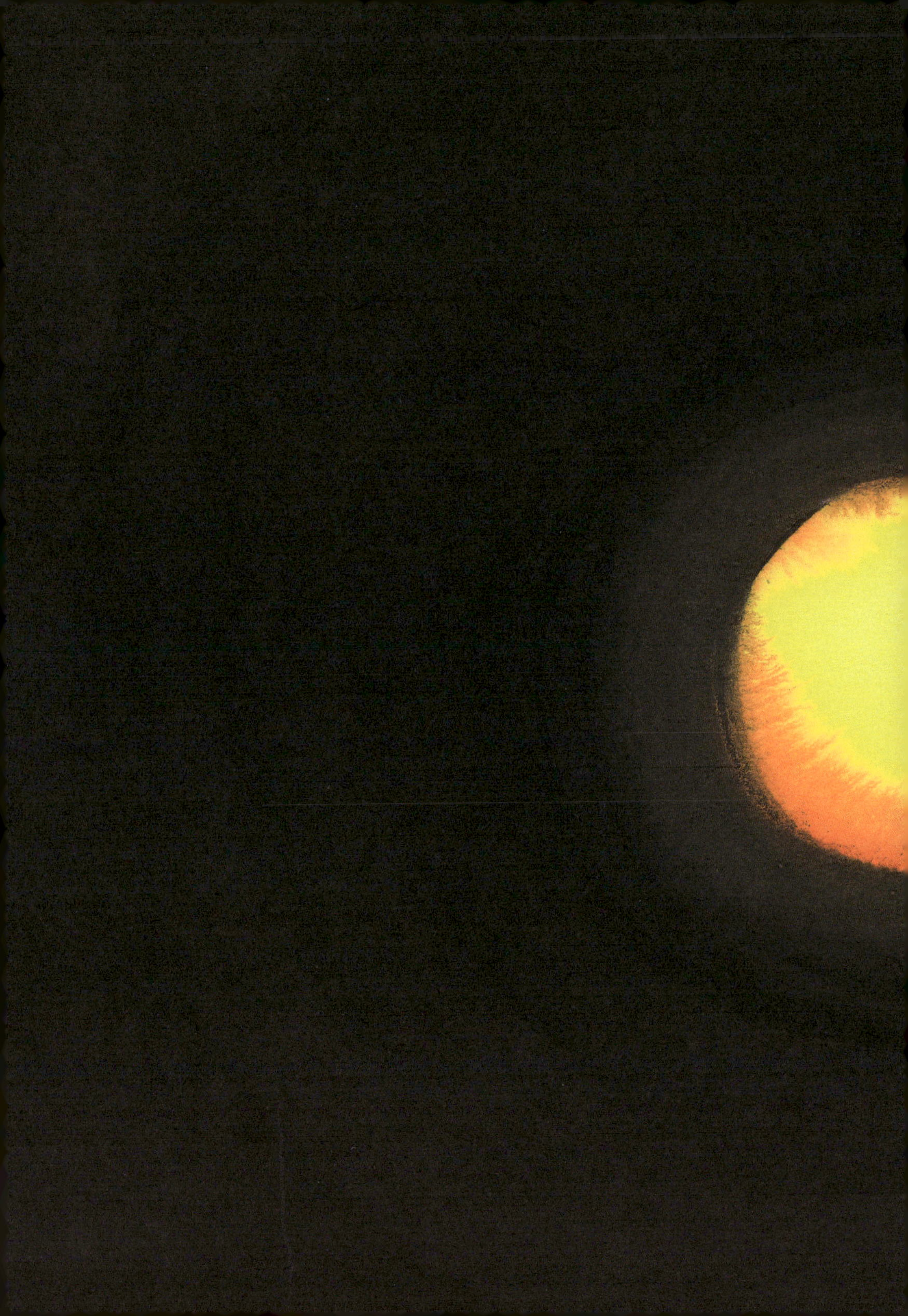

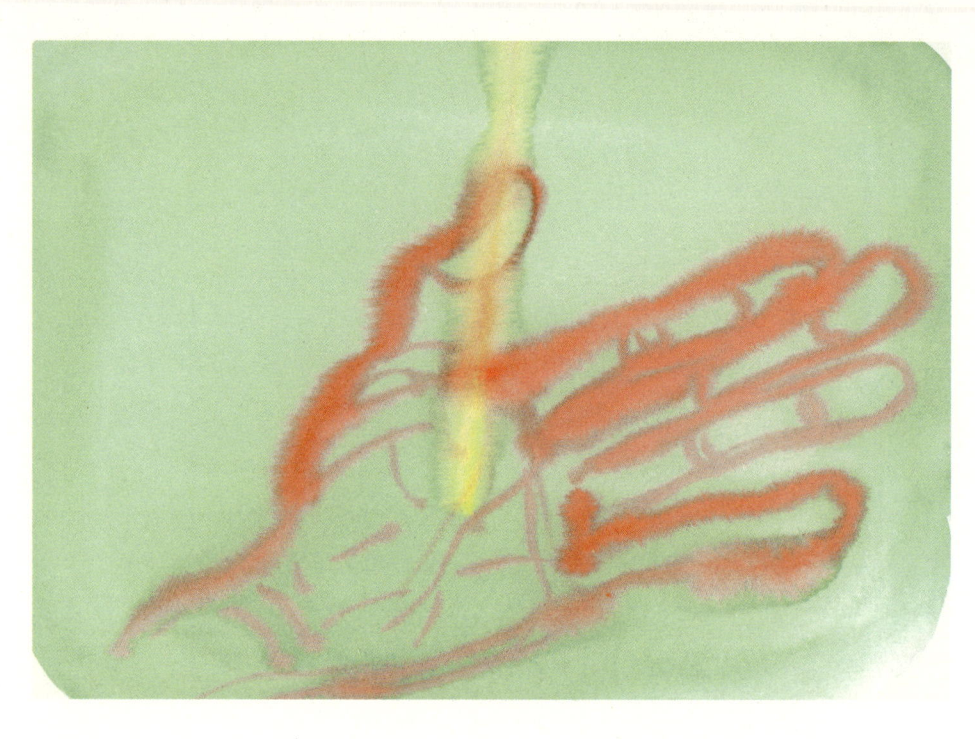

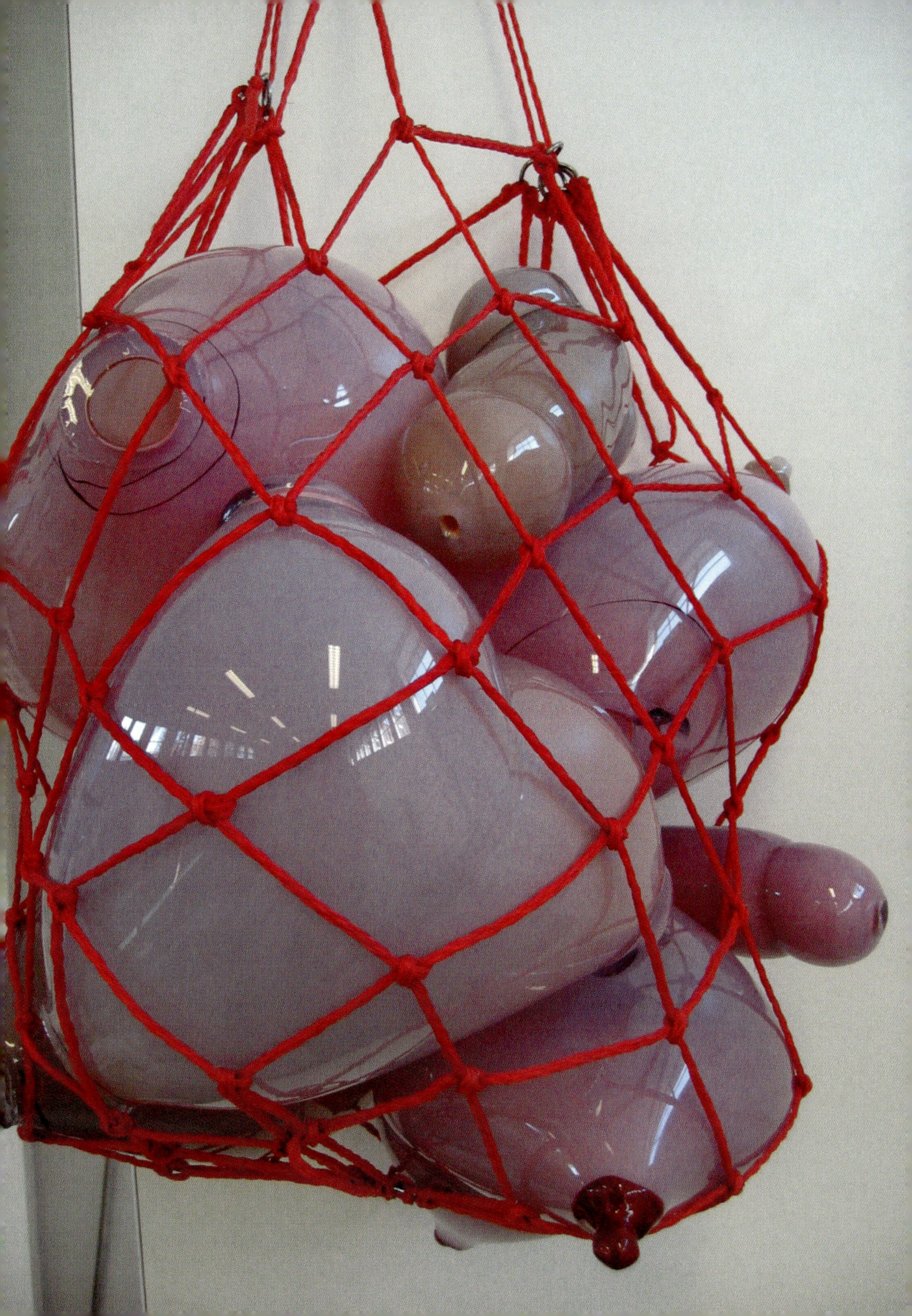

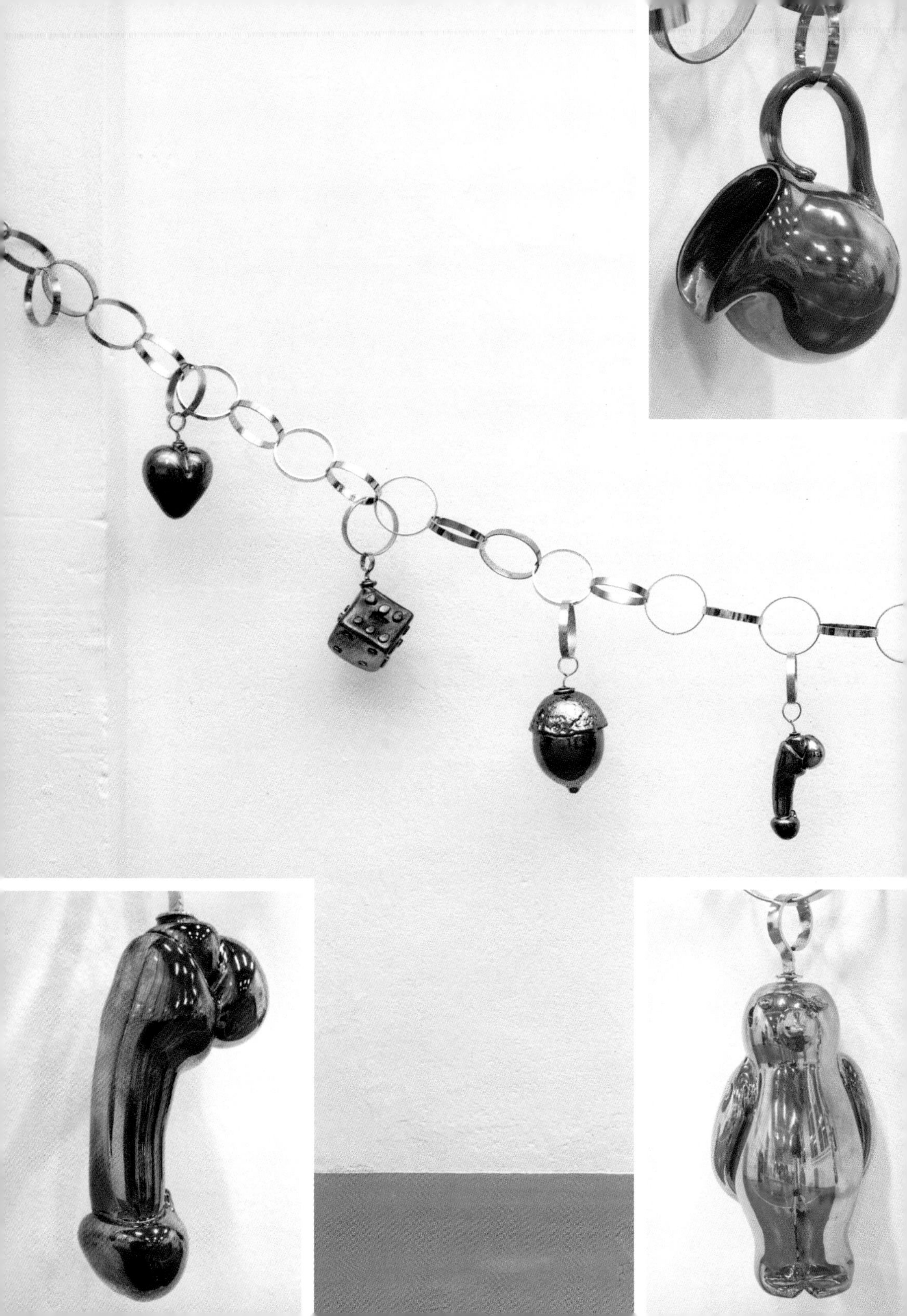

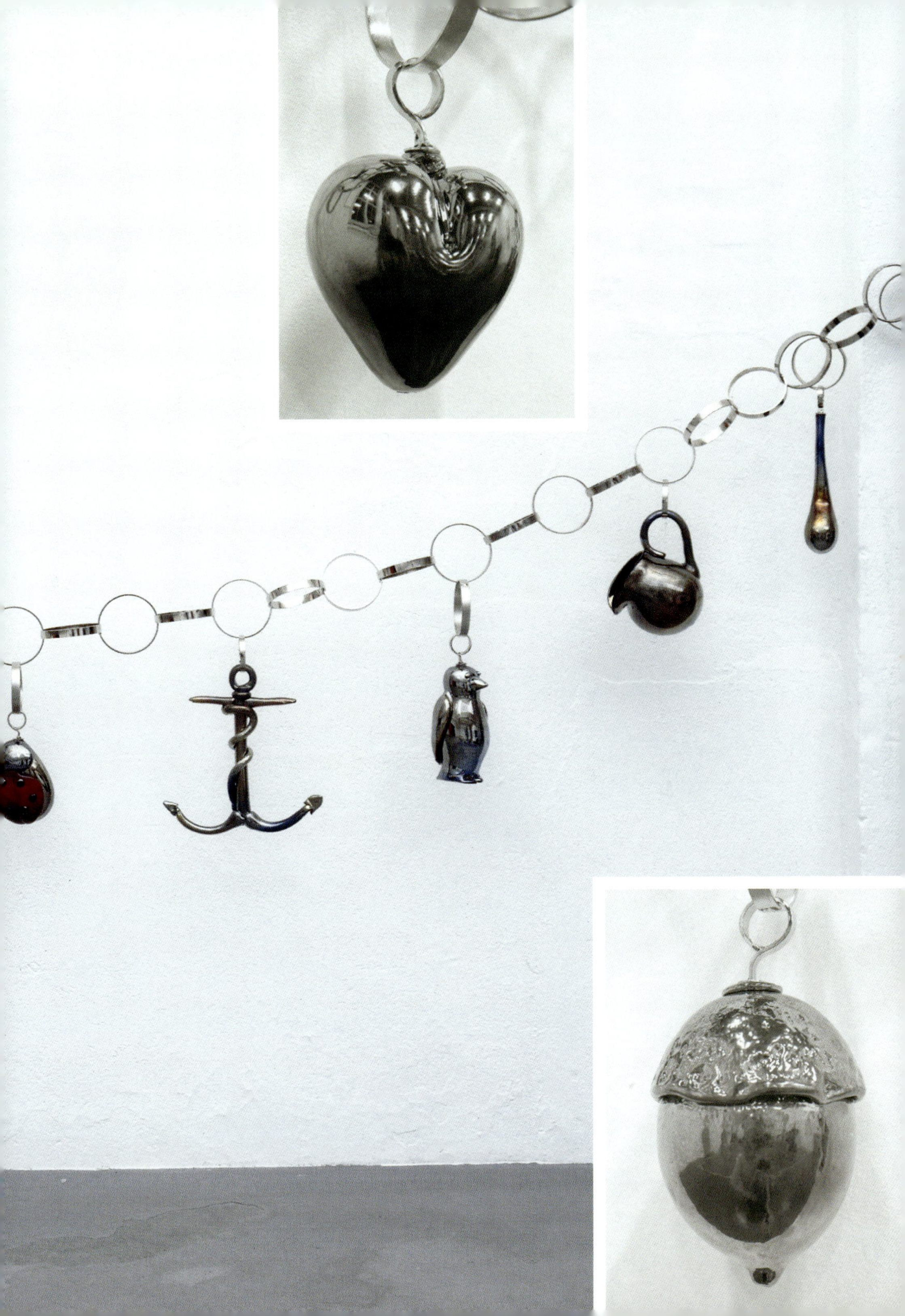

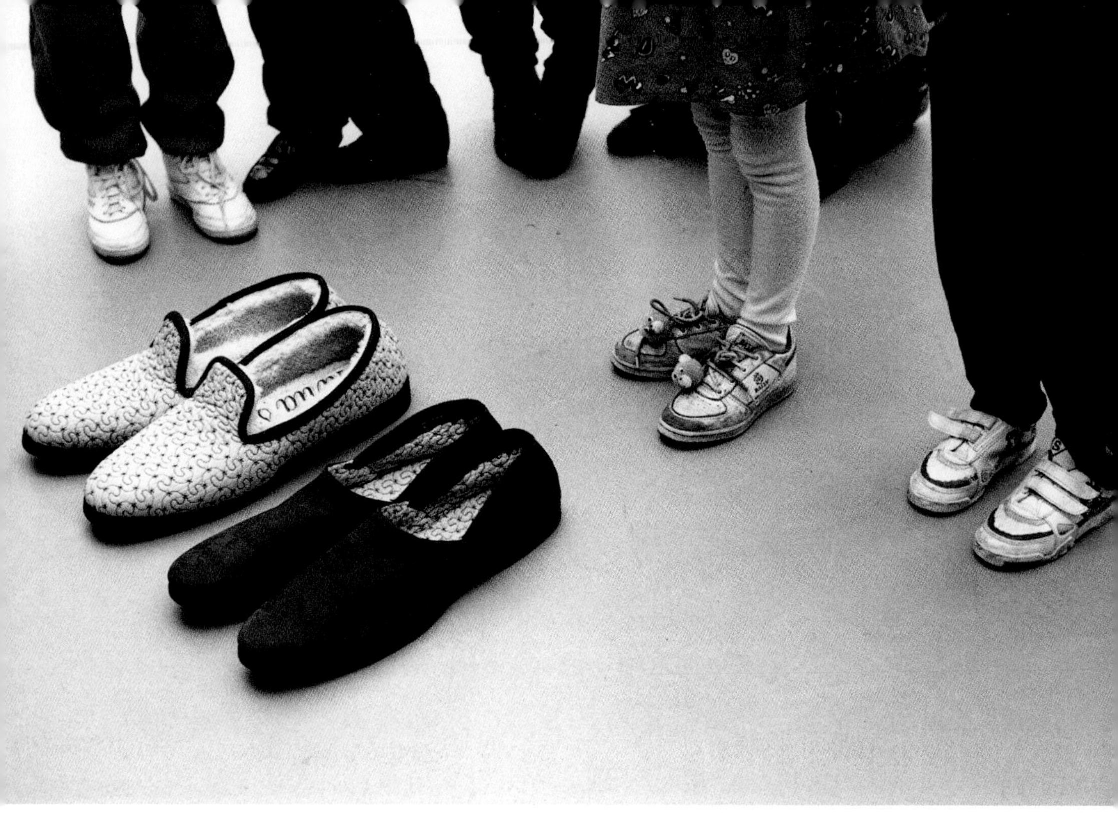

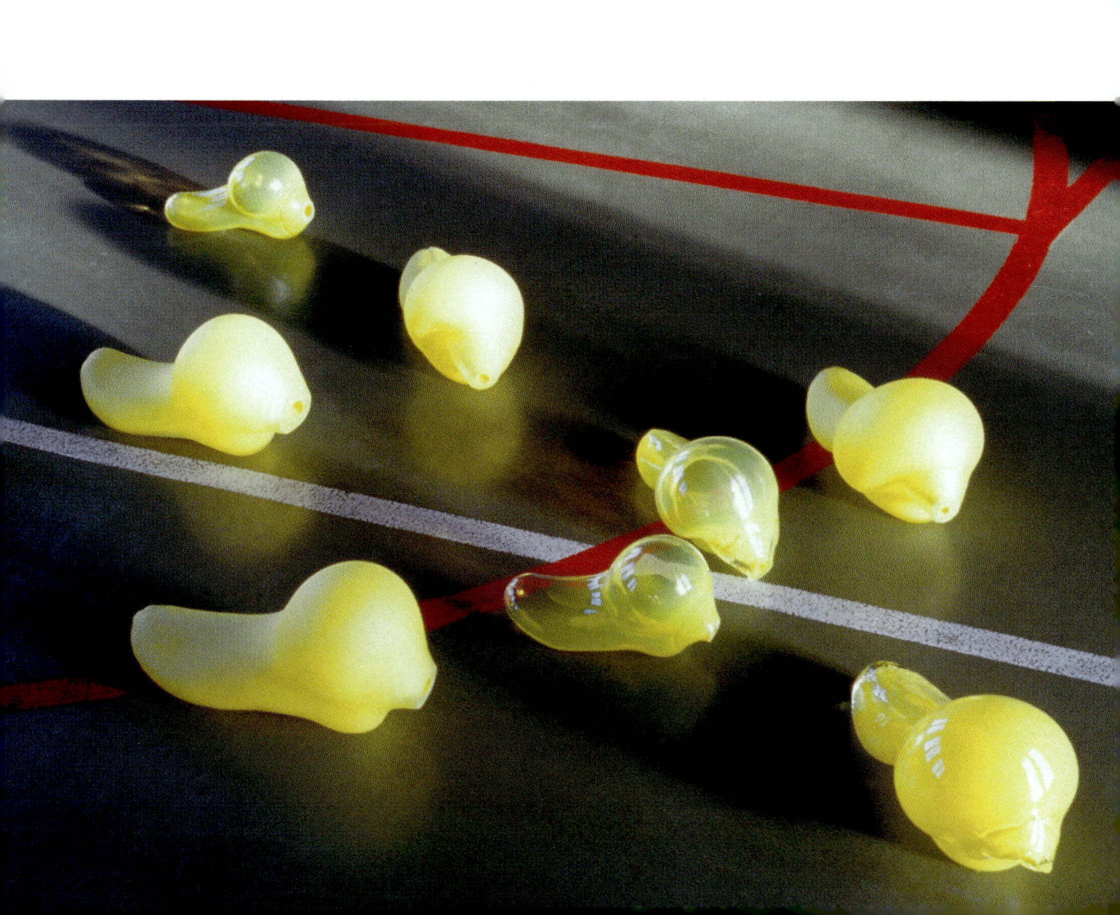

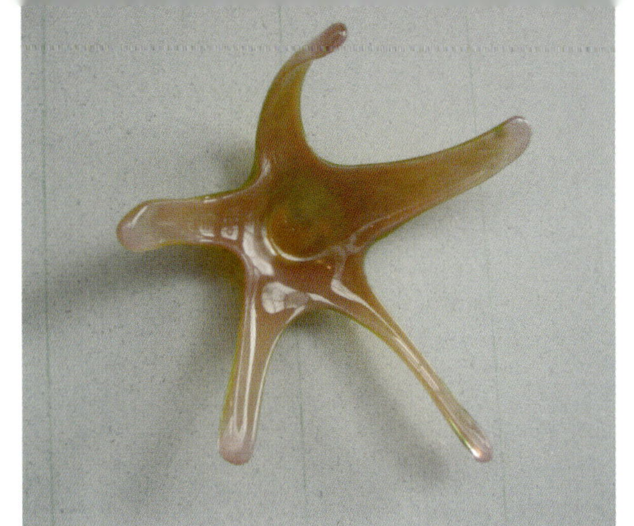

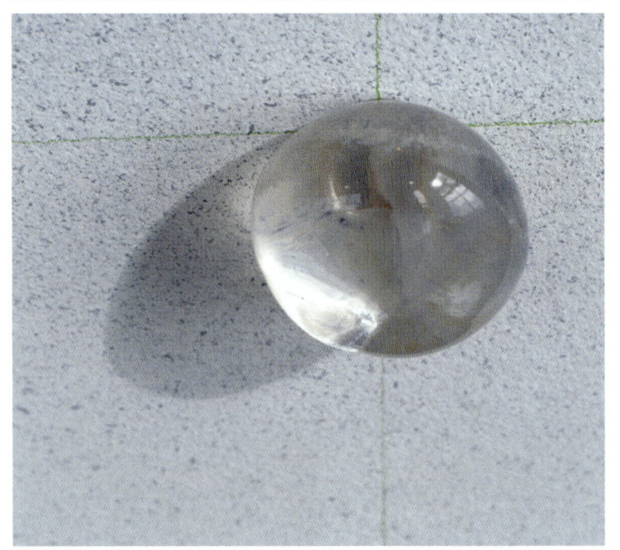

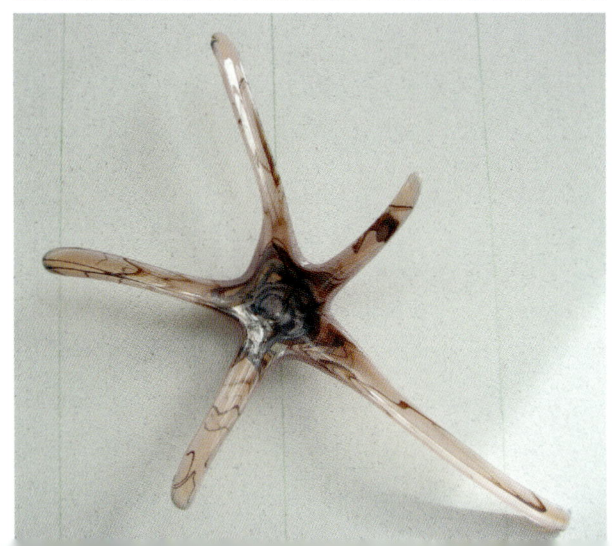

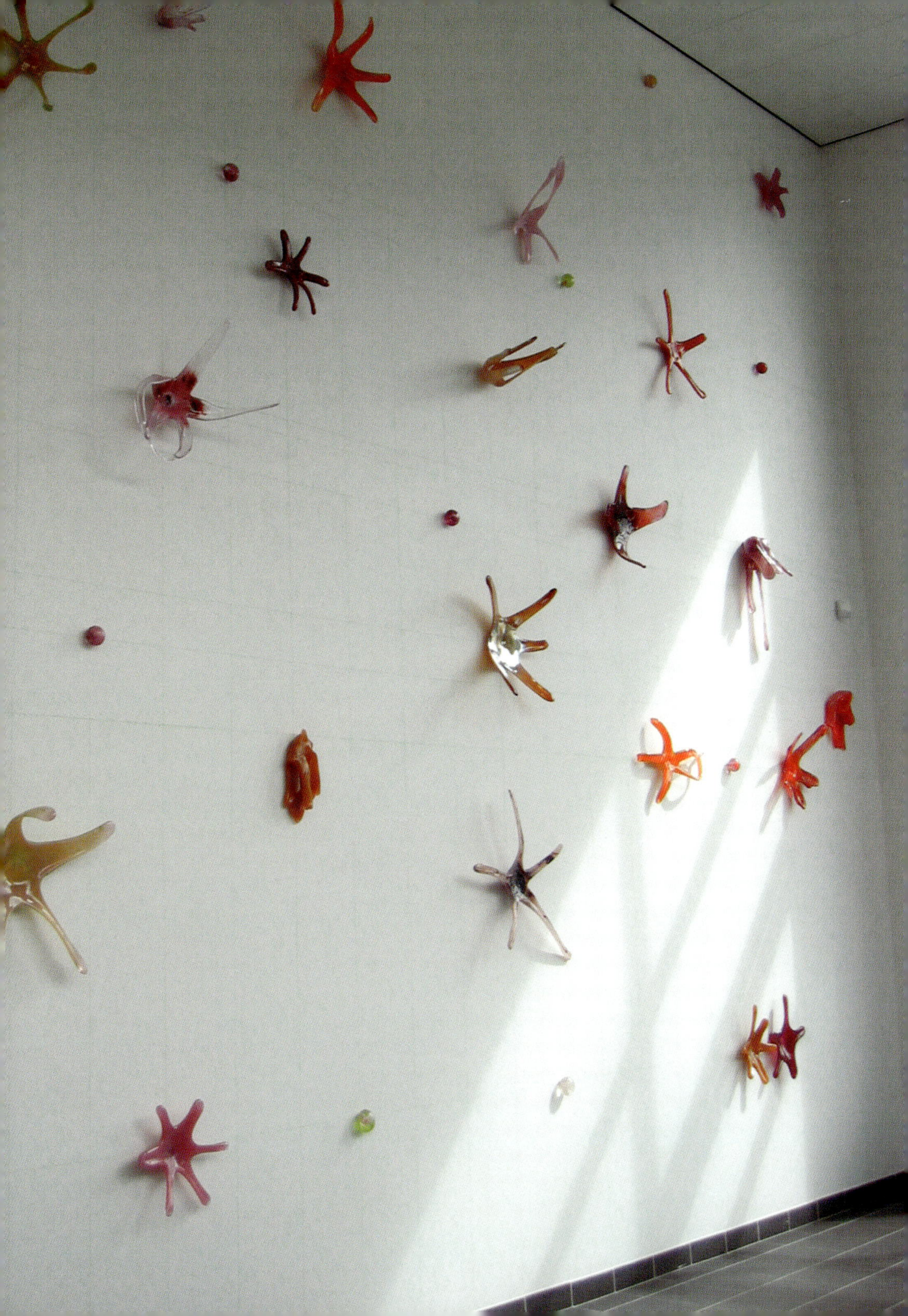

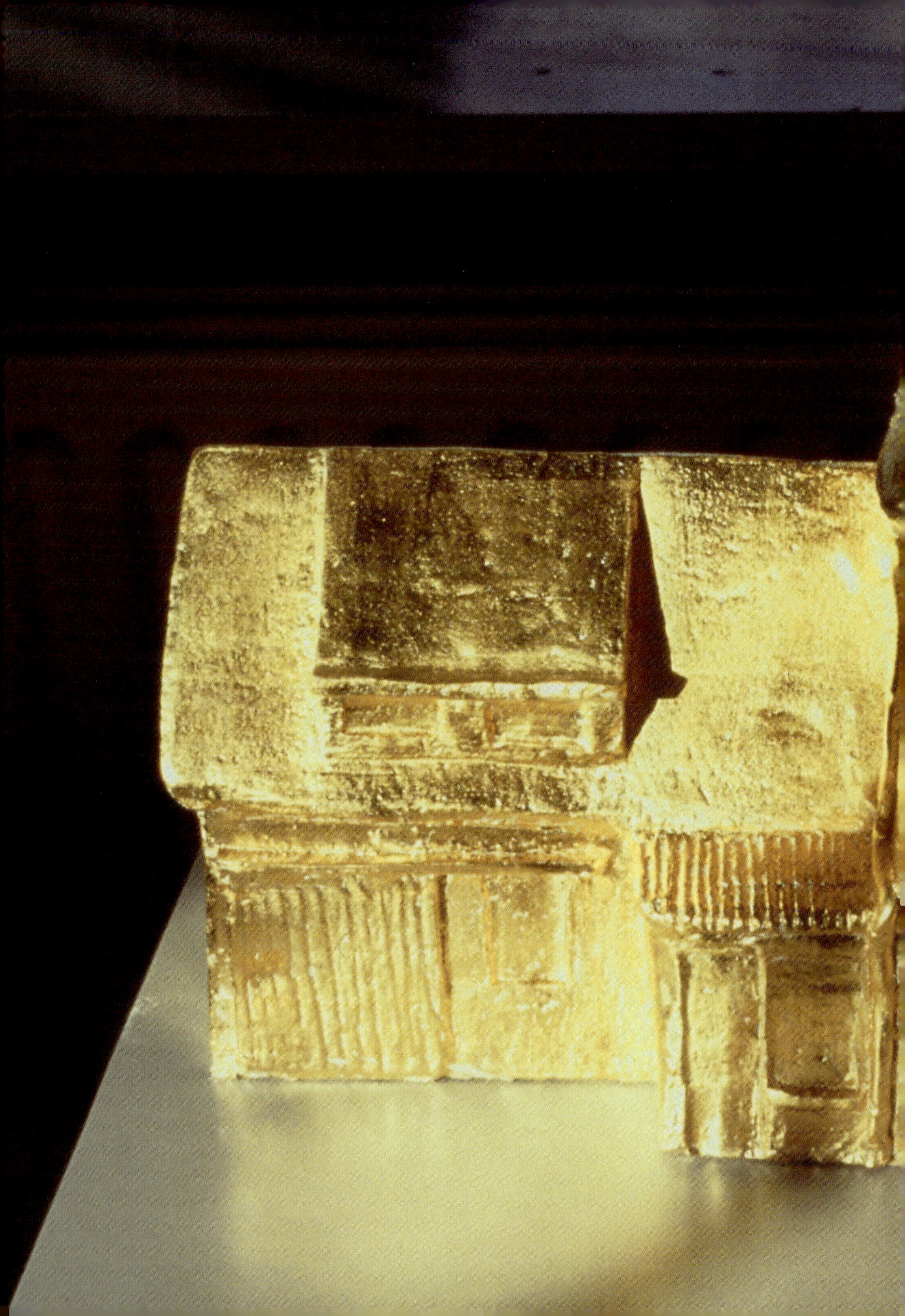

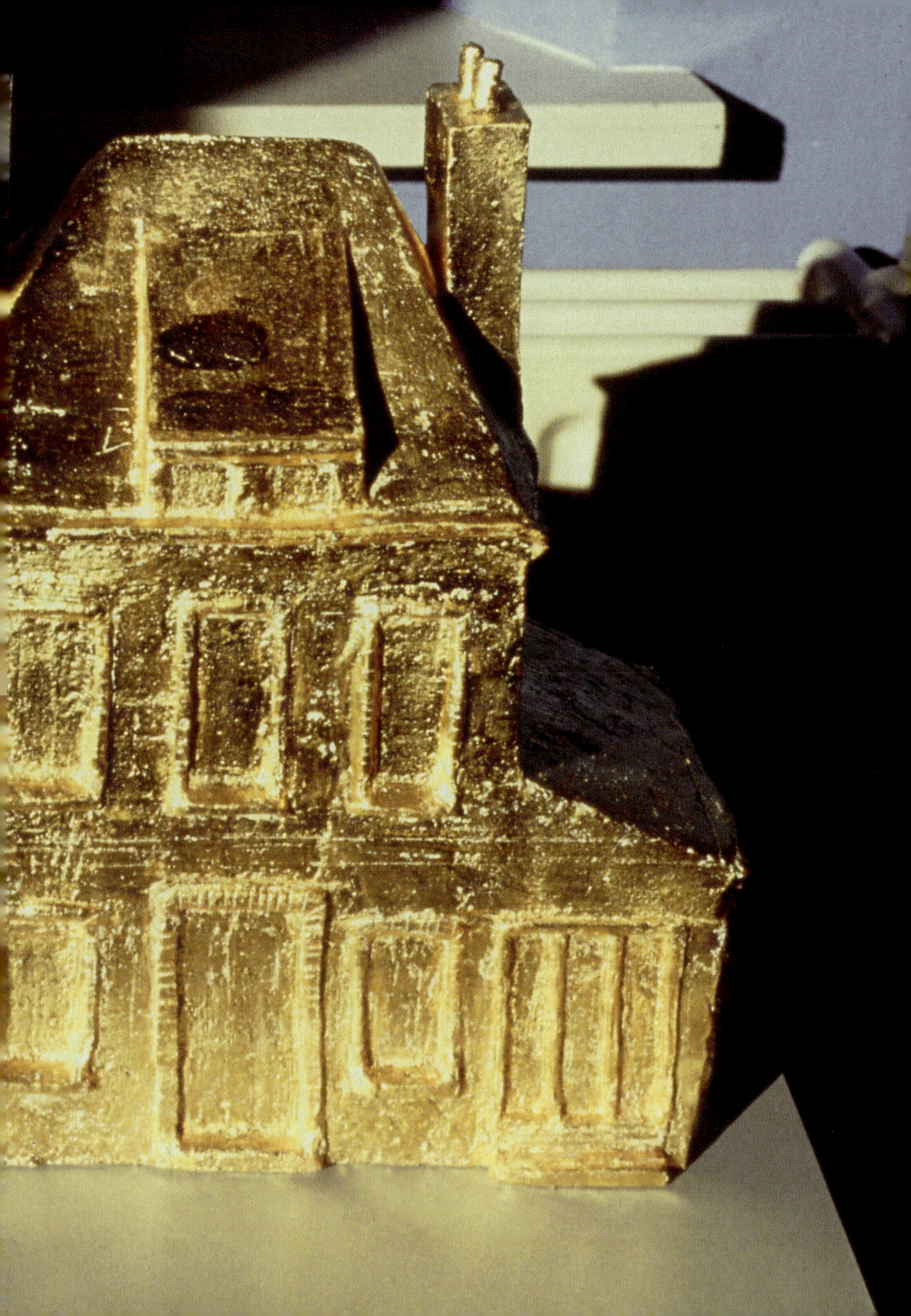

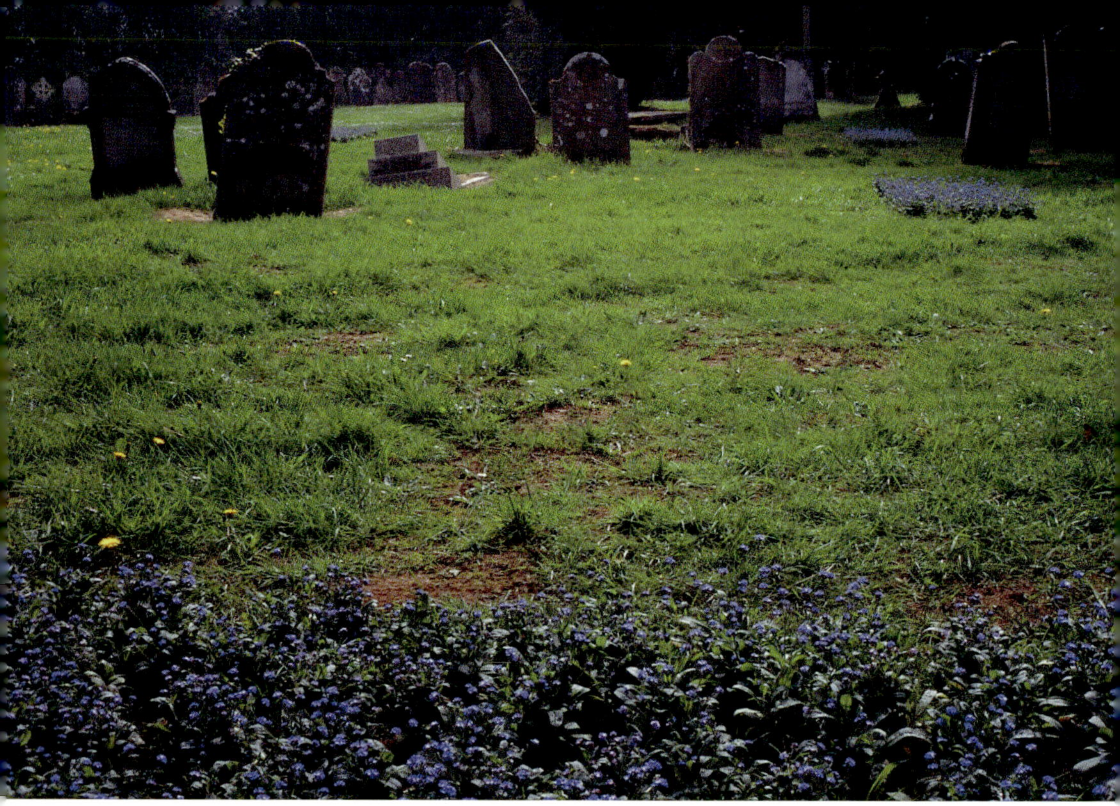

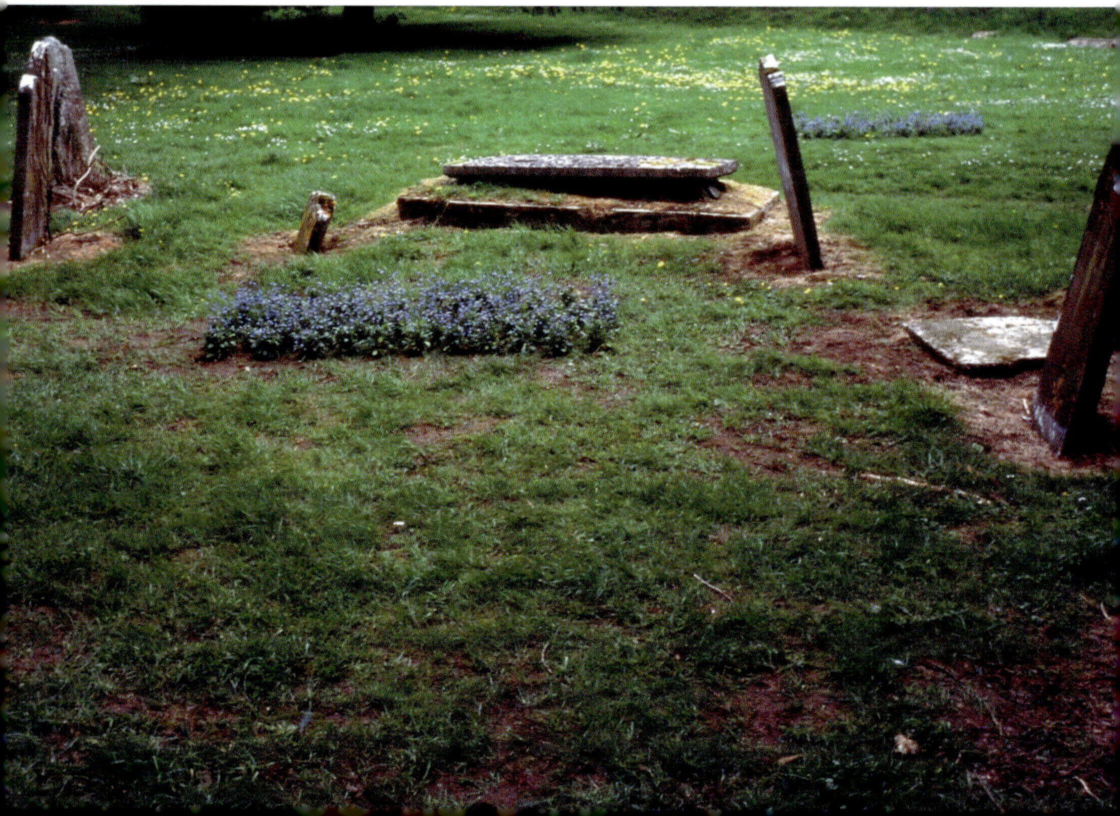

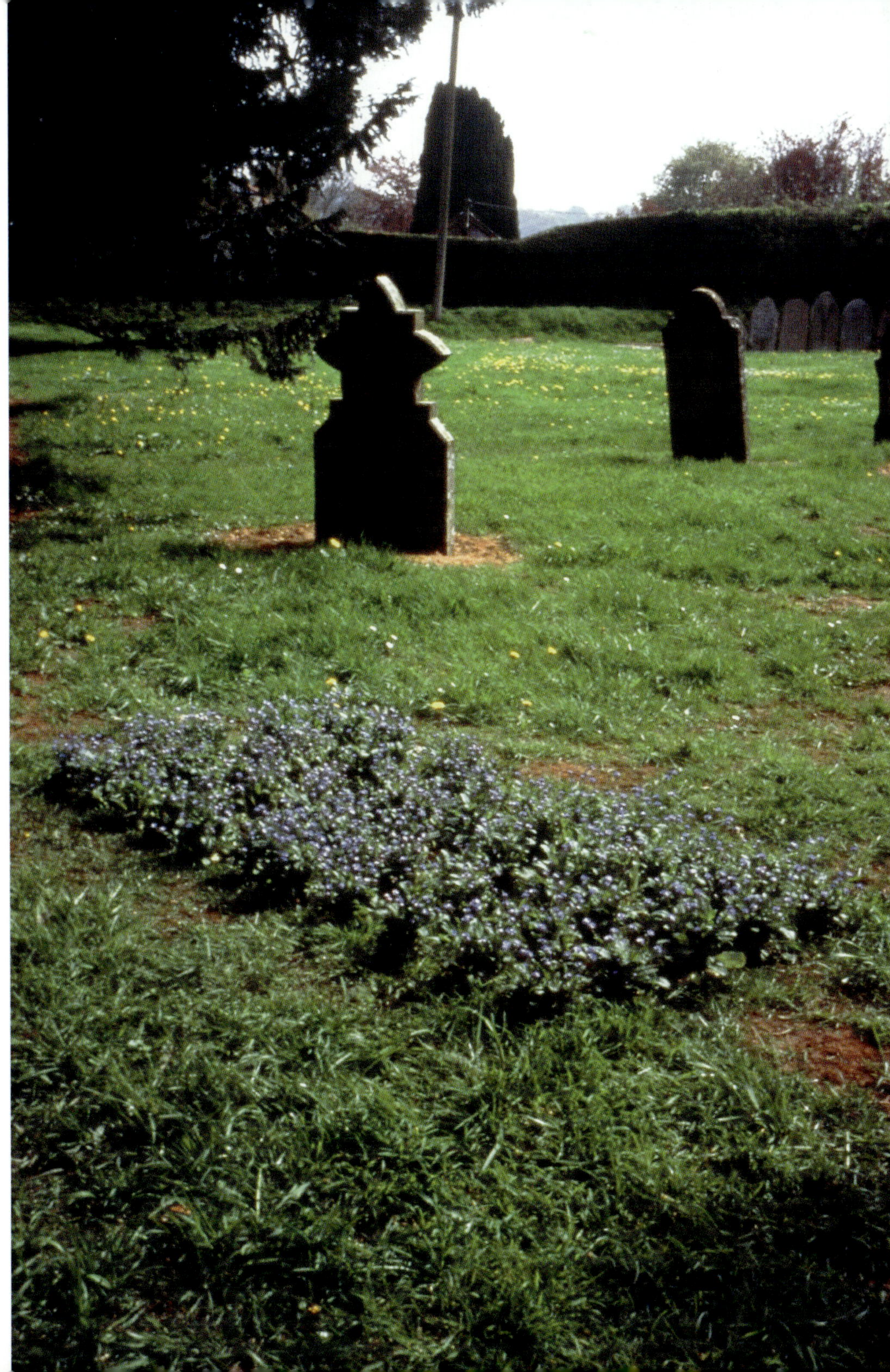

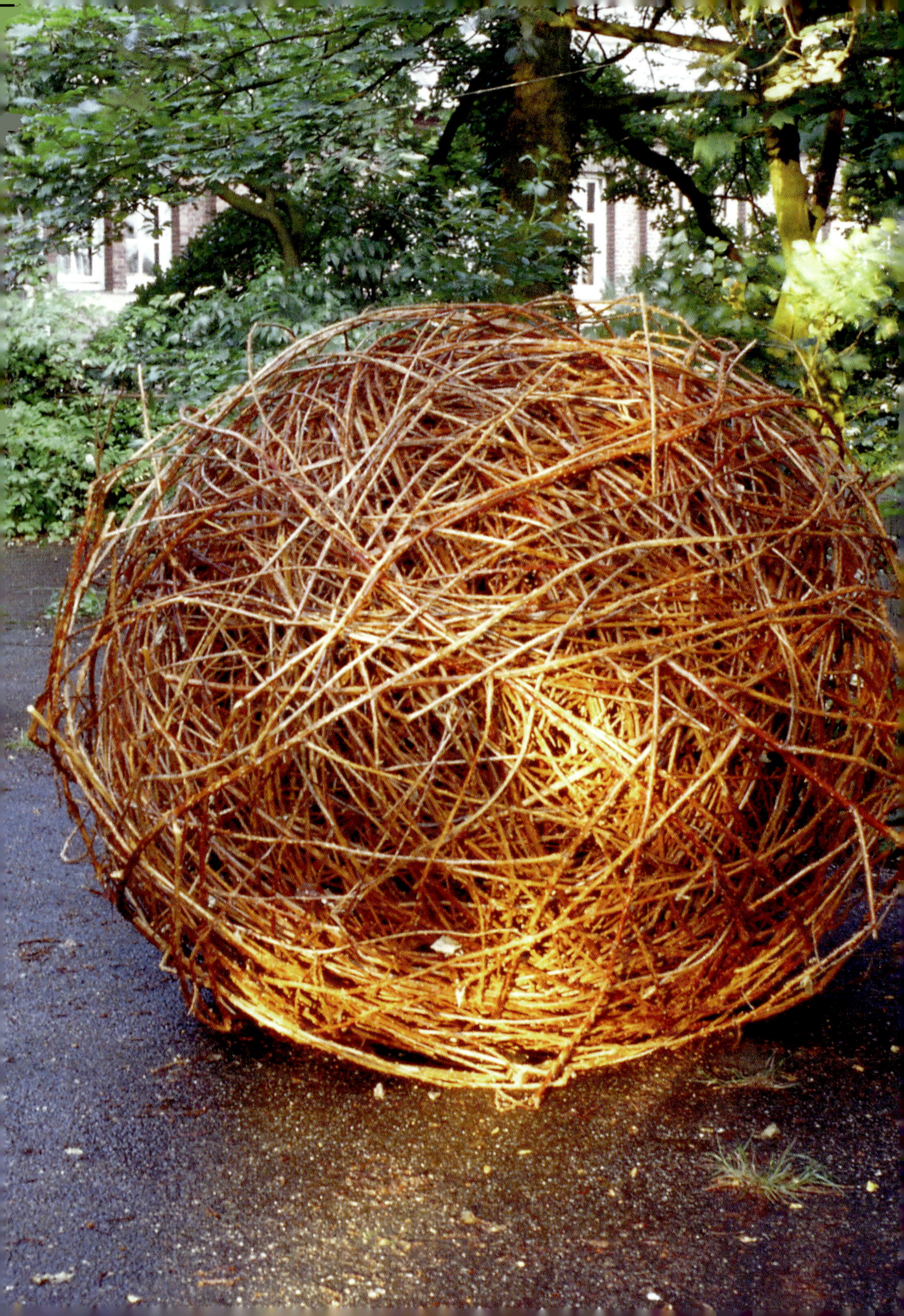

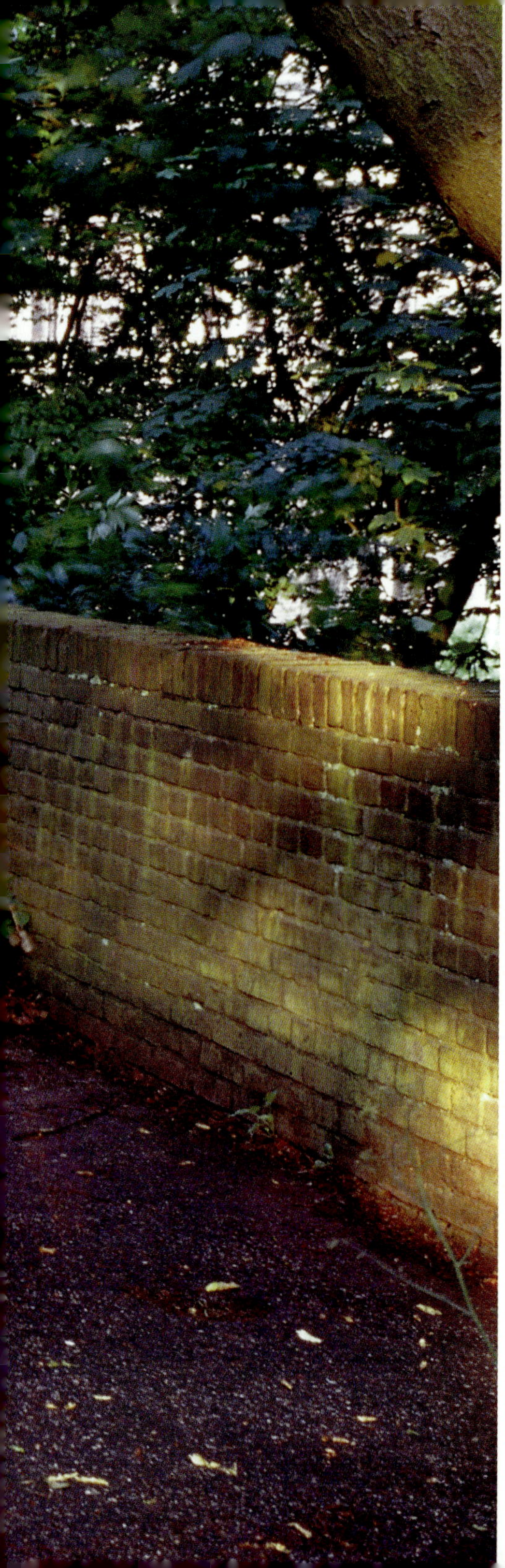

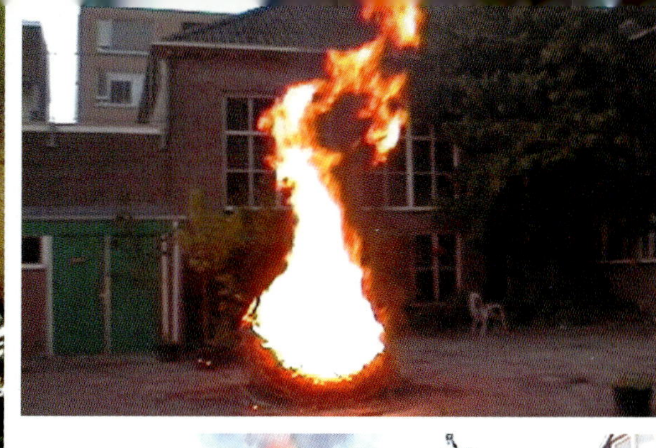
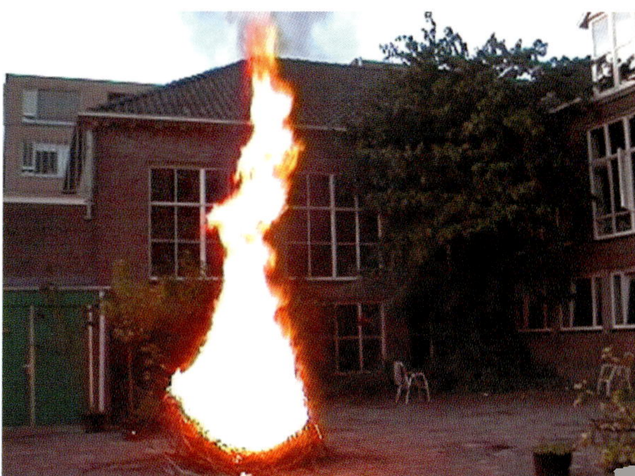
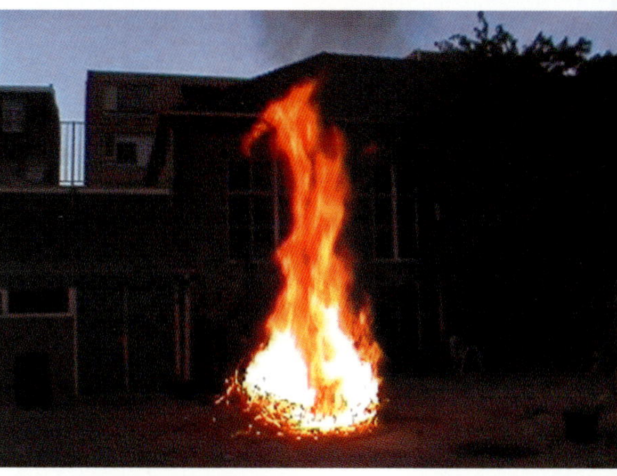
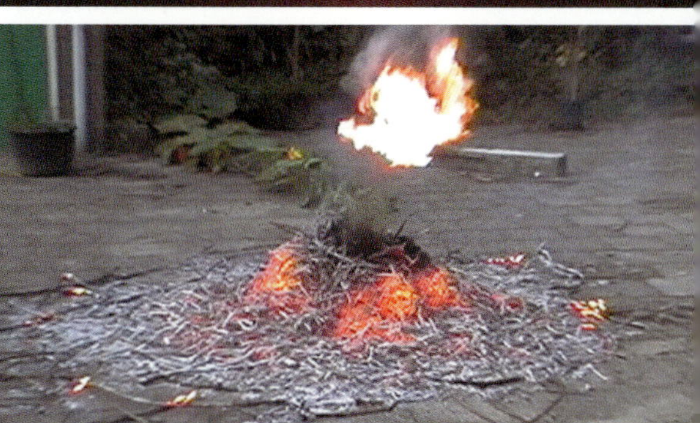

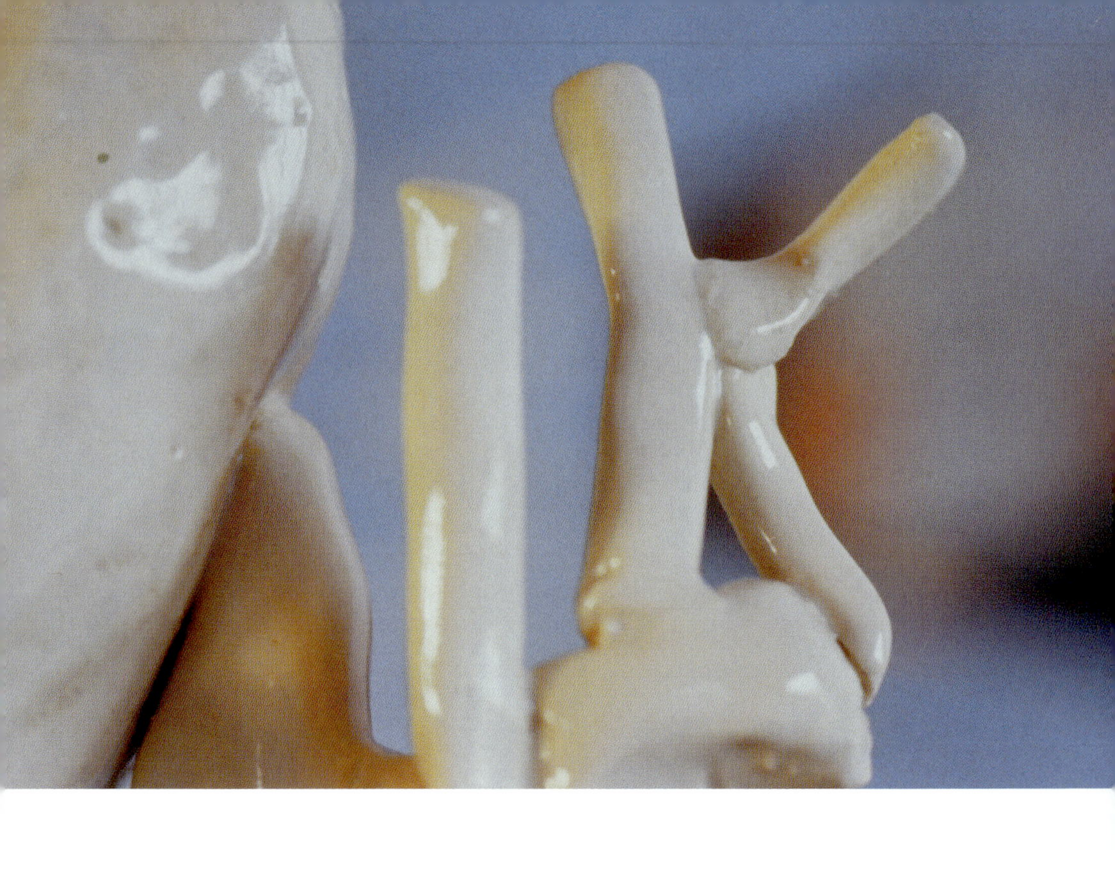

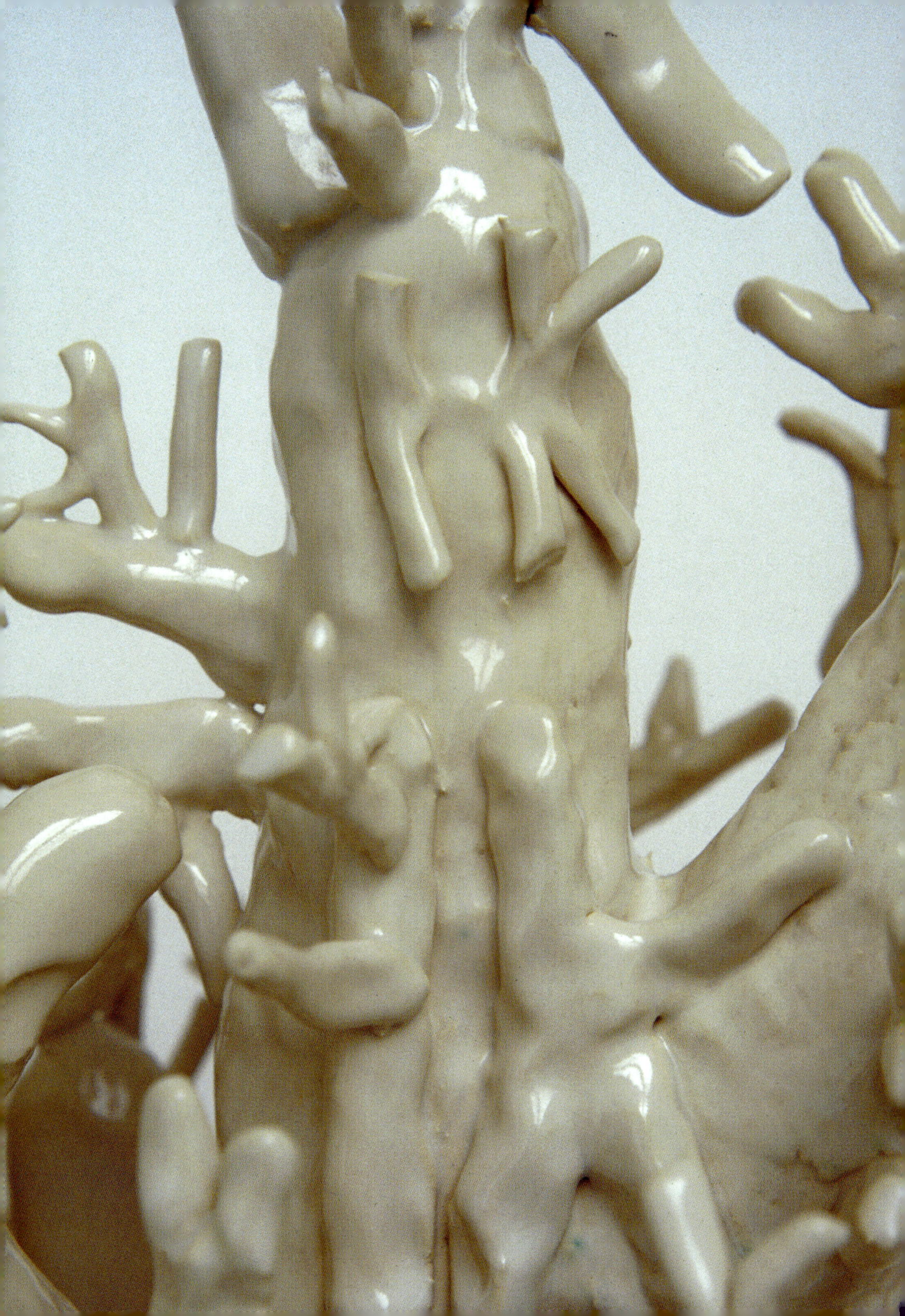

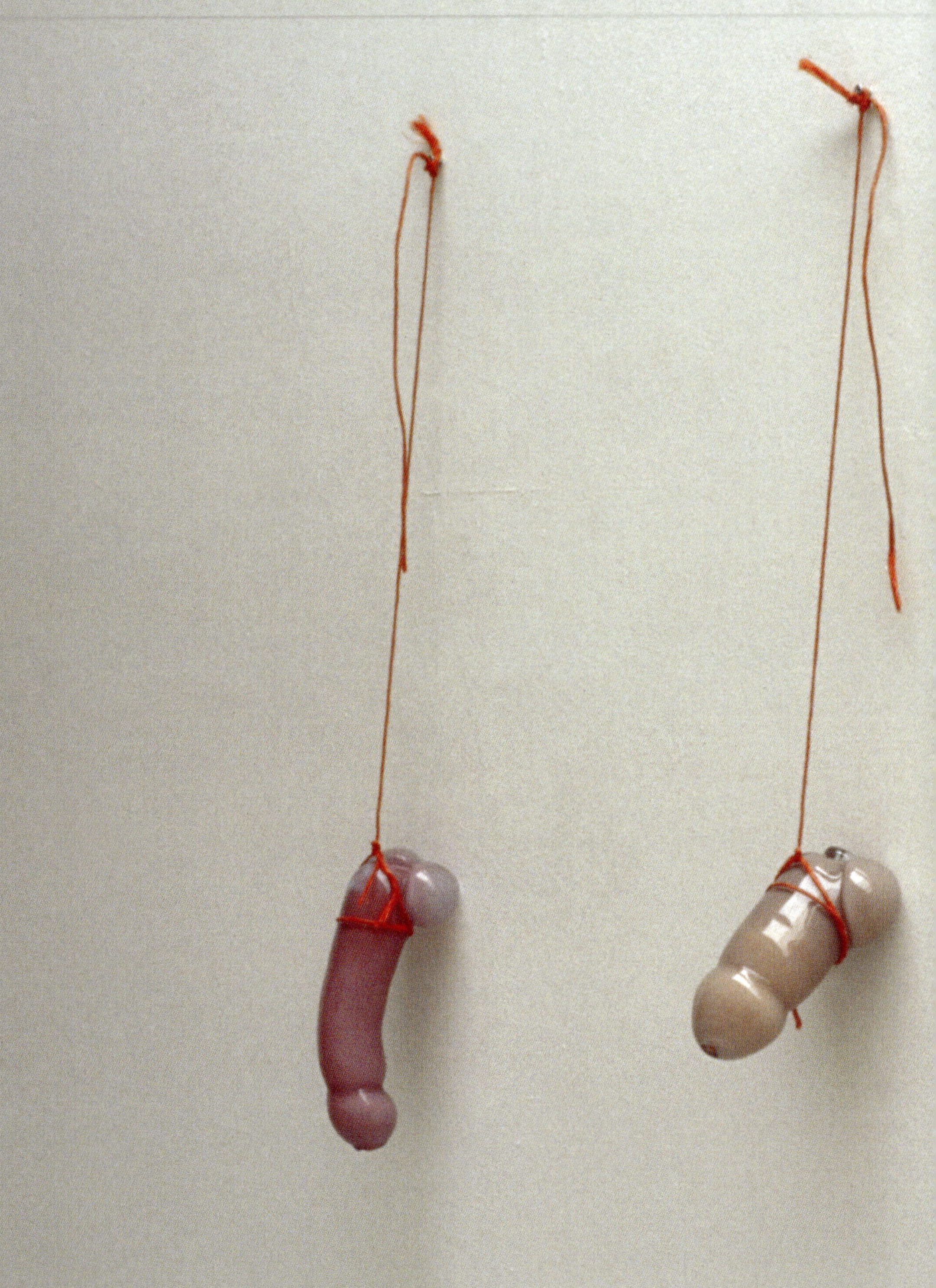

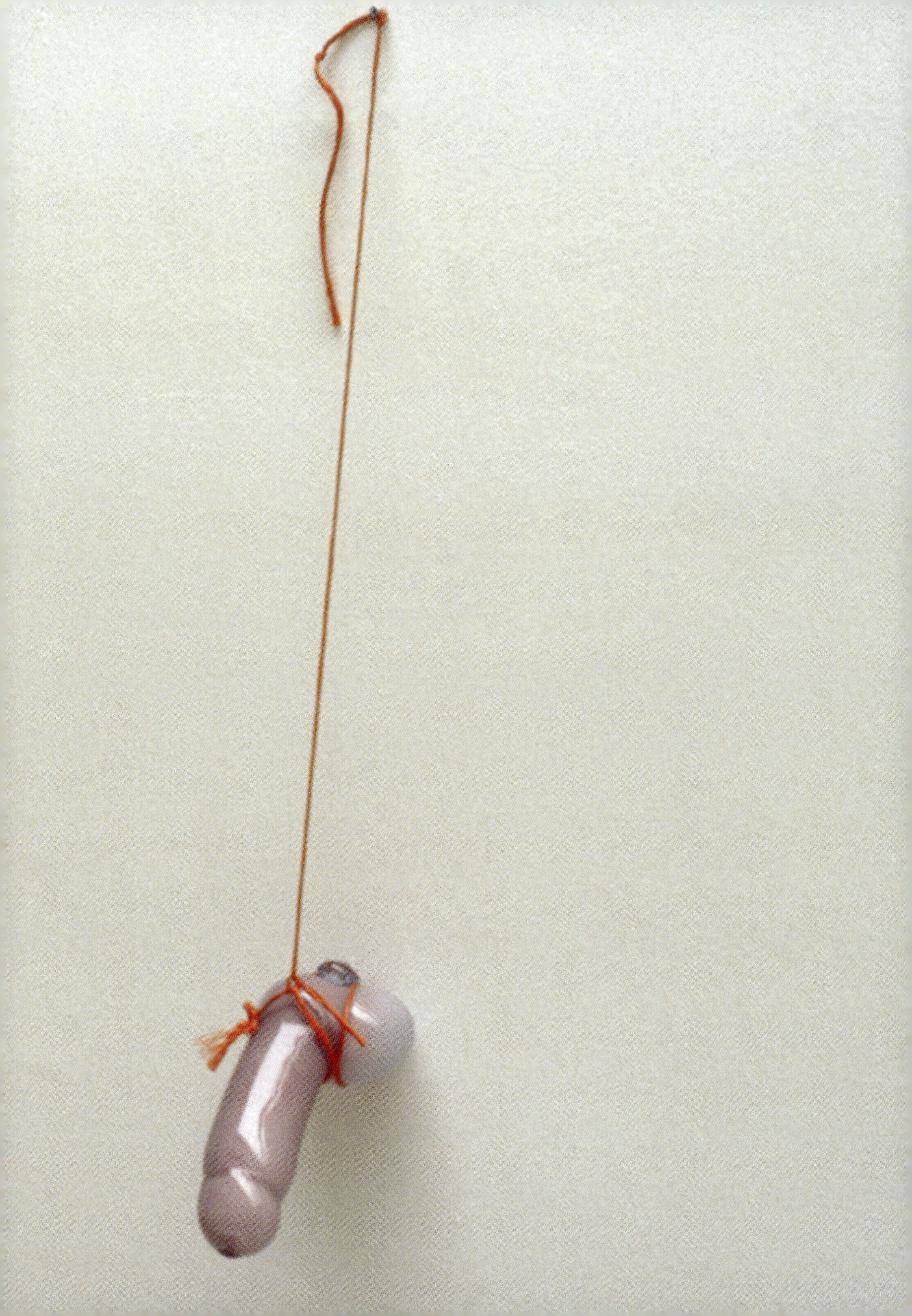

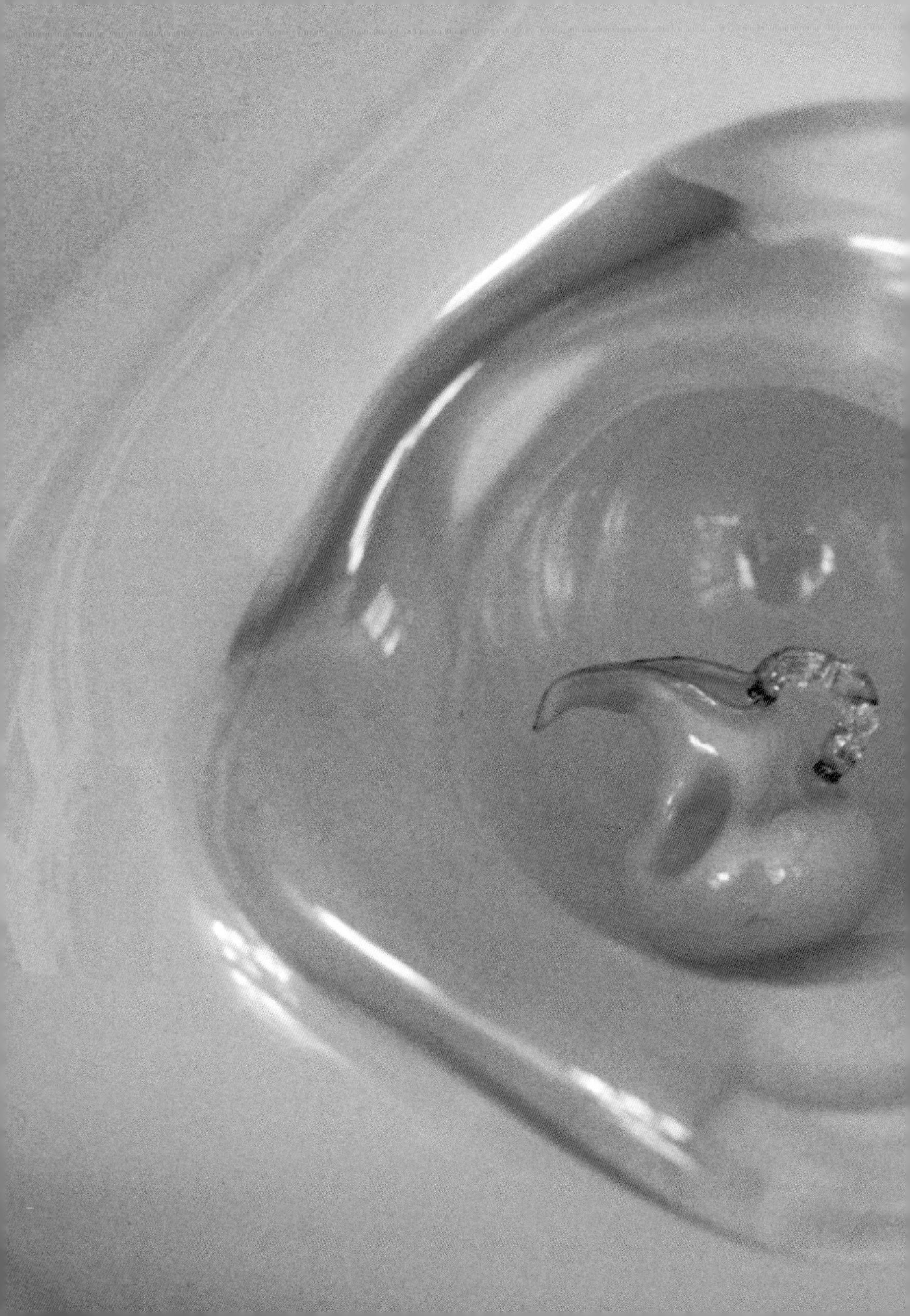

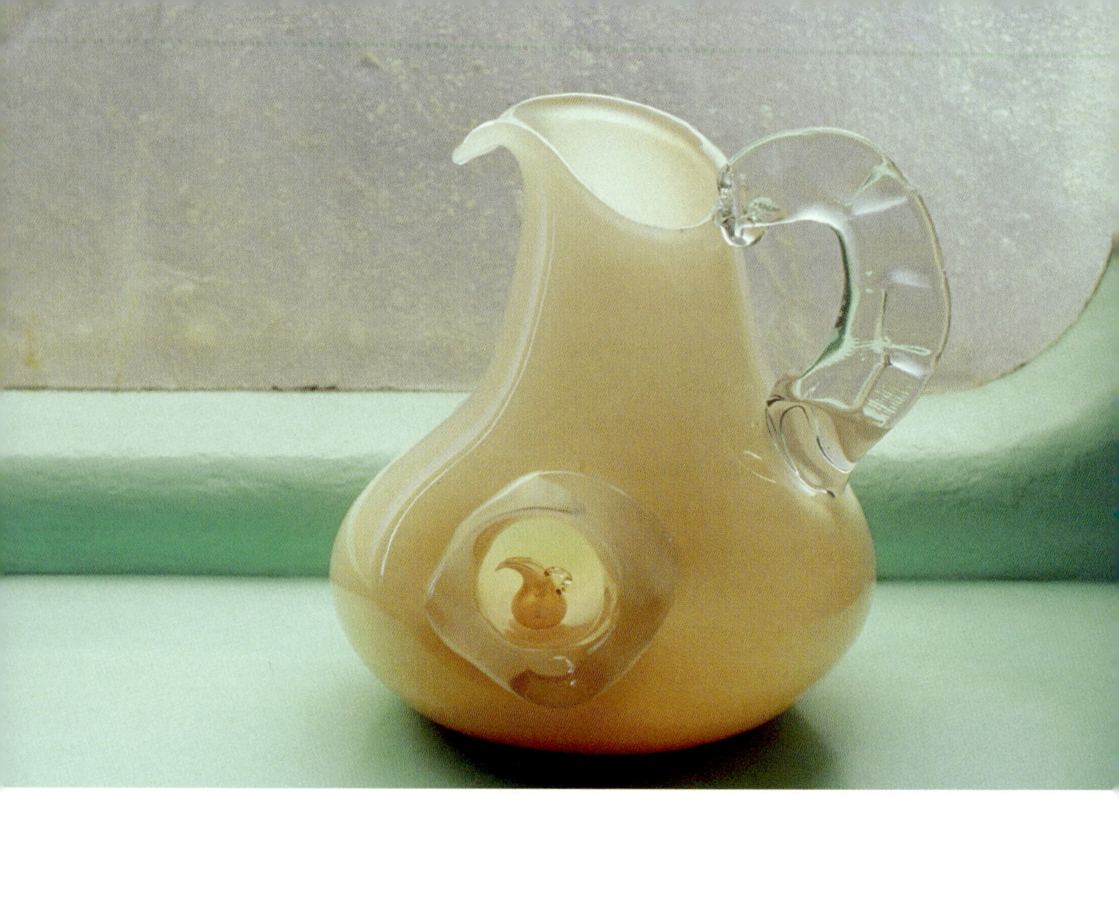

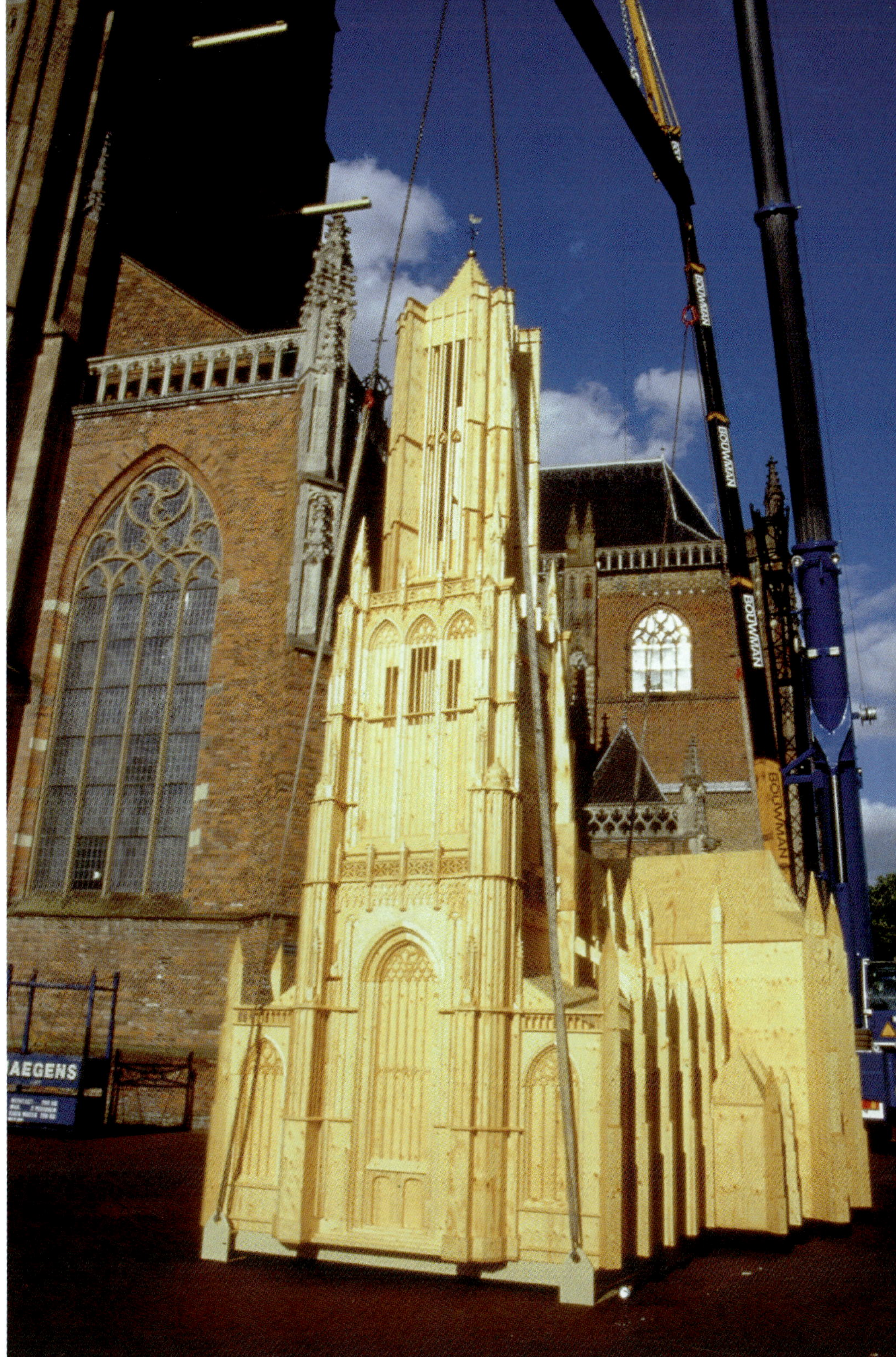

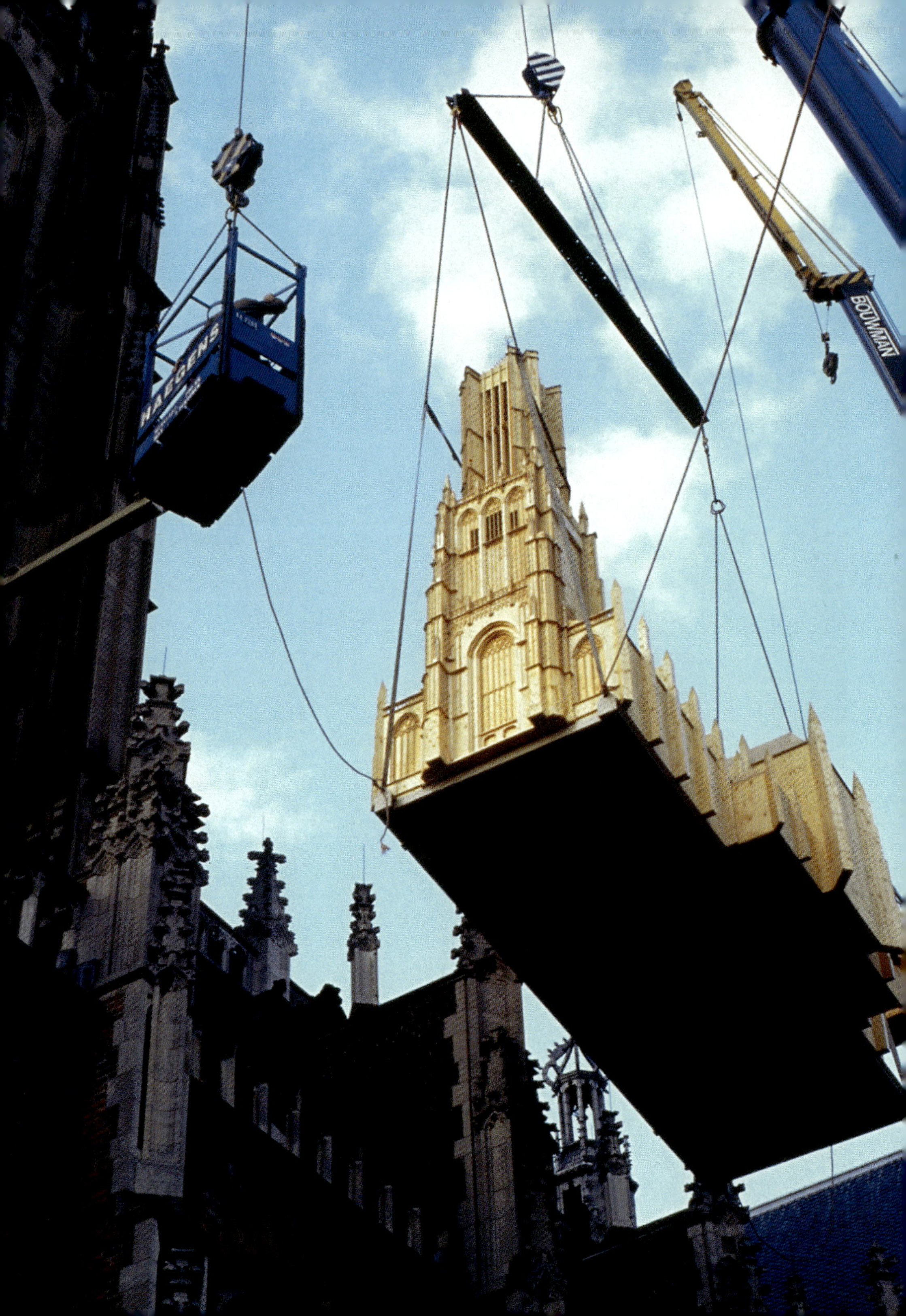
HAEGENS
BOUWMAN

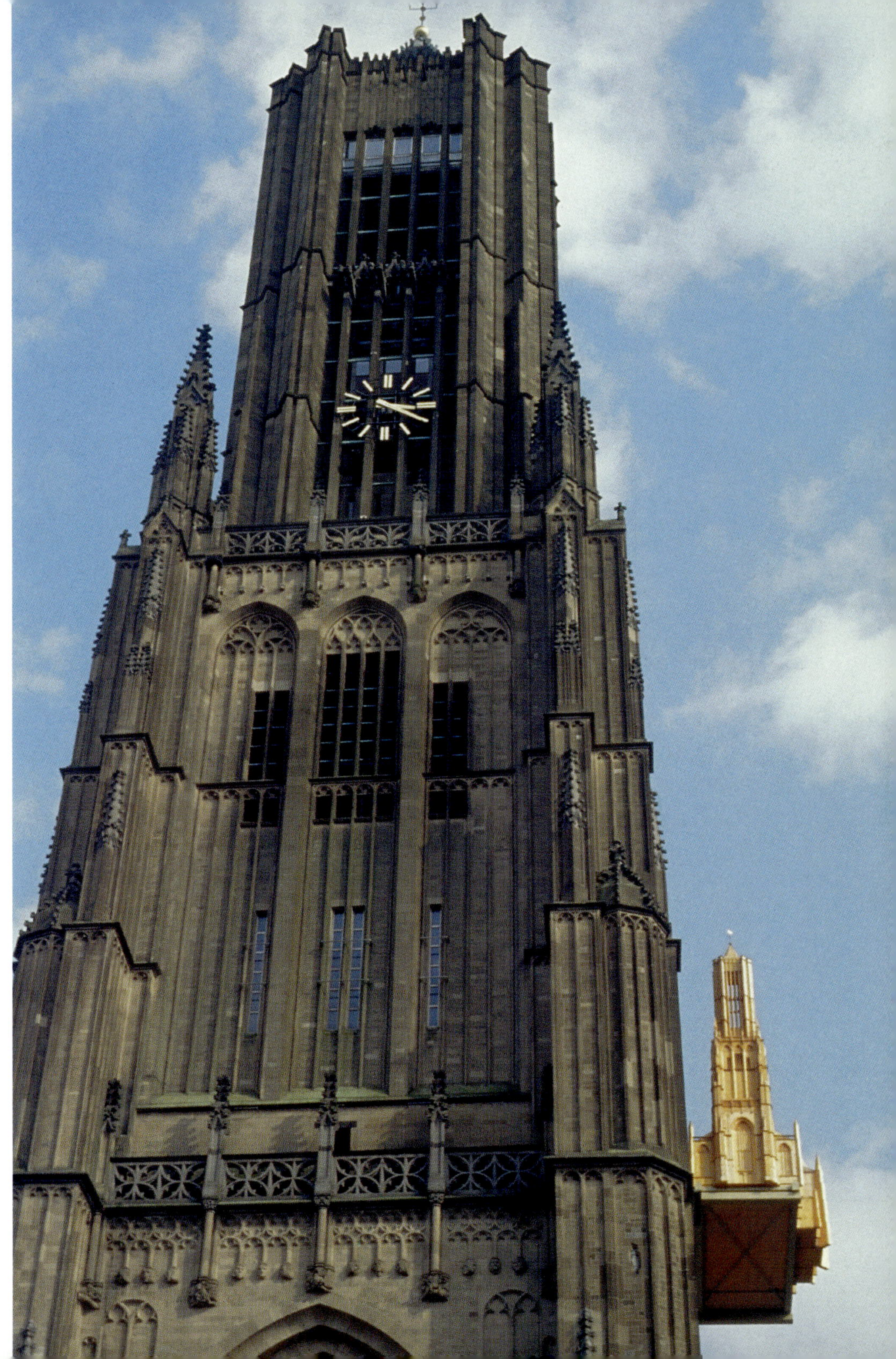

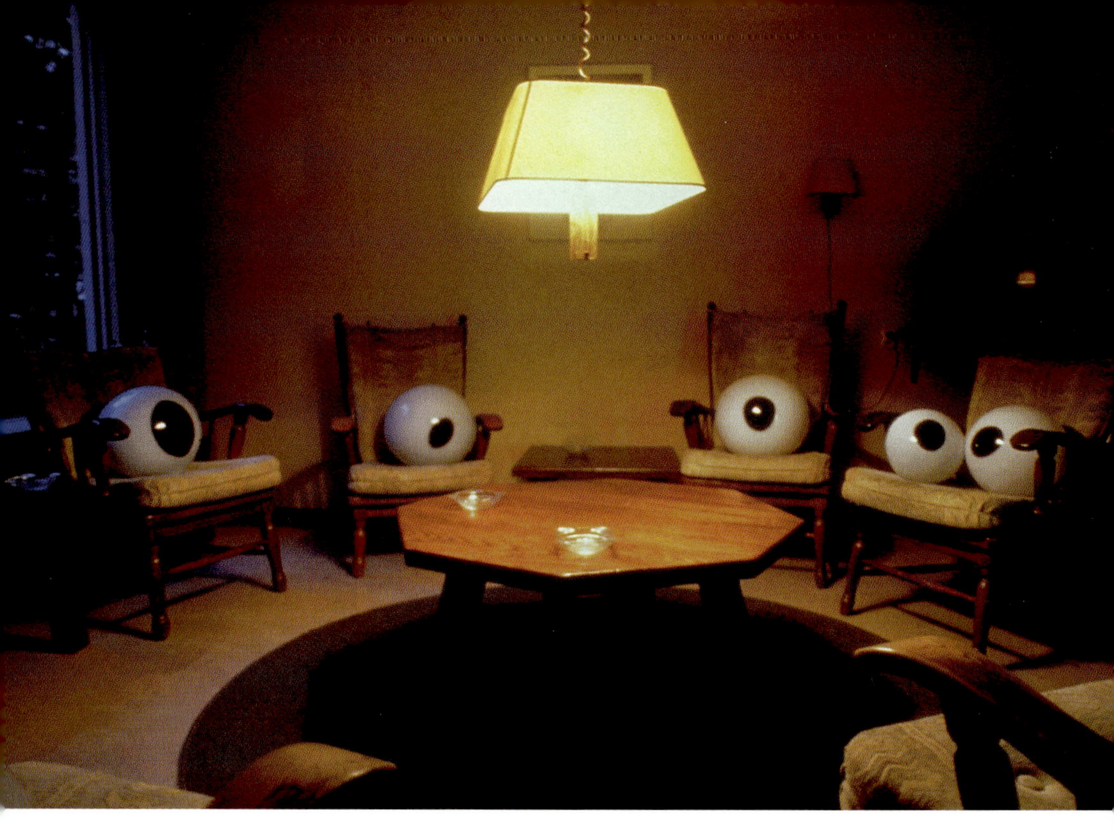

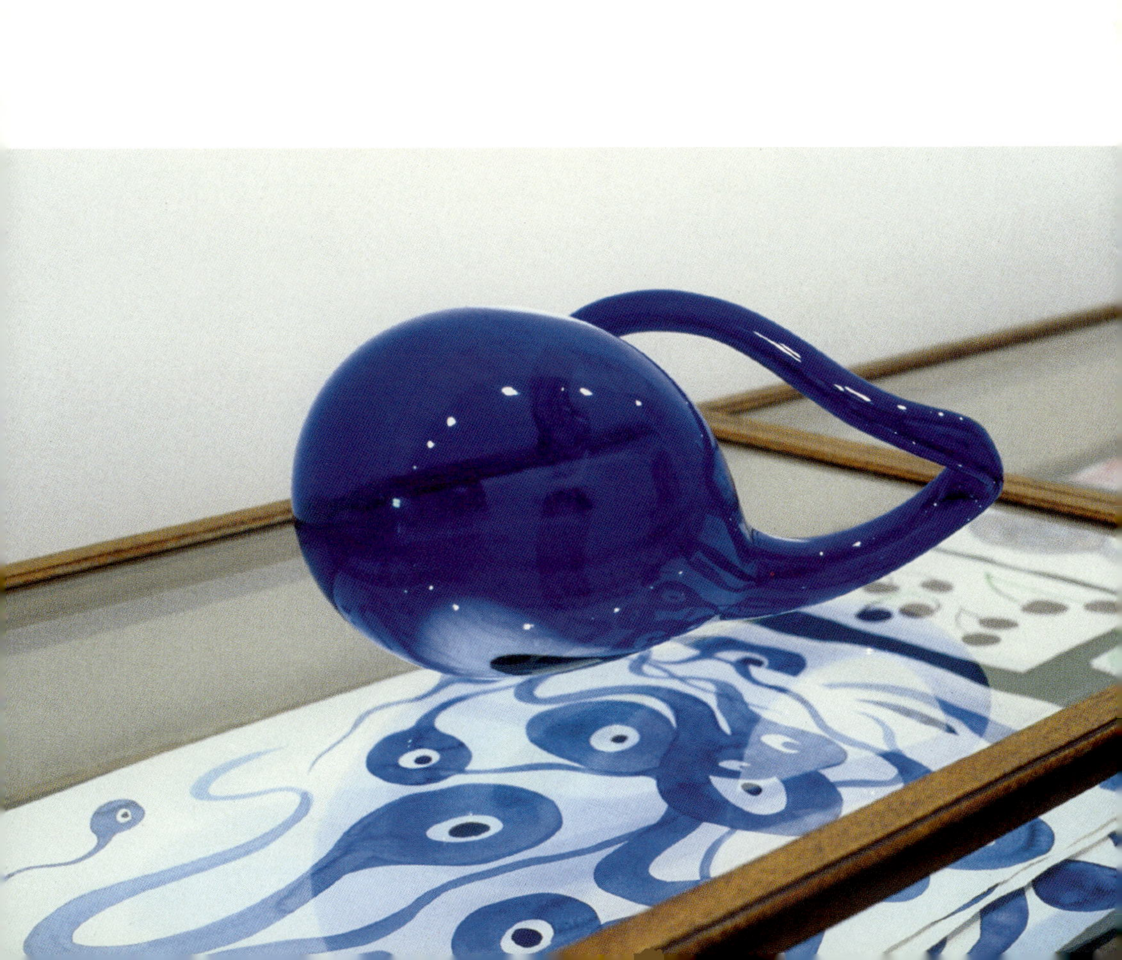

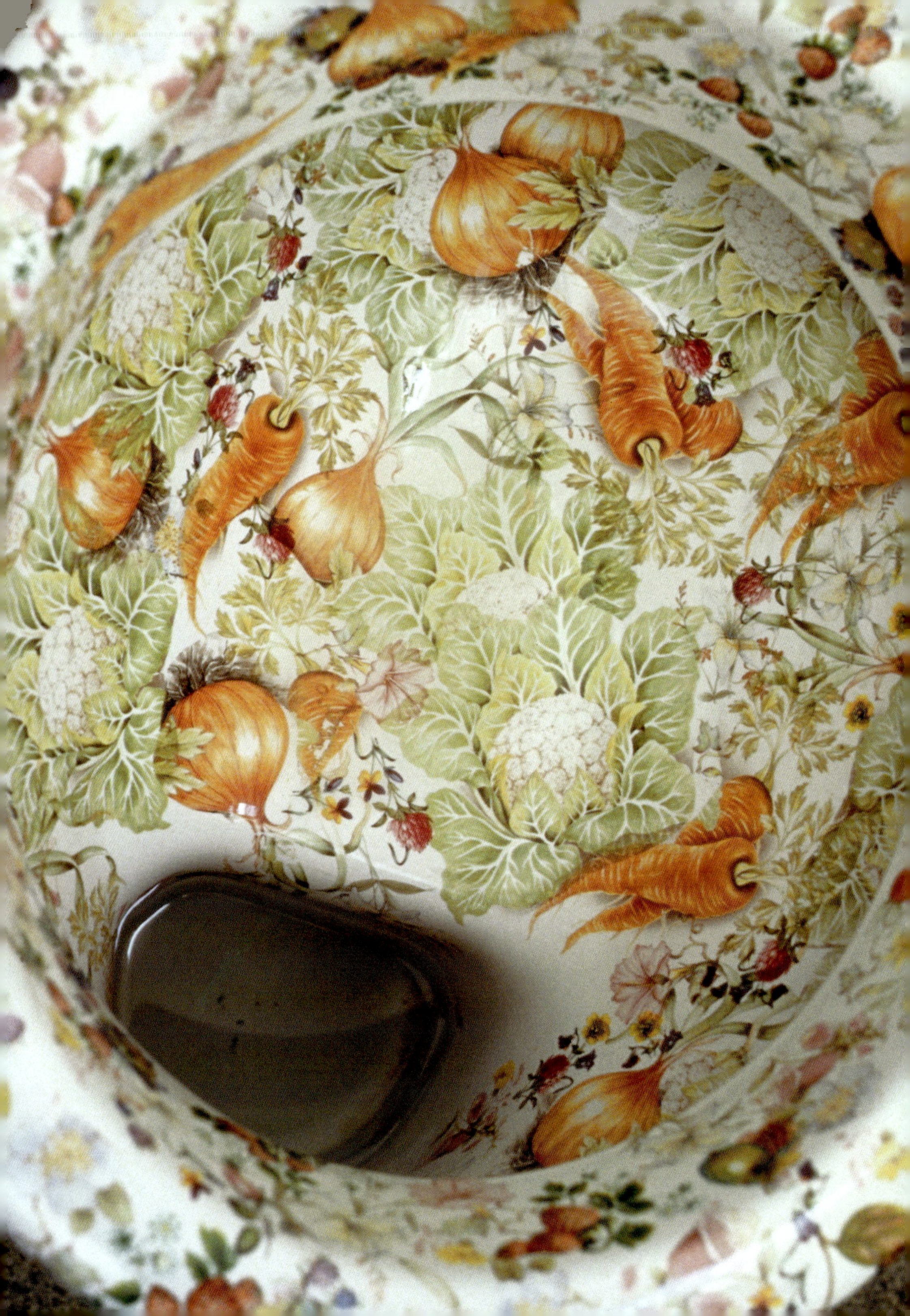

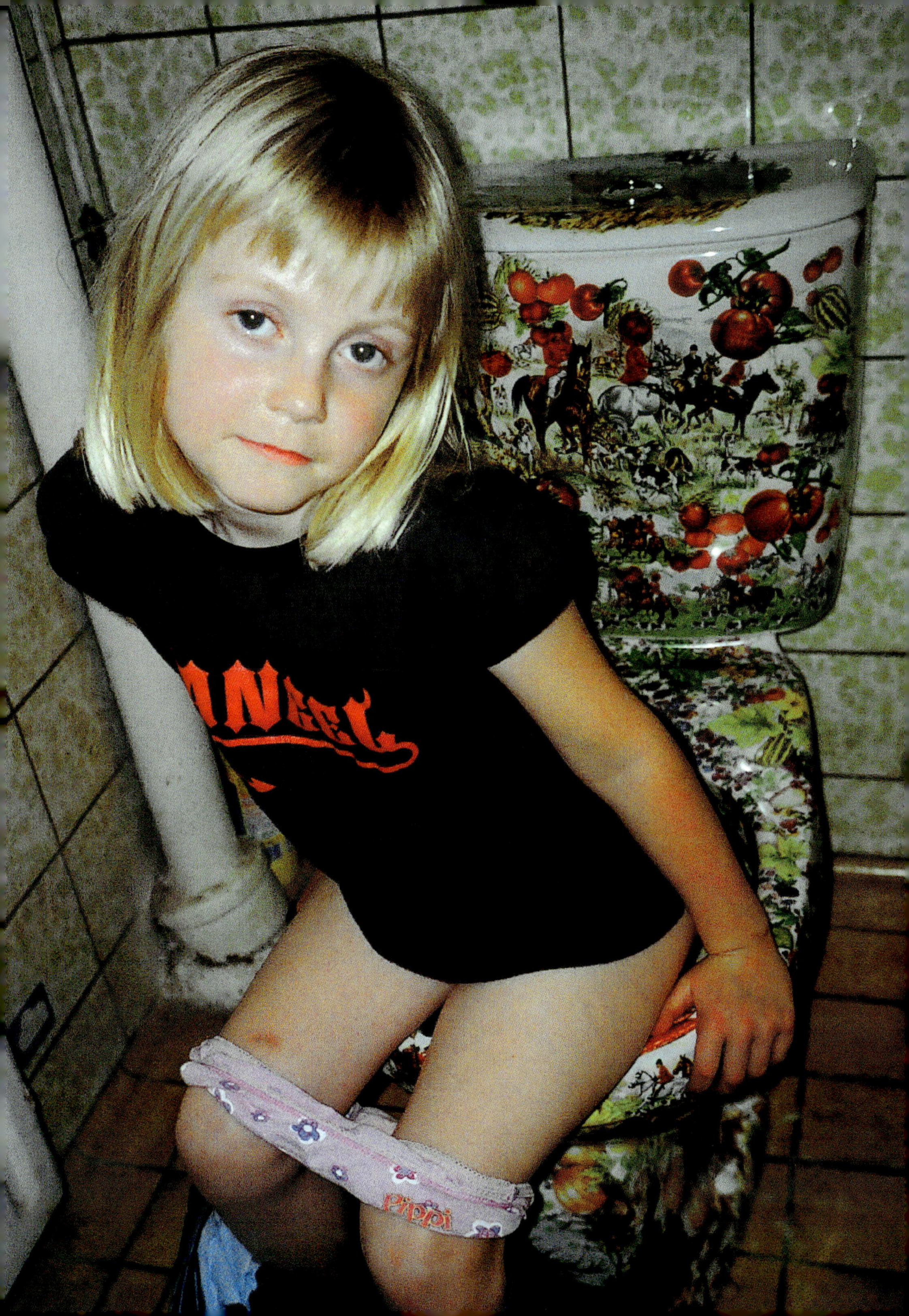
ANGEL
Pippi

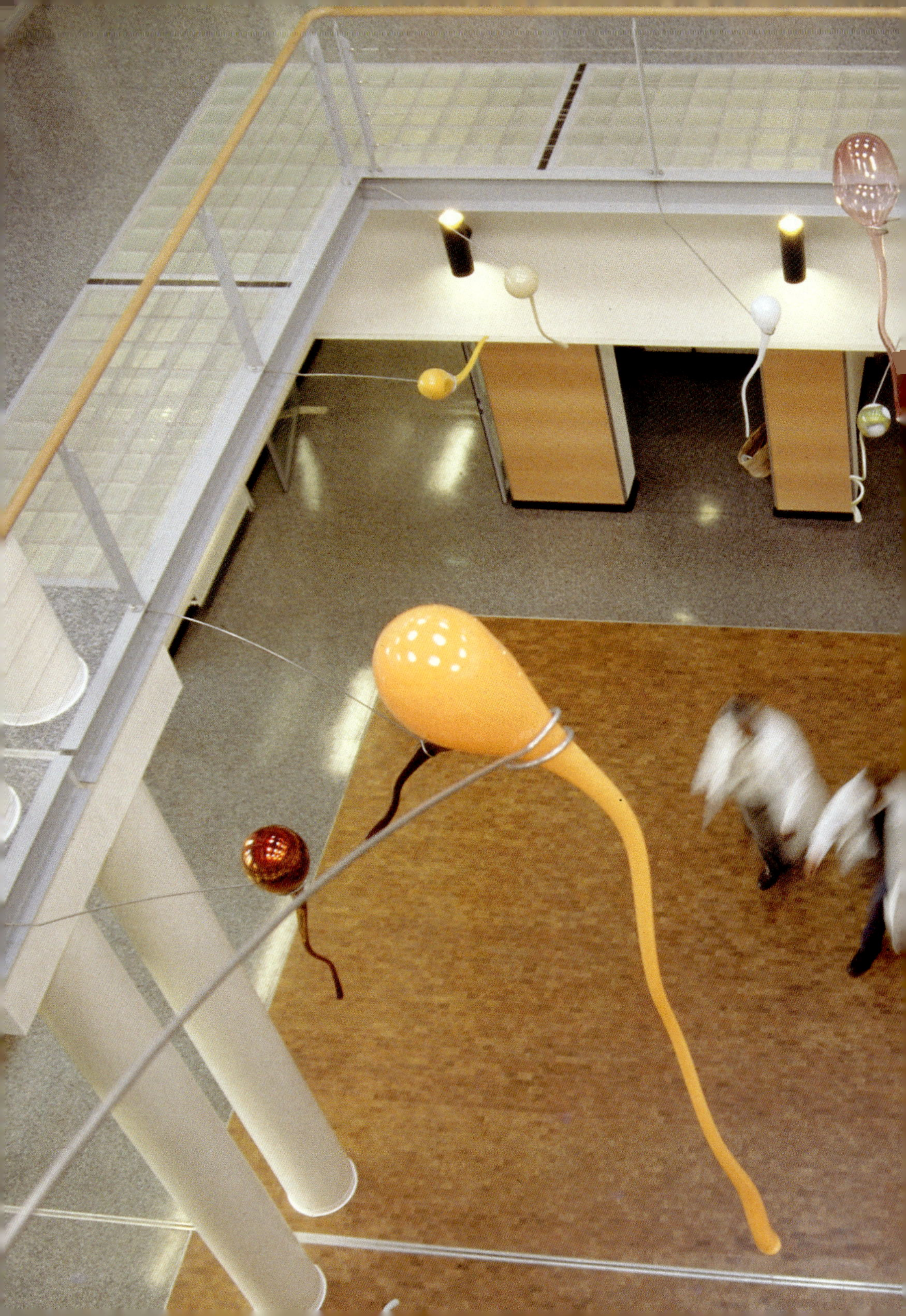

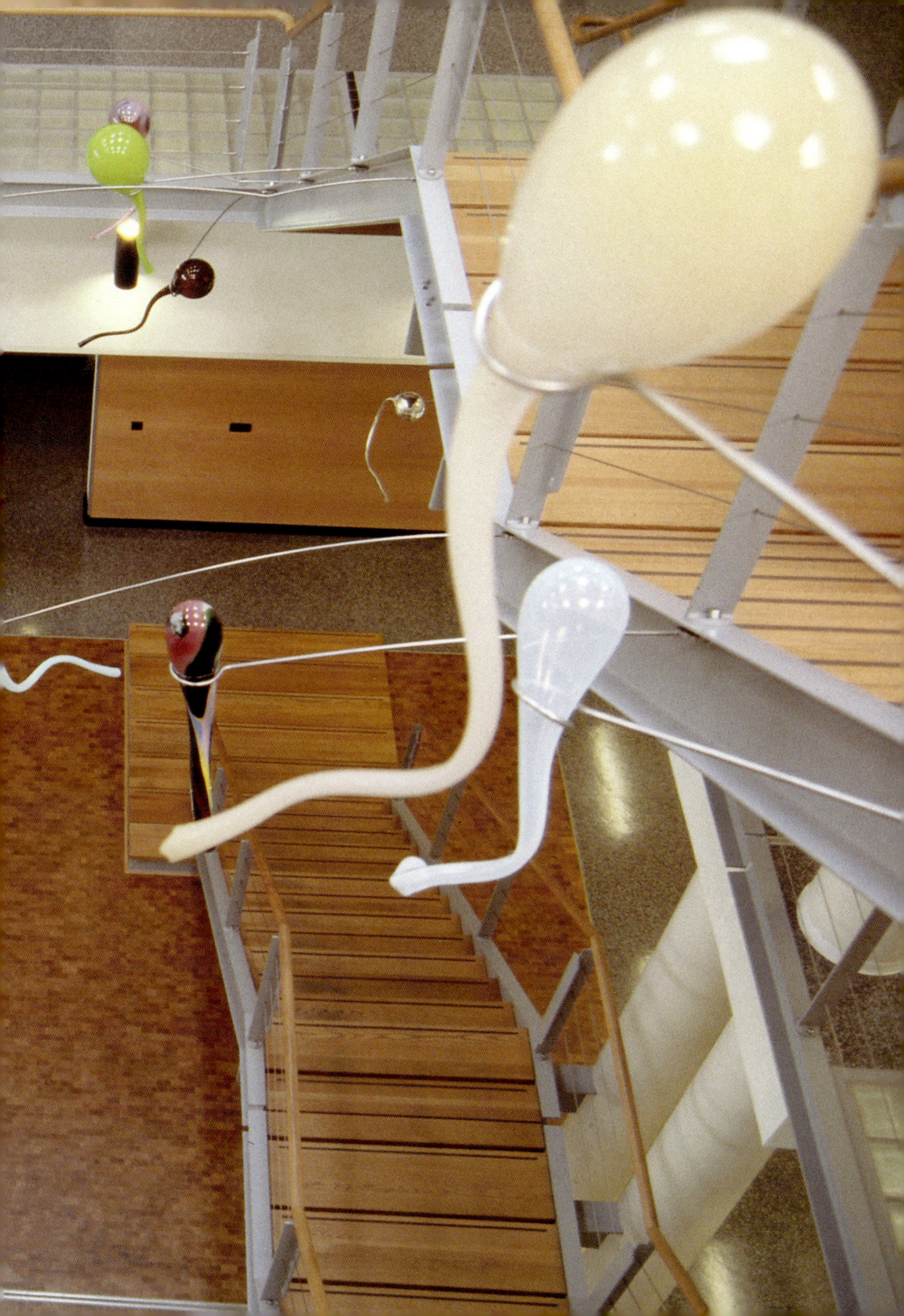

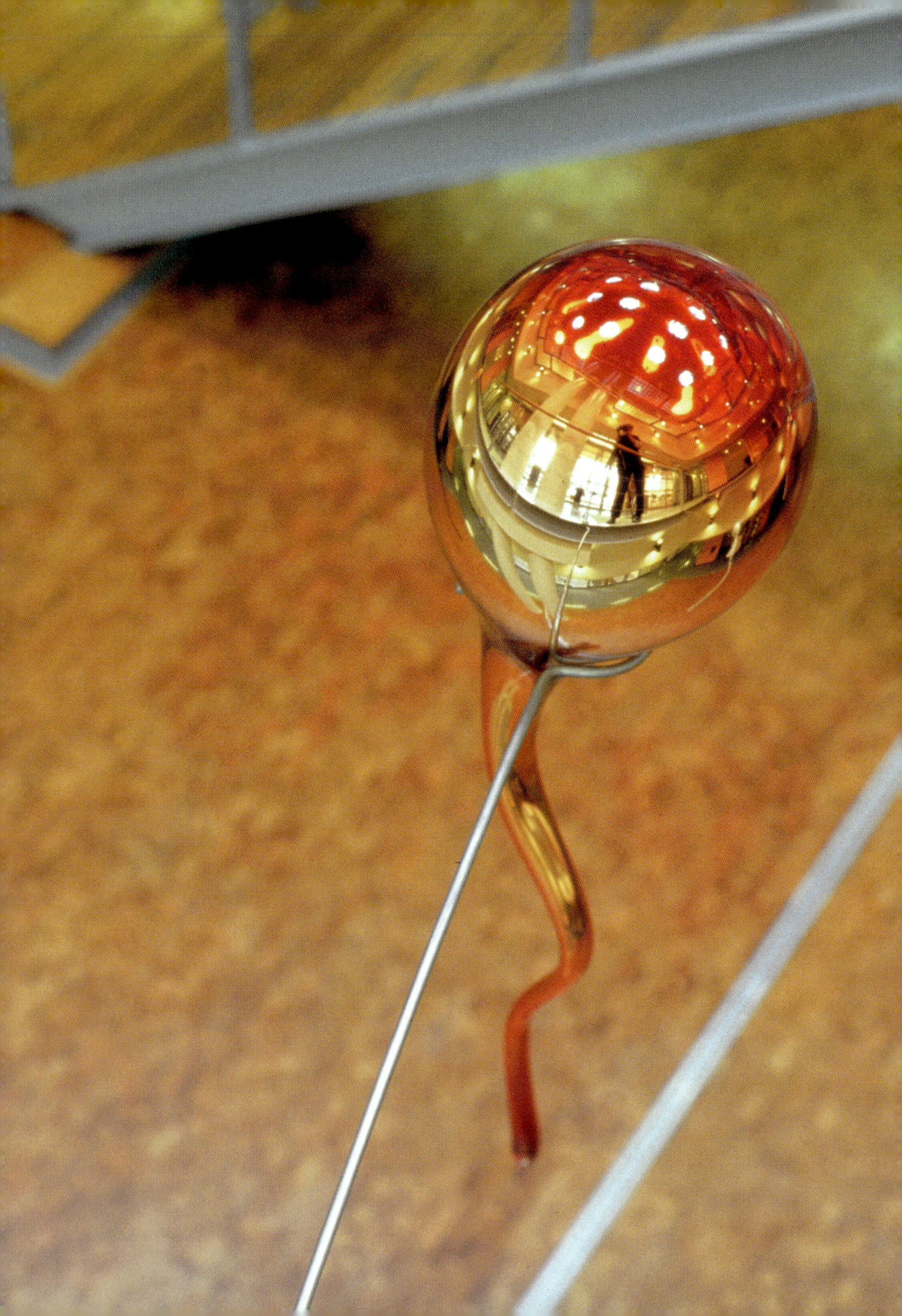

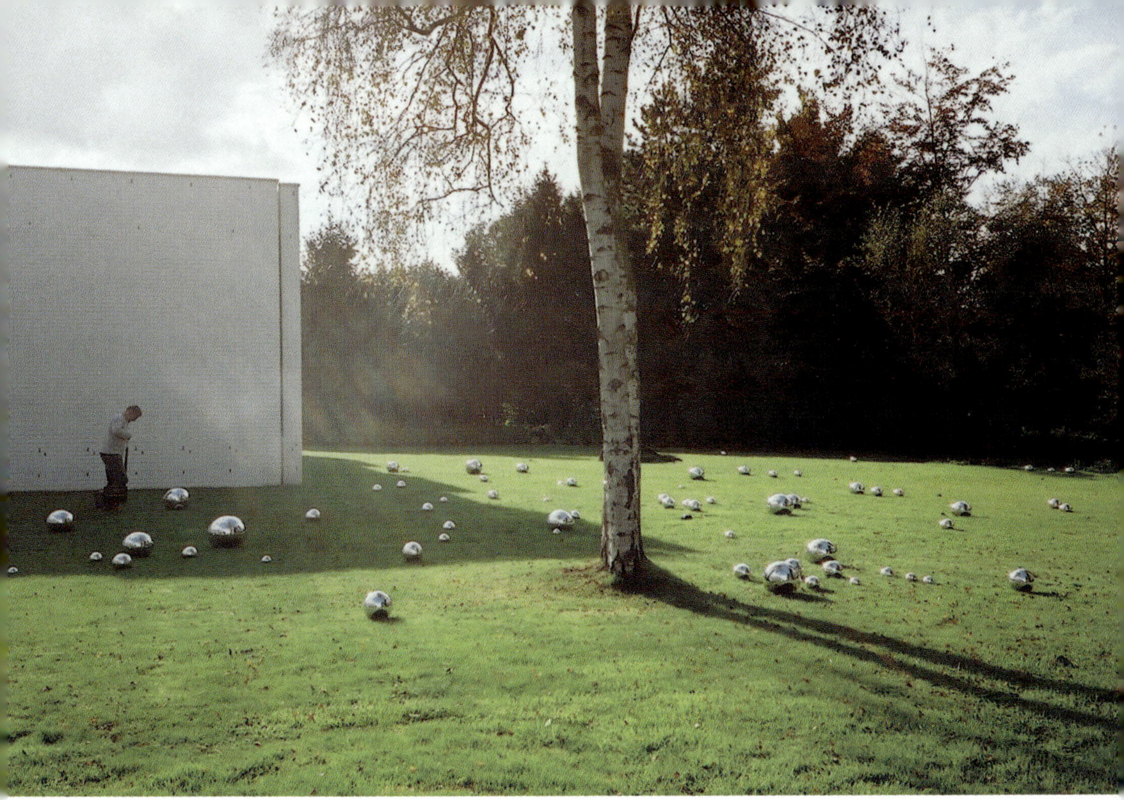

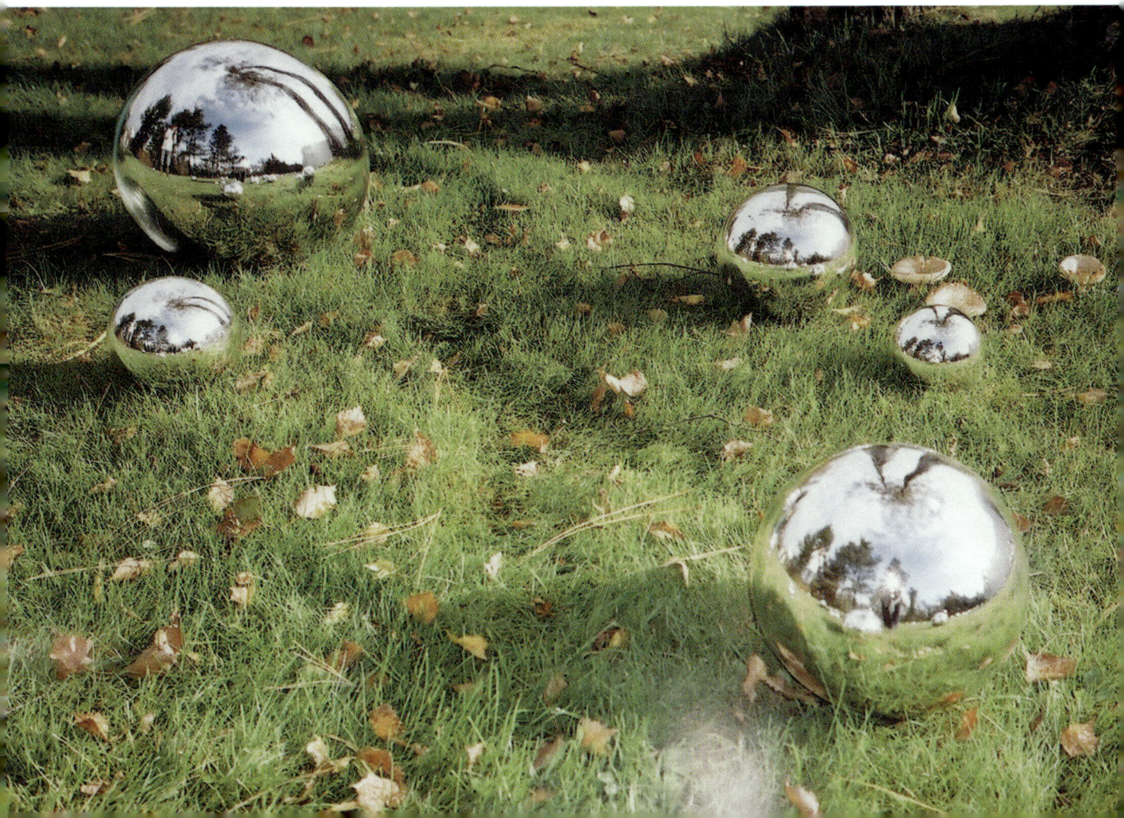

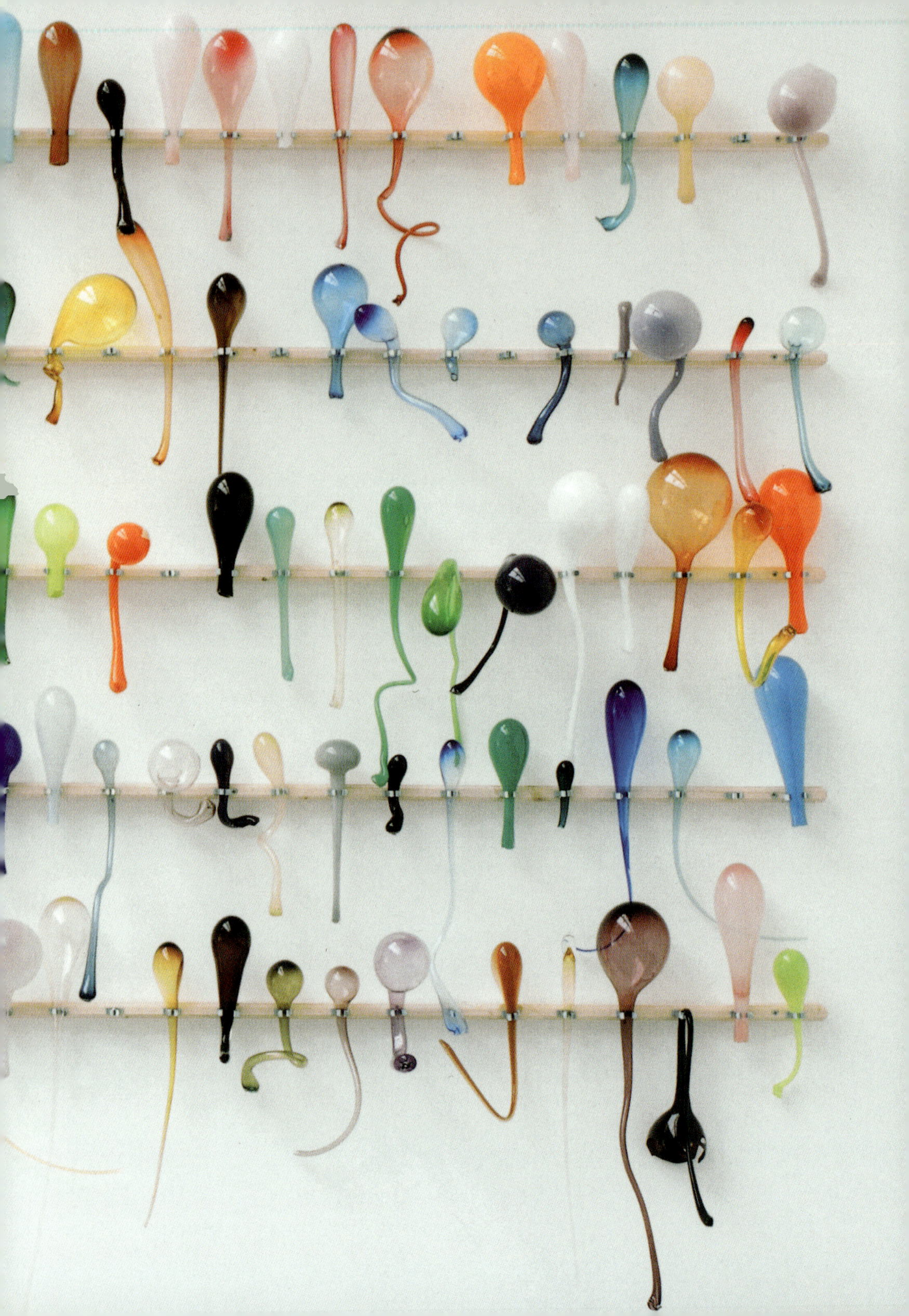

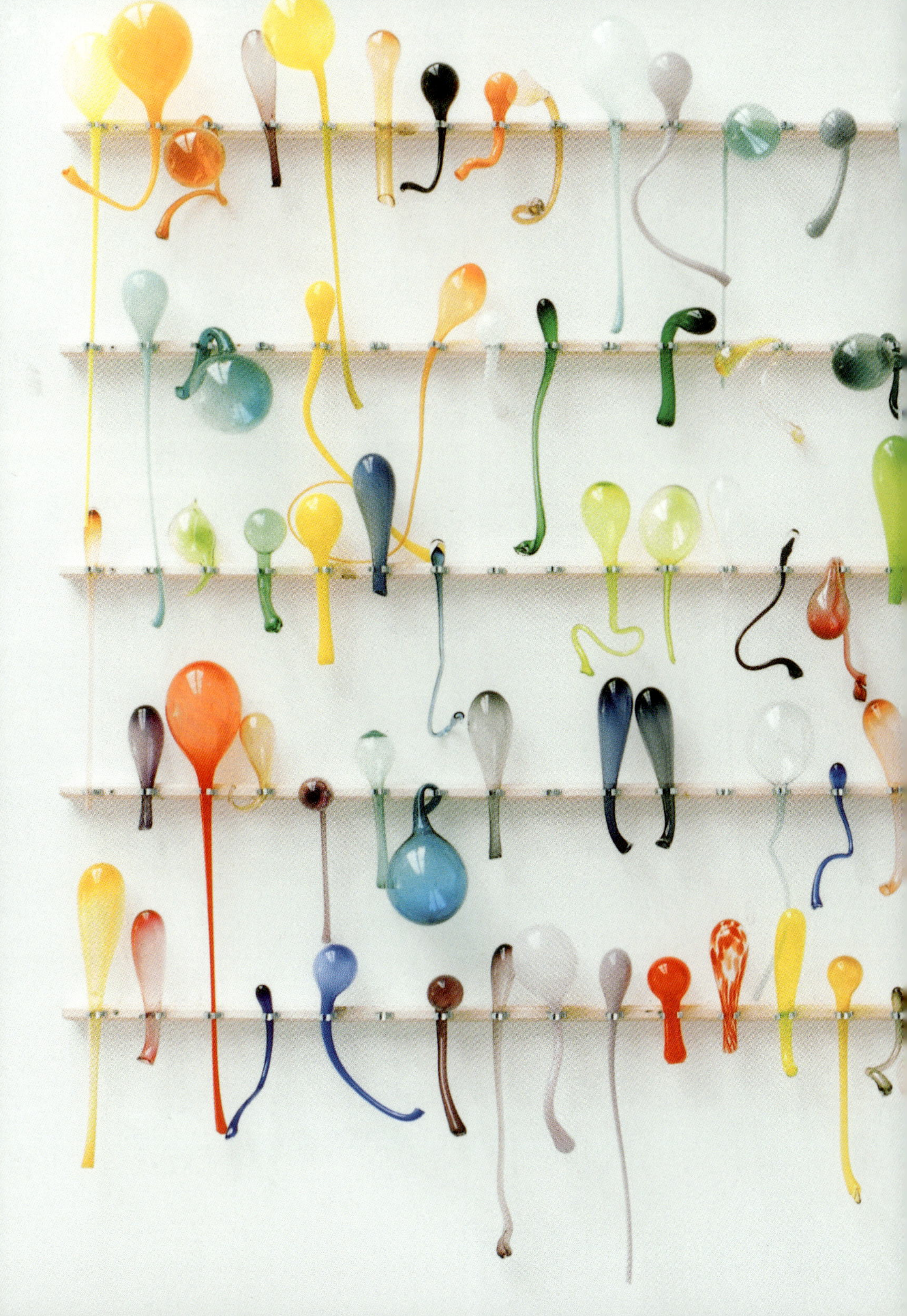

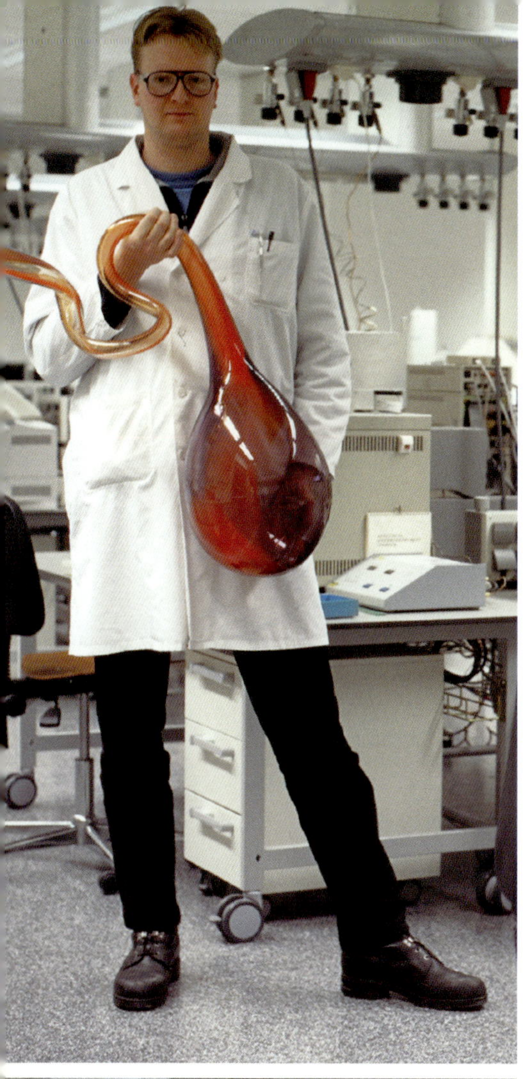
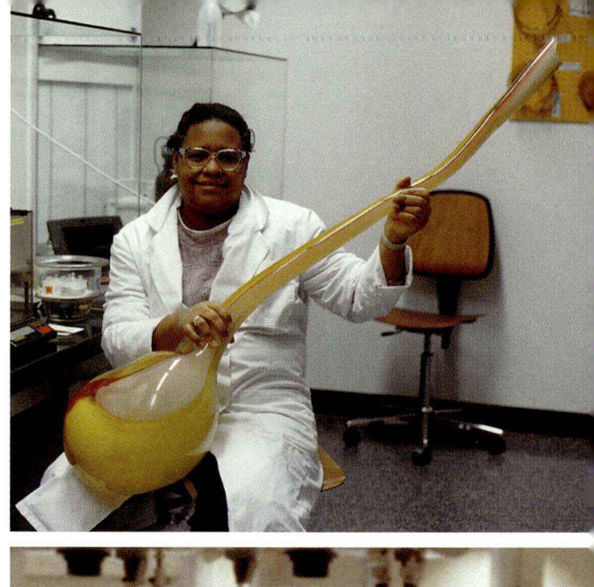
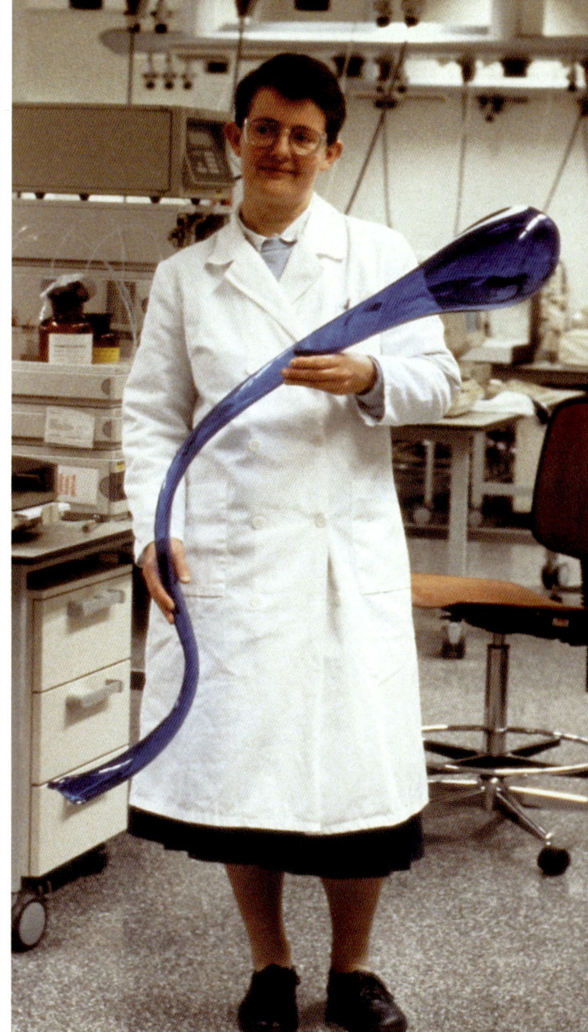
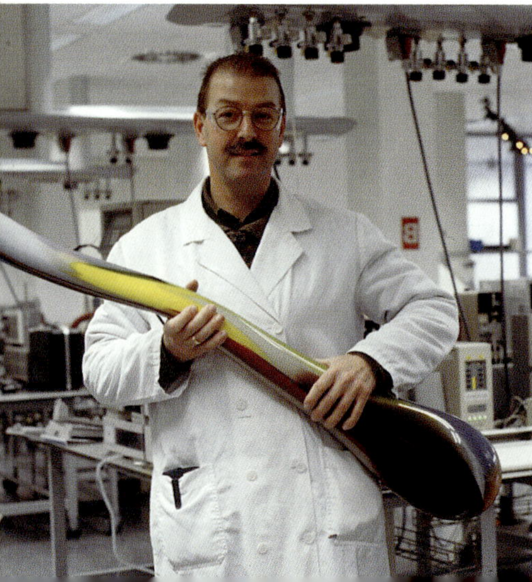

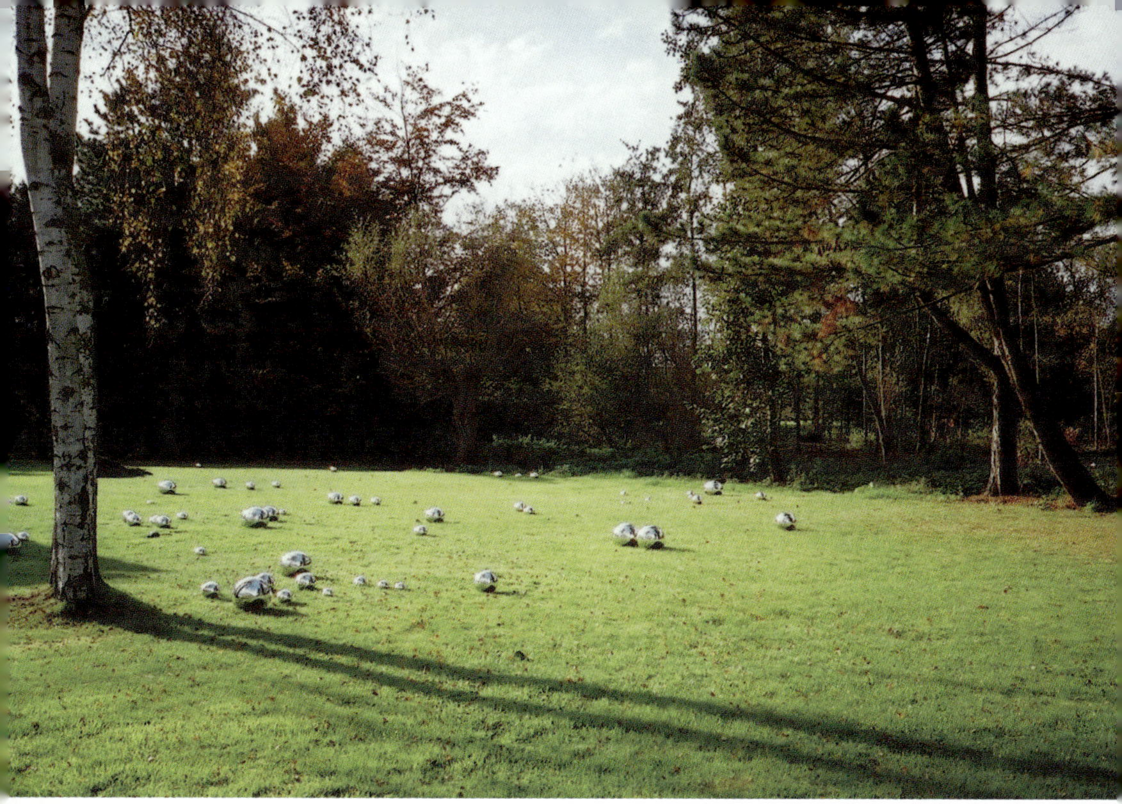

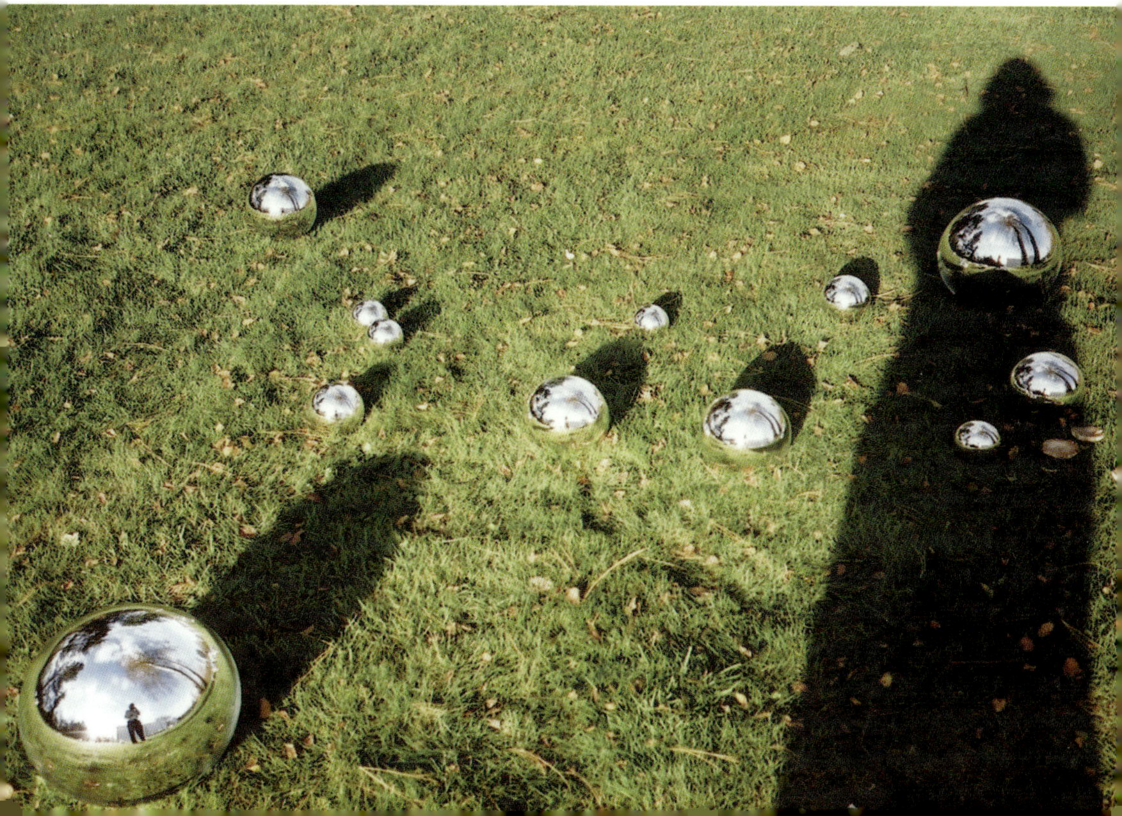

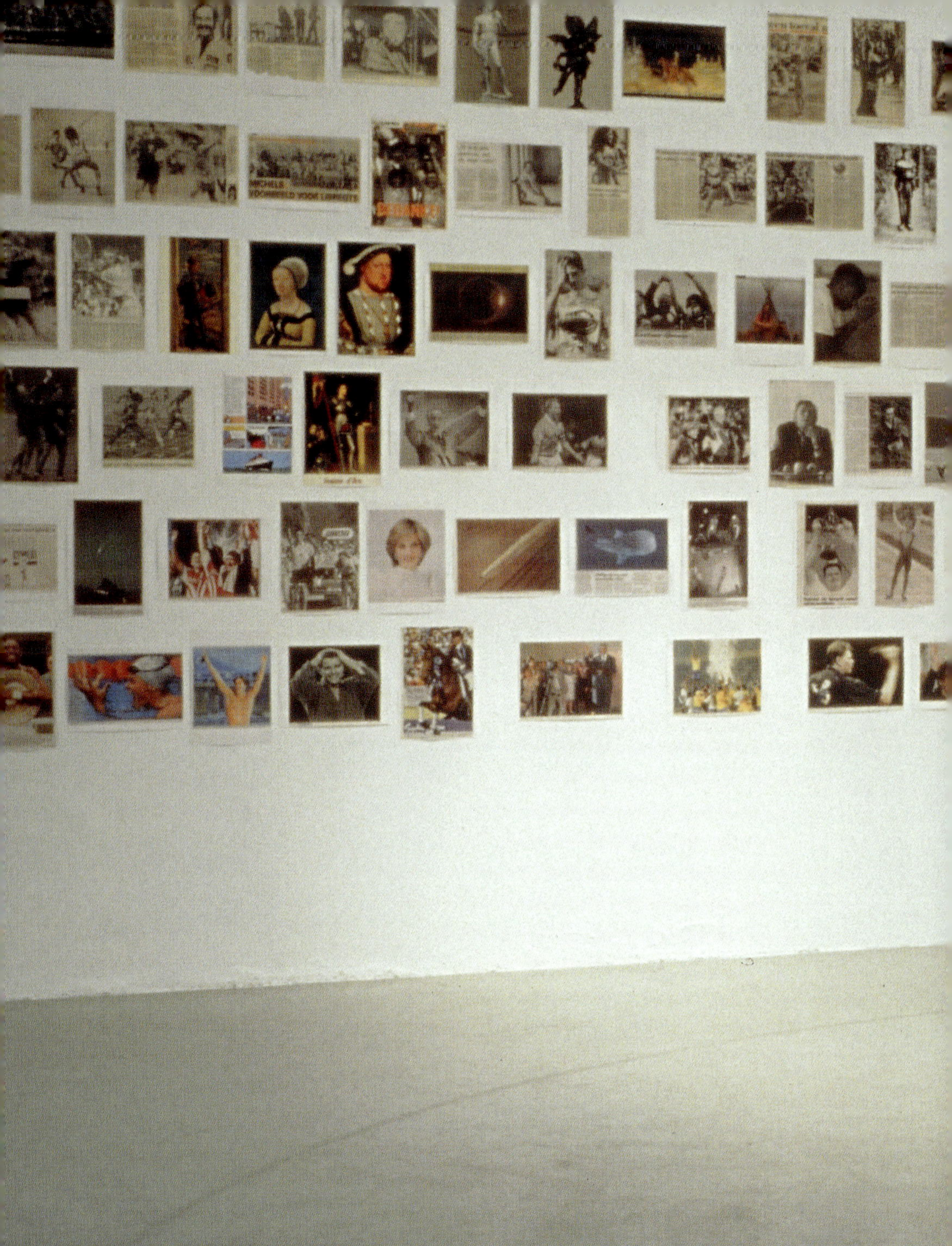

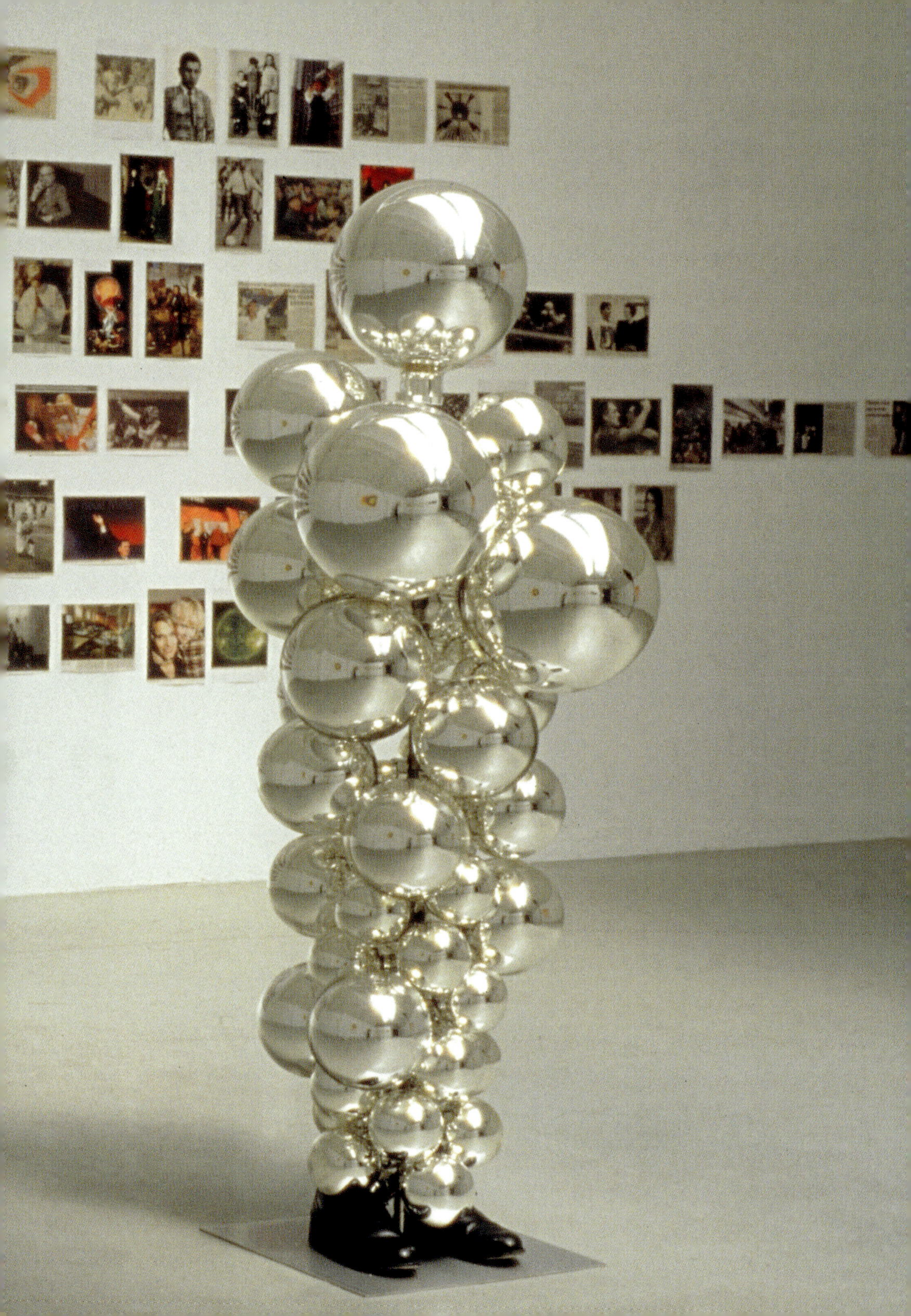

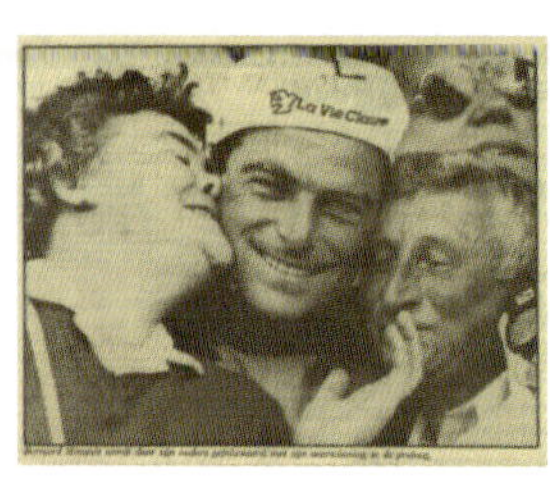

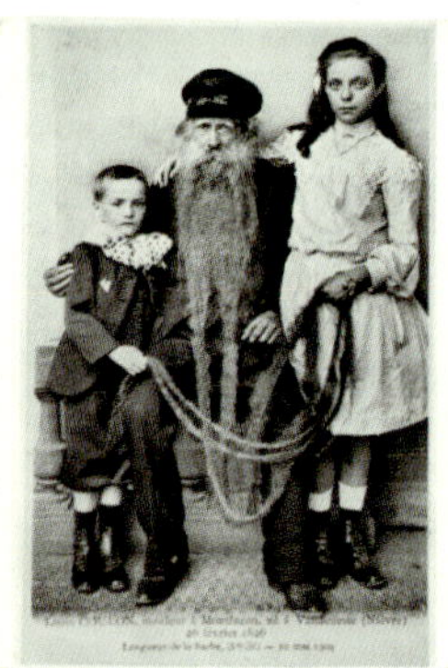

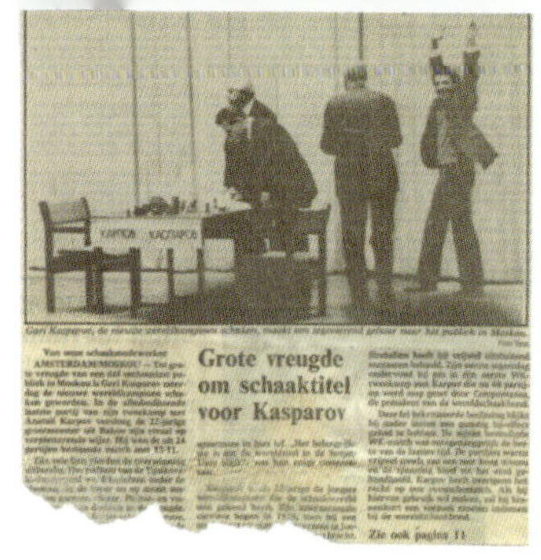

Gary Kasparov, de nieuwe wereldkampioen schaken, maakt een zegevierend gebaar naar het publiek in Moskou.

Grote vreugde om schaaktitel voor Kasparov

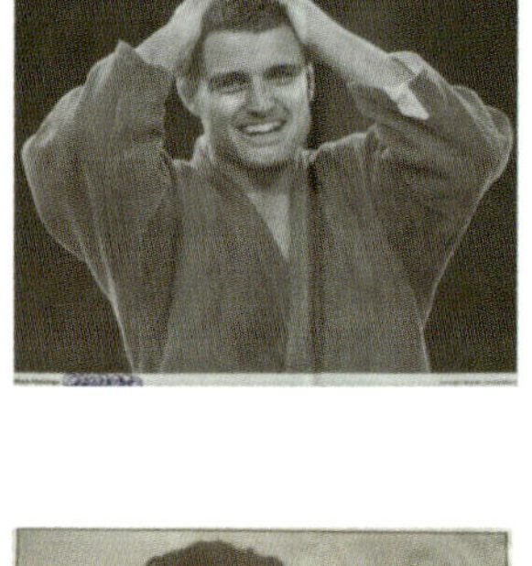

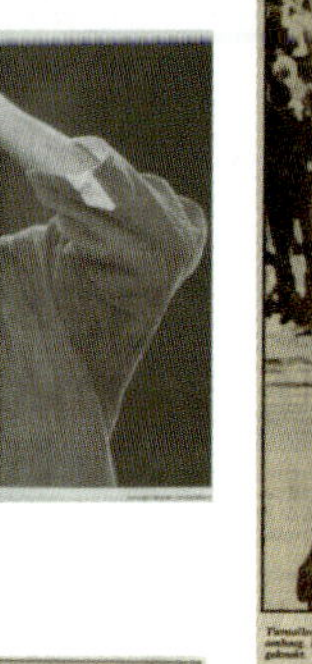

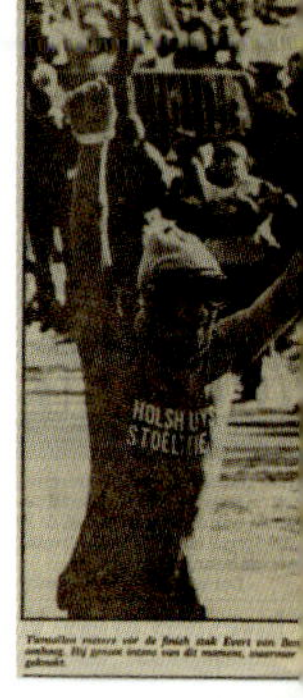

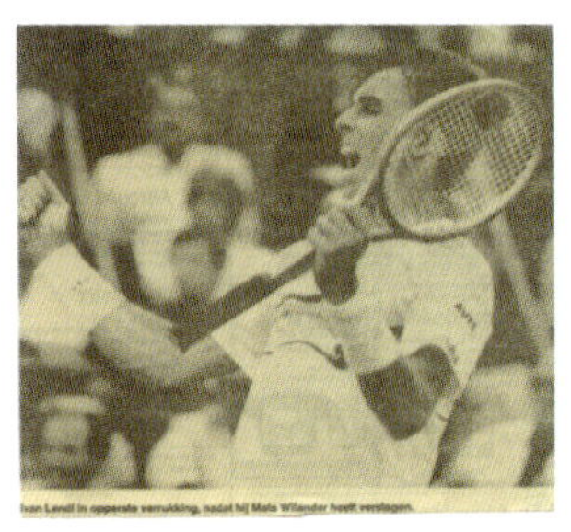

Ivan Lendl in opperste verrukking, nadat hij Mats Wilander heeft verslagen.

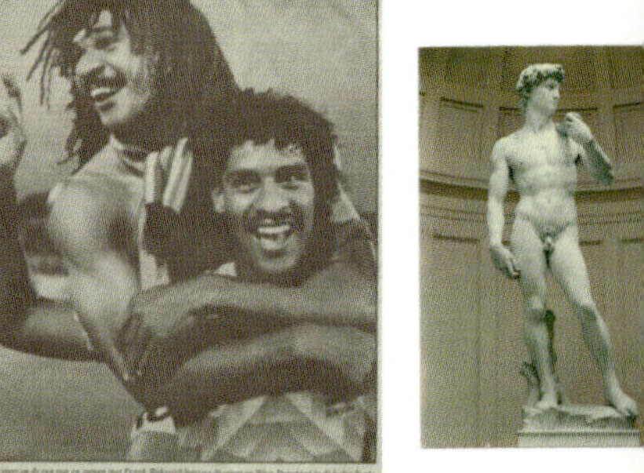

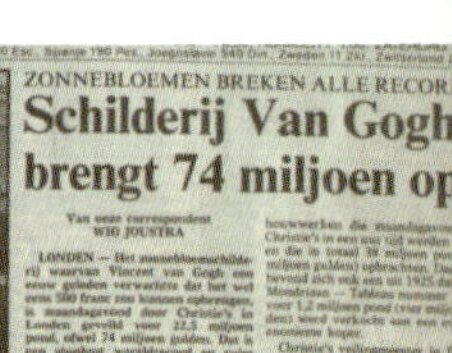

ZONNEBLOEMEN BREKEN ALLE RECOR

Schilderij Van Gogh brengt 74 miljoen op

Van onze correspondent
WIO JOUSTRA

LONDEN — Het zonnebloemenschilderij waarvan Vincent van Gogh een eeuw geleden verwachtte dat het wel eens 500 franc zou kunnen opbrengen, is maandagavond door Christie's in Londen geveild voor 22,5 miljoen pond, ofwel 74 miljoen gulden. Dat is een absoluut wereldrecord en ruim twee keer zo hoog als door het veilinghuis was verwacht.

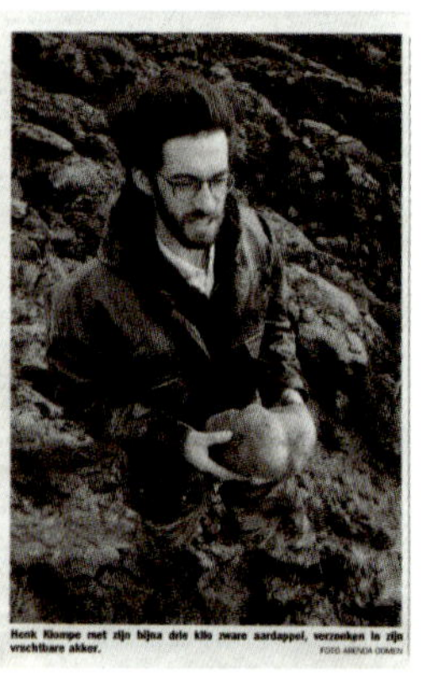

Henk Klompe met zijn bijna drie kilo zware aardappel, verzonken in zijn vruchtbare akker. FOTO AMANDA OOMEN

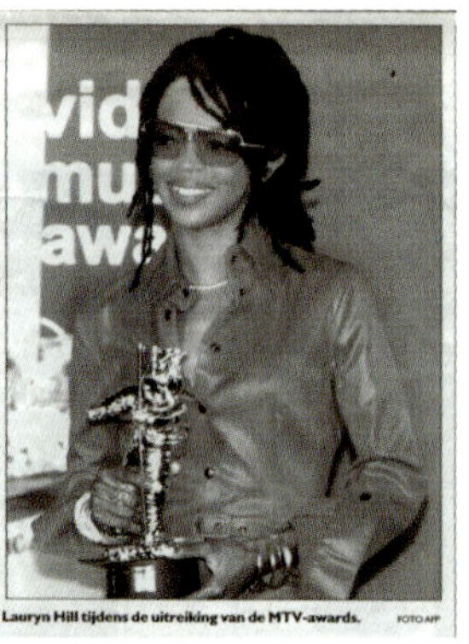

Lauryn Hill tijdens de uitreiking van de MTV-awards. FOTO AFP

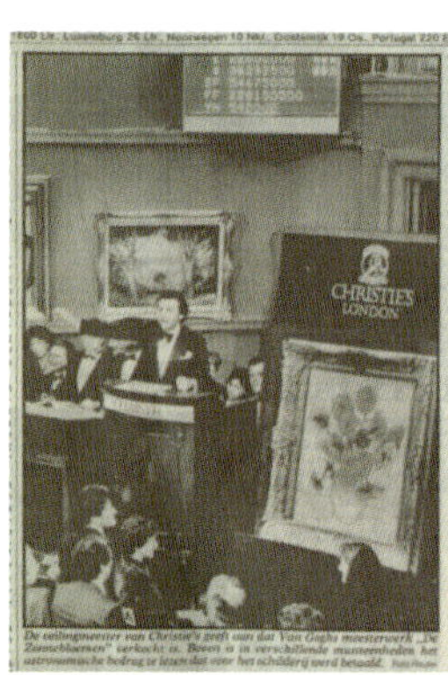

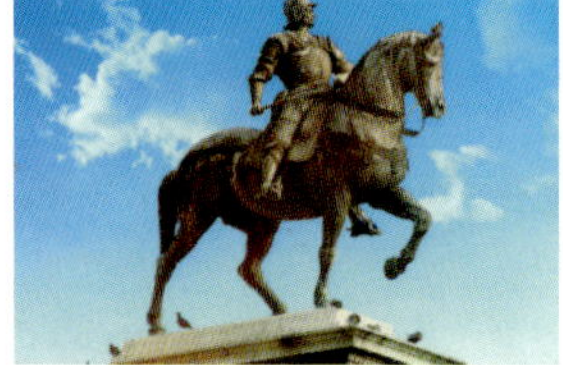

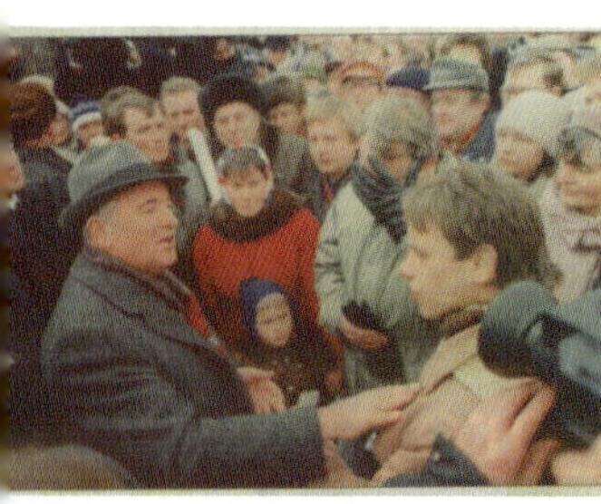

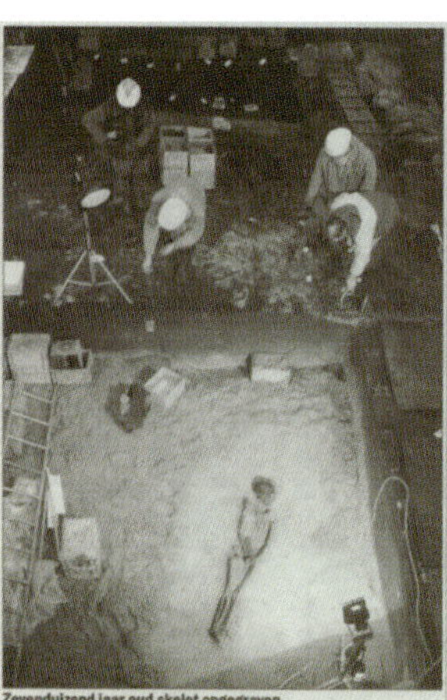

Zevenduizend jaar oud skelet opgegraven

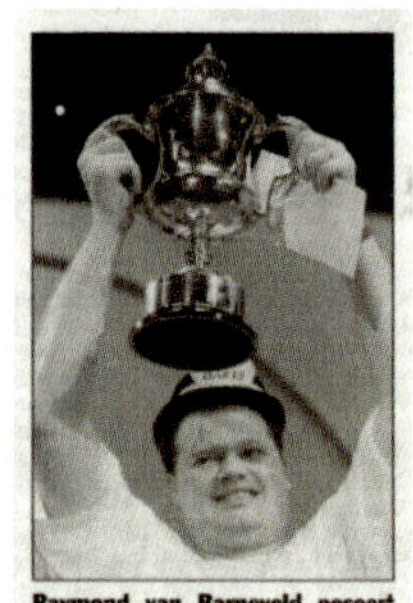

Raymond van Barneveld poseert met de wereldbeker. FOTO ALL SPORTS

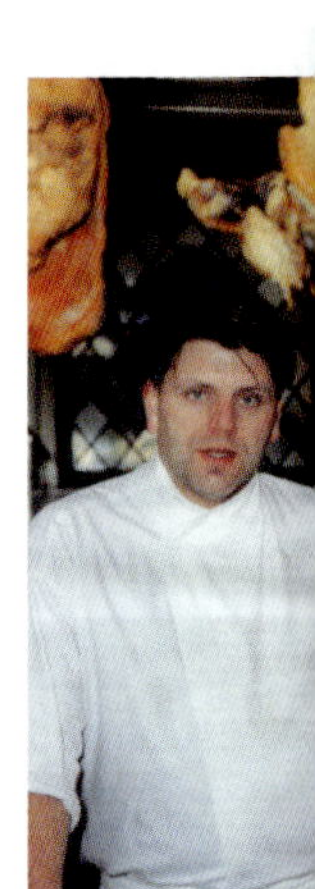

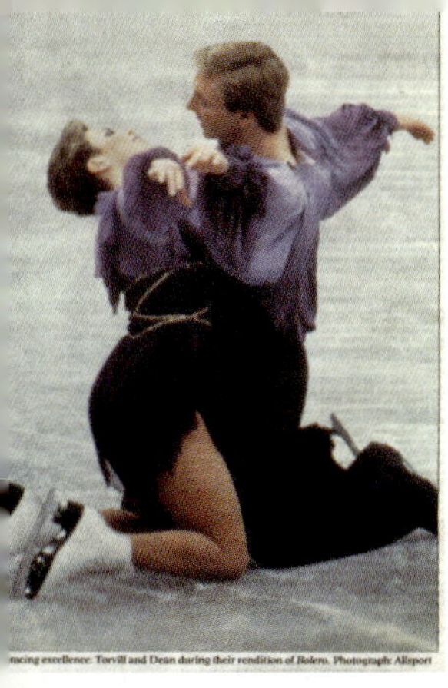

...racing excellence: Torvill and Dean during their rendition of *Bolero*. Photograph: Allsport

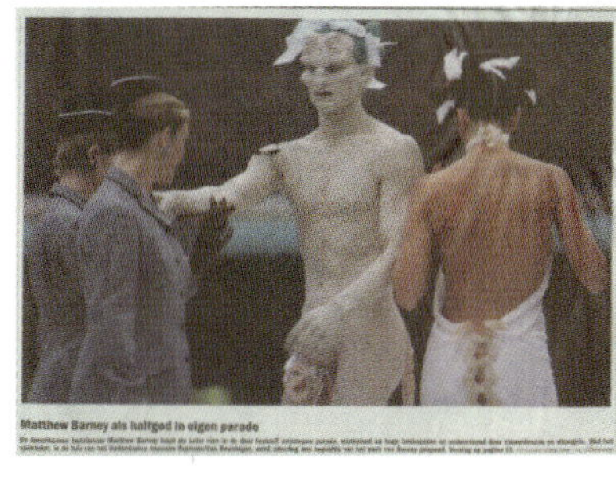

Matthew Barney als halfgod in eigen parade

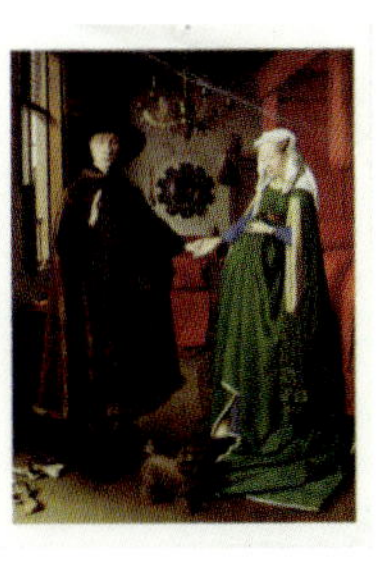

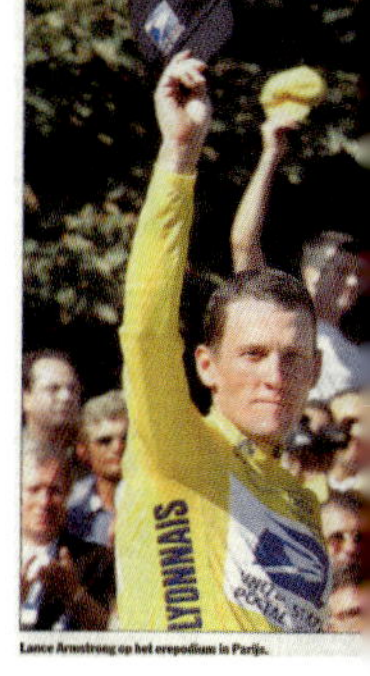

Lance Armstrong op het erepodium in Parijs.

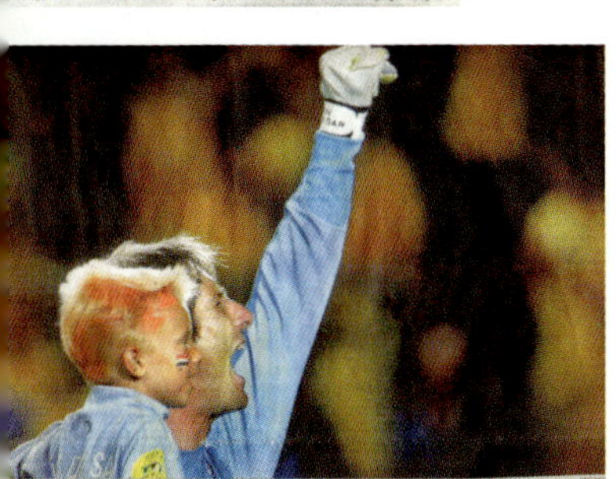

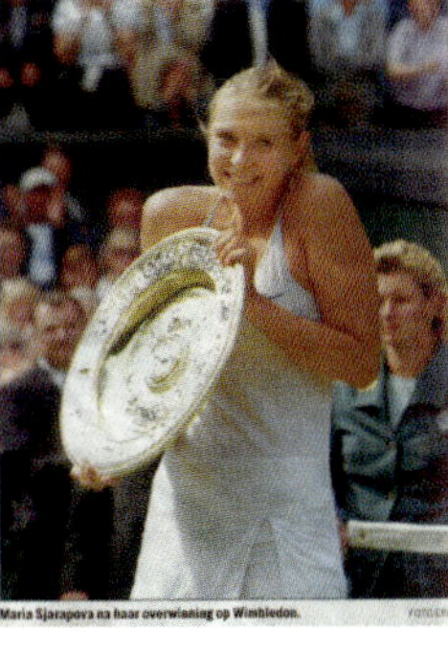

Maria Sjarapova na haar overwinning op Wimbledon.　FOTO EPA

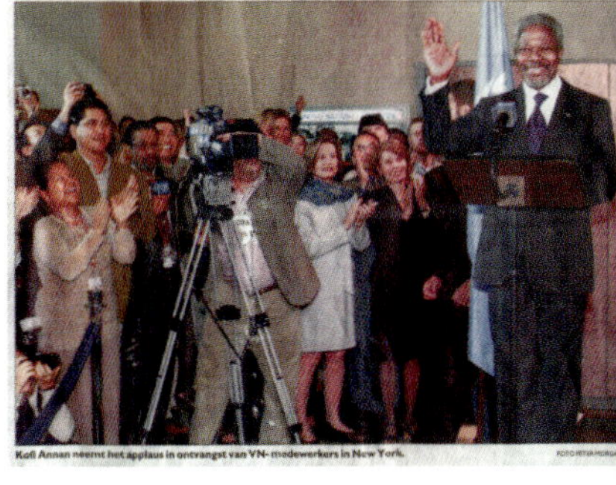

Kofi Annan neemt het applaus in ontvangst van VN-medewerkers in New York.　FOTO PETER HORGAN

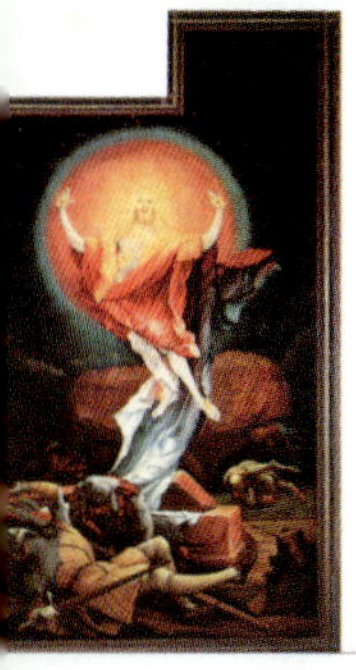

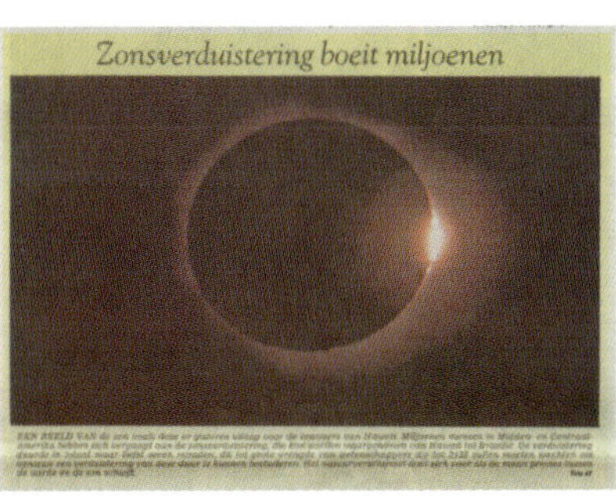

Zonsverduistering boeit miljoenen

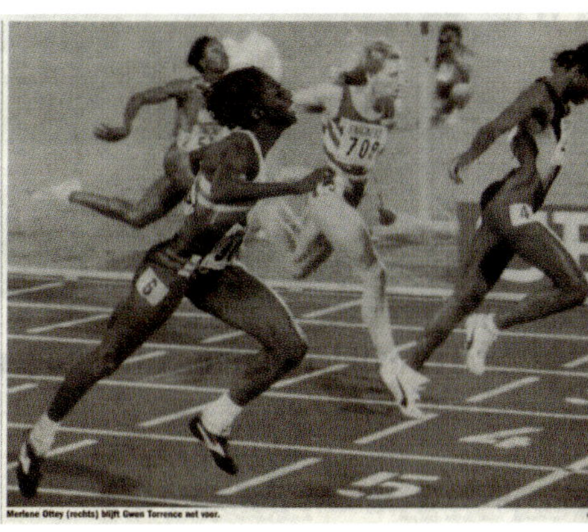

Merlene Ottey (rechts) blijft Gwen Torrence net voor.

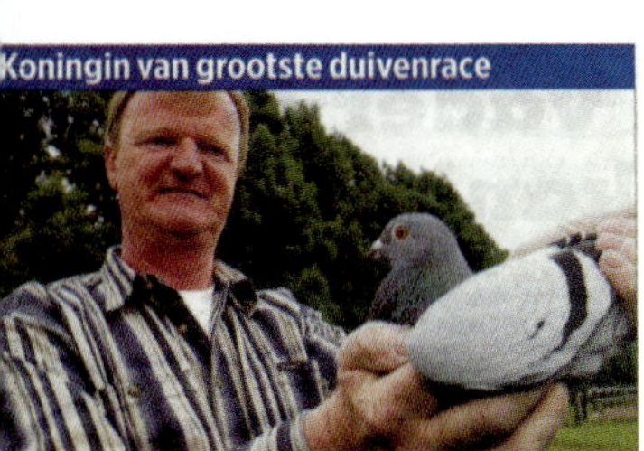

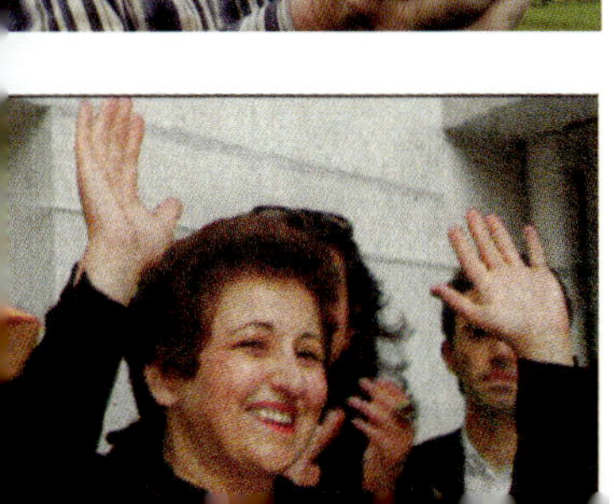

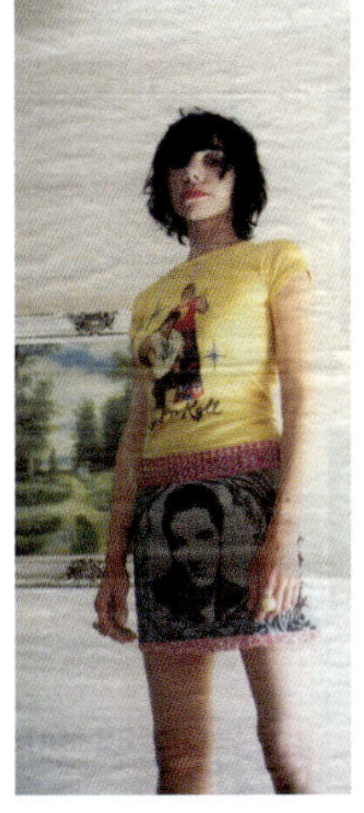

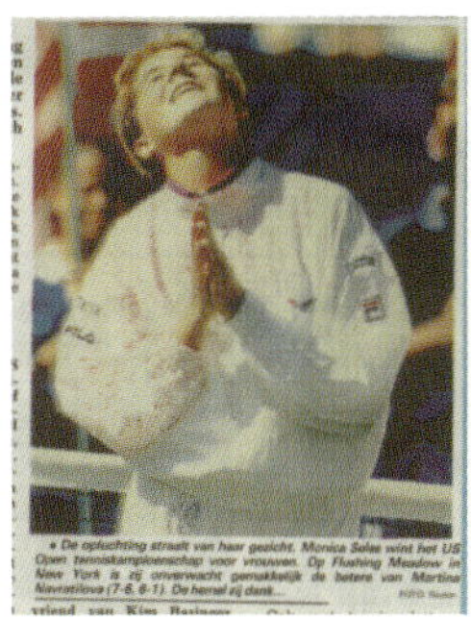

• De opluchting straalt van haar gezicht. Monica Seles wint het US Open tenniskampioenschap voor vrouwen. Op Flushing Meadow in New York is zij onverwacht gemakkelijk de betere van Martina Navratilova (7-6, 6-1). De hemel zij dank...

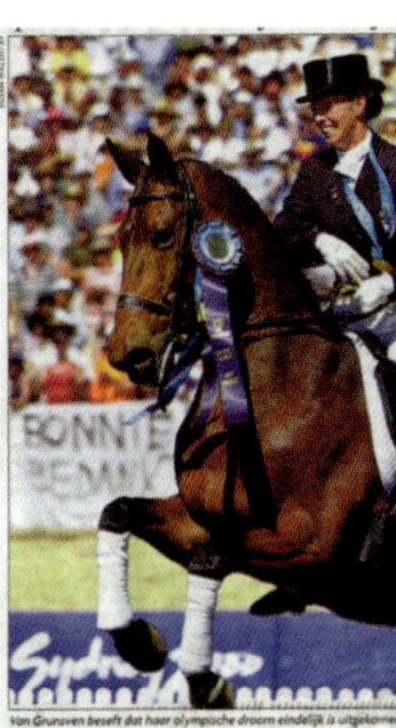

Van Grunsven beseft dat haar olympische droom eindelijk is uitgekomen.

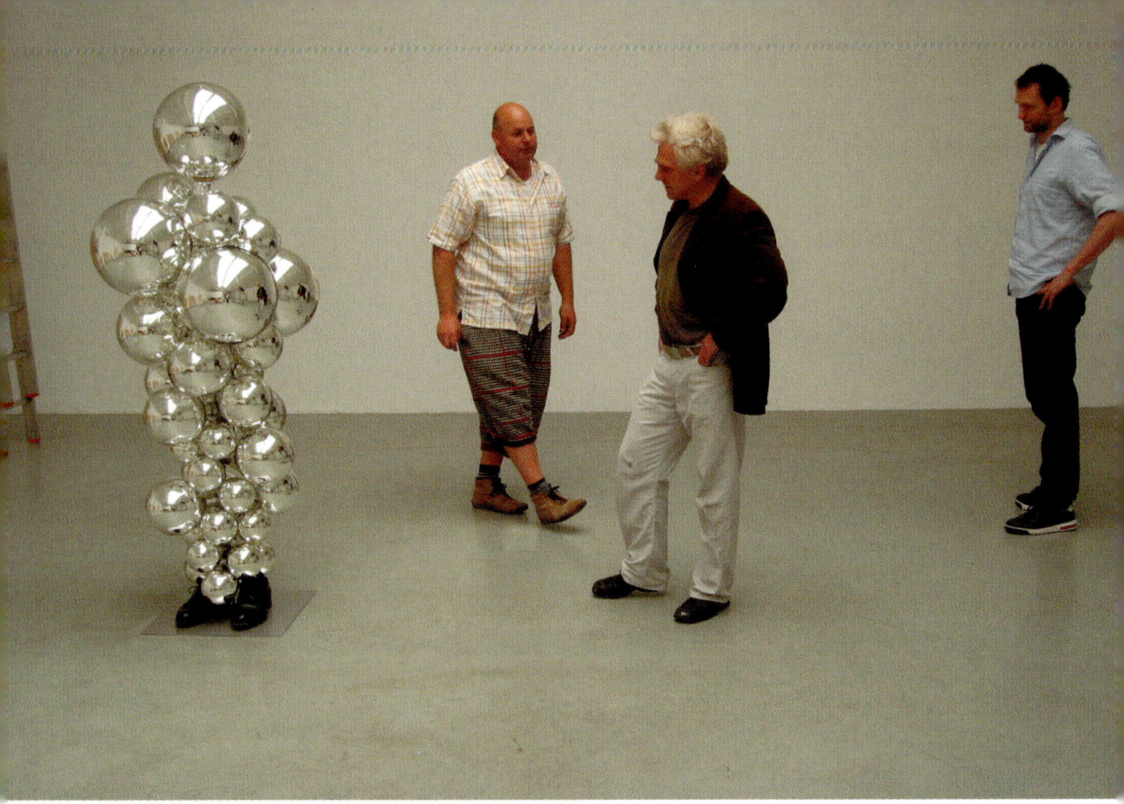

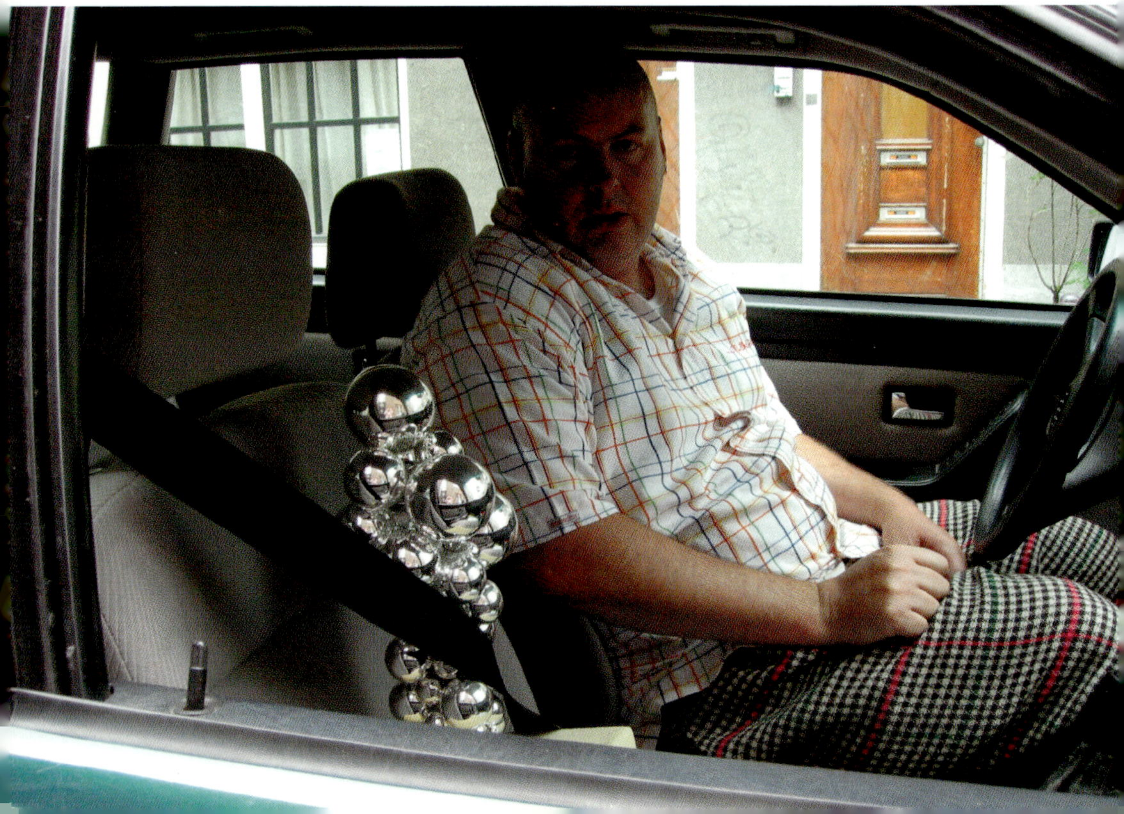

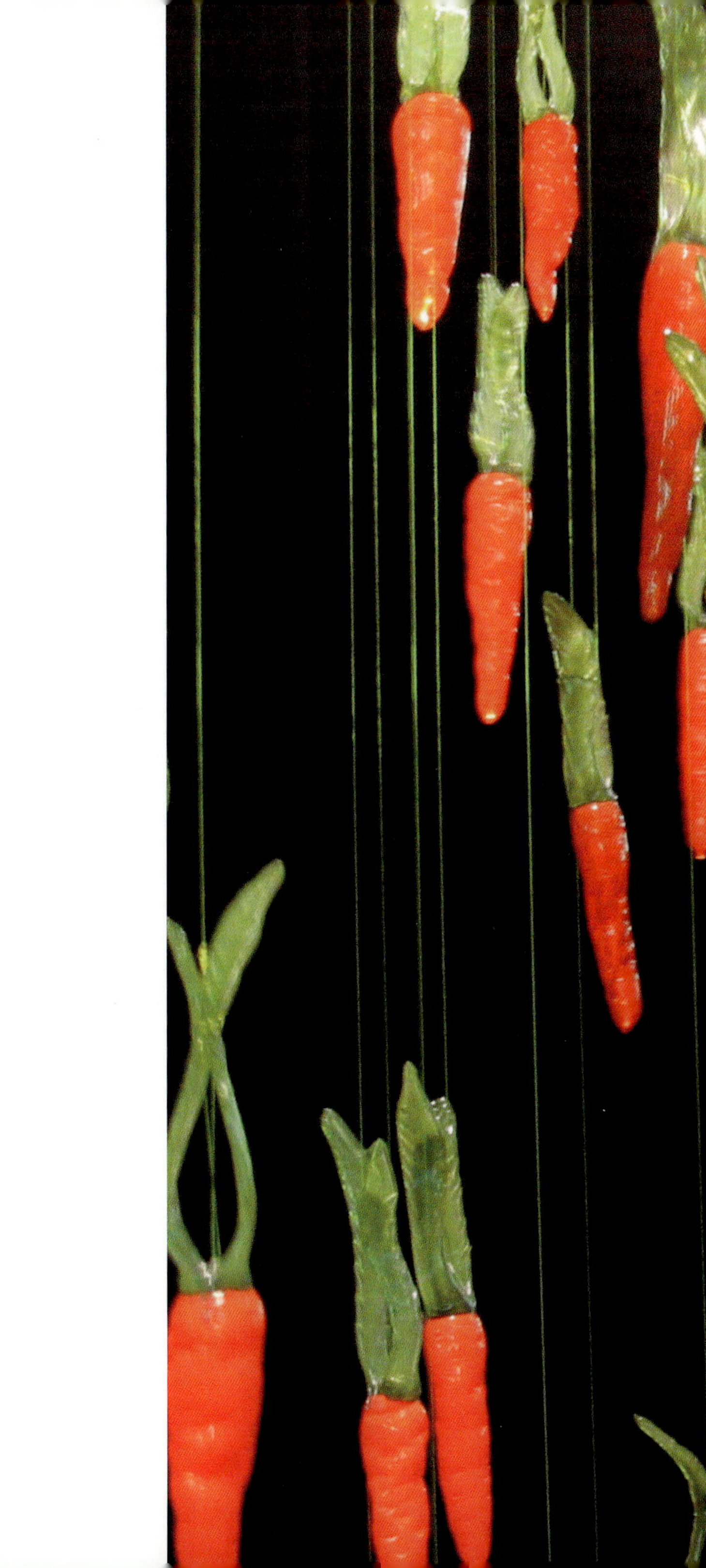

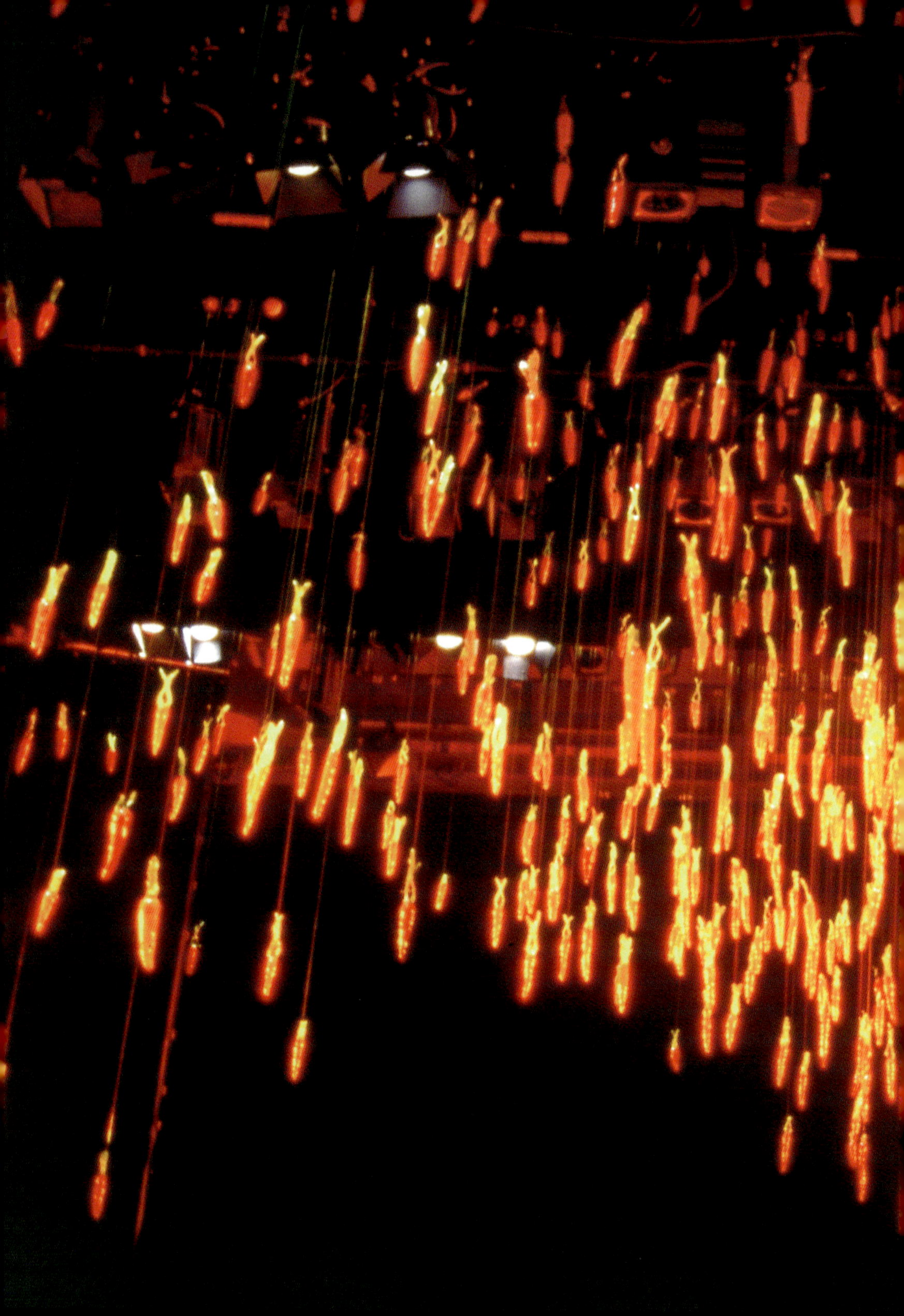

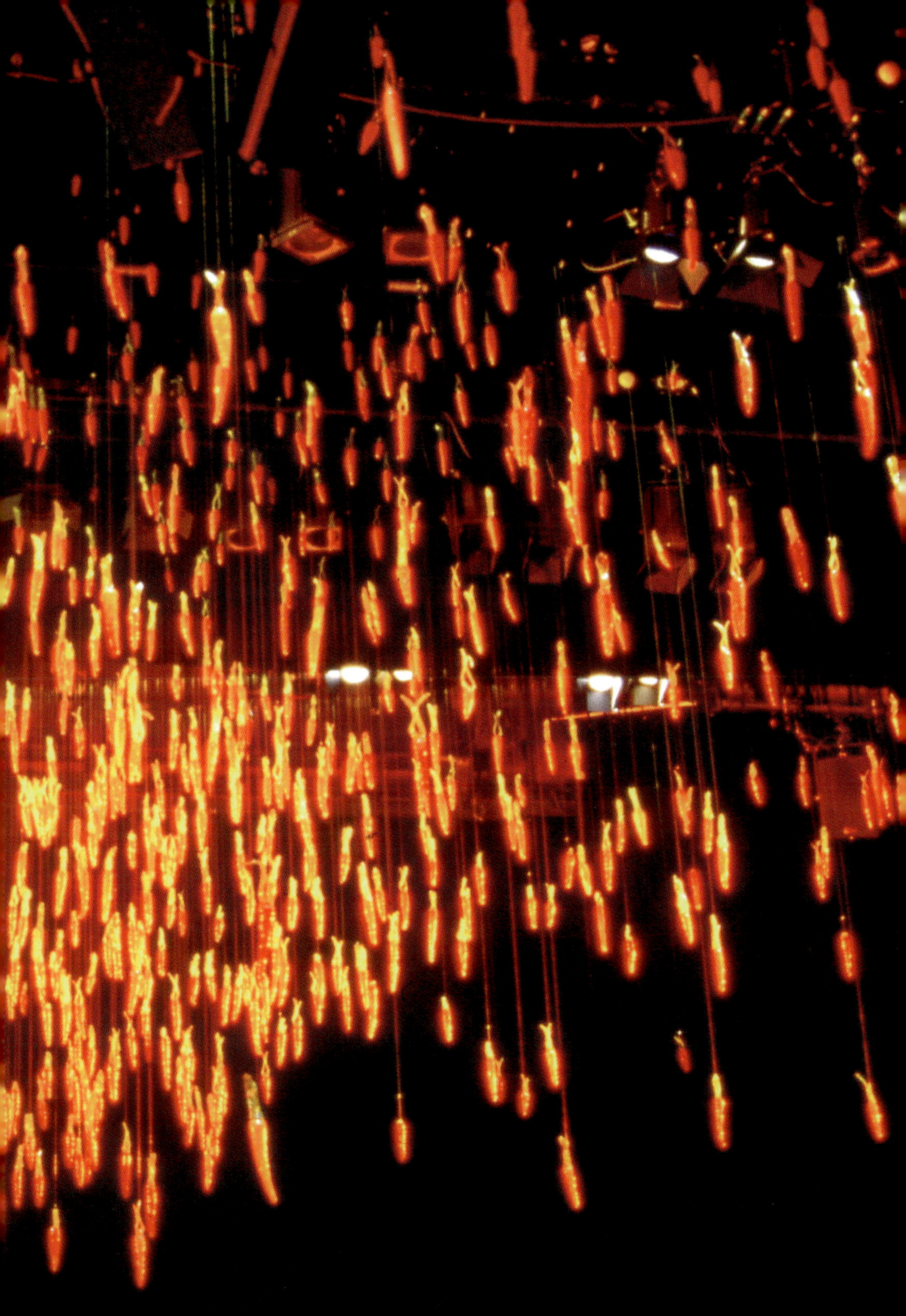

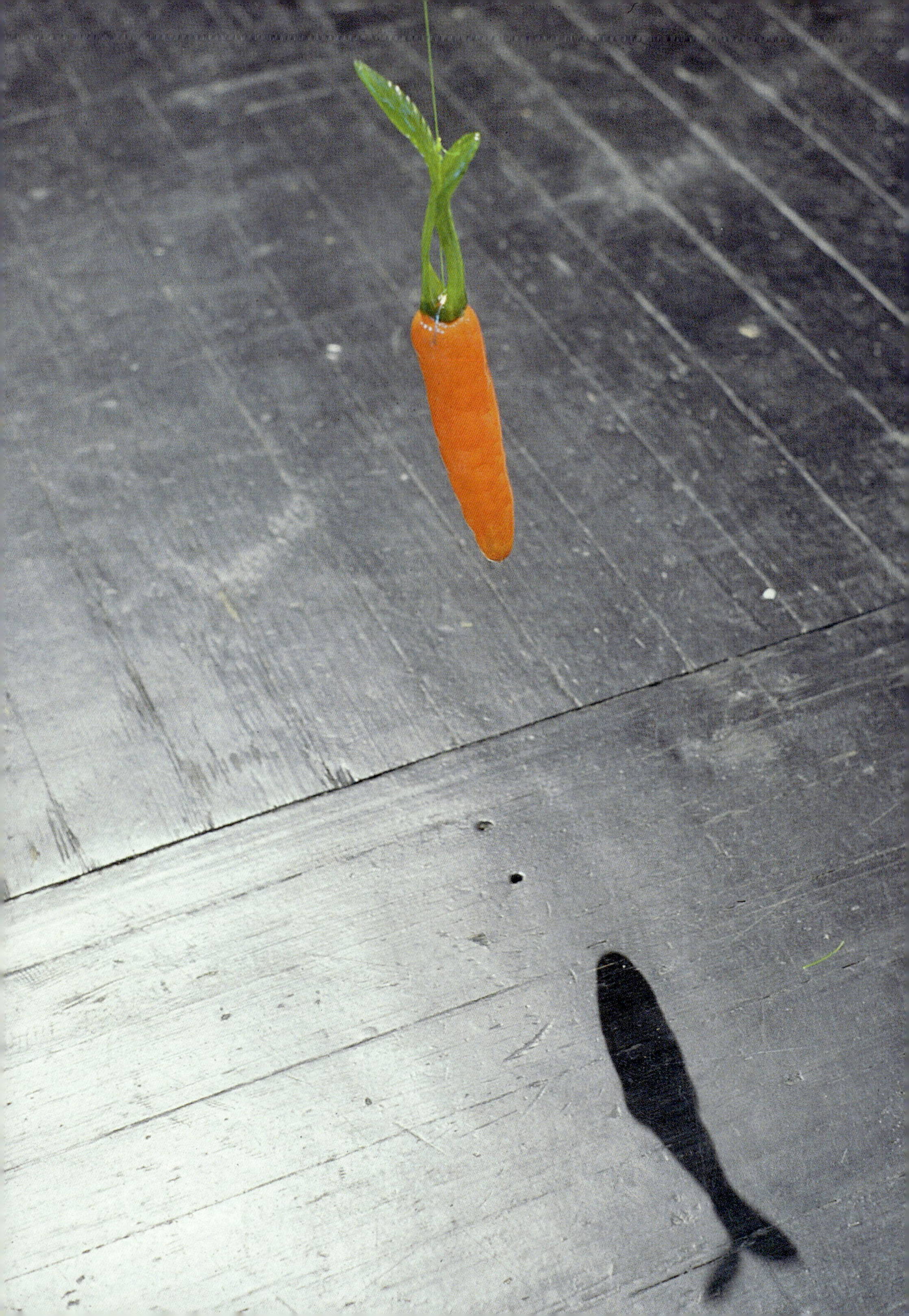

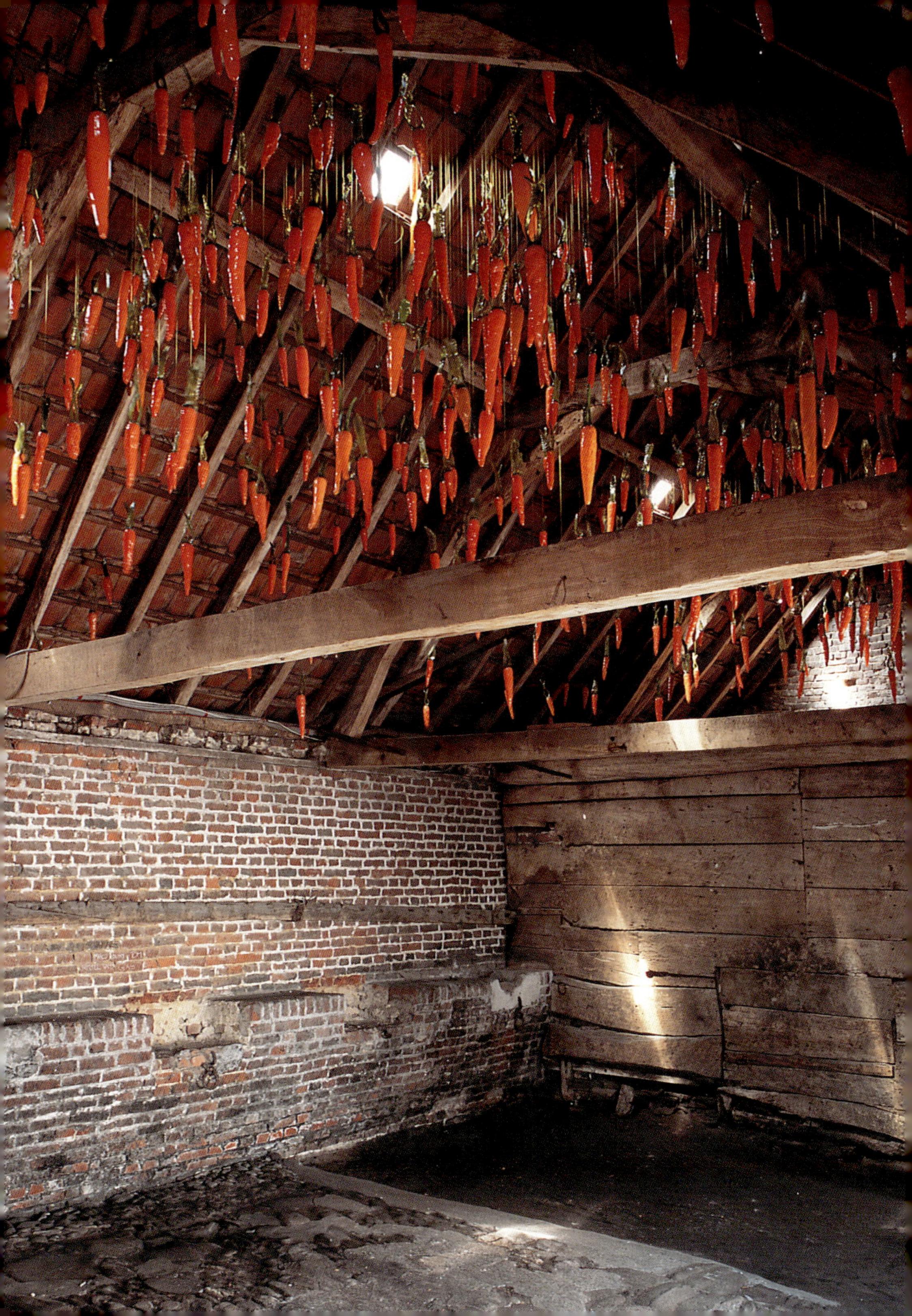

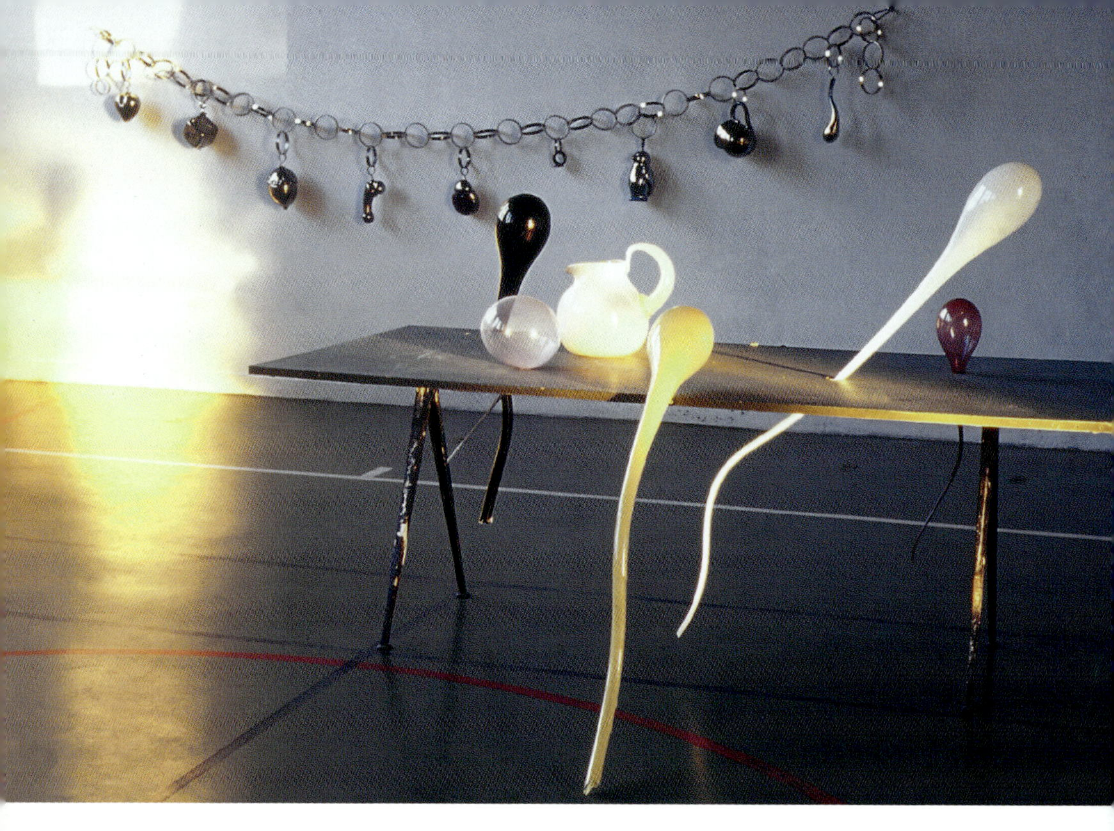

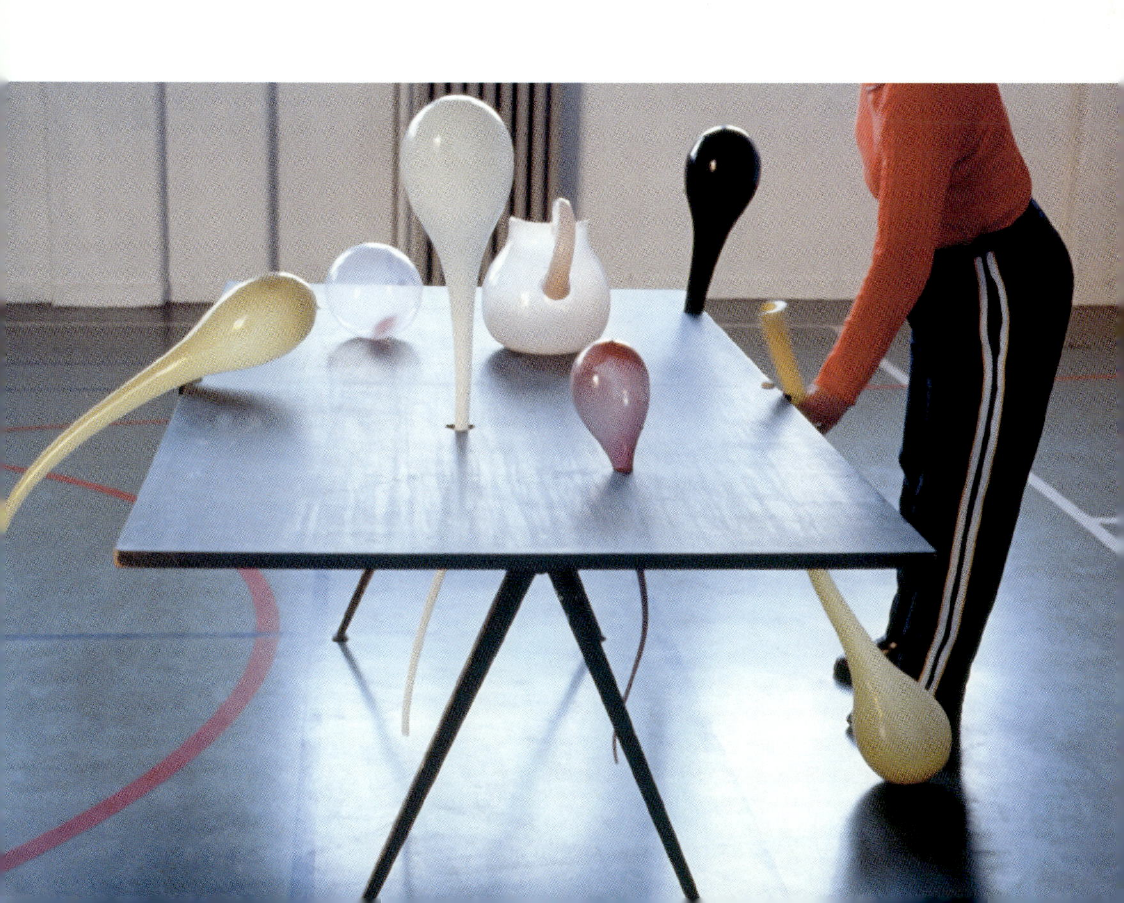

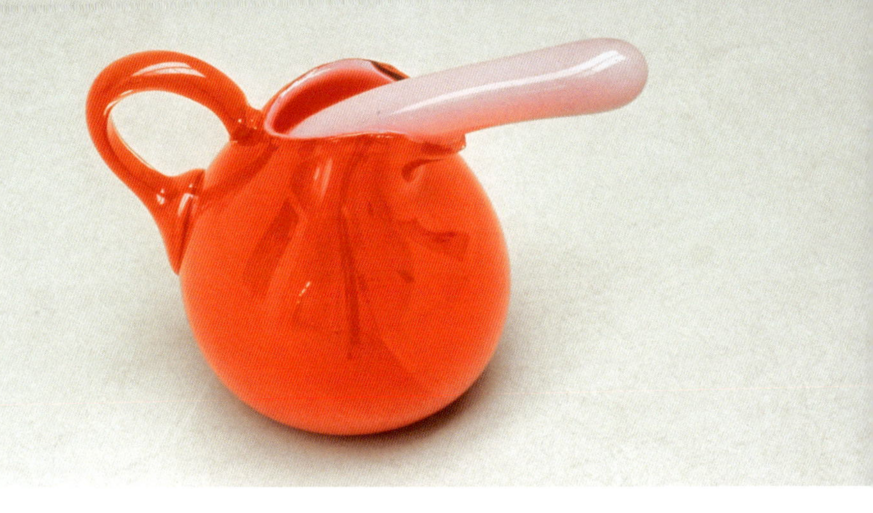

She Comes in All Sizes

JENNIFER ALLEN

Things get big in Maria Roosen's work. VERY big. Or tiny. Teeny tiny. Take those glass milk jugs: large enough to be embraced by both arms and small enough to fit into the palm of a hand. Shaped by the warm breath of a glassblower, they are then filled with chilled cow's milk, ten litres or ten drops. Roosen's mirrored orbs, scattered across the garden of the Boijmans Van Beuningen Museum, reflect their surroundings with the compactness of a period at the end of a sentence that has summarised the entire landscape, from blades of grass to clouds in the sky. Dried sunflowers, knitted in white and brown wool, become towering versions of their former selves. There are the many glass penises, overblown to supersizes that must evoke envy from both sexes. The breasts, copious twin pendants made of coloured mirror glass, are tucked into beds or lounge in leather arm chairs for a tête-à-tête. Recently, Roosen has expanded – and shrunk – into architecture with parasitic additions that do not belong to their hosts yet could not exist without them. She added a cast-iron circular staircase to a two-storey tree in a forest and hung a long orange fringe of shipping-rope around the top of a watertower at a harbourfront. Architectural models like the golden house – a model of her home

sealed in gold leaf – look more like dwarfs from a fairy tale than prototypes for buildings. Her diminutive wooden doppelganger of a stone church (*Mirakel*), 2001 – stuck to the side of the structure's massive tower, like a calf clinging to the whale, or a slim shadow cast around high noon.

Growing or shrinking, Roosen's oeuvre constitutes a unique collection of giants and miniatures. However miraculous, her works are not the stuff of divine intervention but belong to a secular world of wonders where ordinary objects – sunflowers or jugs – suddenly become extraordinary. Roosen seems to extend the seven wonders of the world to include the intimate spaces of the body, domestic realms inhabited by chairs and staircases, collective services like faith and water, the natural sites of the forest and the garden. Her project initially appears to be both old and modern, linked with the collectibles in a Renaissance *Wunderkammer* or *cabinet de curiosités* as well as with the sculpted monuments to mass consumption in Pop Art. Yet Roosen's combination of a change in scale along with a change in materials would exclude her from both eras. The Renaissance collector, hoping to glimpse the totality of the divine plan, coveted

81

102-103

natural rarities whose uniqueness lay in their exceptional or deformed character (a sunflower with two heads would be preferable to two XL knitted versions). A Pop artist like Claes Oldenburg, while changing the scale and material of a squeezed toothpaste tube, made a singular monument to a common consumer good while aiming for a resemblance with the original. Roosen not only shies away from reproducing commodities but also maintains a balance between similarity and dissimilarity in her renditions of everyday objects. Her sunflowers come as a giant pair that look like the originals, yet they are visibly knitted in monochrome shades of wool – a material that shares just as little with Andy Warhol's colourful multiple prints of flowers.

Roosen's changes in scale and materials balance realism with a fabrication that does not come entirely from nature, nor from the factory line. Again, her work belongs fully to the wondrous, to the French merveilleux, itself based upon the Latin *mirabilia*, describing remarkable and admirable things, marvels created foremost by God. This realm, despite fusing the object with the reception, has largely escaped the secular creations of contemporary art. The wondrous, once pushed into the profane world, is more common to science and to literature, whether fairy tales, fantasy, satire or magical realism. Consider the wonders revealed by the microscope and telescope, along with other wondrous scientific discoveries and inventions. Tales like *Alice in Wonderland* or *Gulliver's Travels* rely upon exaggerations in scale to maintain a bridge between realism and fabrication. Of course, the dominant contemporary expression of the wondrous occurs in film, in particular, in the realist fabrications of Hollywood special effects, although one may argue that film replaces

the unexpected amazement of the wonder with the expectation of entertainment. In her study of the merveilleux, Marie-Françoise Christout notes several characteristics that resonate with Roosen's works.[1] The wonder is essentially dynamic and always involves growth, transformation, accelerations and decelerations. These changes are exaggerated and therefore allow for extremes to be confronted with each other, whether giant or elf, good or evil. Wonders startle because they unsettle familiar relationships with credible resemblances. Since the laws of causality remain visible, the wonder falls short of illusion, whether the deceptive artifice of trompe l'oeil or the magician's slight of hand.

Roosen expresses the dynamic central to the wonder by favouring organic elements that are linked to growth, life, metamorphosis. Penises and breasts are body parts that change in size while playing a role in reproduction. There are also giant sperms in hand-blown glass along with big eyeballs, with changing dilated pupils. Roosen had glass blown into the empty shells of wooden shoes and leather pants – organic and flexible coverings for the body that also come in a wide variety of sizes. Indeed, her materials tend to be naturally occurring ones which are invariably moulded into something else, once they are extracted from nature. Glass, wool, gold, metal and wood are endlessly malleable materials, which are proper to craft, precisely because they can take on innumerable shapes and forms, even in restricted amounts. The craftspeople, whom Roosen engages to execute her works, play an equal role in the wonder's dynamic: the glass blower expertly transforms an inchoate chunk of glass into one of many body parts. In Roosen's exaggerations from the miniature to the gigantic, several extremes

62

1-3

3

meet each other. By attaching a small church to a big one, the artist effects an exceptional shift in proportion while reflecting the reduction in the number of the faithful as Christianity wanes in Europe. The extremes of human waste and nourishment meet in the toilet bowl decorated with a cornucopia of vegetables or with pastoral hunting scenes. Odour meets odourlessness in Roosen's suspended empty perfume bottles, also formed in glass, which of course does not smell. And life confronts death in the perennial forget-me-nots, planted in a minimalistic rectangular shape in the cemetery. In her entire oeuvre, however dynamic, life is often curbed by death. The materials may be organic, but they rob organic matter of its vitality, like King Midas's golden touch. The glass penises – as odourless and empty as the perfume bottles – will never ejaculate; the breasts will give no milk; the eyeballs reflect but see nothing. Yet this 'death,' far from a final destiny, appears as a temporary suspension of life, like a spell that has been cast but could always be broken, undone through the very same processes that brought about the enchantment. The glass works could be melted down and blown into other forms; the sunflowers could be unravelled and knitted into socks, sweaters, mittens; the gold could be removed from the model house to cover the lip of a chalice or the thin edges of pages bound in a hardcover book.

In addition to creating a dynamic of extremes, Roosen's wonders unsettle familiar relationships with entirely credible resemblances. The small church, apart from its size and colour, perfectly resembles the original church. Yet its sudden appearance, high up on the side of the tower, must have startled locals who are used to seeing a solitary structure. *Mirakel* belongs and does not belong; the

sculpture is a copy that venerates its model (to the extent of aping its lofty height) and a charge that burdens its origin. Roosen's architectural pairings the staircase with the tree and the fringe with the watertower – may recall the odd pairings of surrealism, except the artist's additions fit their hosts functionally. Trees can be climbed; stairs facilitate the task. Watertowers are tall; fringe must be suspended to swing freely. Roosen's glass works, while resembling body parts, have lost their familiar relationship to the human body. The penis does not appear between a man's legs or even as a strap-on but exists in a series of three, hanging from strings on a wall. The mirrored orbs faithfully reflect the landscape – including spectators, who can readily verify their reflections – yet barely take up any space. Those who cannot experience Roosen's works first hand will nevertheless get a sense of their startling effects. The artist has her works photographed, not as solitary sculptures, but as installations within a particular setting, usually inhabited by people. Her mini-jug resembles her maxi-jug, but it would be impossible to confuse the two works in photographs, since the former rests in an open hand and the latter appears in a living room by a woman knitting a jumper for it. And there is no doubt that Roosen's glass sperms are giant because they are held by scientists in laboratories. Since the scientists do research in reproduction, their habitual visual relationship to the sperm – enlarged under the microscope – becomes an unsettling reality. Finally, Roosen's wonders display the laws of causality behind them. There is a resemblance but no illusion behind the glass body parts because they are patently made of glass. There is no secret, nor deception, in how the wool sunflowers were made; there is only the skill of the craftsperson who knitted them. Roosen's

83

40-41

golden house is not paint masquerading as the precious metal but a small amount of real gold that has been thinned to cover a modest house. If part of the wonder in Roosen's work lies in changes in scale, the other part lies in the visible tension between a rudimentary material and its crafted final form. Gold becomes a house and yet stubbornly remains gold, just as the model house remains true to its immense origin.

Body Scales

The touchstone for Roosen's entire oeuvre remains the human body. The miniature and the gigantic exist in relation to each other, but the human body is the point of reference for all her exaggerations. Not one body, nor anybody, but the body of the viewer. As Susan Stewart notes in her study of miniatures and giants, the body is our mode of perceiving scale. We take the place of the original for the detailed symmetry of a doll house, which offers us a total perspective, or the grotesque distortions of a gargantuan, which overshadows us.[2] Although Roosen explicitly represents the body in a figurative form (penises, breasts, eyeballs), she implicitly refers to viewers who will perceive her exaggerations in relation to their own bodies and experiences. Those who view Roosen's works in photographs gain their sense of scale by identifying either with the people in the surroundings, whether scientists or knitters, or with the surroundings themselves, like the museum and the gym, two collective corporeal sites where the twin breasts lounging in bed were installed and photographed. To sharpen the viewer's sense of scale, Roosen also chooses objects designed to fit the human body, from handles to houses. Instead of sculpting a complete figure, the artist implies the body through its absent parts; instead of the sculpted foot, she

66-67
6-7

offers the staircase or the inside of a worn shoe. Viewers gain a sensation of their own bodies by being excluded from familiar spaces they might normally occupy.

92
3

The artist's model man – composed of several mirrored balls stacked over a pair of sensible black leather shoes – confronts viewers more or less eye to eye, depending on their height. Yet, whatever their height, every viewer sees himself or herself reflected as a wee dot in the surroundings, as the mirrors are spherical. Part anamorphosis, part carnival funhouse, the reflection recalls Jan van Eyck's surprise self-portrait in the rounded mirror in the depths of the Arnolfini painting, if not the mirrored eyeball of a security camera. Coming closer may increase the size of the viewer's body but at the cost of distortion. This distorted representation is continually reaffirmed because the same reflection can be found on the spherical surface of every mirrored ball that makes up the man's bulbous body. While keeping several eyes on the global picture, this man has the ability to make others look slight or askew, many times over. Our distance is much too far; our proximity, far too close.

68-6

Daily Victors, Slumbering Giants and Bubble Heads

Roosen's most expansive work to date is her on-going series *Overwinnaars* (Victors), 1985–now. The 190 images, mostly cut out from daily newspapers, constitute a wondrous collection of people and things that have made the news for their exceptional nature. While there are many athletes celebrating victories in various sports (cycling to soccer), there are also objects (a large potato and a small microchip), oddities (a man with the longest beard, and the oldest female skeleton), statesmen (e.g. Mikhail Gorbatchov), public women (Princess Diana and Mother

68-

Theresa), entertainers (Nick Cave and P.J. Harvey), artists (from Jan van Eyck to Matthew Barney). Despite her seemingly broad survey, Roosen does not choose just any victors. Friends who send along images of exceptional people for her collection tend to find their clippings politely returned. Confronted with a cornucopia, Roosen selects only the figures that are victorious for her. The Dutch soccer team celebrating its Europe Cup victory in 1988 shows a tinge of national pride; the potato – found in Flevoland – offers another homage to home-grown fare while Bettine Vriesekoop and Anky van Grunsven, selected in 2004, reflect a local, personal history, intertwined with gender. The passage of time can play a significant role. The man with the 3.3 metre beard was born in 1826, photographed in 1904 and collected by Roosen in 1987; the 7000-year-old skeleton belonged to a woman who died at age forty-five – then the same age as the artist. Some victors – like Michael Jackson, who joined Roosen's collection in 1996 – have since fallen from her favour. Others – like Nick Cave, who claimed 'The muse is not a race horse' in 1996 – have not lost any of their authority for her over the years.

By relying upon ready-made images from the press, Roosen seems to valorise the mass media circulations of the spectacle. Yet her collection – with its specialised and intimate labour – opposes the collection of the newspaper, which tries to impose an objective order on current events while assuming to exhaust them. The vastness of *Le Monde* and the infinity of *The Times* are reduced to a portable space that can be consumed in one day. The newspaper uses the miniature to effect a harmonious shift from public to private space; its exteriority (every page is printed, every space filled) matches its interiority (the opened pages enclose, if not house, the reader). Roosen, by cutting out

her favourite victors, liberates the giant from the confines of the miniature; too big for the newspaper, her victors are freed from the common news to inhabit a separate sanctuary made especially for their kind; their images are saved from the garbage bin to persist as art and history. Part historian, part editor, Roosen replaces the newspaper's mediation from public to private with her own personal pantheon that spreads across an entire wall. The newspaper's format – the unwieldy 'handles' of the fold-out spread – has been visibly cut out with a pair of scissors, another uniquely individual way of holding and shaping history. Later victors have been left in the context of the news that first surrounded them. Yet throughout her collection, the illusion of totality – and objectivity – in the newspaper is eclipsed by another history that remains incomplete because it is linked to Roosen's life. Her choices reflect not only her personal tastes but also the biological time of her body, if not the changing values that come with age itself. The woman's skeleton was both 7,000 and forty-five years old, both the oldest skeleton and the skeleton of a woman the same age as the artist. The athletic victors are gradually replaced by women with exceptional life stories – a shift in interest from the collective to the individual native. Growing – if not ticking away – with the artist's life, this collection remains incomplete, open. It is an organic, living thing that maintains a tension between the public life of the victor and the private life of the artist.

It is significant that Roosen prefers to translate the Dutch title 'overwinnaars' with the English word 'survivors'. While related to the victor, the survivor describes her figures' endurance beyond the ephemeral newspaper while recalling the French word *survivre*, literally, to overlive. Such an excess of living belongs to the hero exceptional yet mortal individuals whose superhuman feats lie between earth and the gods.[3] Yet the excess of living in *survivre* also belongs to the organic exaggerations that can be found in one of Roosen's earlier works: the slippers she had crafted for the Rotterdam giant. The work refers to a real giant who lived in the city and died in the 1950s; after seeing his shoes in a museum, Roosen had the slippers custom-made by a German workshop that specialises in crafting shoes for large people around the world. Roosen's victors and giants – understood as an excess of life (overperformance and overgrowth) – manifest an evolution in one body which symbolises changes in the collective space. Of course, the giants belong to the first race of human beings; mentioned in the Old Testament, they were then attributed with extreme topographical and meteorological phenomena, from rocky shores to heavy storms, before being tamed as the mythological patrons for cities and states.[4] Consider Gargantua's role in Mont-Saint-Michel or Gog's and Magog's London. Roosen's giant slippers – donned at bed and worn in the house – show the giant's domestication; his flight from the open natural landscape to the sheltered cultured home; and his transformation from folklore into bedtime fairytales. After shaping nature for civic life, the giant is retired, only to appear in the occasional parade or carnival; his great size is no longer a source of terror, but a mere incident of birth, as fortuitous and freakish as the big potato from Flevoland. Roosen's *overwinnaars* – victors, survivors, heroes – take over from the giant and reflect our own withdrawal from nature. Their feats of over-living are not the result of nature, but personal choice and dedication (even the man with the longest beard has decided not to cut it); they do not make rocky shores, nor

cause heavy storms, but shape our media landscape. Measuring ourselves against their spectacular feats, we understand the limit, if not the frame, of the public world that we inhabit, albeit on a smaller scale.

In the historical shift from giants to heroes, Roosen's recent project attempts to create a space for the individual. Using old newspapers, the artist made large balls with paper mâché and then gave the hollow white forms to her friends with the explicit instructions to decorate them as they wished and to wear them over their heads. At once generic and individualised, the 'bubbles' are the result of the specialised and intimate labour of craft – a collectivised labour that does not come from the artist's hands but from her wishes, executed by others. More like a head dress than a mask, these bubbles do not so much hide the individuals as exaggerate their personalities along with their size and height. While reminiscent of dialogue bubbles in cartoons, if not cartoon figures themselves, these works also recall the costumes in a carnival or parade. Indeed, Roosen allows her friends to embellish their heads so that the fine details of their personalities – usually experienced at close range in the context of private social gatherings can be seen from a great distance. To this exaggeration, Roosen also adds mobility, proper to our era of perpetual movement in travel. The paper heads, once custom-decorated, were taken along to Roosen's exhibition openings at galleries and museums in other cities outside Arnhem. Since her friends could not always make the trip to attend, the artist asked other guests to wear the bubble heads at the openings. In this shift from the heads of close friends at home to those of fresh acquaintances in foreign cities, the bubbles become portable doubles, living keepsakes of private relations. Despite their origin in the personal realm, the heads are destined for a larger public space. Unlike Roosen's golden miniature house, which eases the pain of separation by appearing to shrink distance, her oversized heads use scale in another way: to dwarf the unfamiliar guests and to shrink their overwhelming anonymity. Like the giants in a parade or even the enlarged faces of the victors in the newspapers, these decorated heads float high above the crowd. They are moving beacons that do not warn travellers away from a rocky shore but transform a sea of unknown faces into a familiar social circle. Here, Roosen's sense of scale follows her desire to have very, very close what is extremely far away.

1. Marie-Françoise Christout, 'Le merveilleux, catégorie esthétique', *Le merveilleux et le 'théâtre du silence' en France à partir du XVIIe siècle,* Paris: Editions Mouton, 1965,
ch. 21. While defining the characteristics of the merveille, Christout focuses on ballet.
2. Susan Stewart, *On Longing. Narratives of the Miniature, the Gigantic, the Souvenir, the Collection,* Durham & London: Duke University Press, 1993, xii.
3. See Anna Makolkin, *Name, Hero, Icon. Semiotics of Nationalism through Heroic Biography*, Berlin/New York, Mouton de Gruyter, 1992.
4. See Walter Stevens, *Giants in Those Days. Folklore, Ancient History, and Nationalism,* Lincoln & London, University of Nebraska Press, 1989.

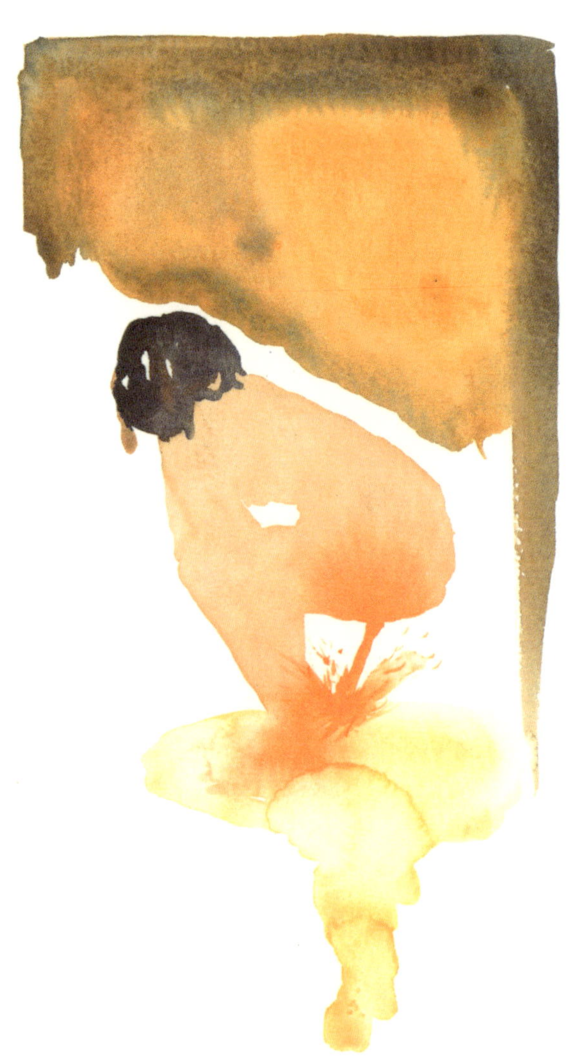

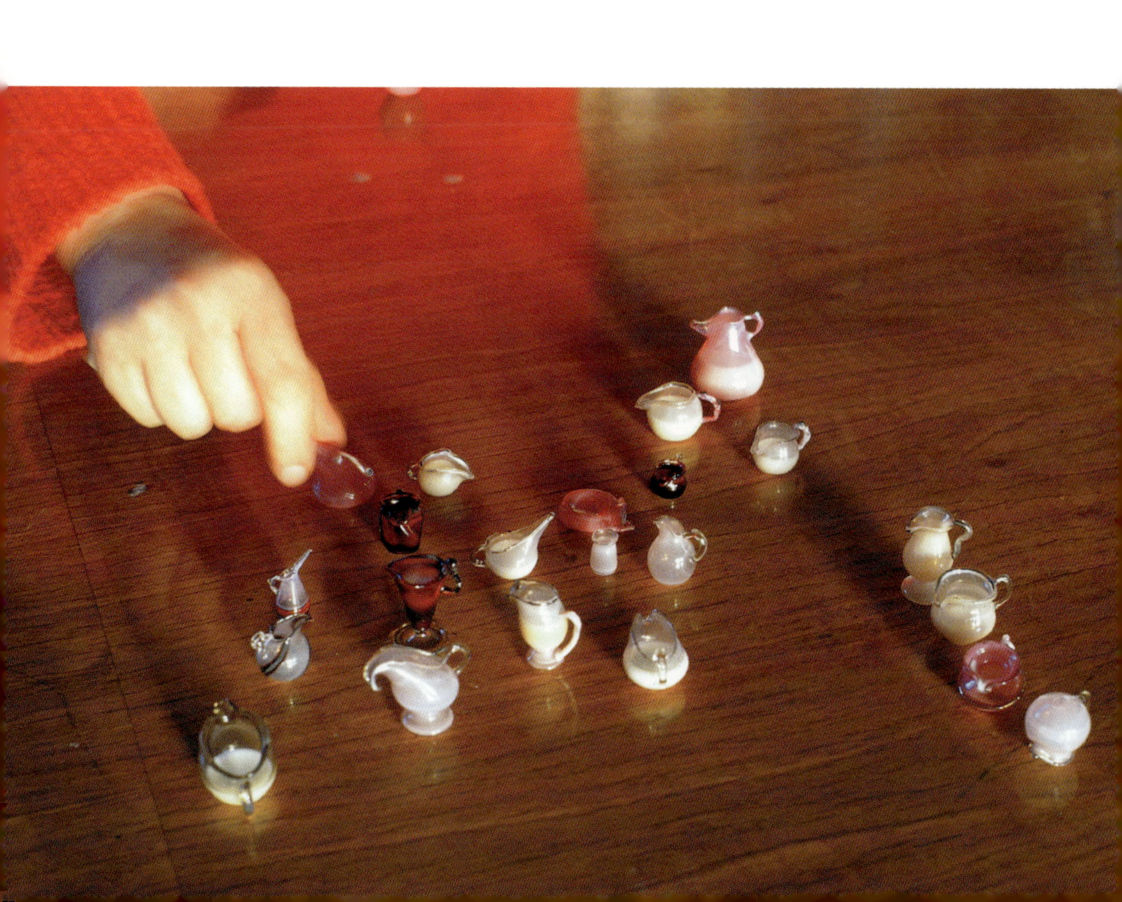

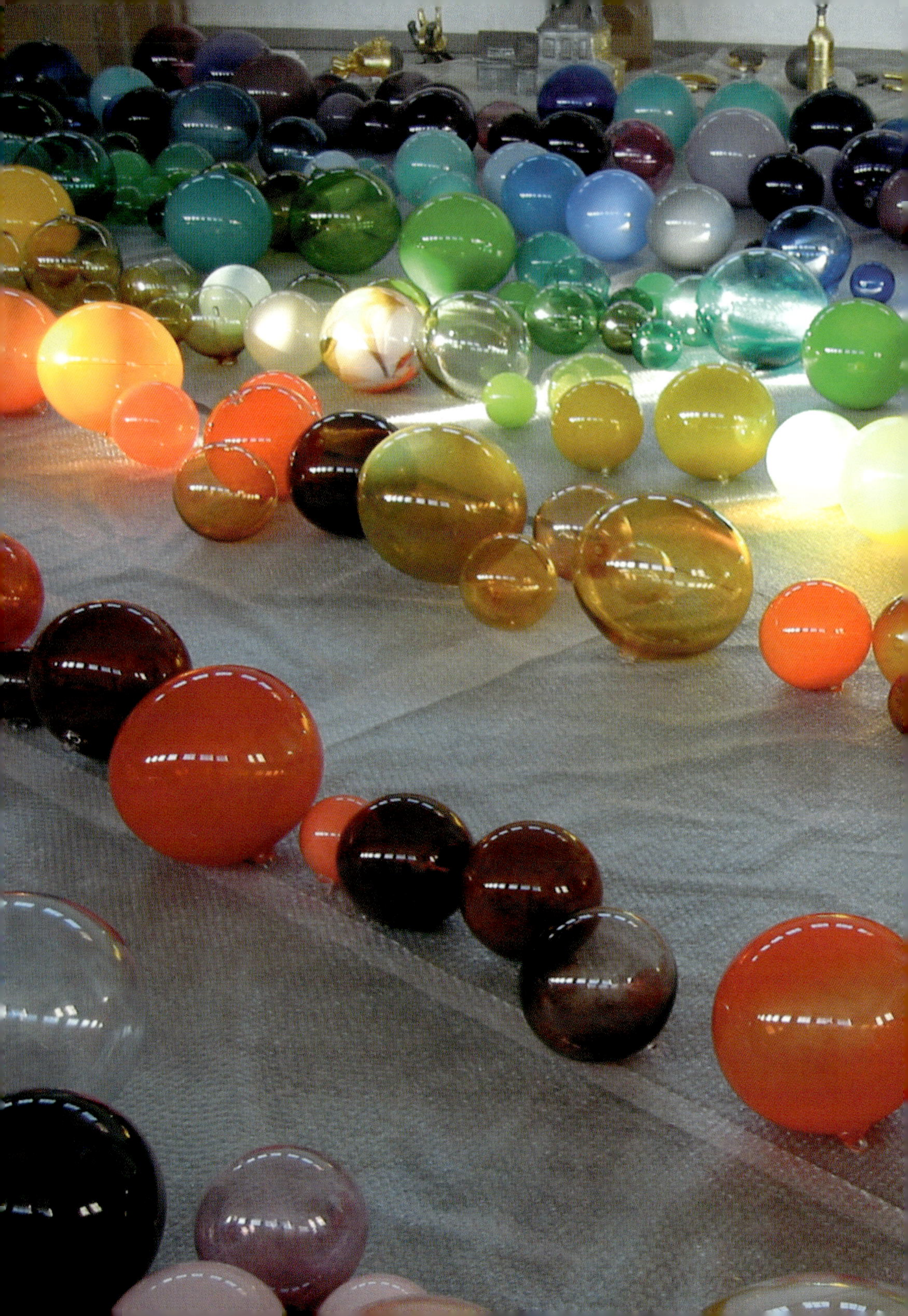

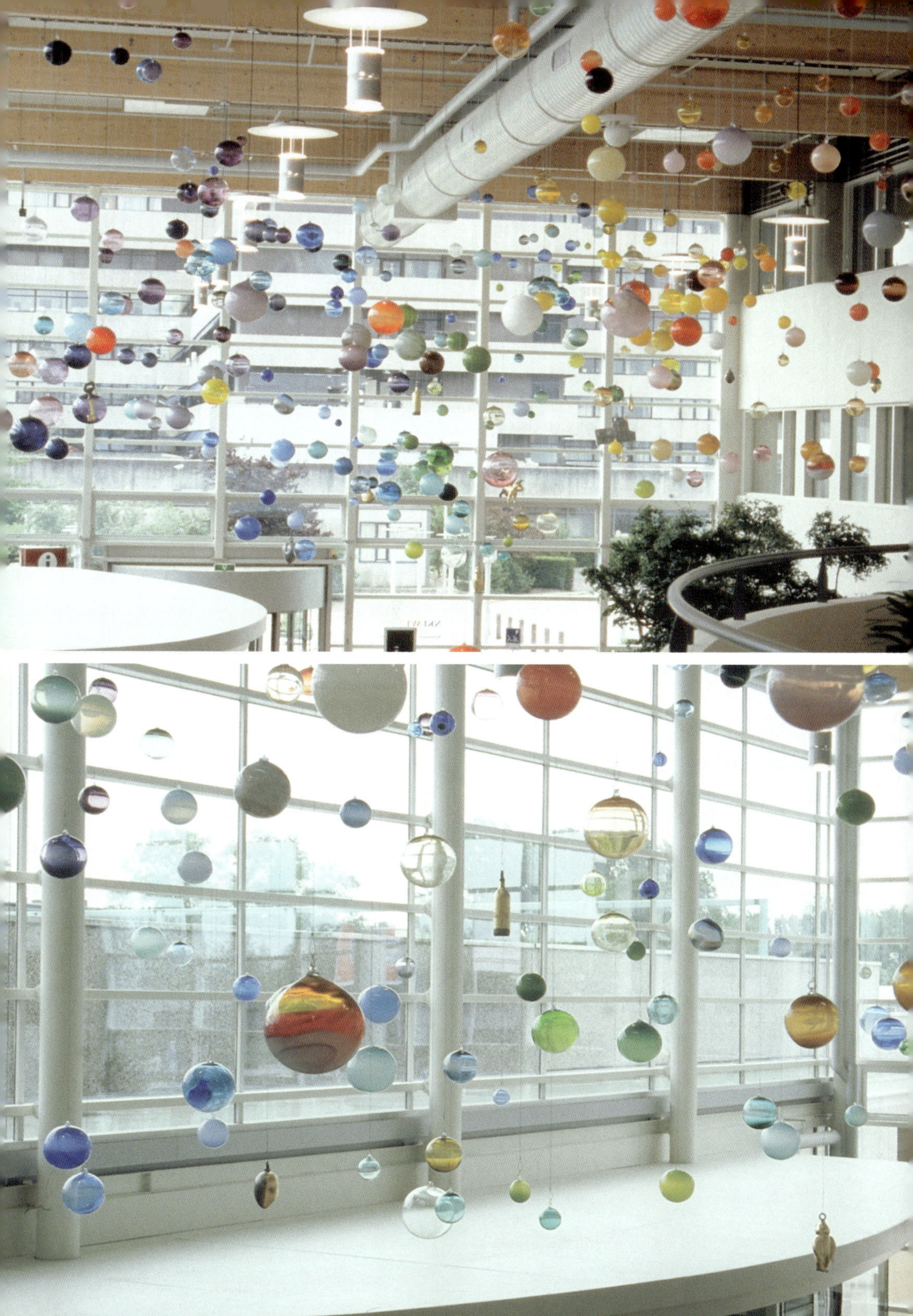

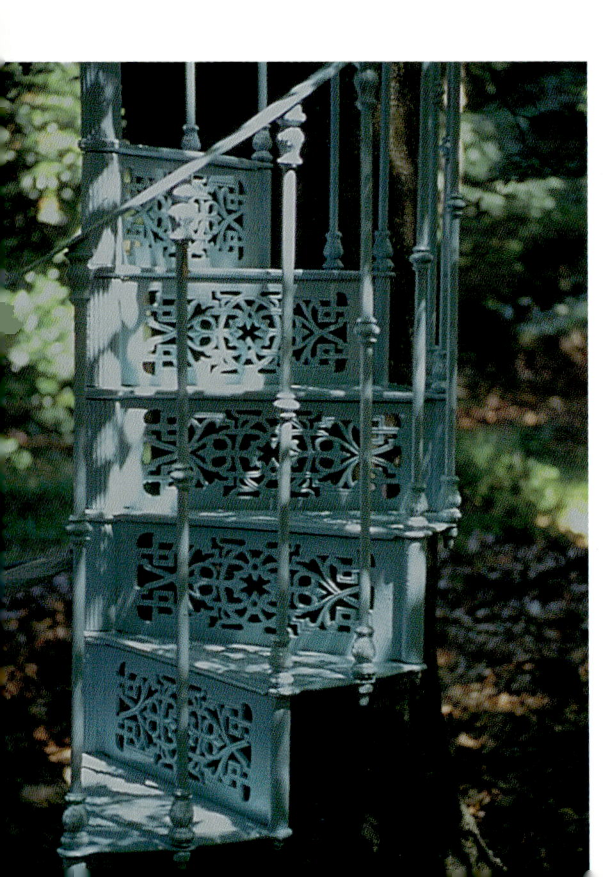

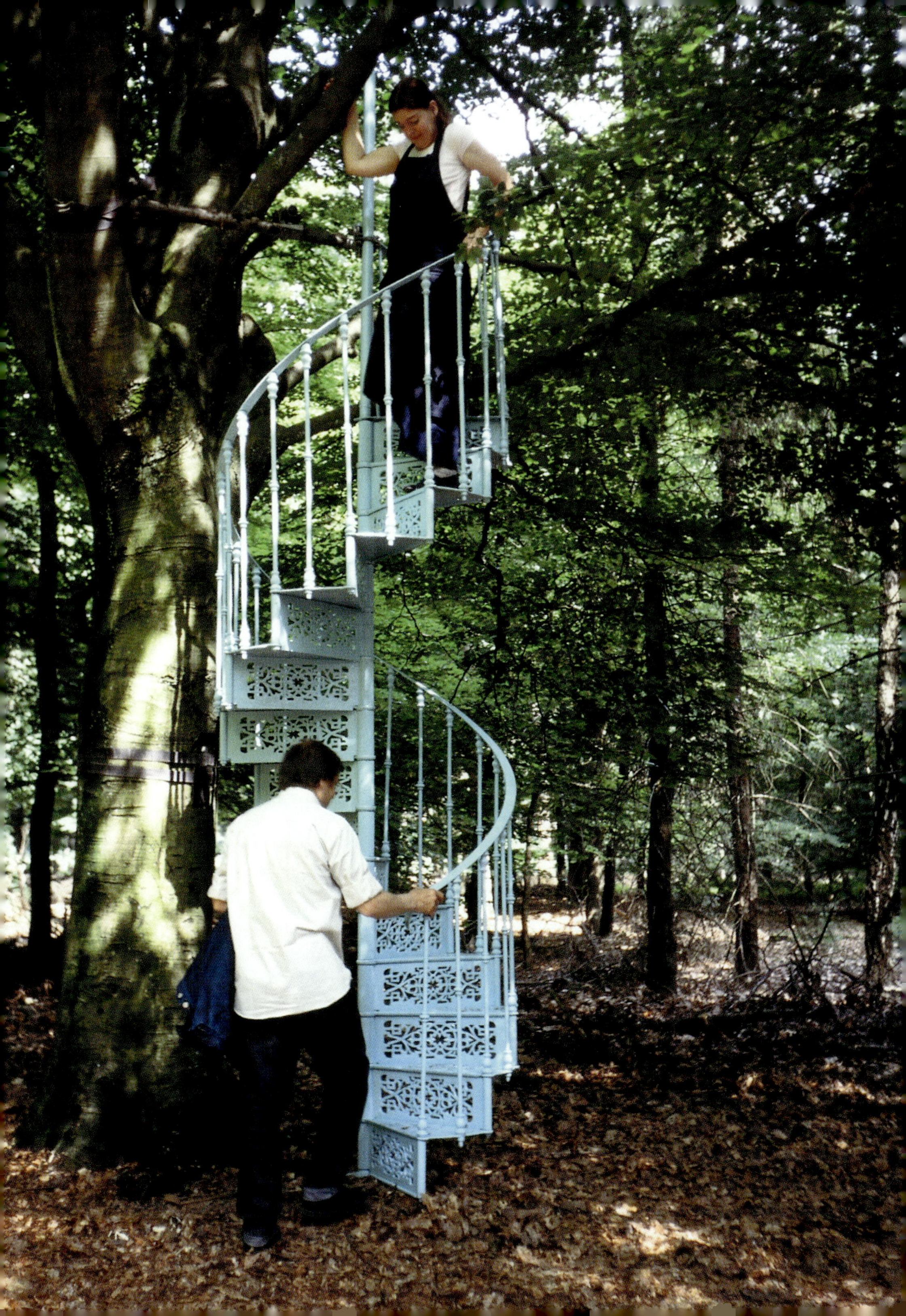

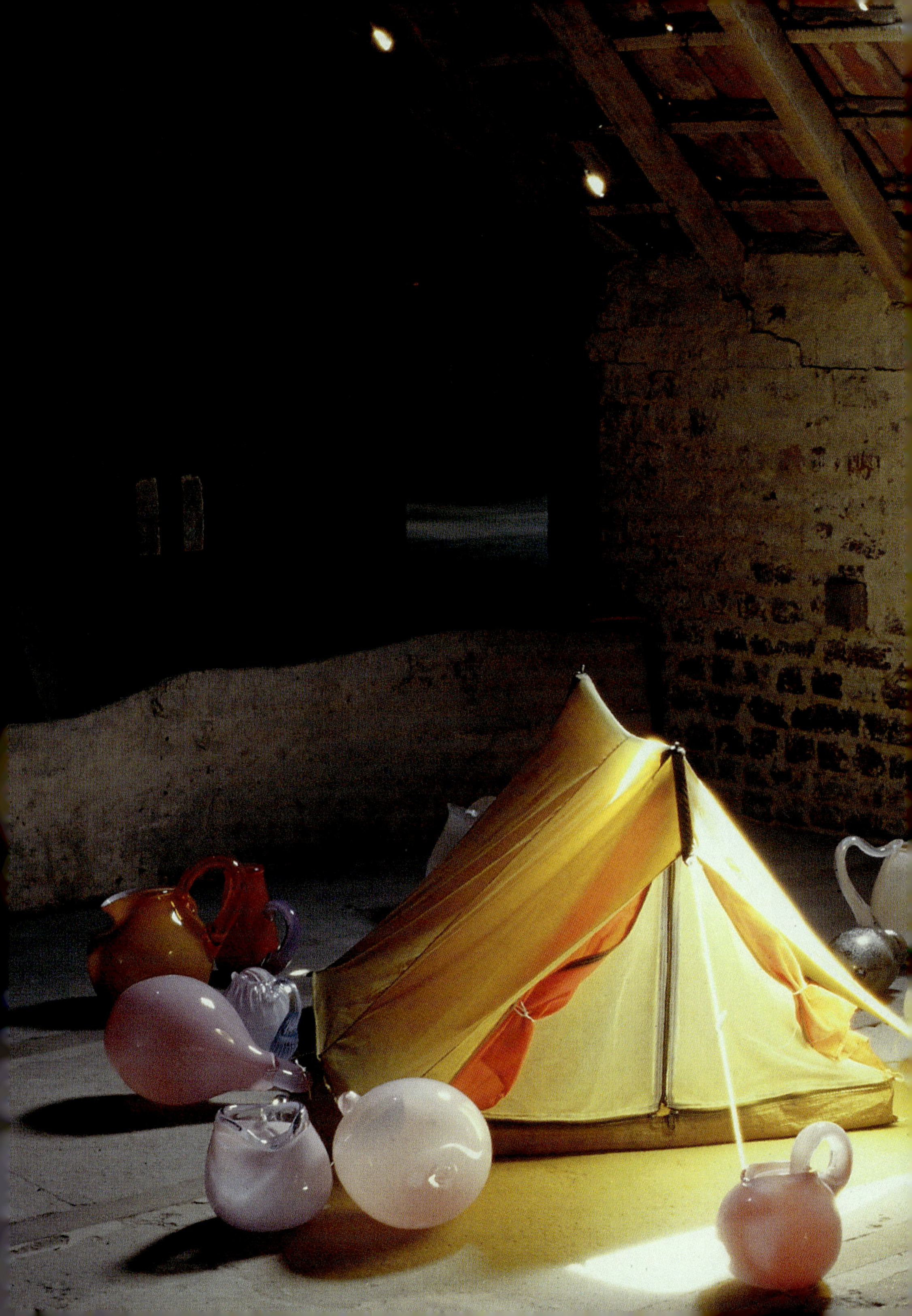

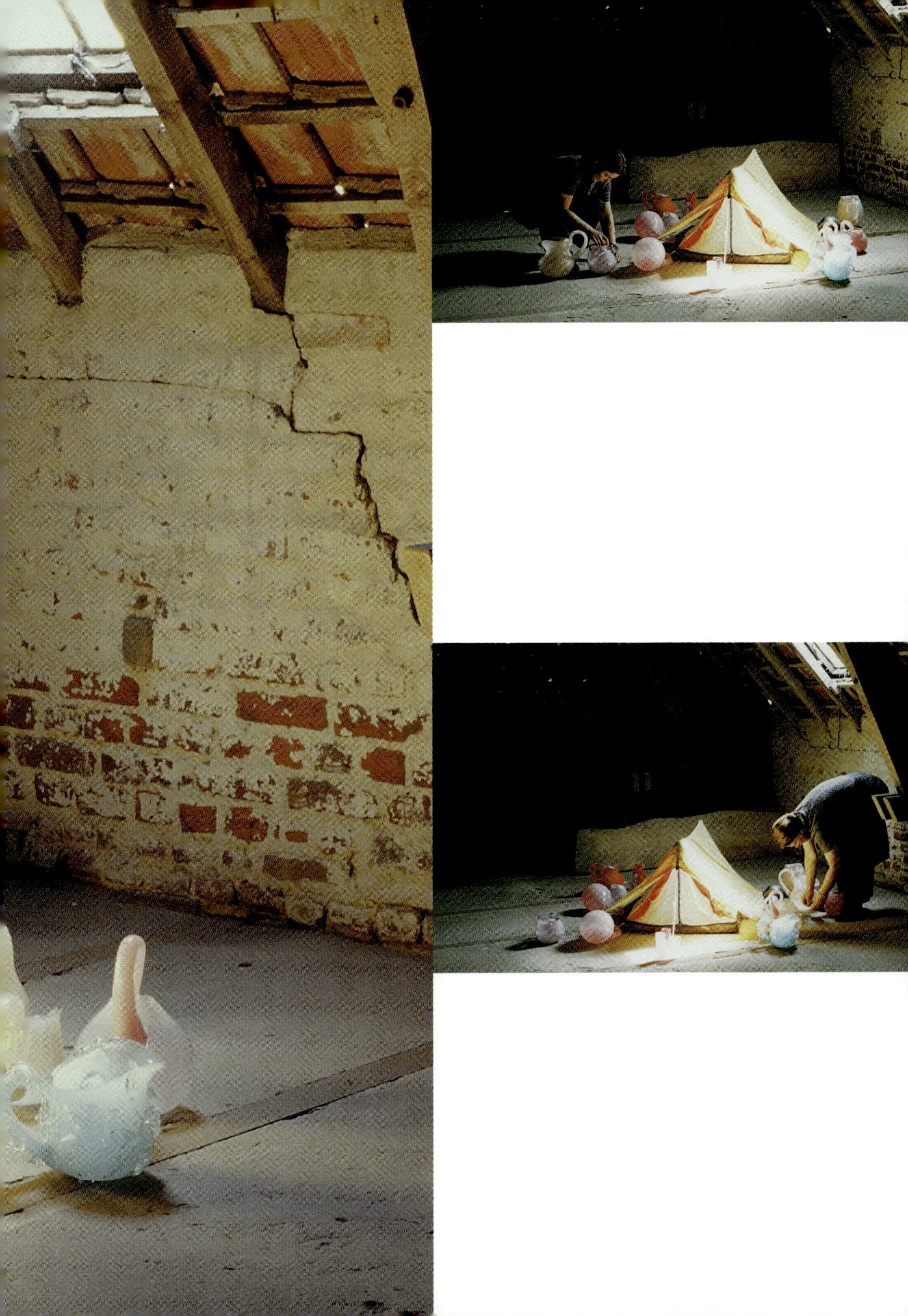

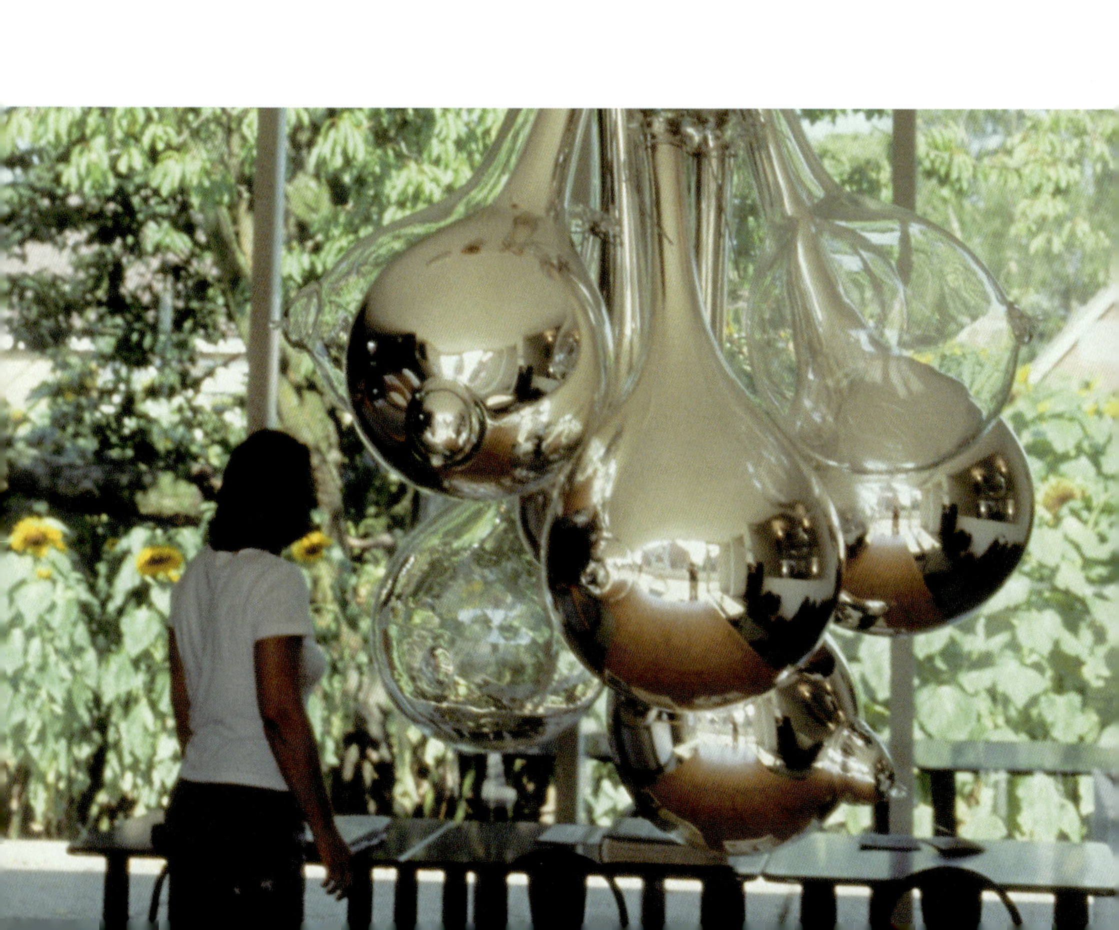

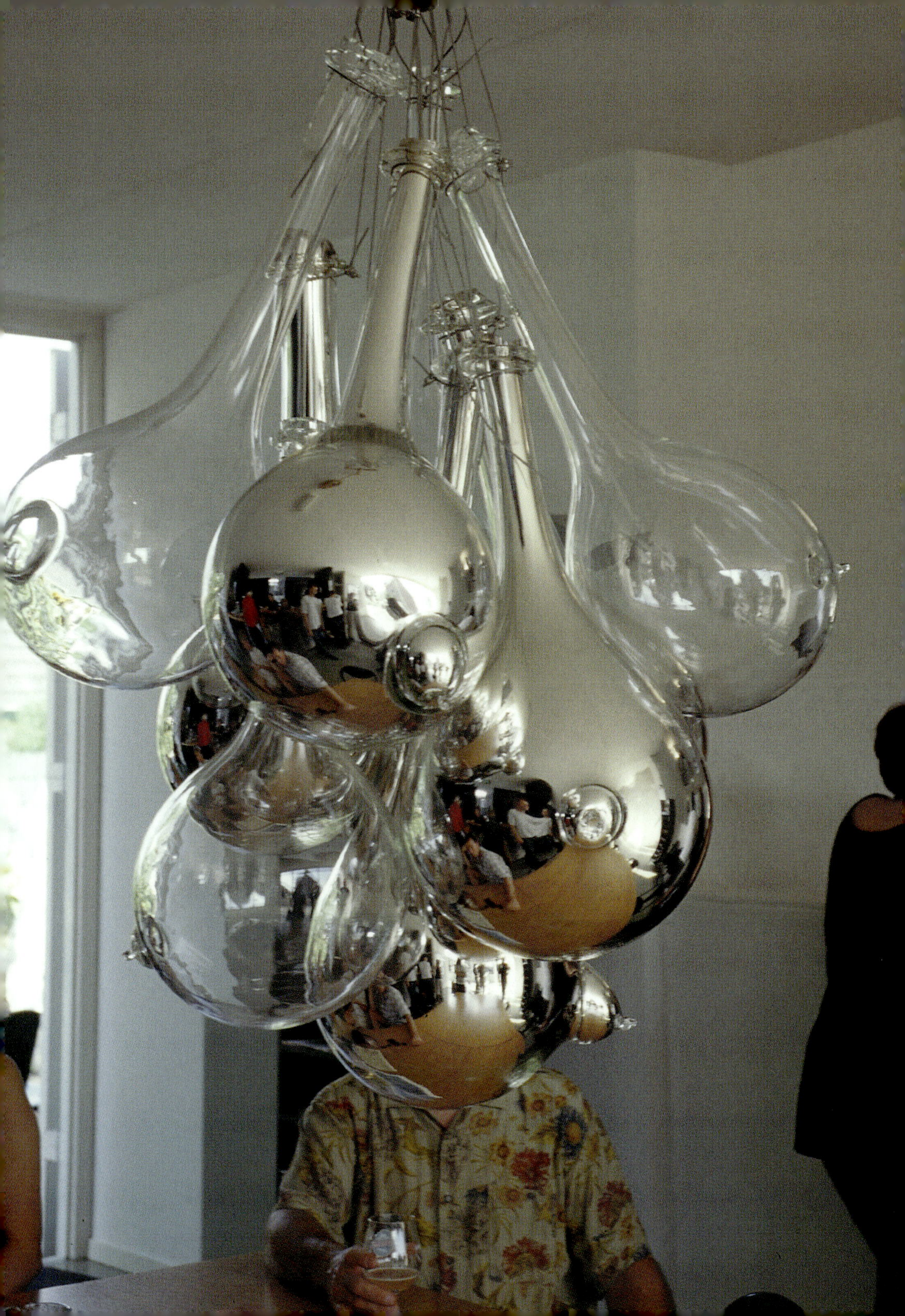

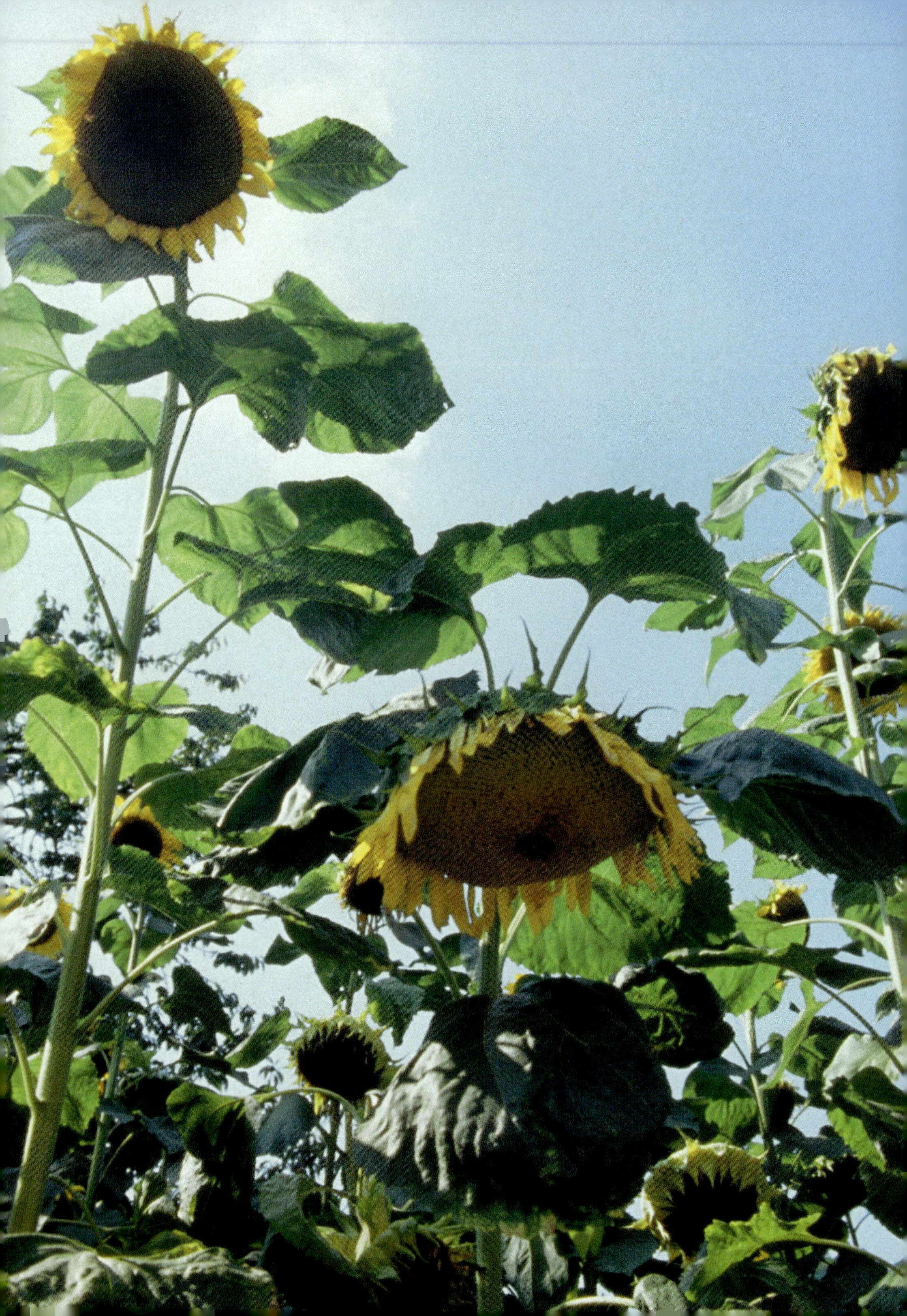

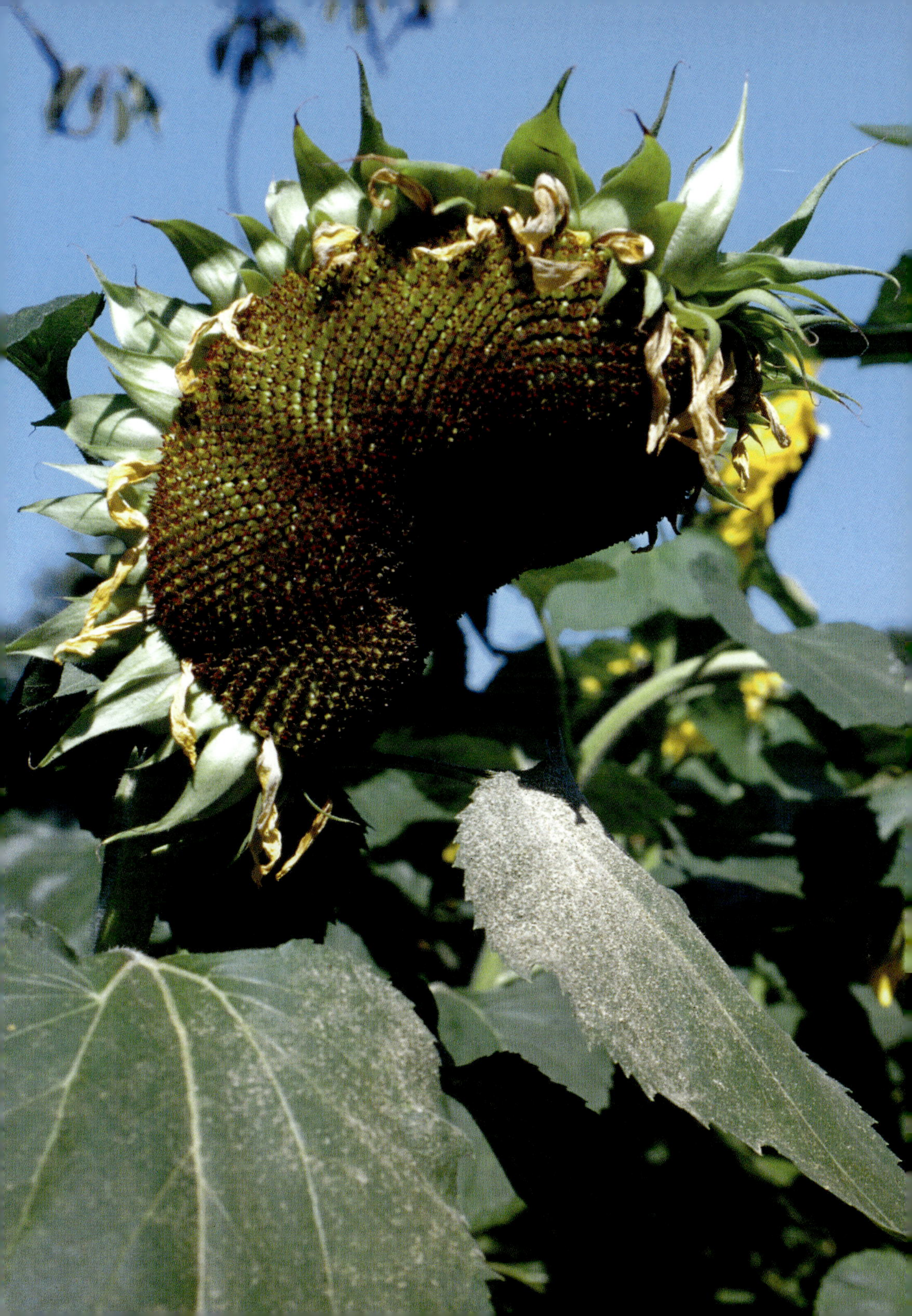

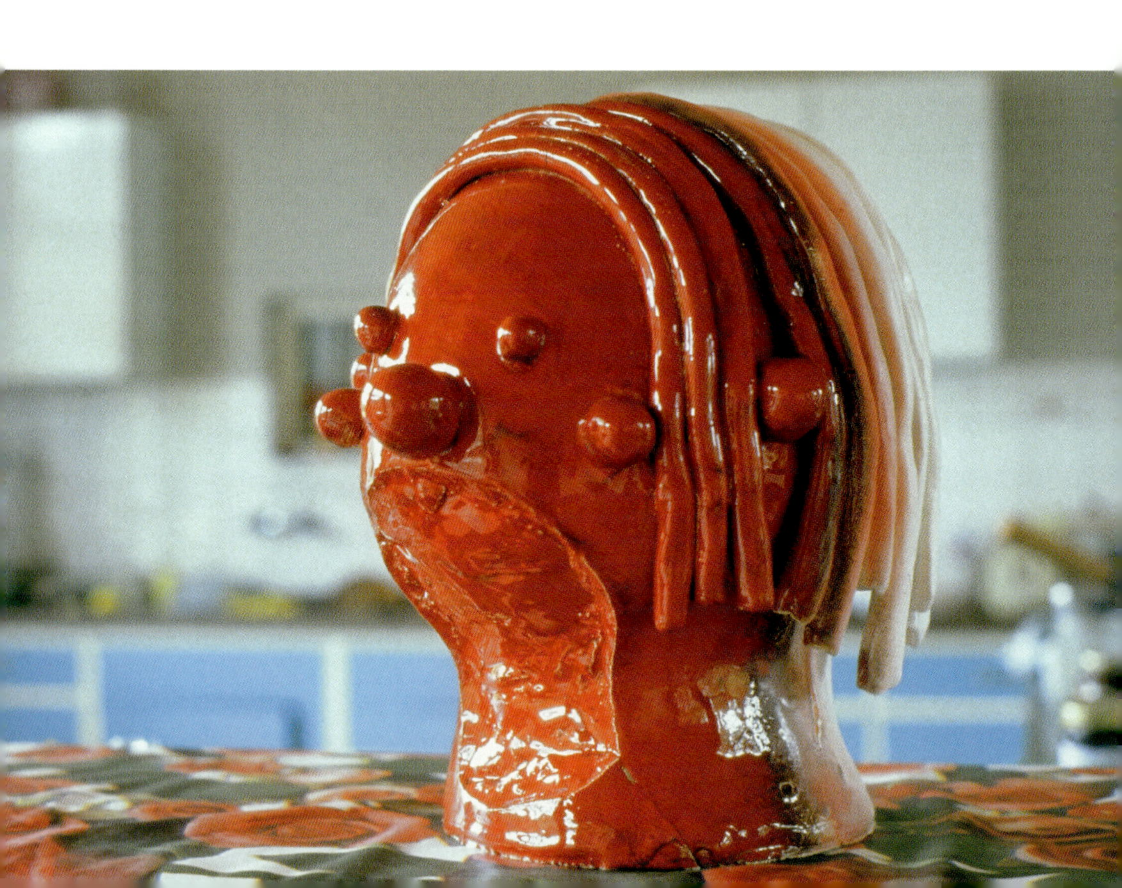

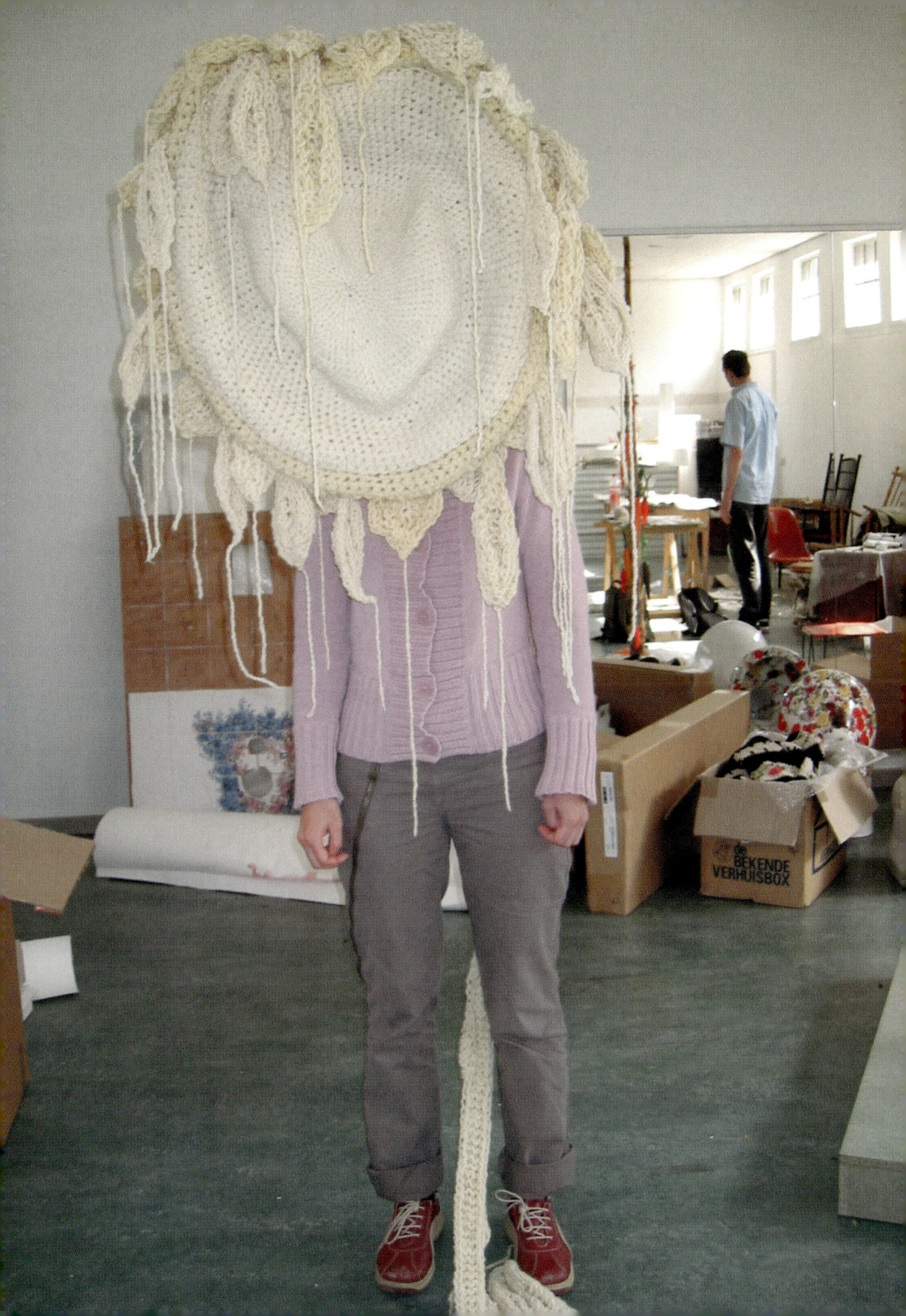

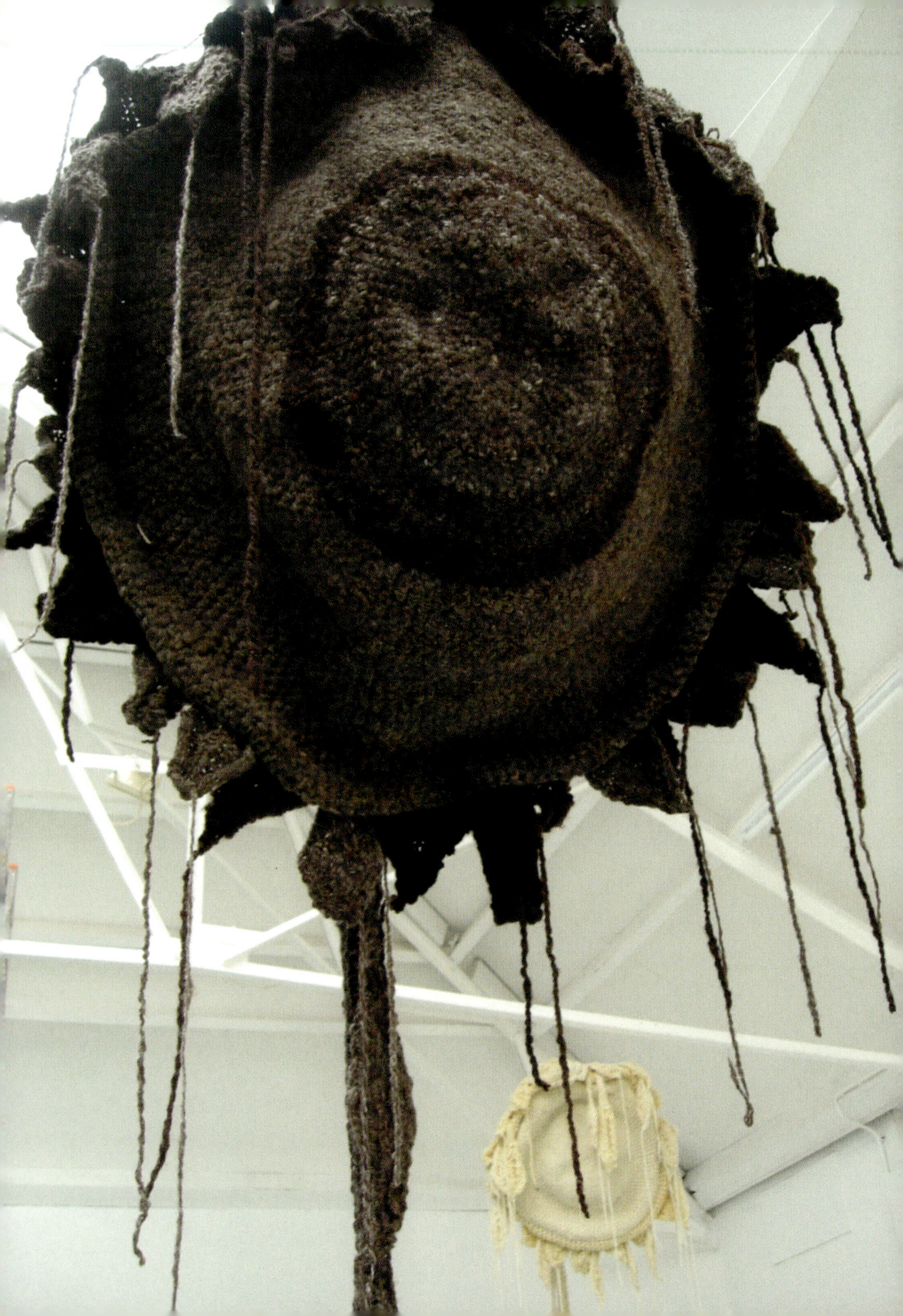

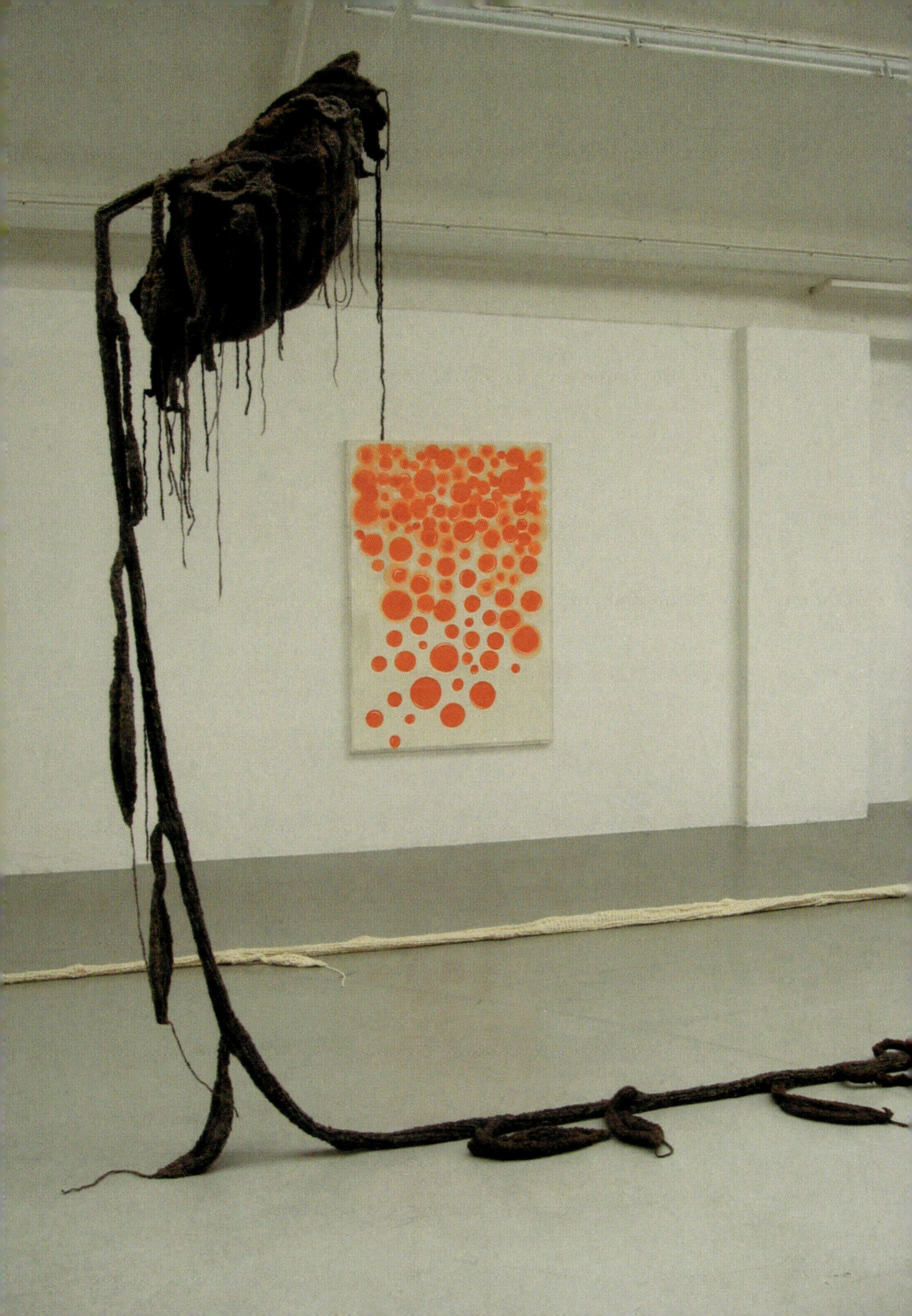

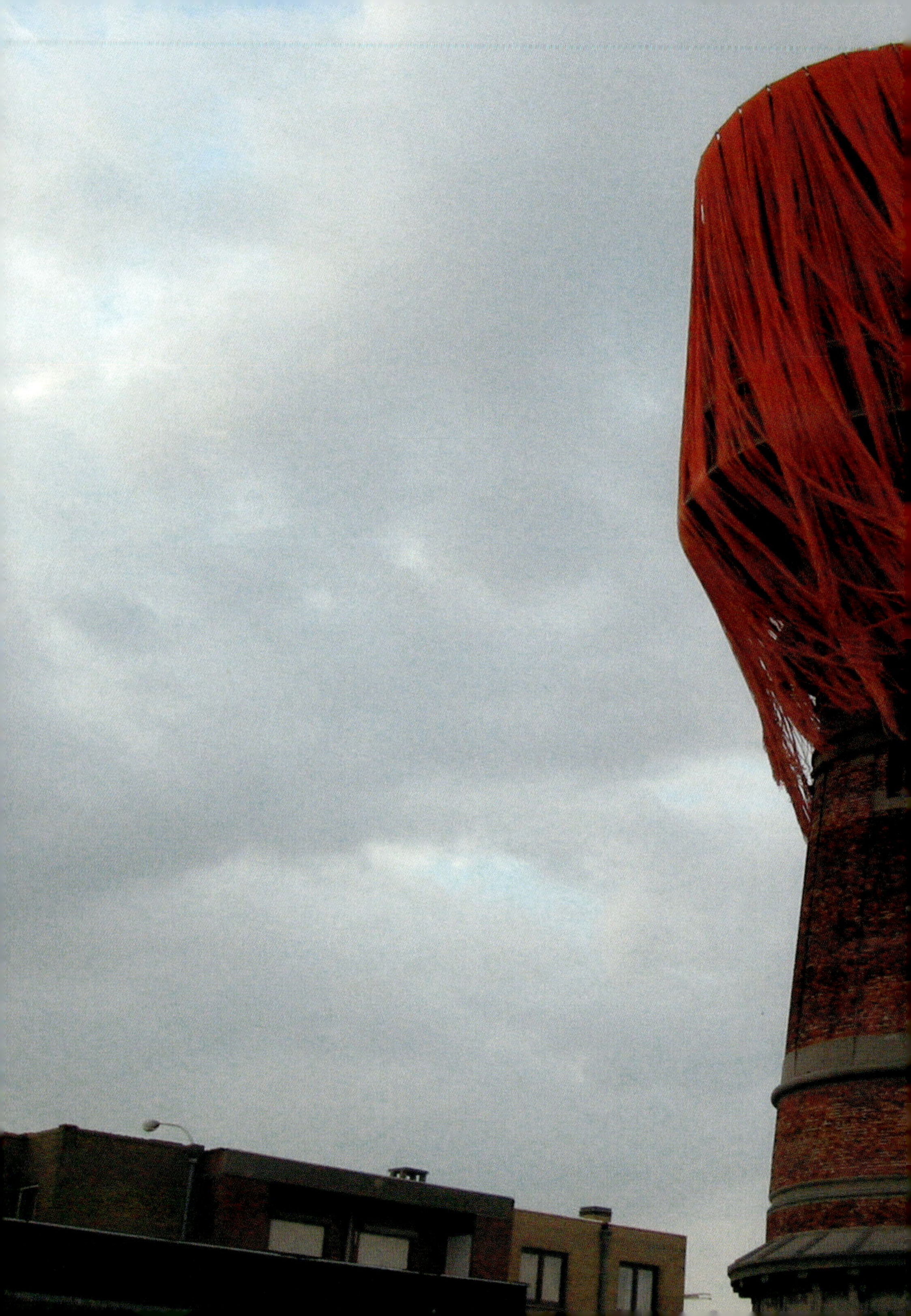

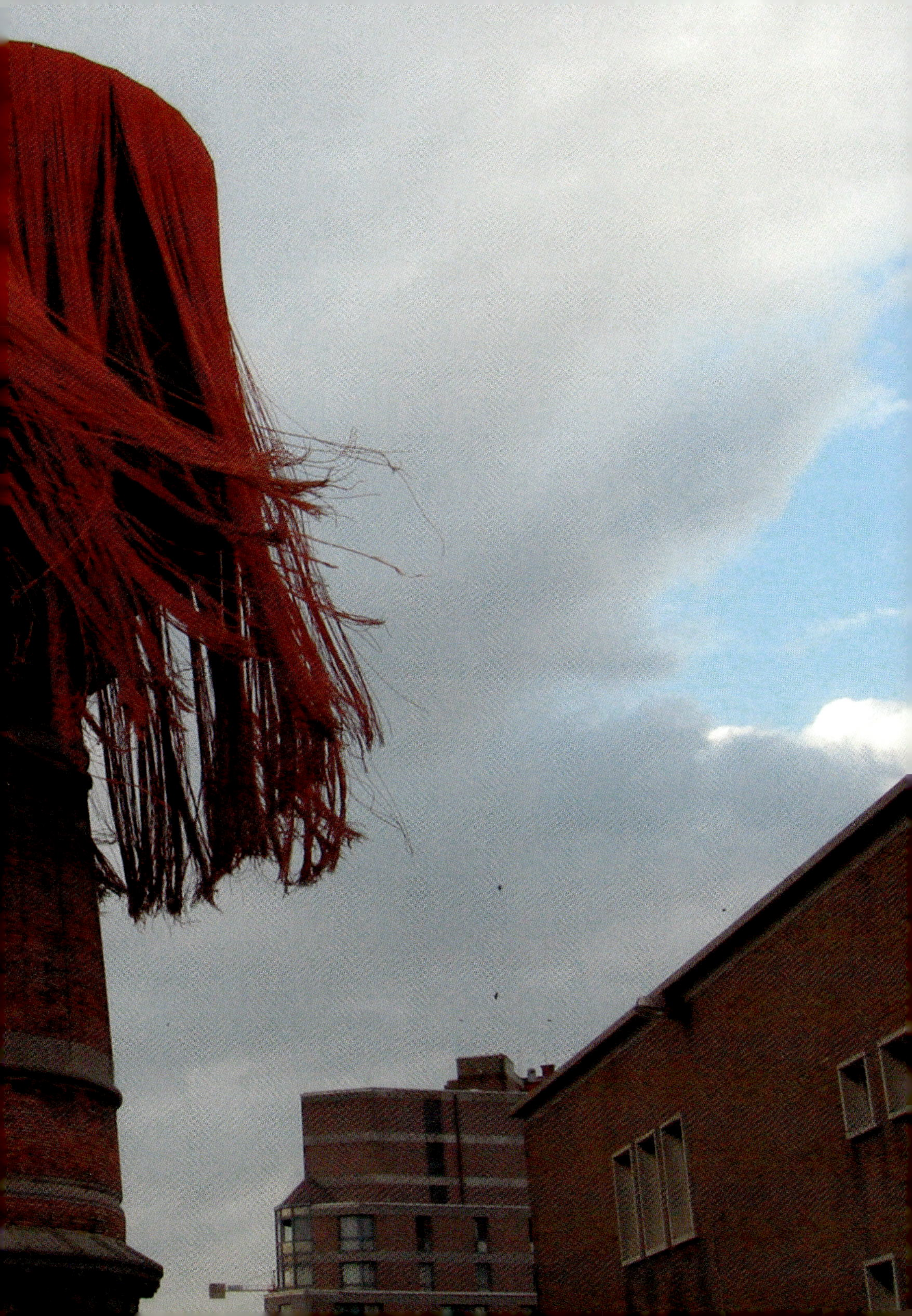

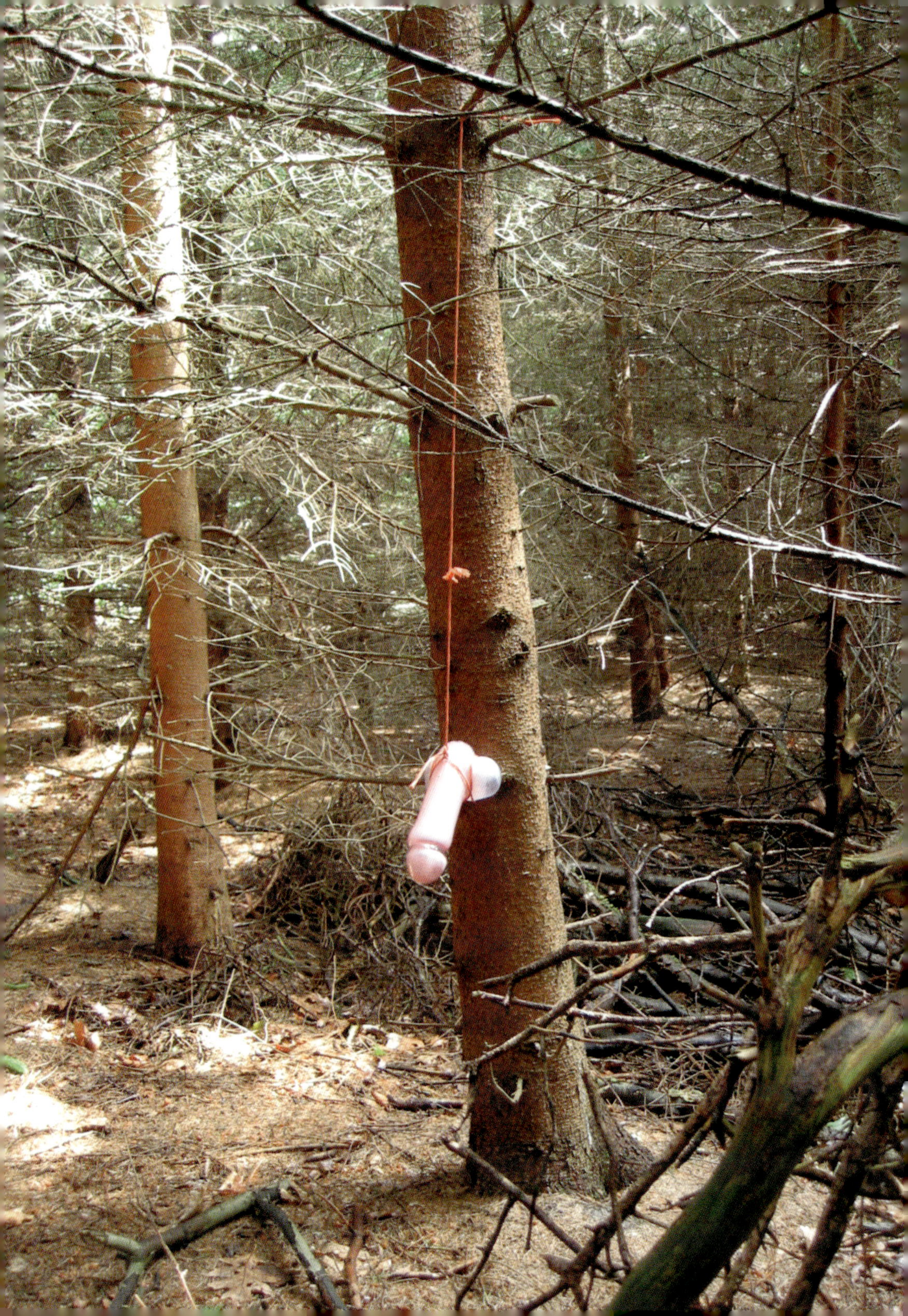

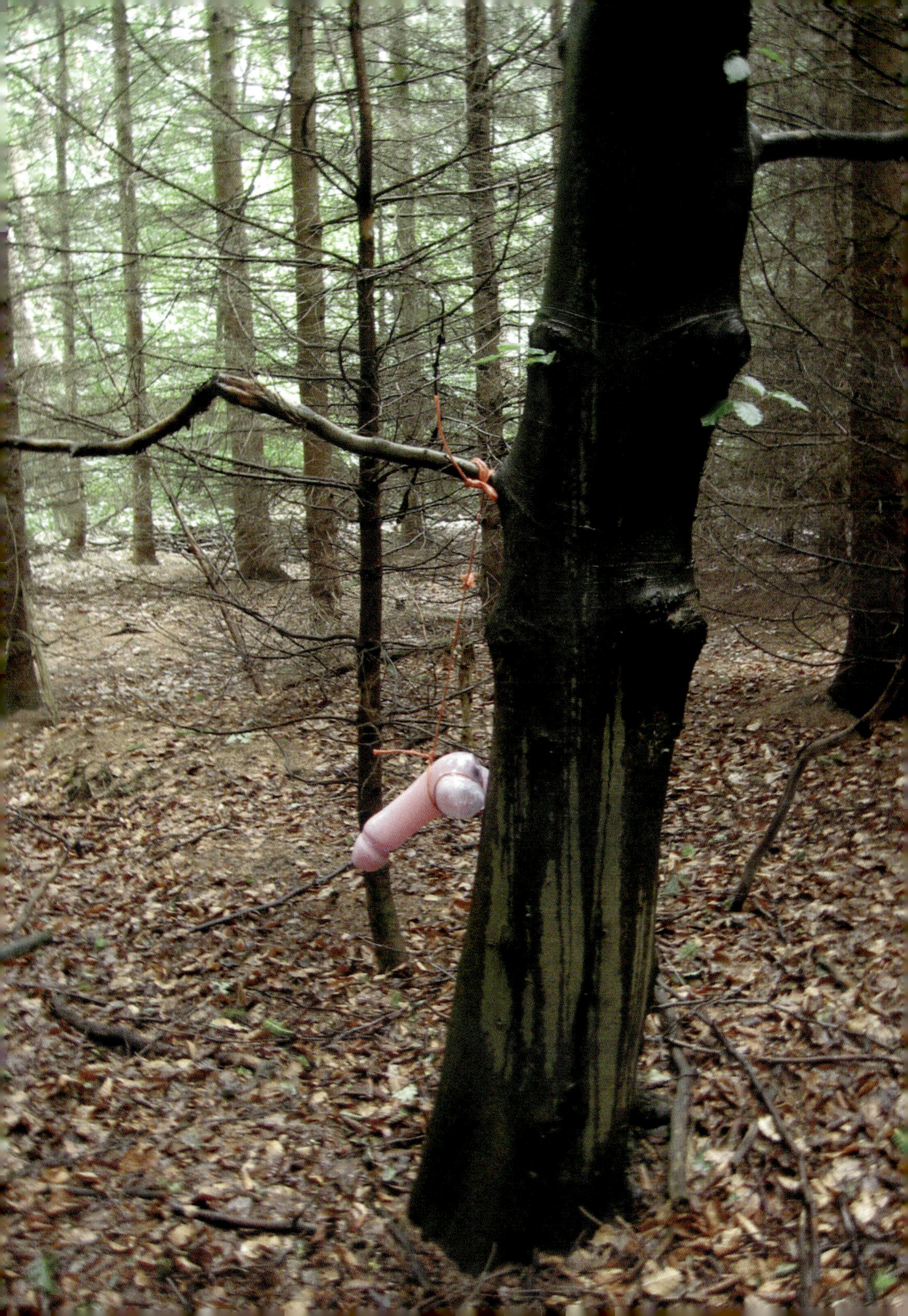

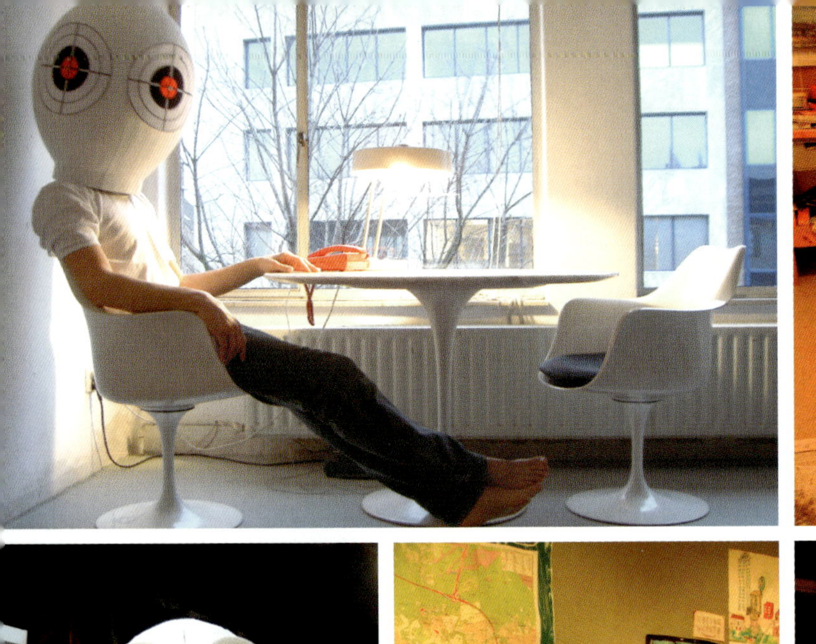
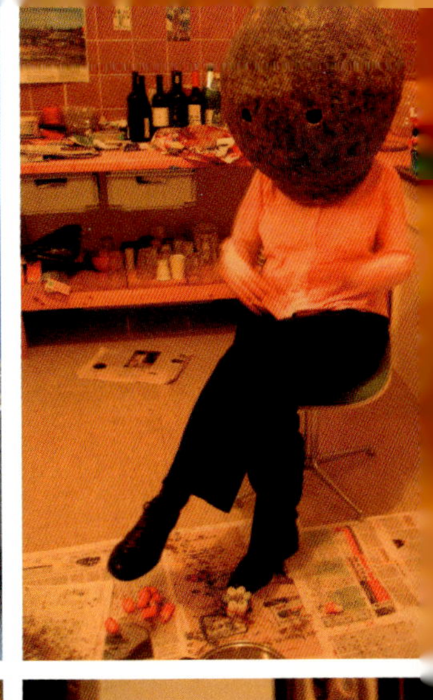
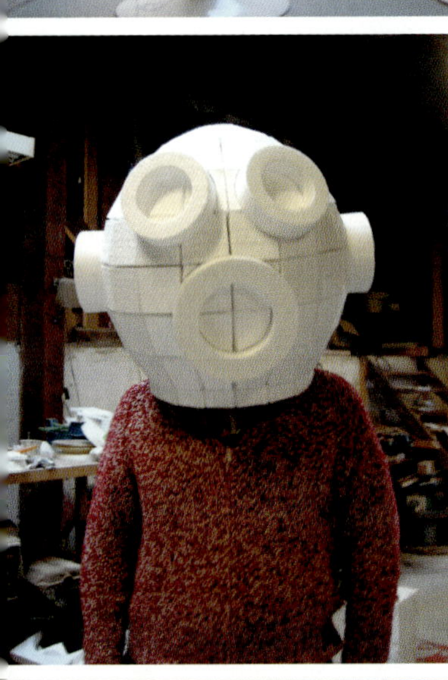
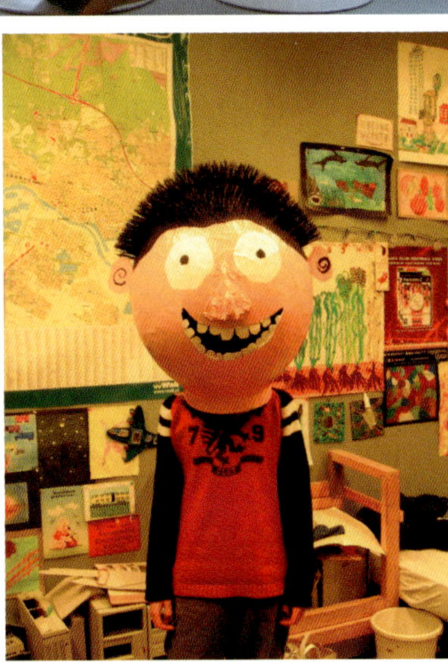
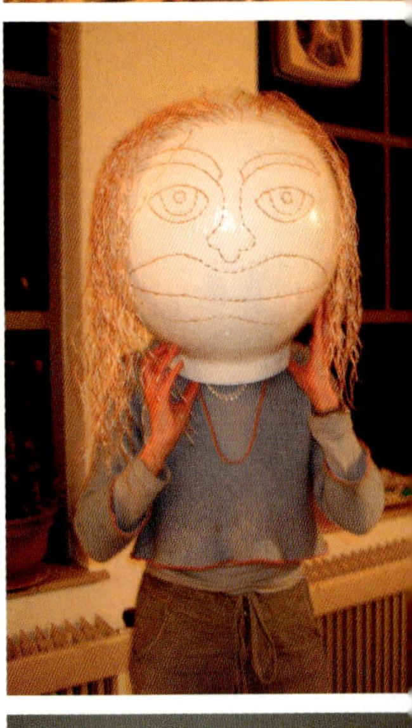
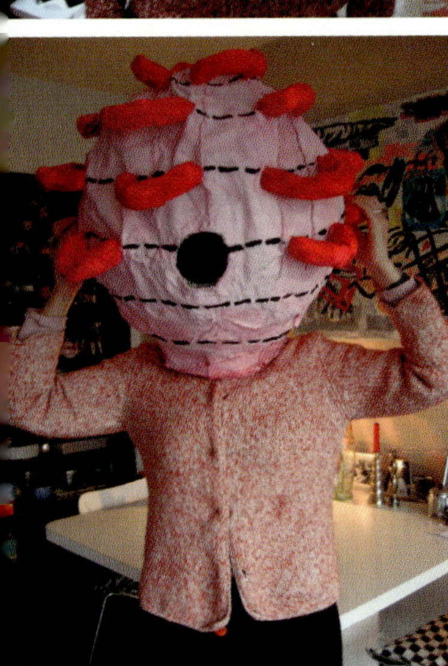
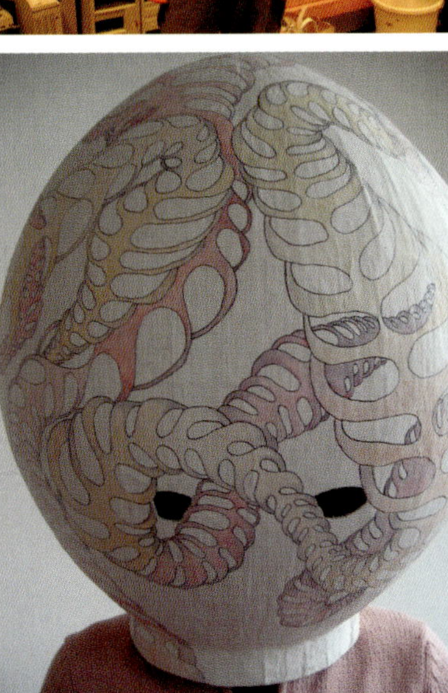
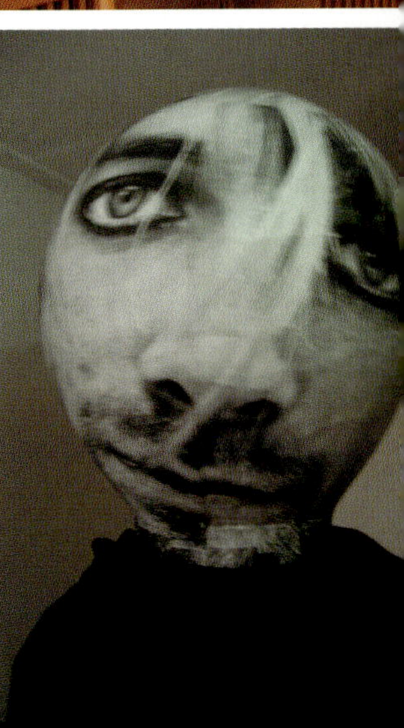

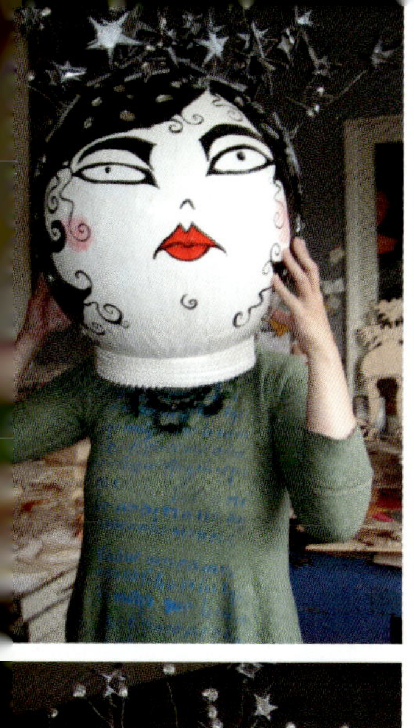
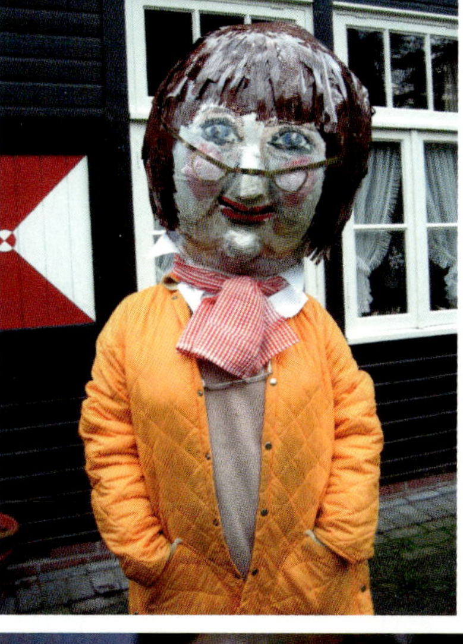
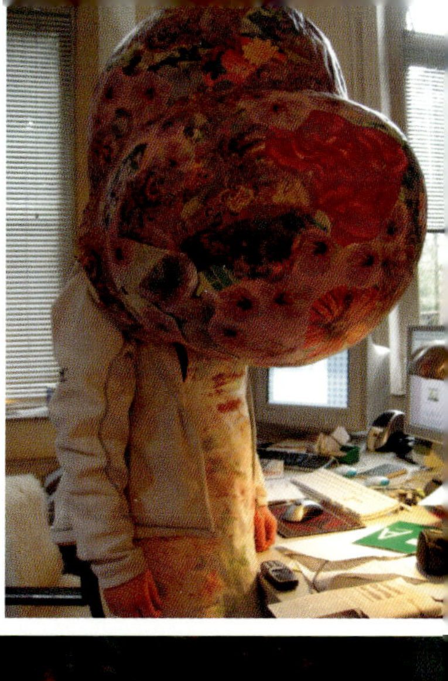
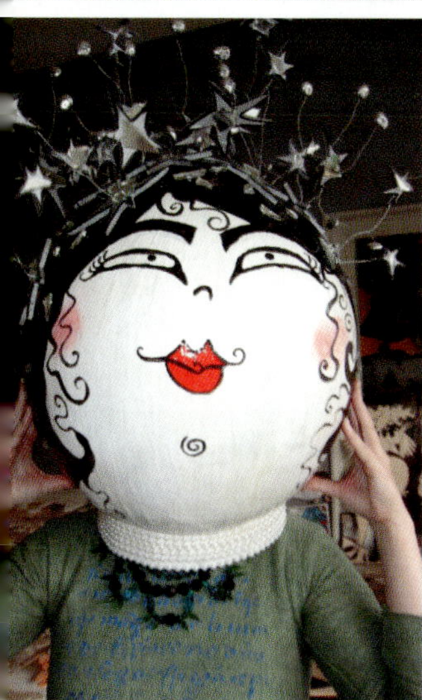
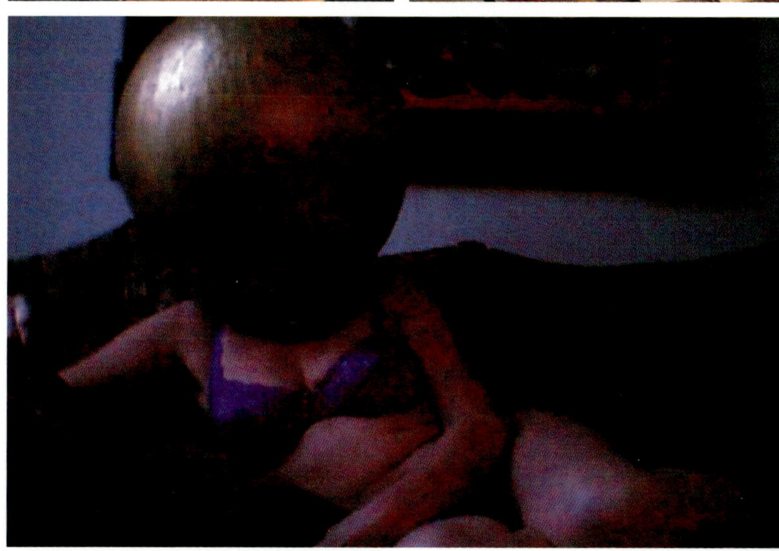
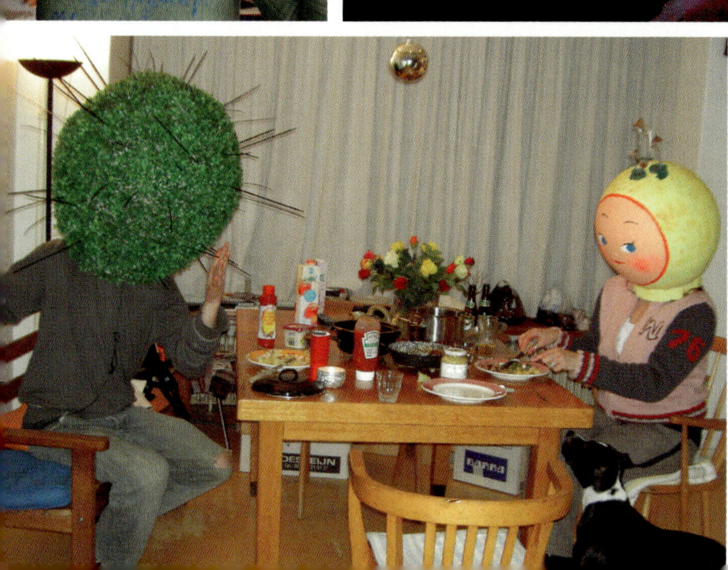
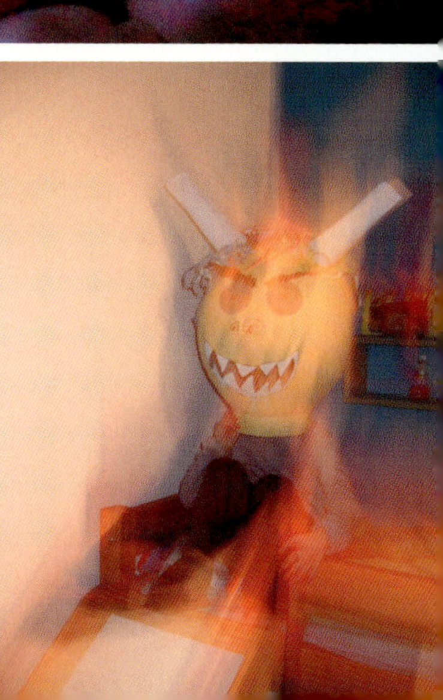

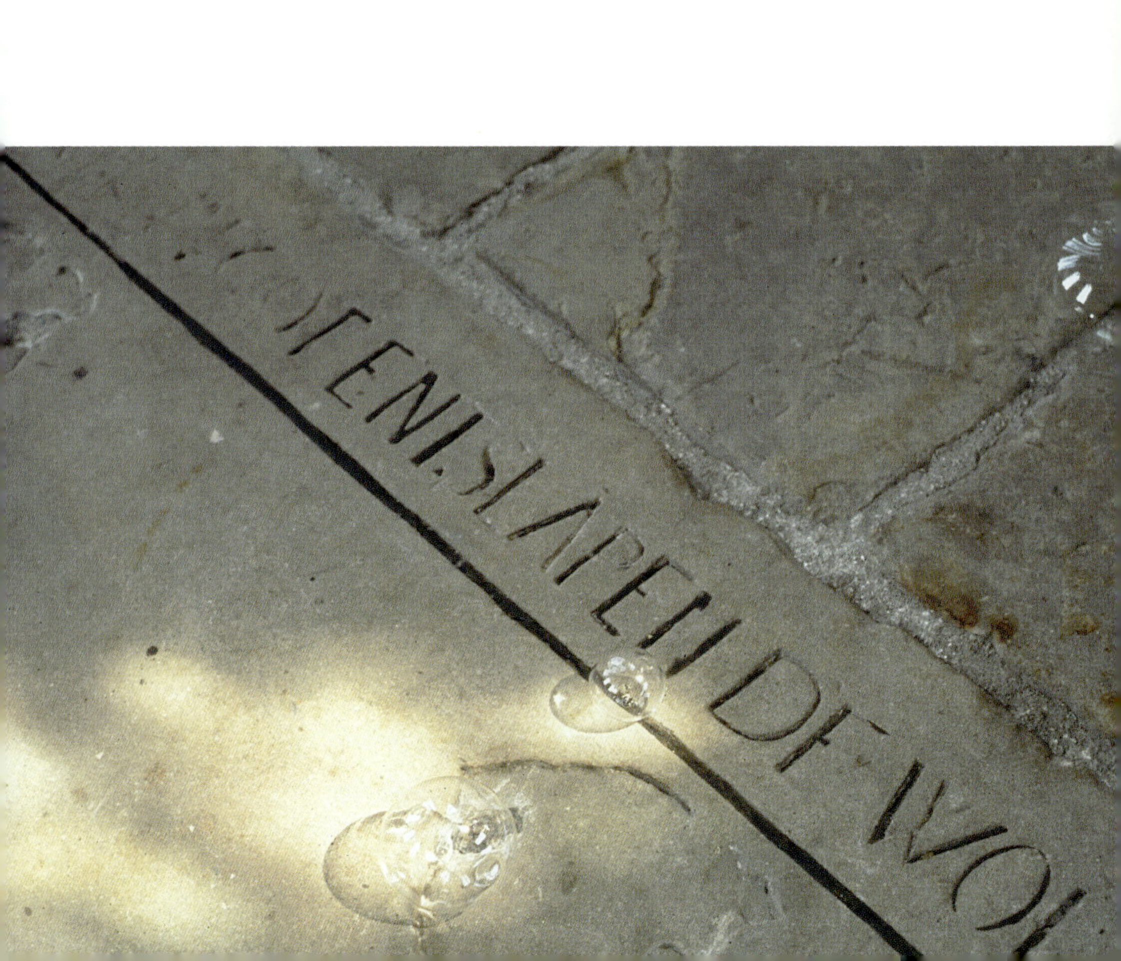
TENI·MAREN·DE·NO

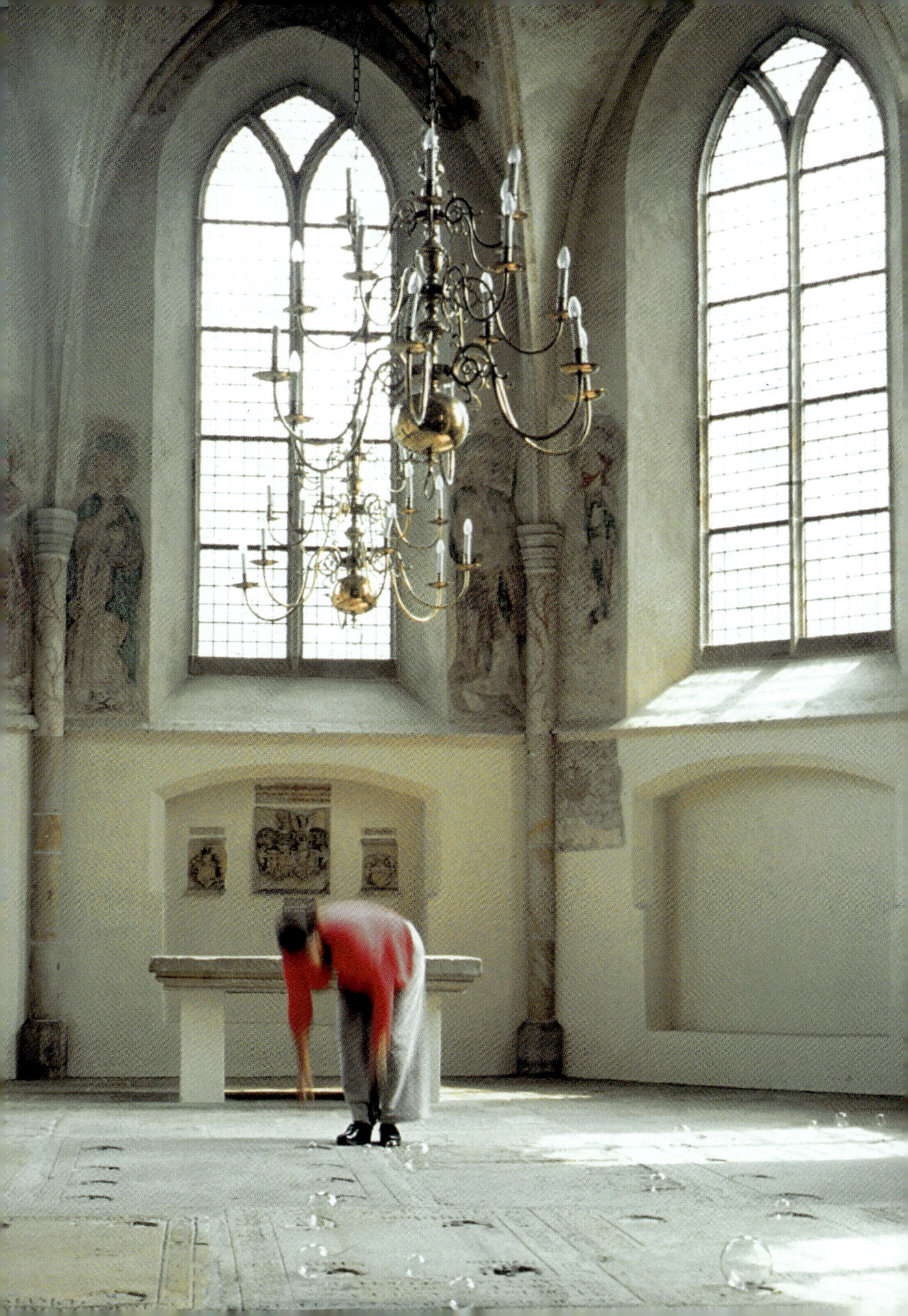

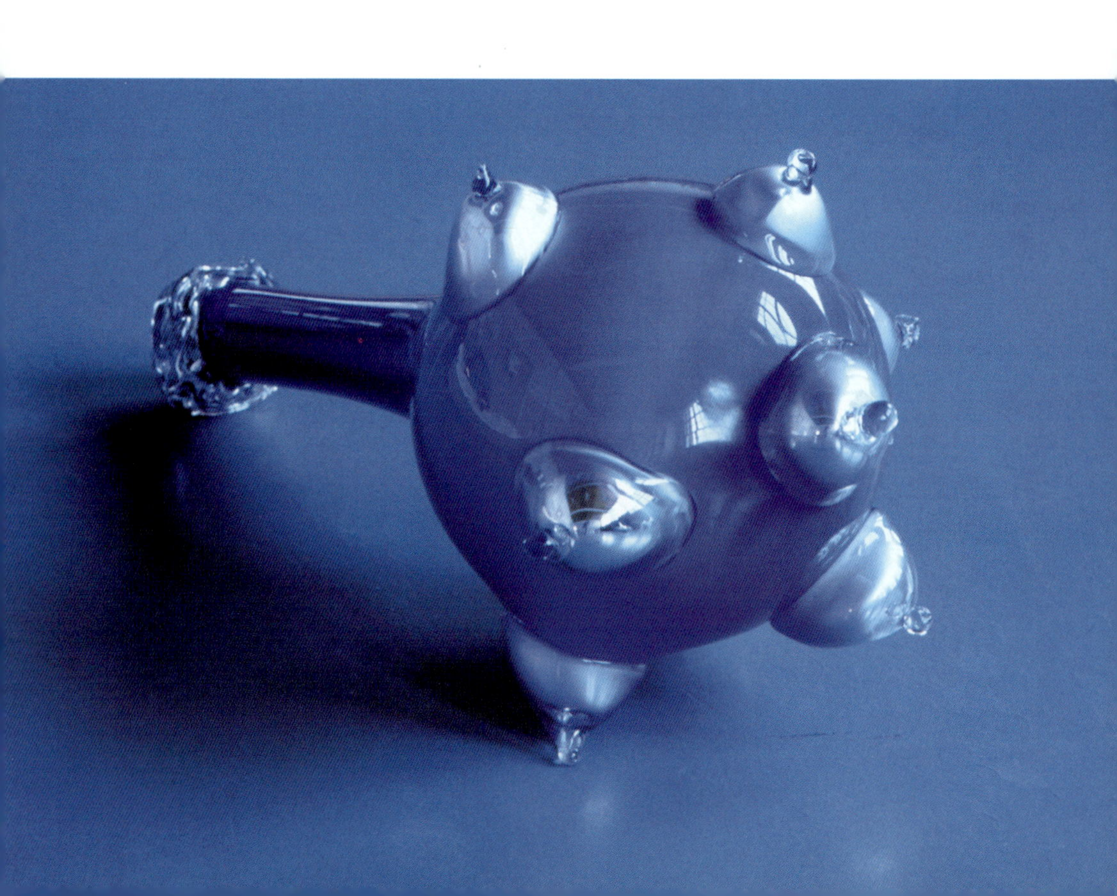

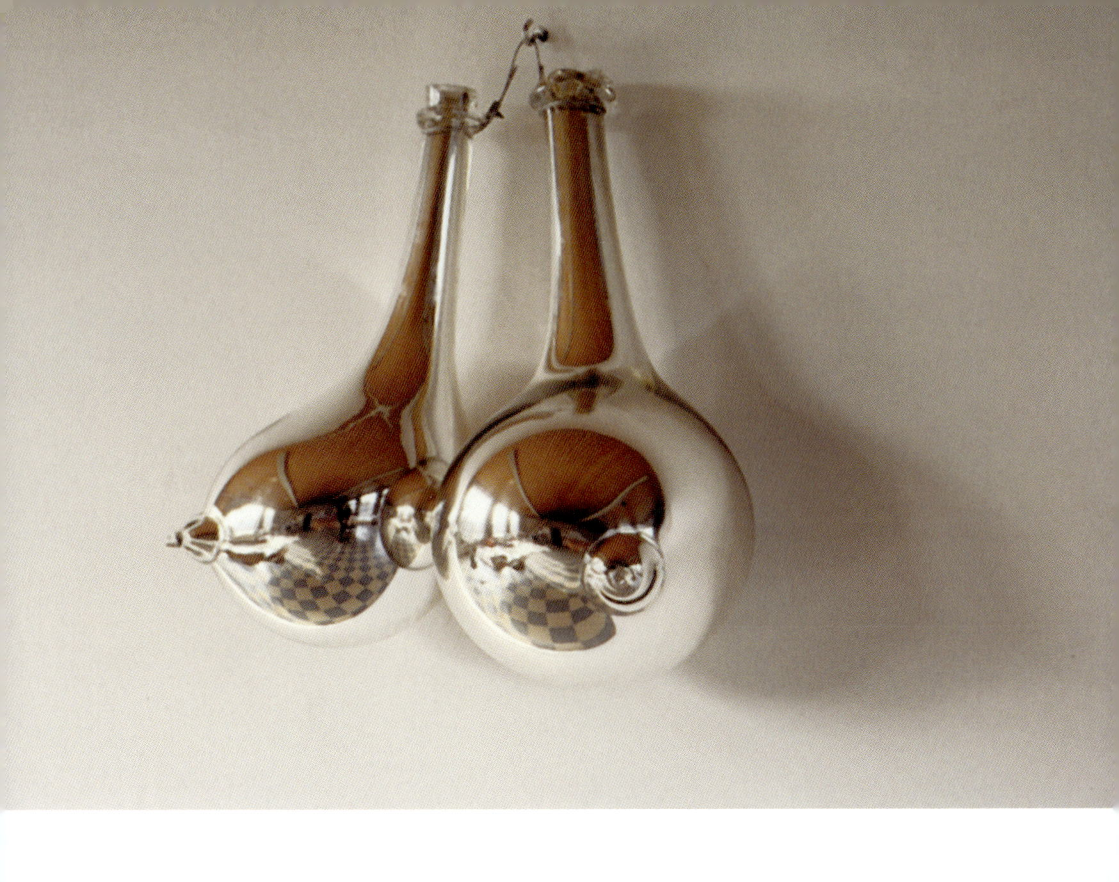

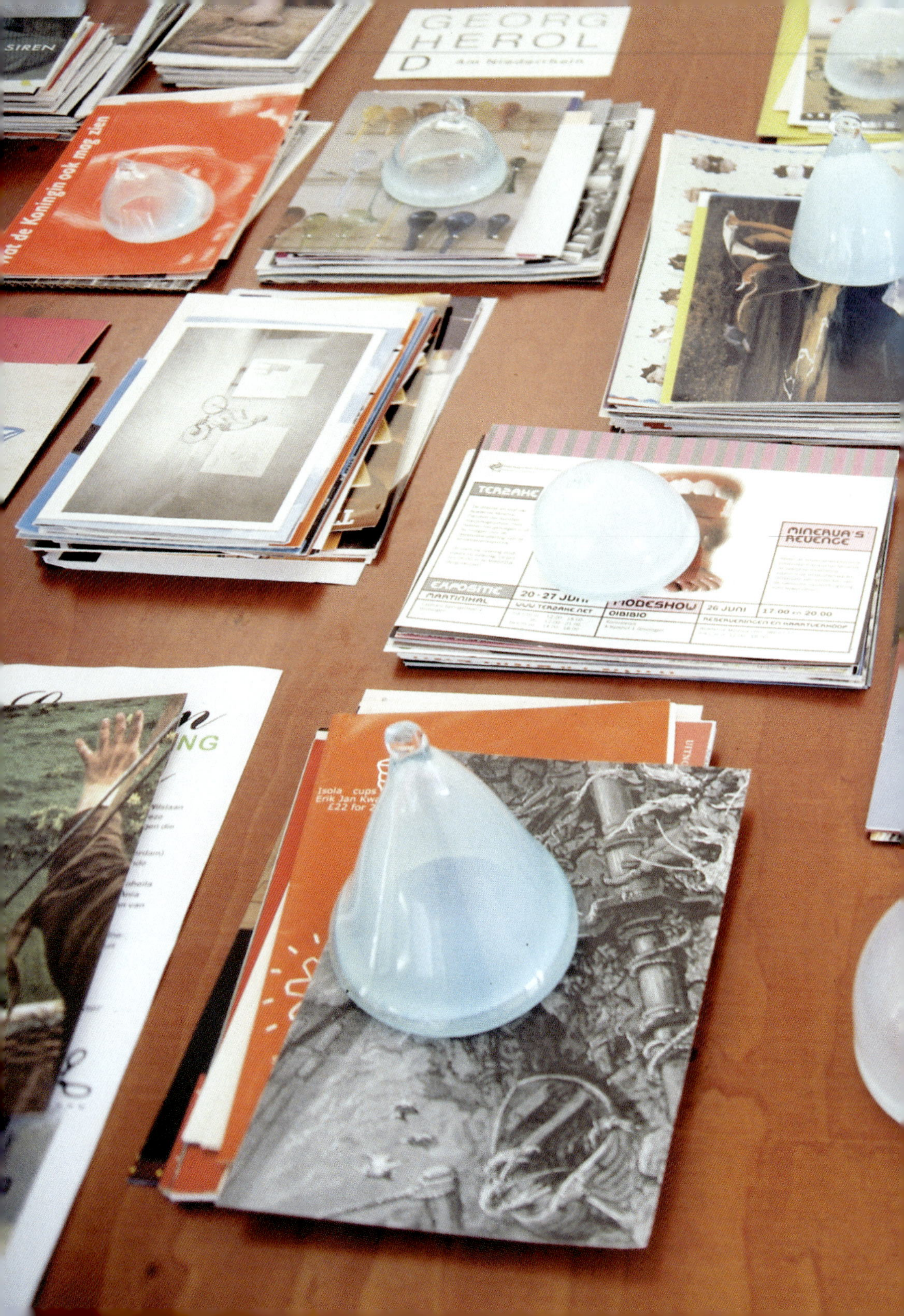

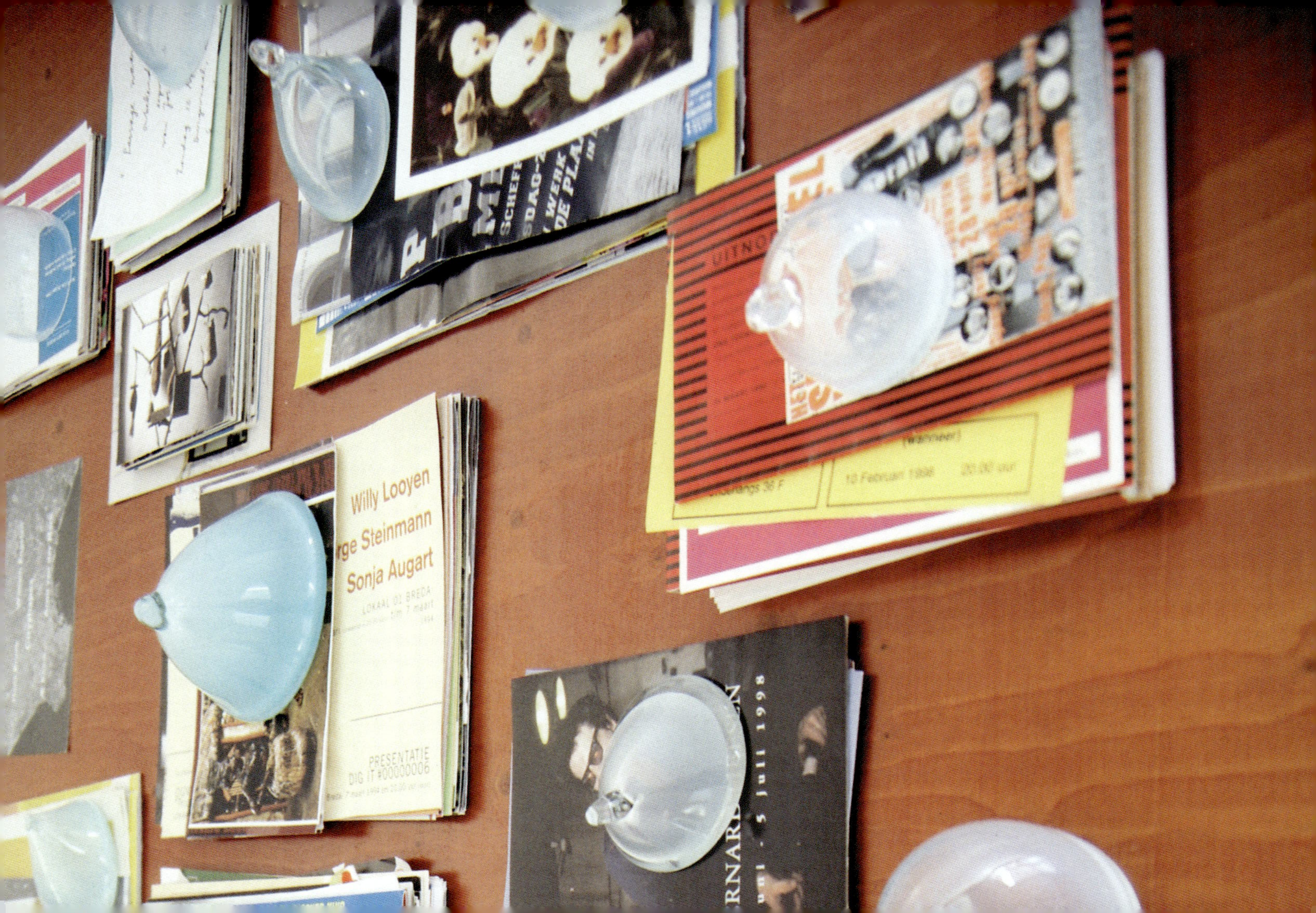
Willy Looyen
rge Steinmann
Sonja Augart
LOKAAL 01 BREDA
t/m 7 maart
1994
PRESENTATIE
DIG IT #00000006
uni · 5 juli 1998
10 Februari 1996   20.00 uur
oorlangs 36 F

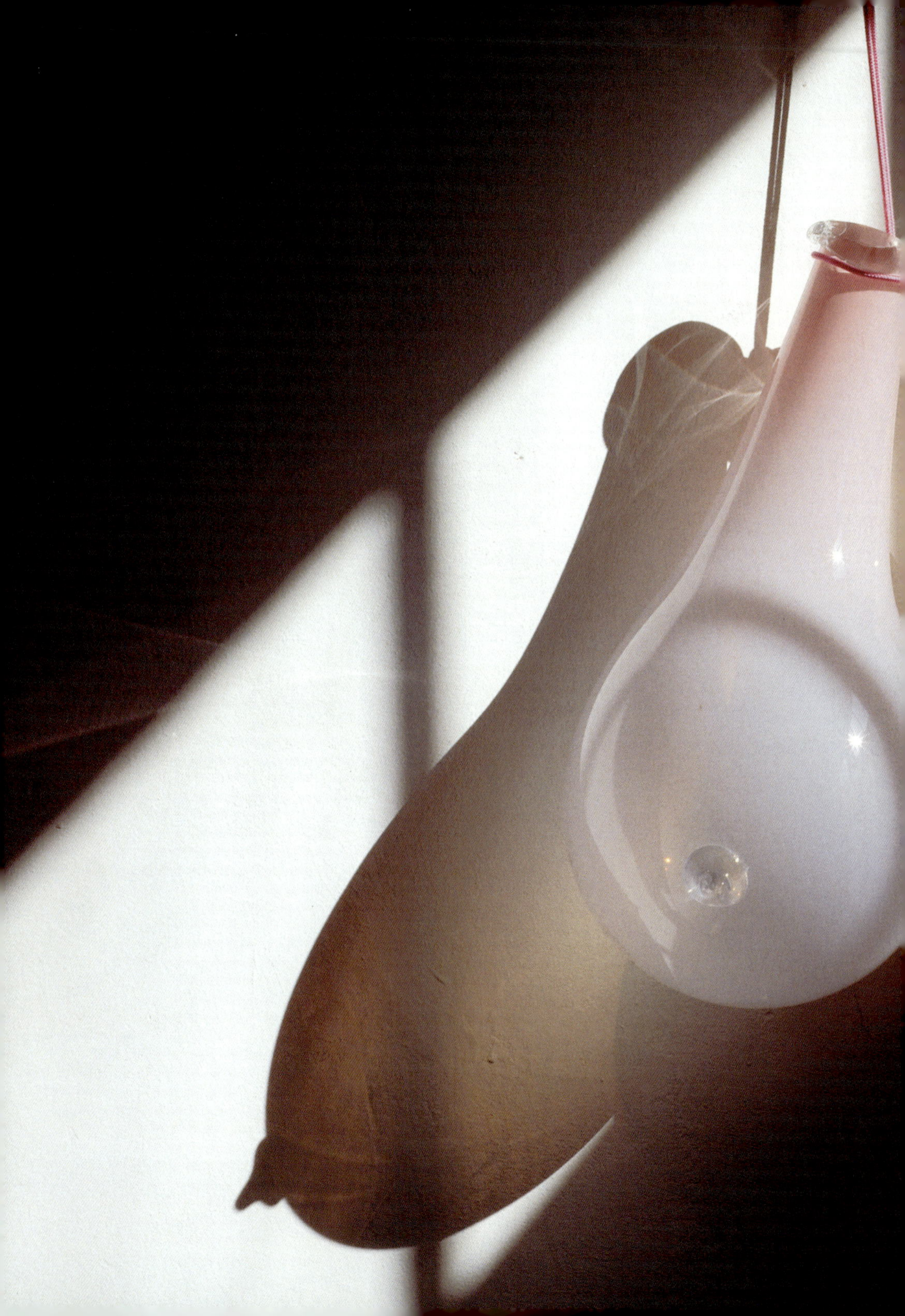

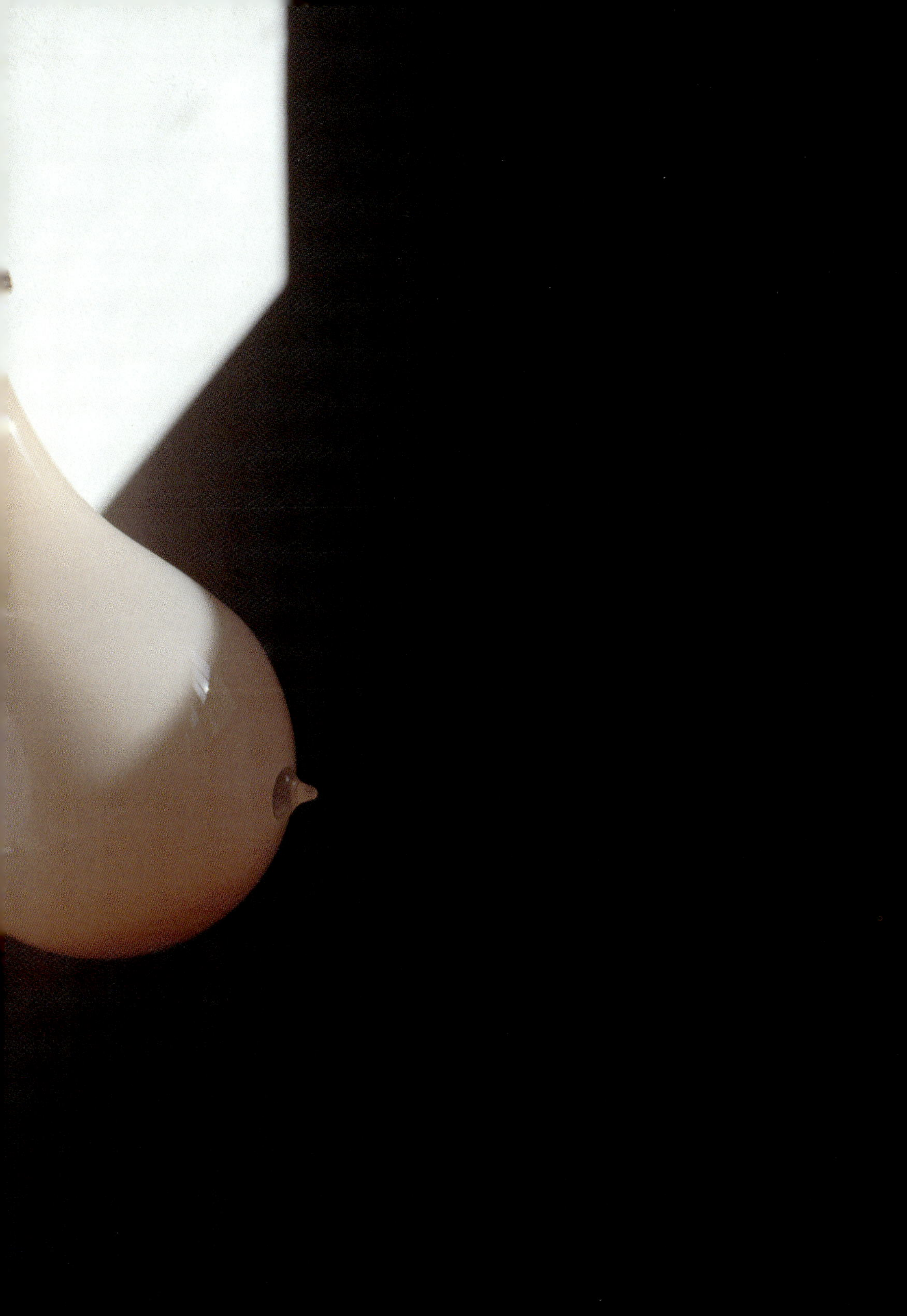

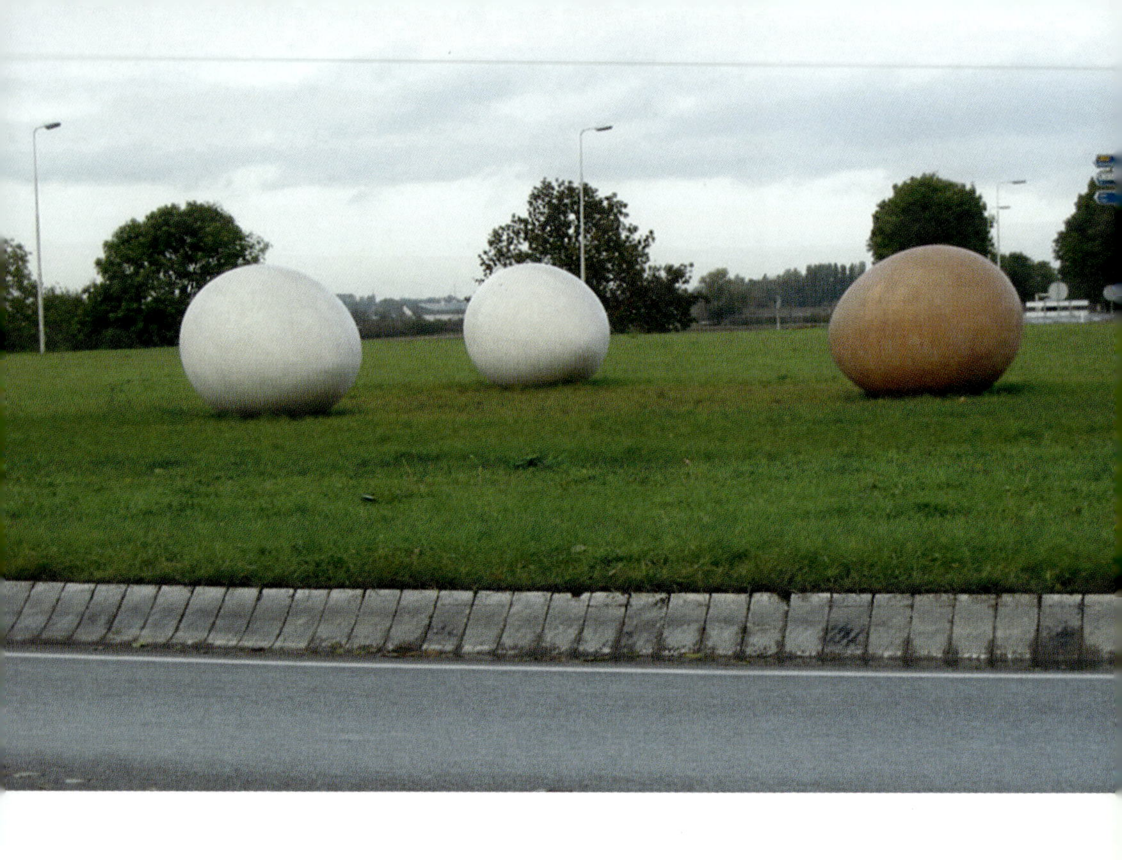

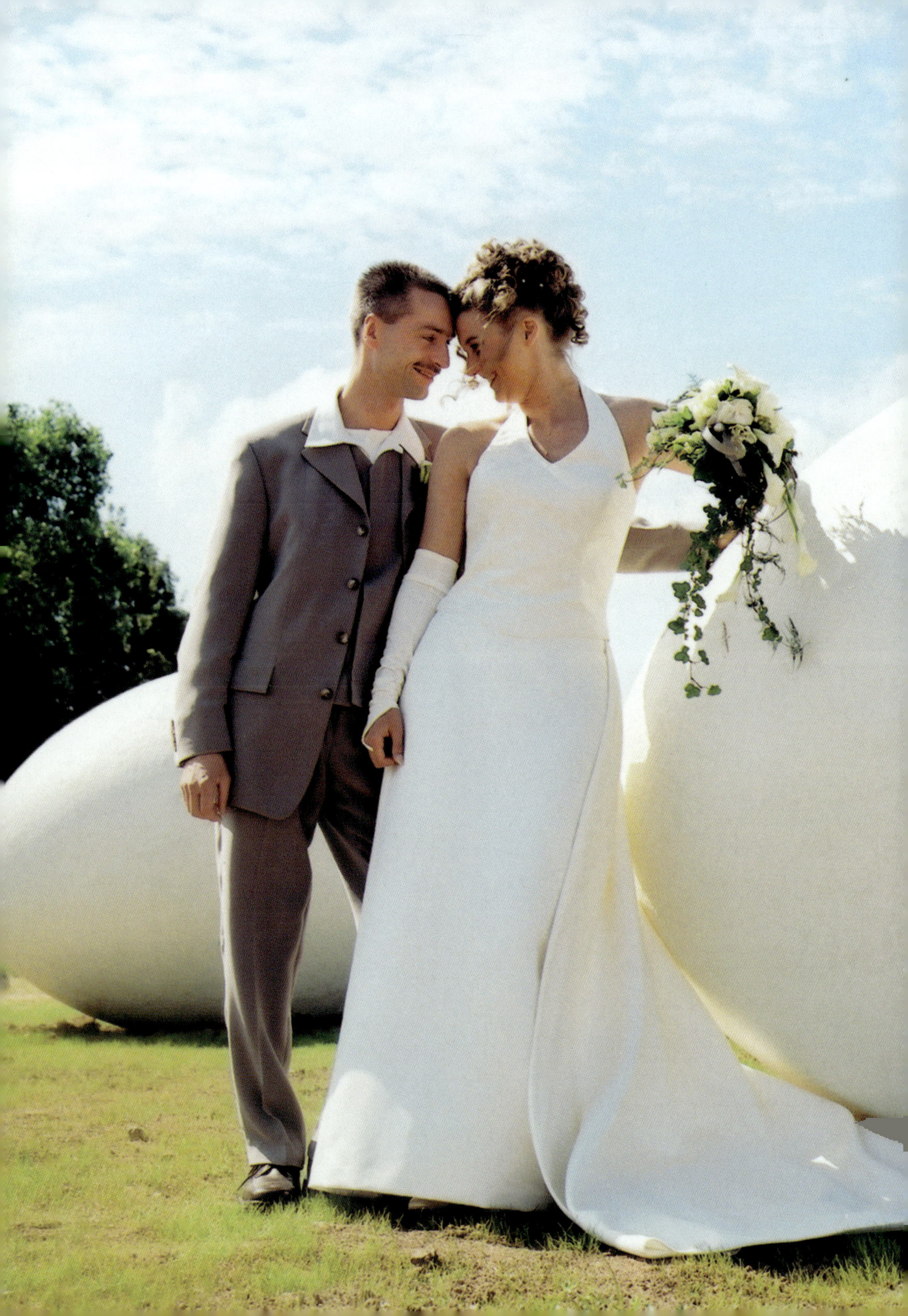

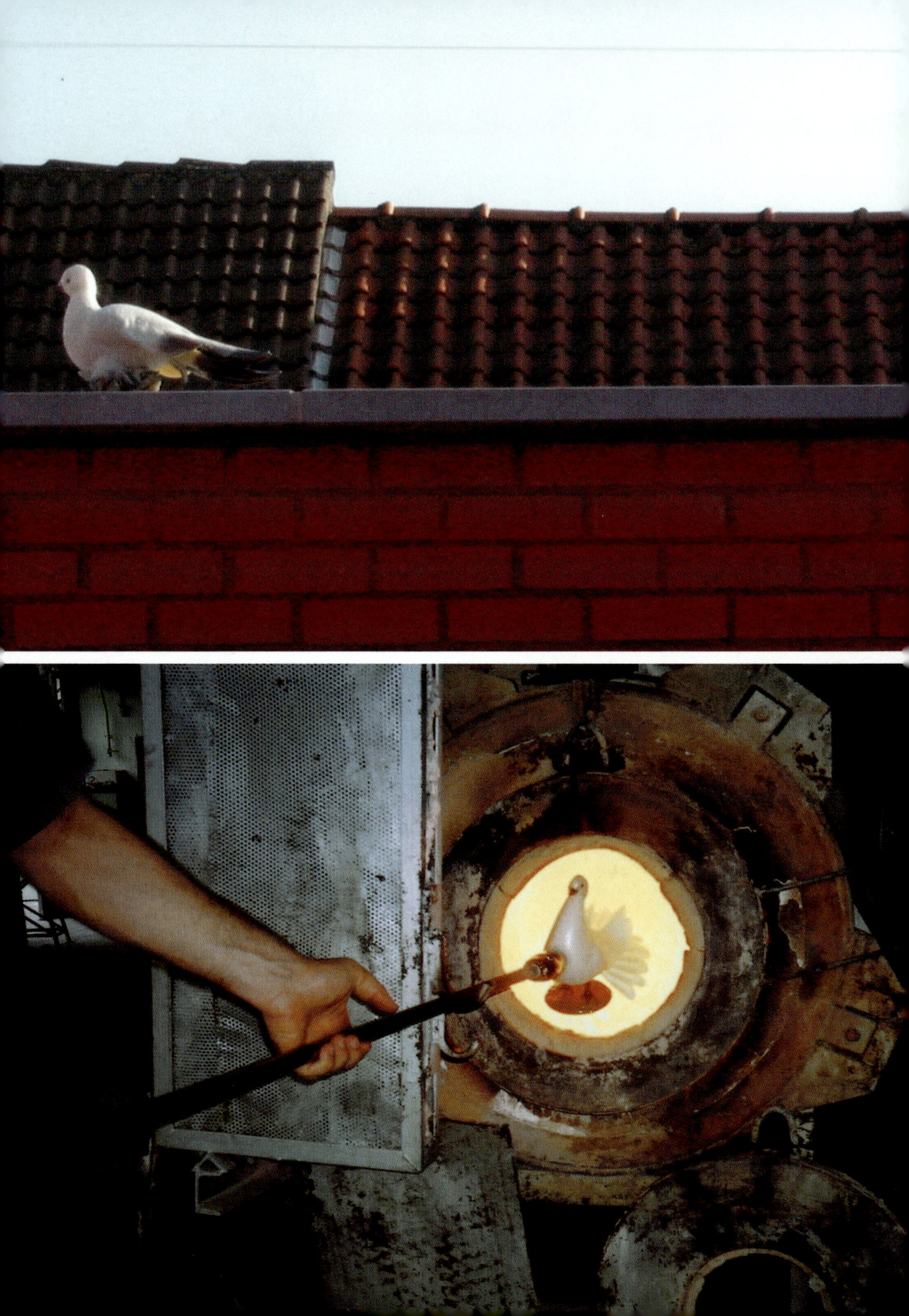

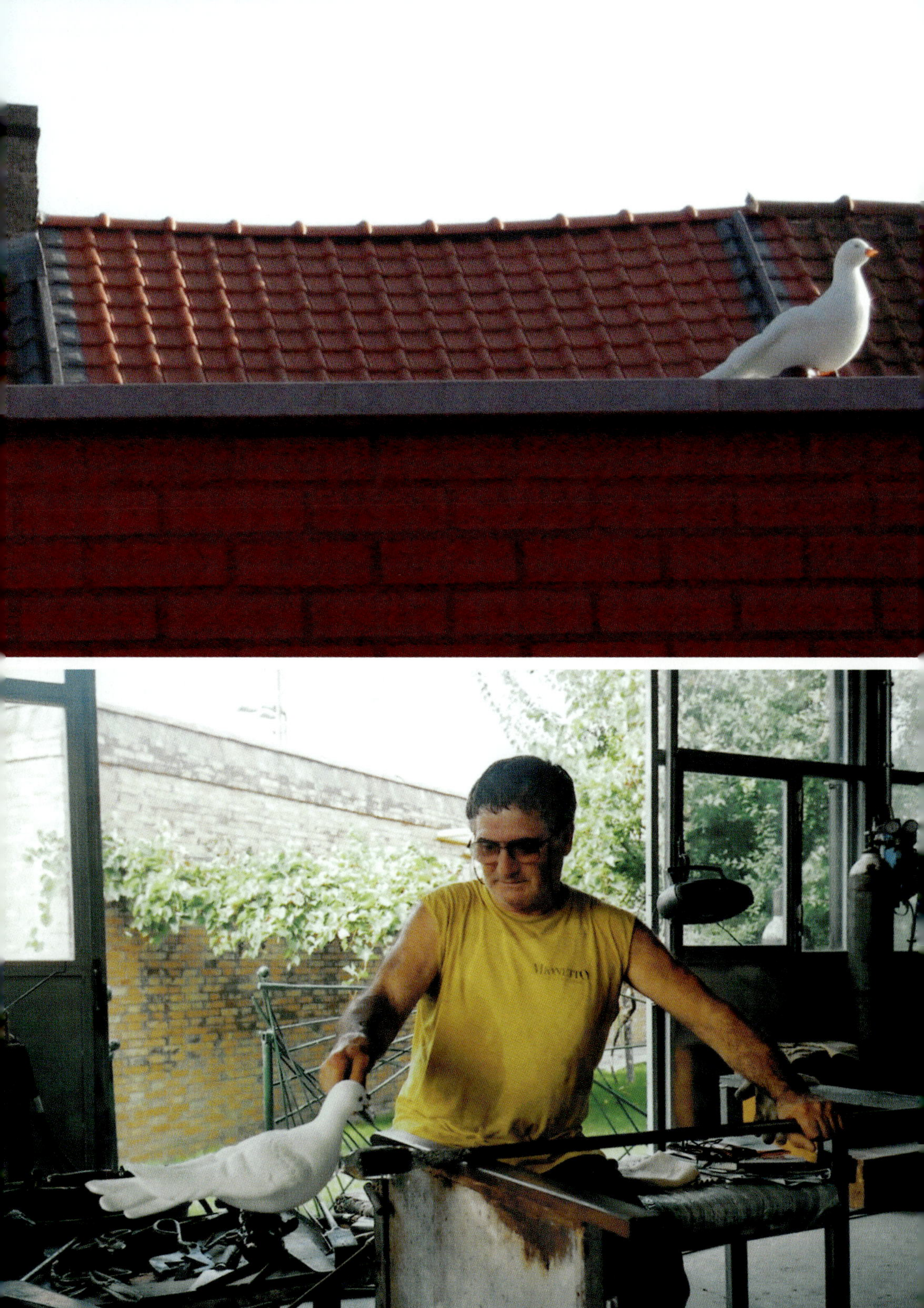

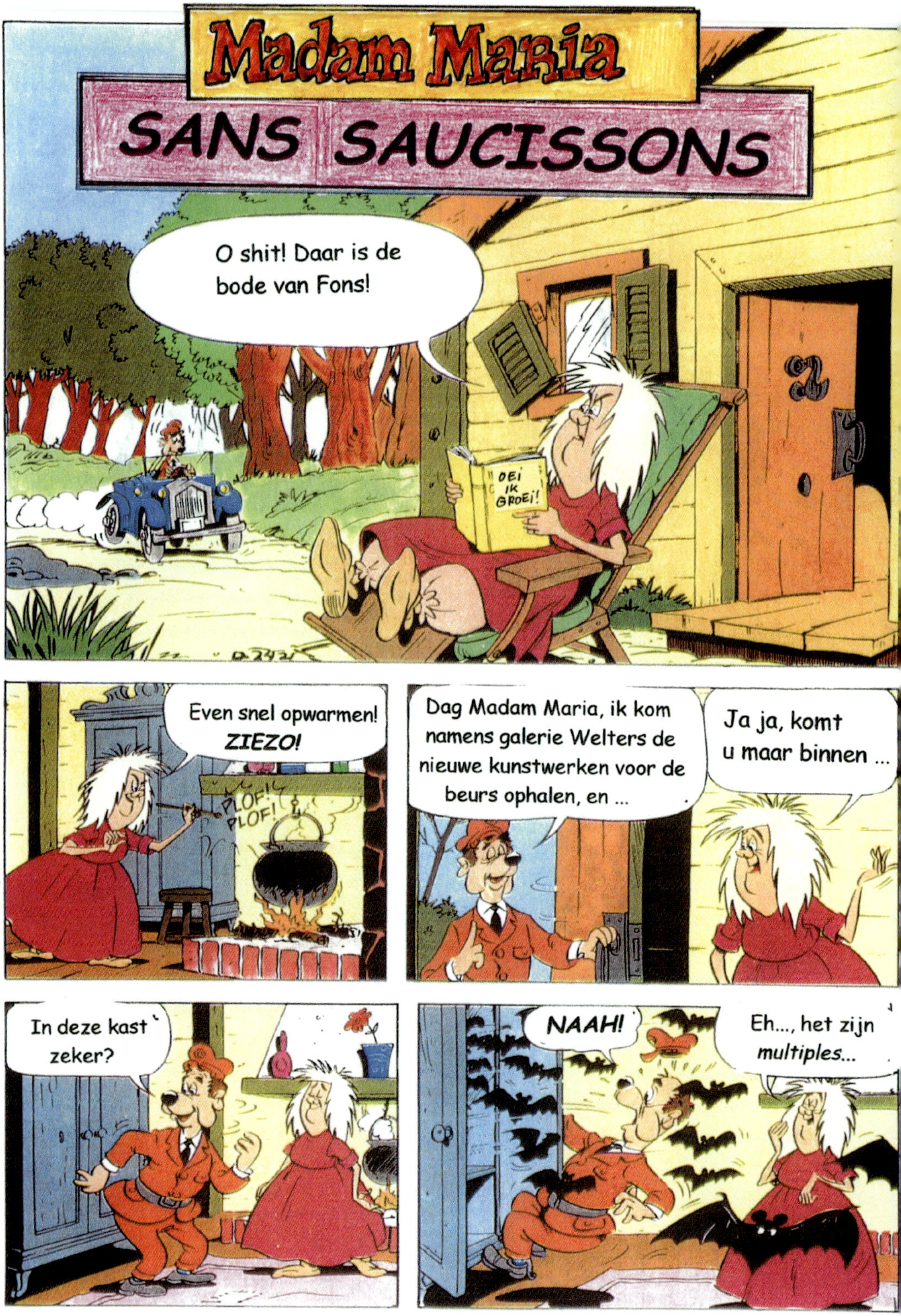

Madam Maria

SANS SAUCISSONS

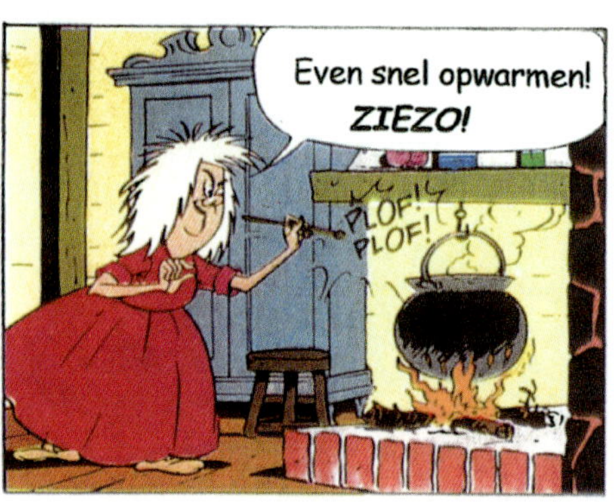

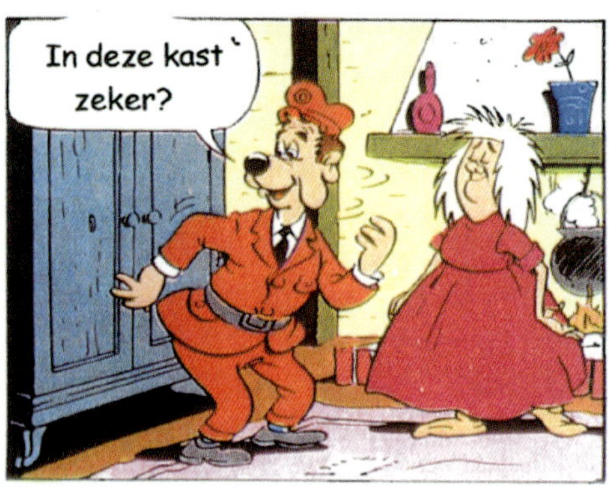

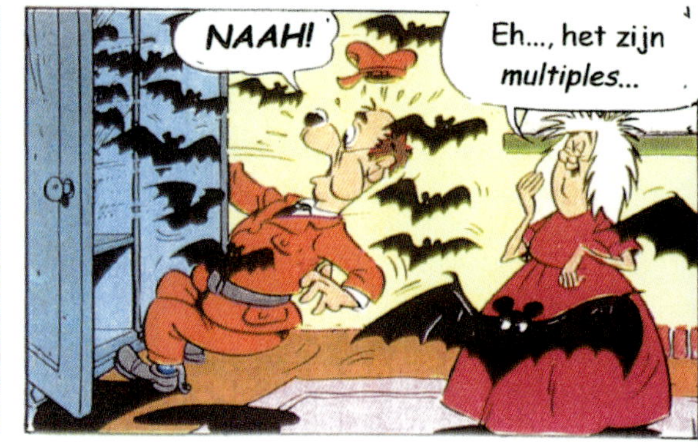

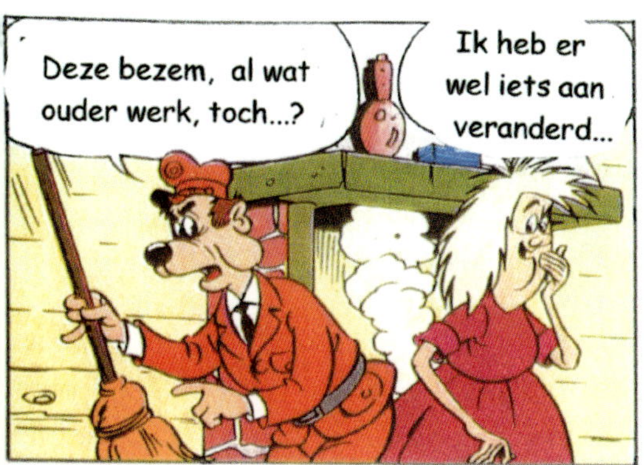

Deze bezem, al wat ouder werk, toch...?
Ik heb er wel iets aan veranderd...

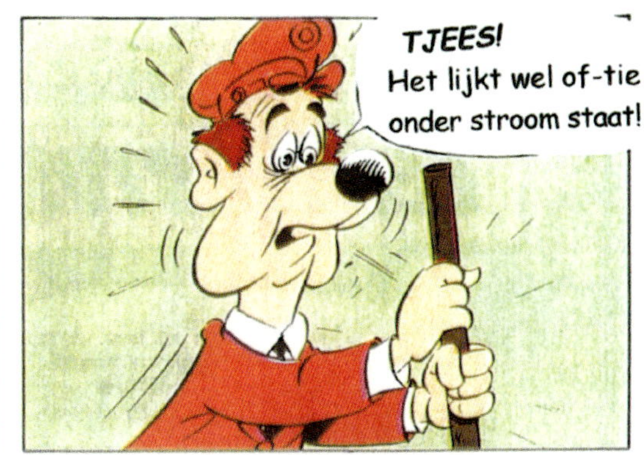

TJEES!
Het lijkt wel of-tie onder stroom staat!

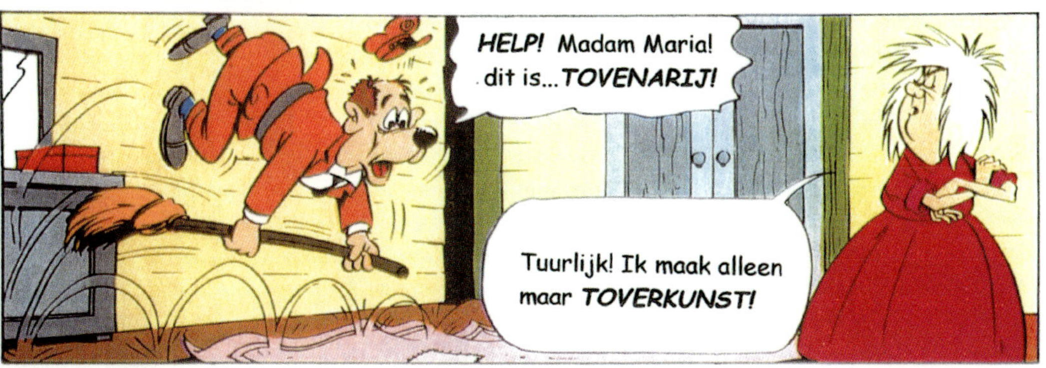

HELP! Madam Maria! dit is...TOVENARIJ!
Tuurlijk! Ik maak alleen maar TOVERKUNST!

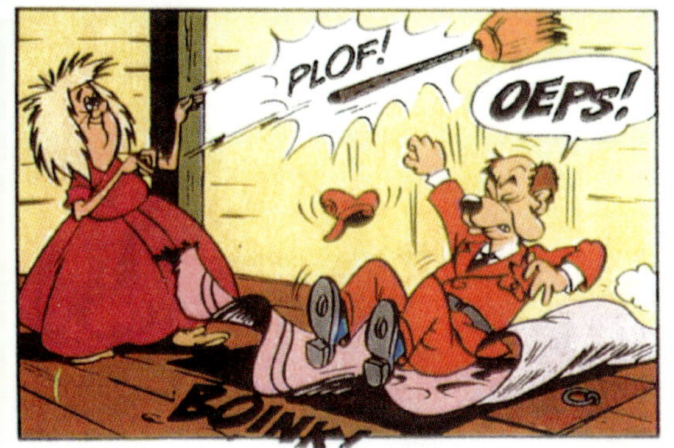

PLOF!
OEPS!
BOINK!

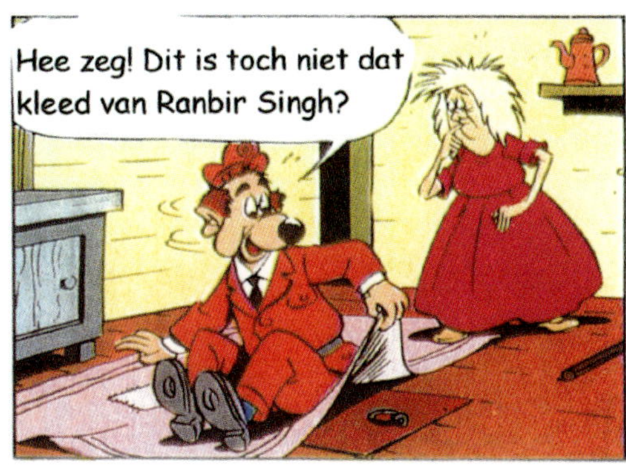

Hee zeg! Dit is toch niet dat kleed van Ranbir Singh?

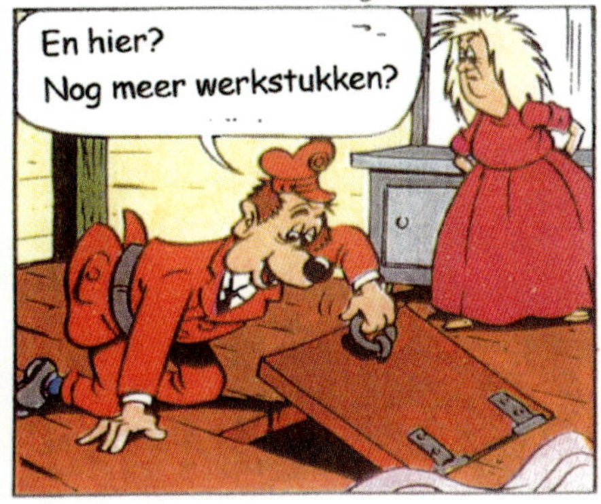

En hier?
Nog meer werkstukken?

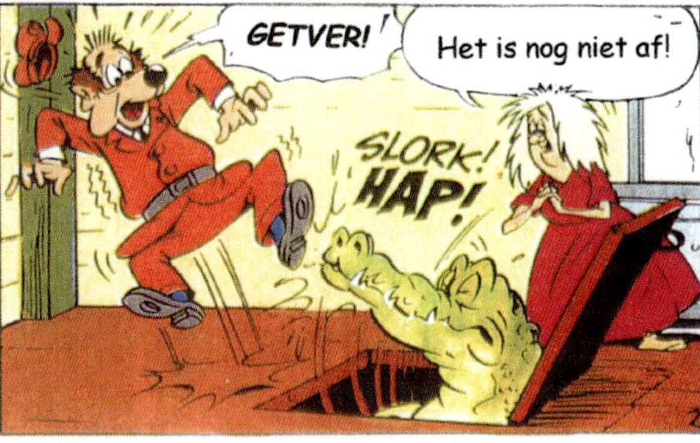

GETVER!
Het is nog niet af!
SLORK!
HAP!

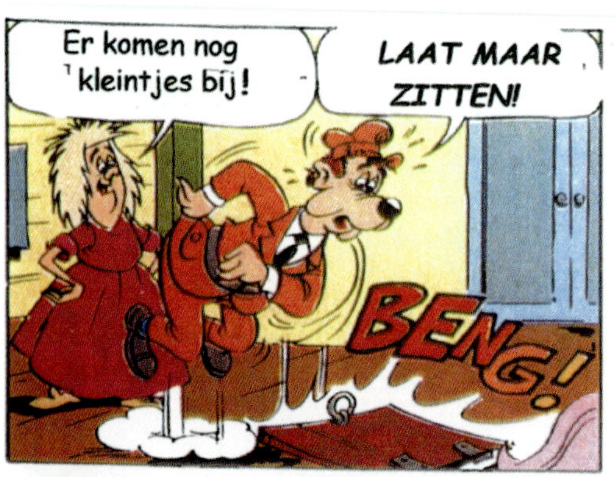

Er komen nog
kleintjes bij!
LAAT MAAR
ZITTEN!
BENG!

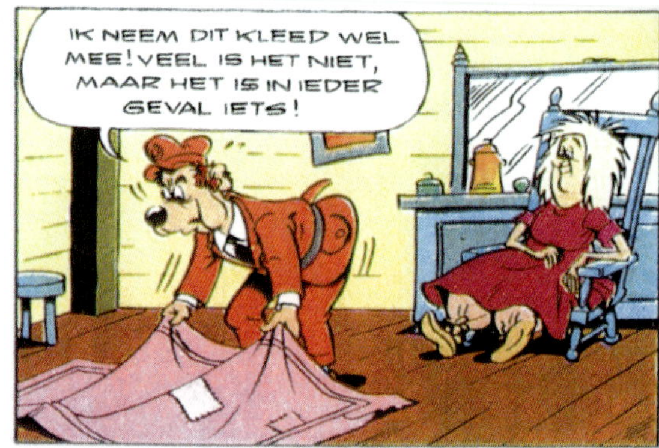

IK NEEM DIT KLEED WEL
MEE! VEEL IS HET NIET,
MAAR HET IS IN IEDER
GEVAL IETS!

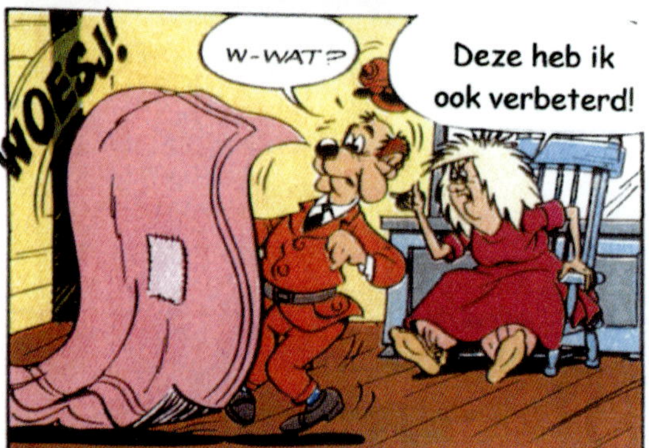

WOESJ!
W-WAT?
Deze heb ik
ook verbeterd!

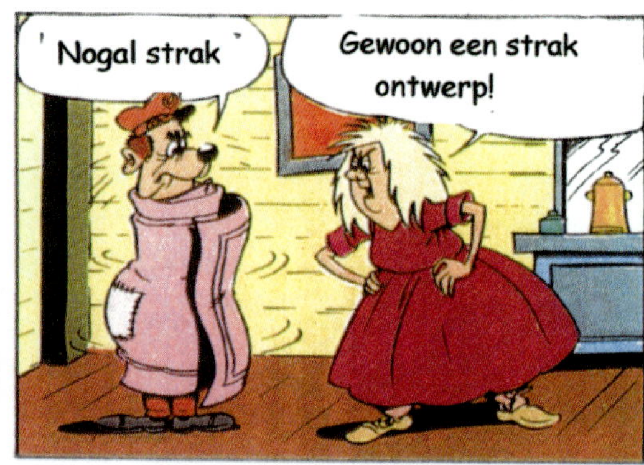

Nogal strak
Gewoon een strak
ontwerp!

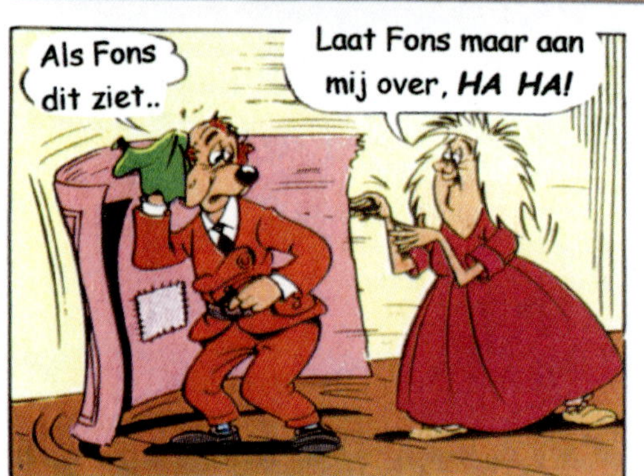

Als Fons
dit ziet..
Laat Fons maar aan
mij over, HA HA!

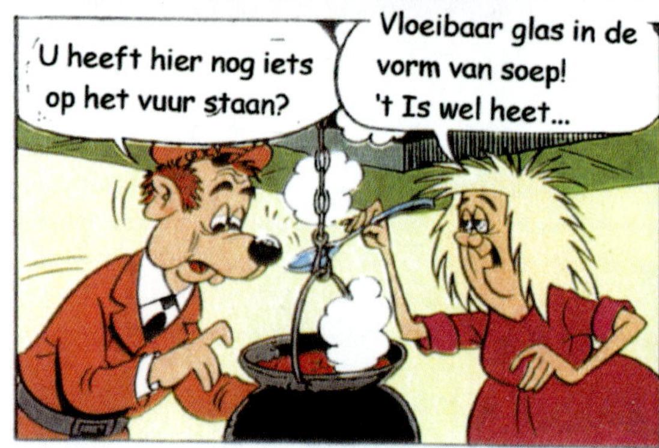

U heeft hier nog iets
op het vuur staan?
Vloeibaar glas in de
vorm van soep!
't Is wel heet...

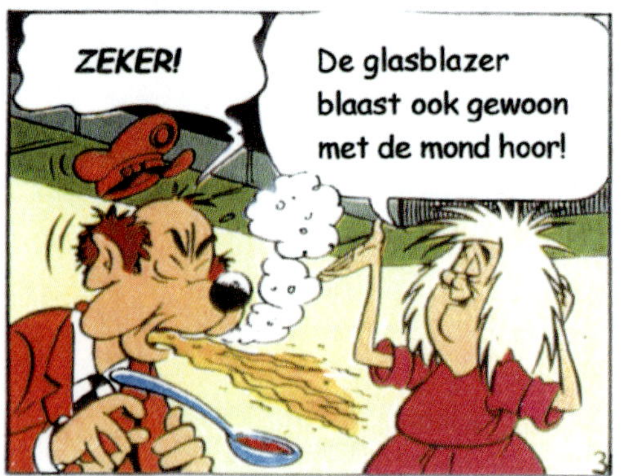

ZEKER!
De glasblazer
blaast ook gewoon
met de mond hoor!

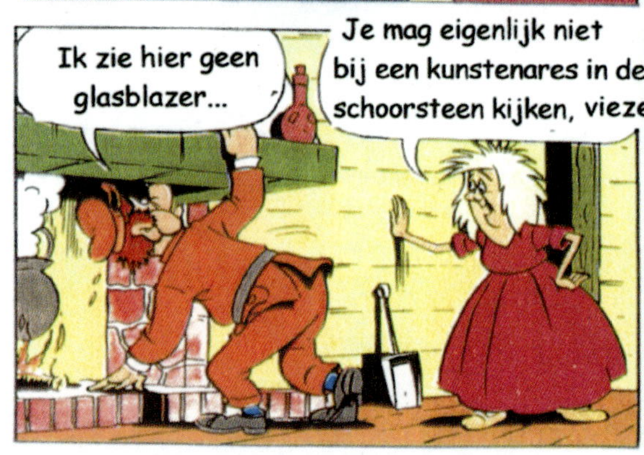

Ik zie hier geen
glasblazer...
Je mag eigenlijk niet
bij een kunstenares in de
schoorsteen kijken, vieze

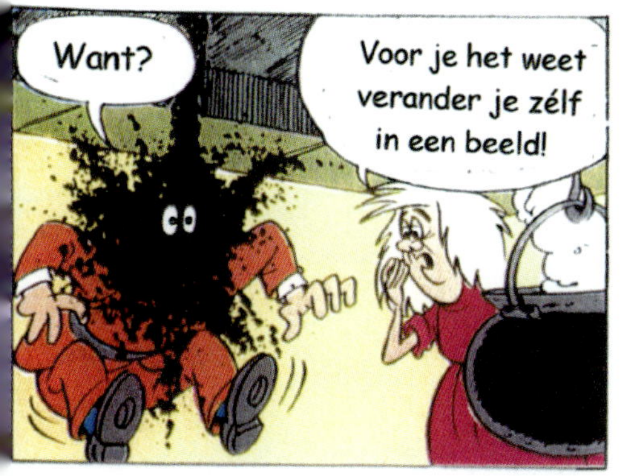

Want?
Voor je het weet verander je zélf in een beeld!

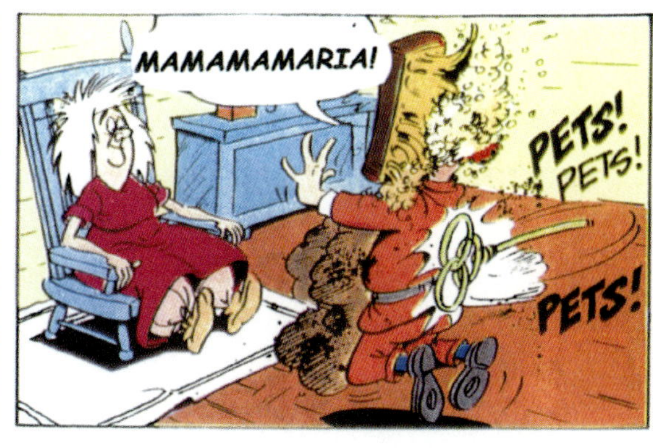

MAMAMAMARIA!
PETS!
PETS!
PETS!

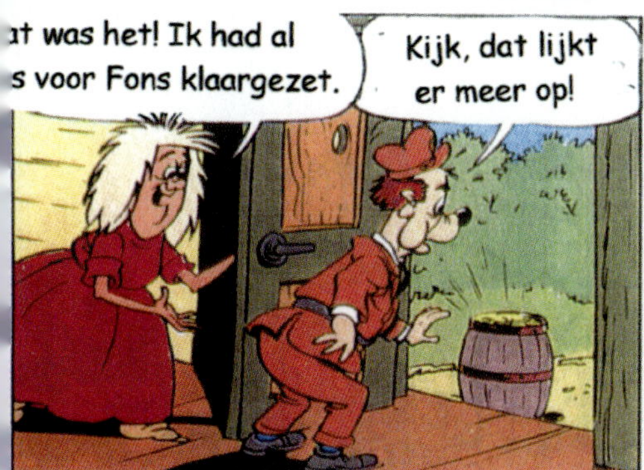

...at was het! Ik had al ...s voor Fons klaargezet.
Kijk, dat lijkt er meer op!

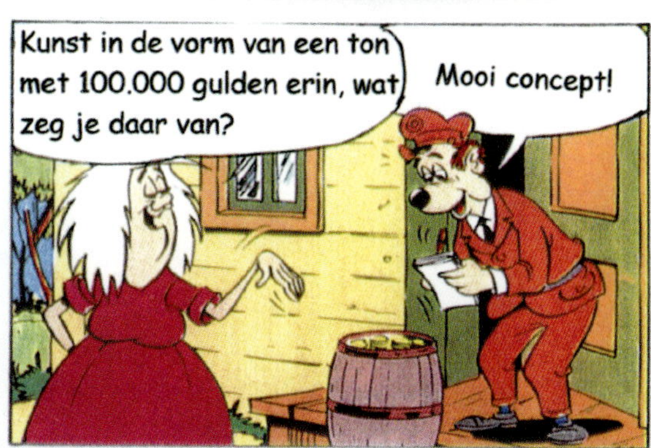

Kunst in de vorm van een ton met 100.000 gulden erin, wat zeg je daar van?
Mooi concept!

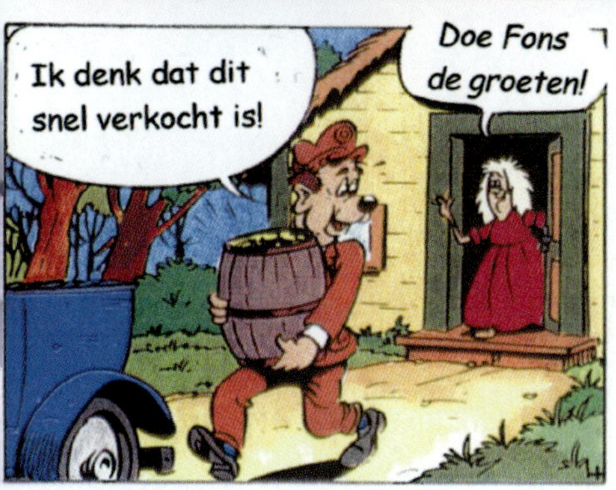

Ik denk dat dit snel verkocht is!
Doe Fons de groeten!

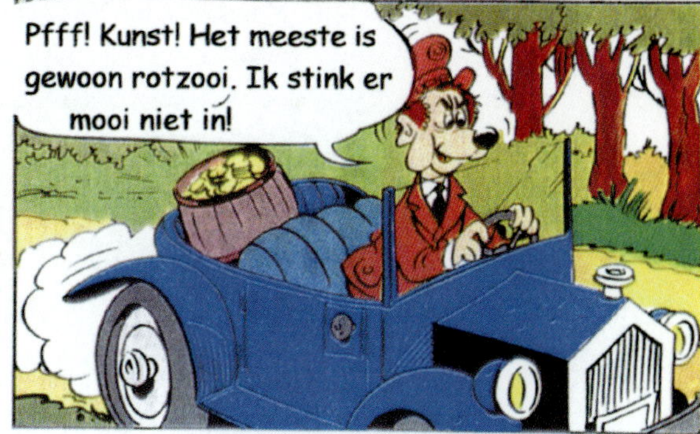

Pfff! Kunst! Het meeste is gewoon rotzooi. Ik stink er mooi niet in!

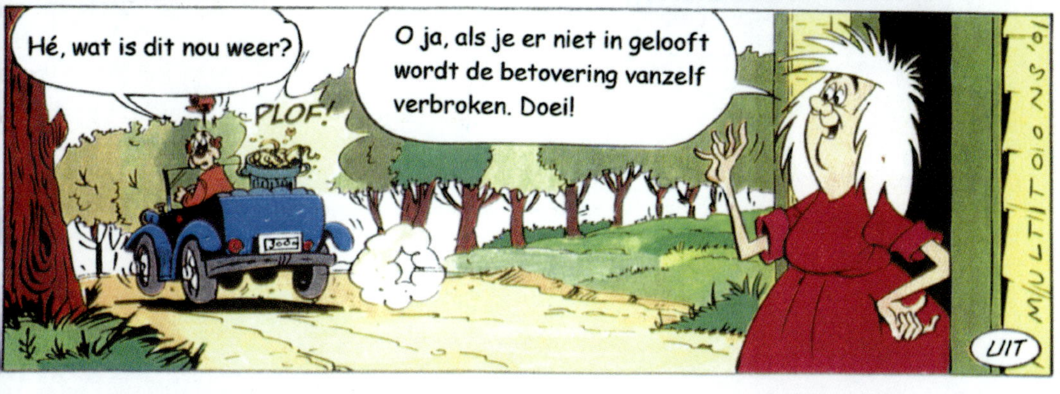

Hé, wat is dit nou weer?
PLOF!
O ja, als je er niet in gelooft wordt de betovering vanzelf verbroken. Doei!
MULTITOONS '01
UIT

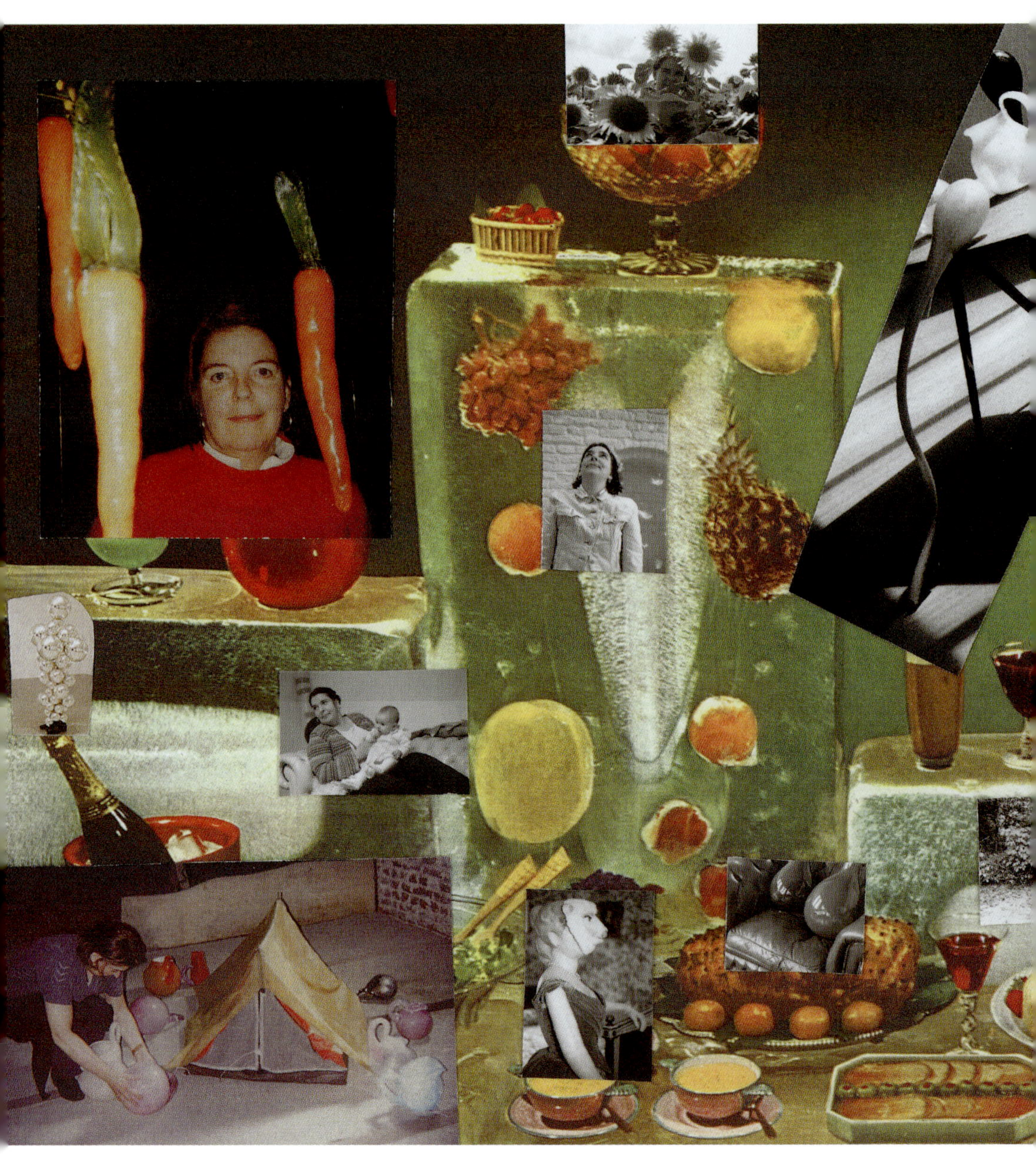

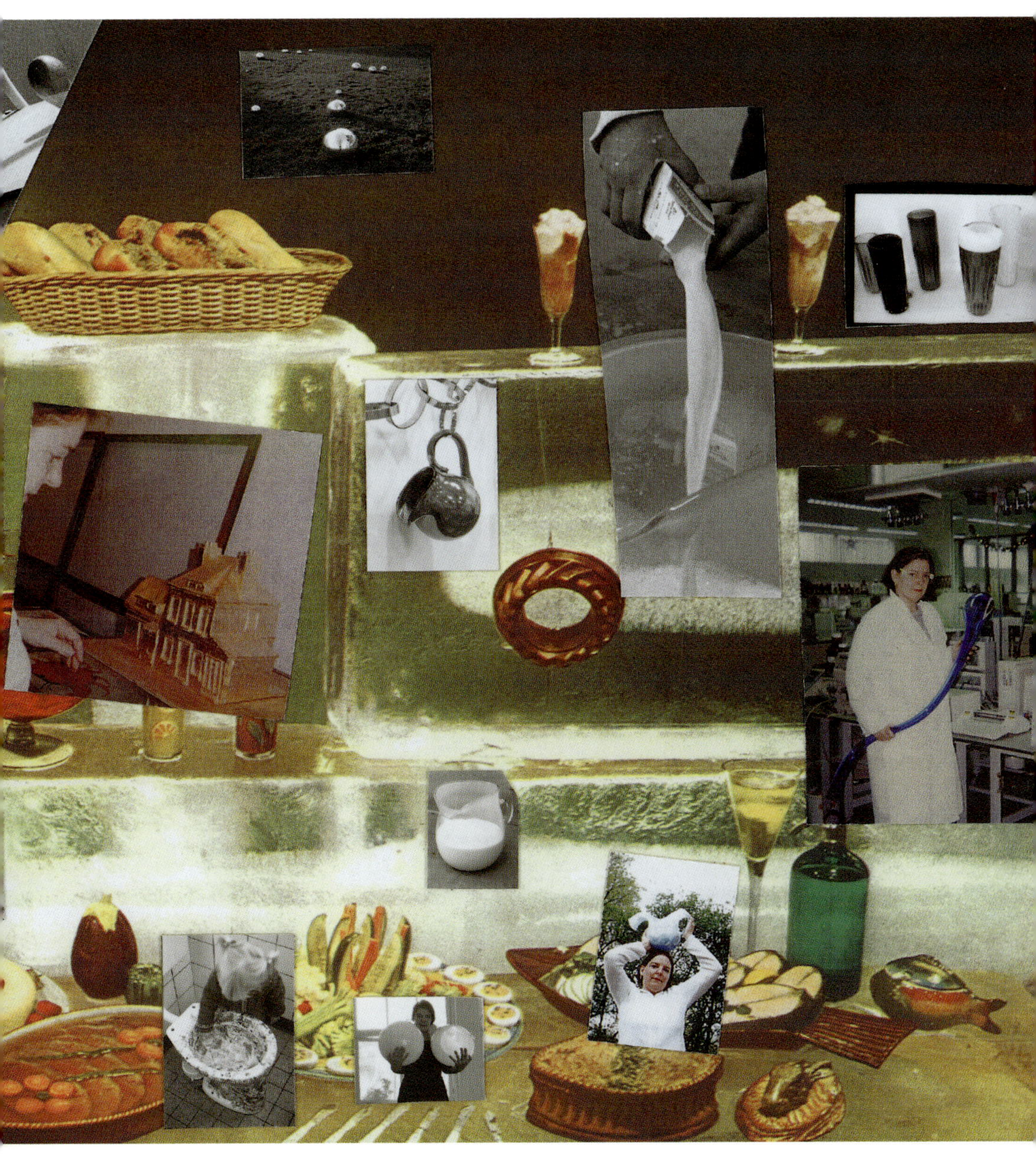

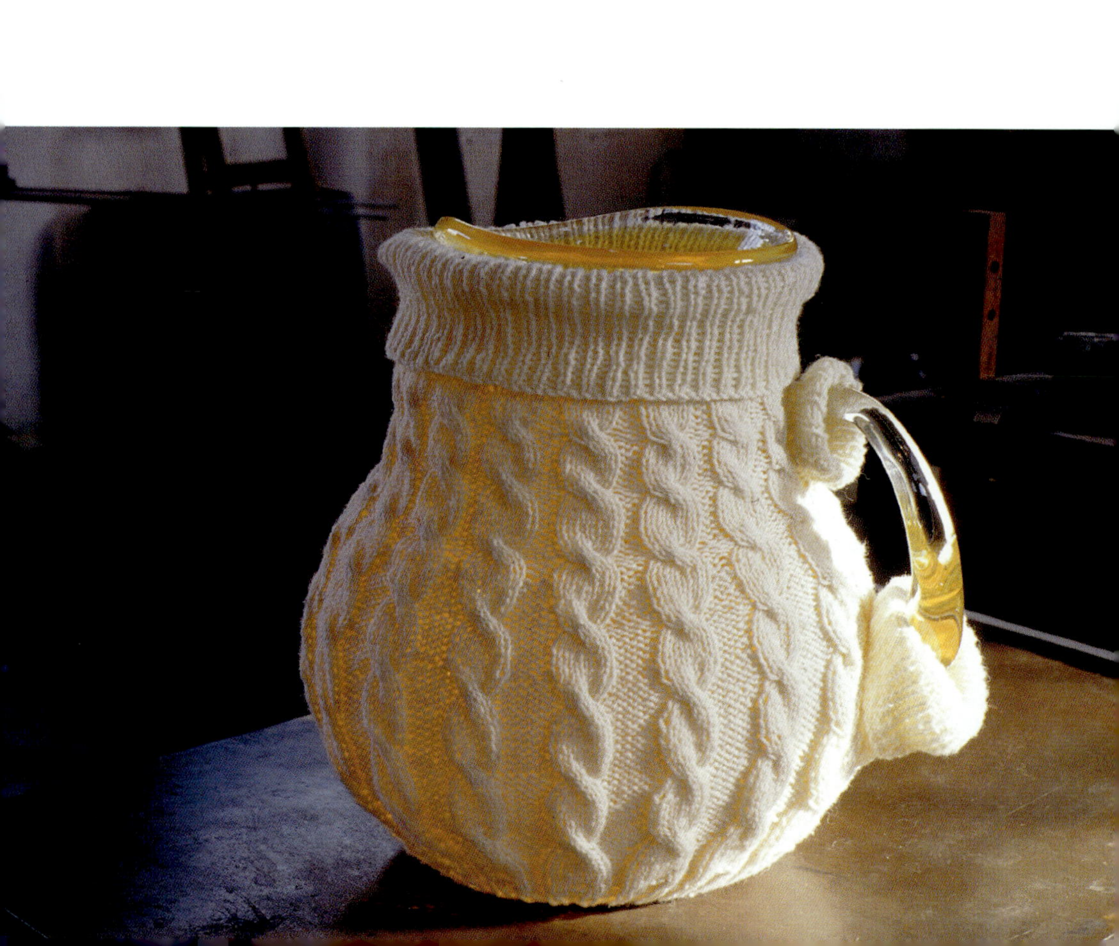

1985
Bernard Hinault
Nationaal Park
  De Groote Peel
Marien Schouten
Le Mont-Blanc (4807 m)
Marienaltar (Henrik
  Douvermann),
  St. Viktorsdom zu
  Xanten
Wubbo Ockels
Gari Kasparov
Gari Kasparov
David (Michelangelo)

1986
Evert van Benthem
Evert van Benthem
Comet Halley
Guido Riccio da
  Fogliano
  (Simone Martini)
Putto alato (Andrea del
  Verrocchio)

1987
Ivan Lendl
Bullfighter, Spain
Louis Coulon (length of
  beard 3.30 m, 1904)
Kevin Costner
Zonnebloemen
  (Vincent van Gogh)
256-Megabit Chip

1988

Tomas Gustafson
Bartolomeo Colleoni
    (Andrea del
    Verrocchio)
S. Giorgio (Vittore
    Carpaccio)
Ruud Gullit, Frank
    Rijkaard
Marco van Basten,
    Ruud Gullit
Ruud Gullit
Rinus Michels
Ruud Gullit, Berry
    van Aerle
Julio Iglesias
Florence Griffith Joyner
Florence Griffith Joyner
Florence Griffith Joyner
Gustet (champion
    mushroom seeker)

1989

Igor Zjelezovski
Tadeusz Mazowiecki
The Marriage of
    Giovanni Arnolfini
    (Jan van Eyck)

1990

Charlton Athletic
Michail Gorbatsjov
Louis XIV

1991

Jim Courier
Sergej Boebka
John Eliot Gardiner
Monica Seles
Andre Agassi
S. Giorgio (Andrea
    Mantegna)
Jörg Fischer's Wife at
    the Age of 34 (Hans
    Holbein the Elder)
Portrait of Henry VIII
    (Hans Holbein
    the Younger)
Solar eclipse
Miguel Indurain
Boris Jeltsin
Kevin Costner
Mike Powell
Mike Powell
Moses Tanui, Richard
    Chelimo, Thomas
    Osano
Monica Seles
Isenheimer Altar
    (Matthias Grünewald)
Young Knight in a
    Landscape (Vittore
    Carpaccio)

1992

Richard Krajicek
Frank Rijkaard
Andre Agassi
Axel Schulz
Regilio Tuur
Allard Budding

1993

Bobby Moore
Rowan Atkinson
Emma Thompson
Jayne Torville,
    Christopher Dean
Paul Cascoine, David
    Burrows
Merlene Ottey
Kuifje the Reporter
Jeanne d'Arc
Shimon Peres
Ronald Koeman

1994

Gunda Niemann, Rintje
    Ritsma
Minister Ien Dales
3-Kilo Potato
Jack Charlton
Jack Charlton
Regilio Tuur
Henrik Larsson

1995
Matthew Barney

1996
Adri van der Poel
Jeroen Blijlevens
Richard Krajicek
Michael Johnson
Henk-Jan Held, Ron
   Zwerver
Michael Jackson
Frits van Oostrom
Nick Cave
Bill Clinton
Edwin van der Sar
Marcello Mastroianni

1997
Henk Angenent
Rudi Fuchs, Markus
   Lüpertz
Ronaldo
Tara Lipinski
Comet Hale-Bopp
Dick Advocaat
Richard Virenque
Diana, Princess of Wales
British Trust
   SuperSonic Car
Whale Shark
A 7000-year-old
   skeleton

1998
Raymond van Barneveld
Gianni Romme
Kofi Annan
Clarence Seedorf
Gerhard Schröder

1999
Raymond van Barneveld
Manchester United
   players
Jupiter and Venus
Venus Williams
Lance Armstrong
Andre Agassi
Lauryn Hill

2000
Michael Schumacher
Militaries,
   St. Petersburg
The French Football
   Team
Venus Williams
Inge de Bruijn
Pieter van den
   Hoogenband
Mark Huizinga
Anky van Grunsven

2001
Kofi Annan

2002
The Brazilian Football
   Team

2003
Raymond van Barneveld
Shirin Ebadi
Shirin Ebadi
Mother Teresa
Bettine Vriesekoop
The Sun

2004
Renate Groenewold
Jonnie Boer
Haitian Woman
P. J. Harvey
Edwin van der Sar
Anky van Grunsven
Maria Sjarapova

2005
Champion Pigeon

Oh shit! It's the man from Fons!
[title of book: *Oh no, I grow!*]

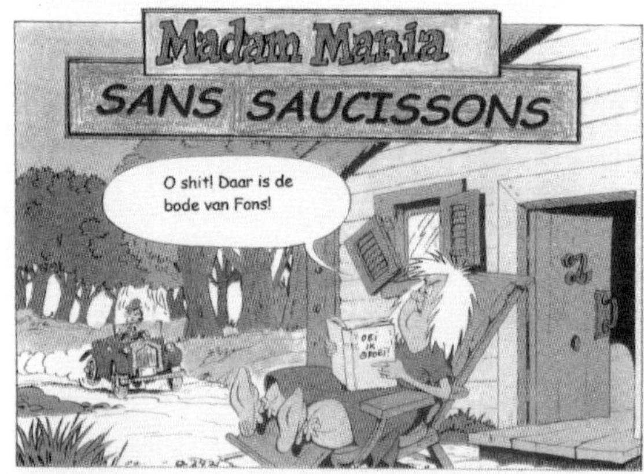

I'll just put it
on to boil!
There we are.

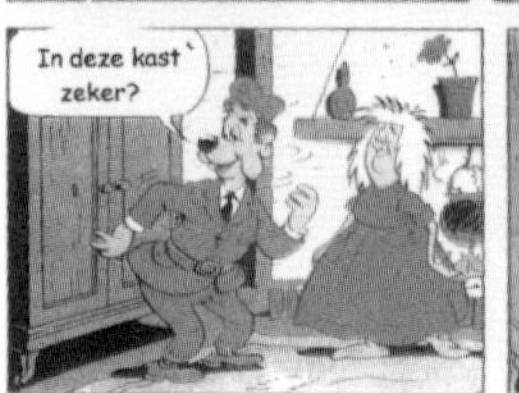

Hello, Madam Maria,
I've come on behalf
of Gallery Welters to
collect the new art-
works for the fair,
and...

Yes, yes, come on in...

I suppose they're
in this cupboard?

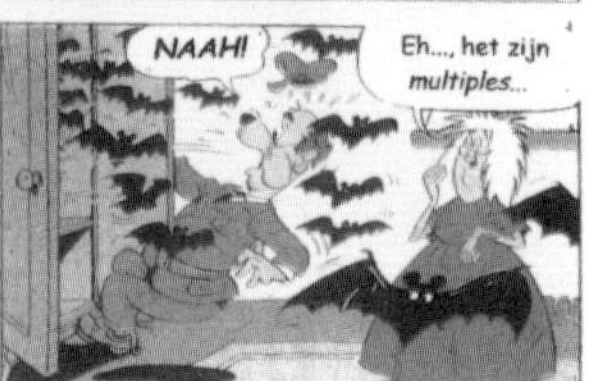

AAARGHH!   Er..., they're multiples...

This broom, older work, isn't it?

I've changed it a bit

Crikey! It seems to be electrified!

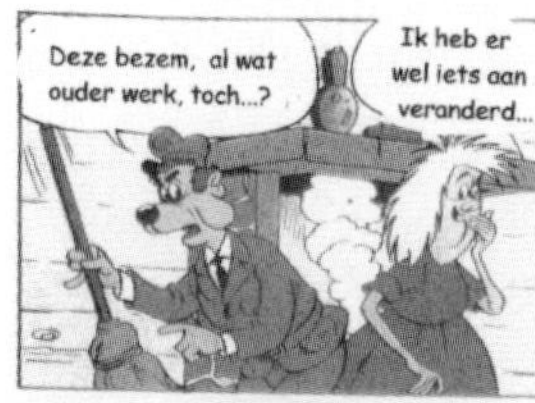

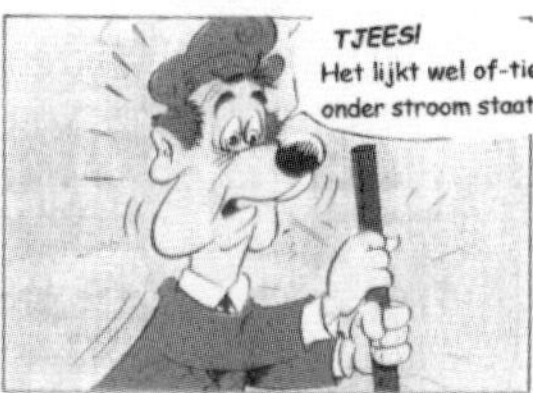

HELP! Madam Maria, this is MAGIC!

Of course! I only practise the MAGIC ART!

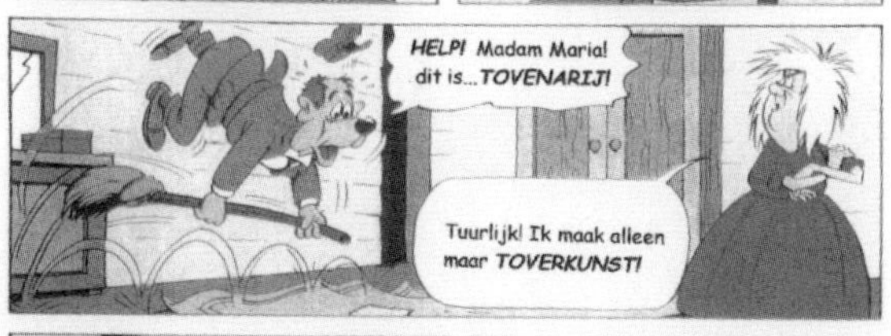

CRASH!

OOPS!

BONK!

Hey, isn't this the rug of Ranbir Singh?

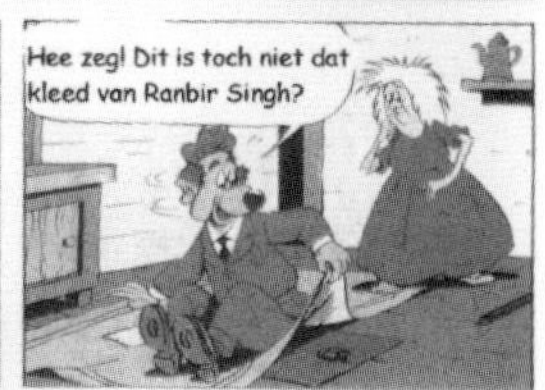

And here? More artworks?

UGGGGH!

It isn't finished yet!

GULP!
CHOMP

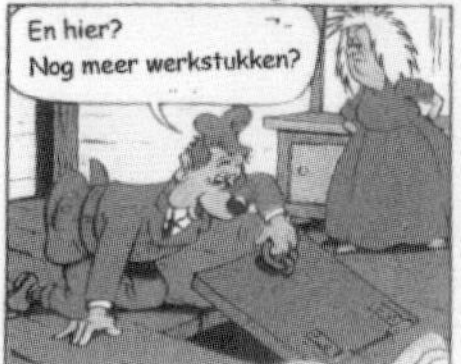

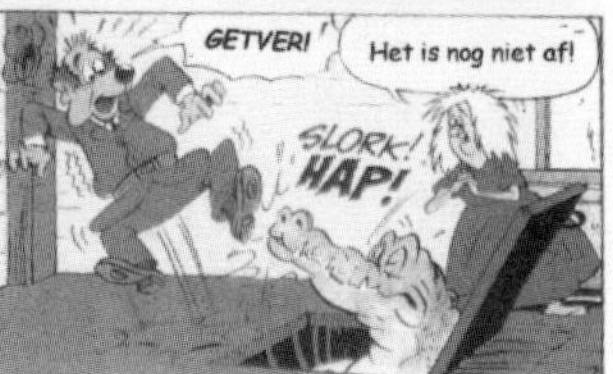

FORGET IT !
CLANG!

I'm working on some baby ones!

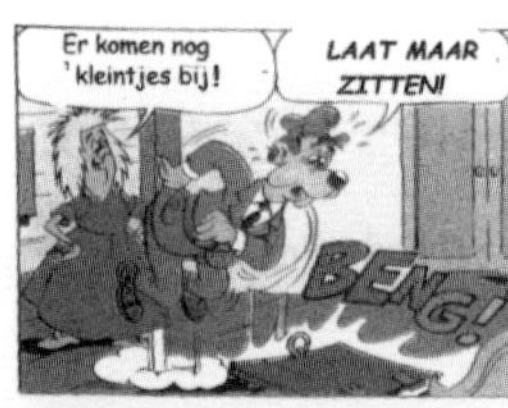

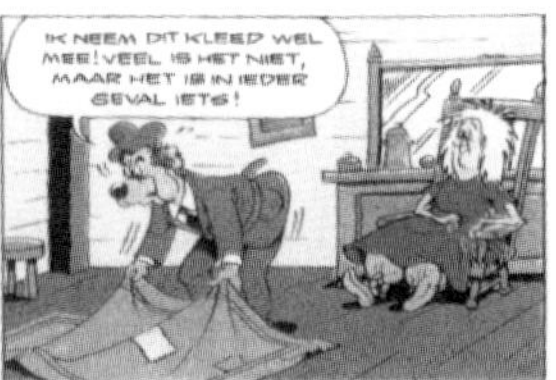

I'll take this rug!
It's not much, but at least it's something!

WOOSH!

WH-WHAT?

I've improved this one as well!

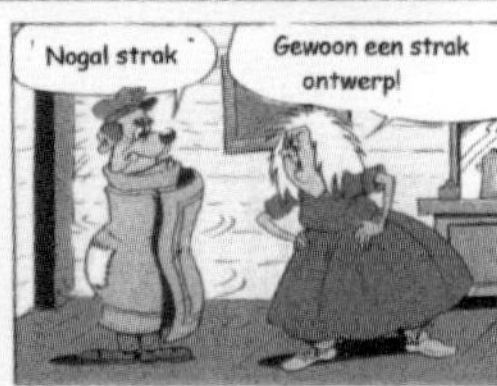

A bit hot

Just a hot design!

If Fons sees this

Just leave Fons to me, HA HA!

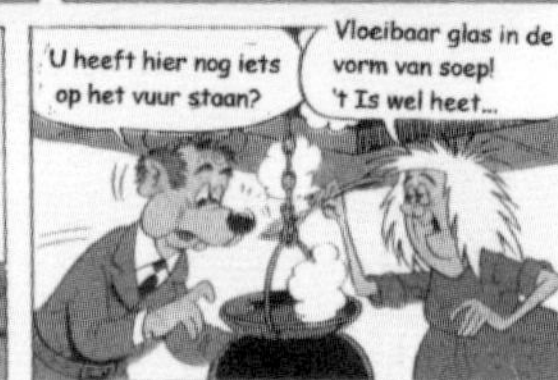

You've got something cooking here?

Liquid glass in the form of soup! It's hot.

IT CERTAINLY IS!

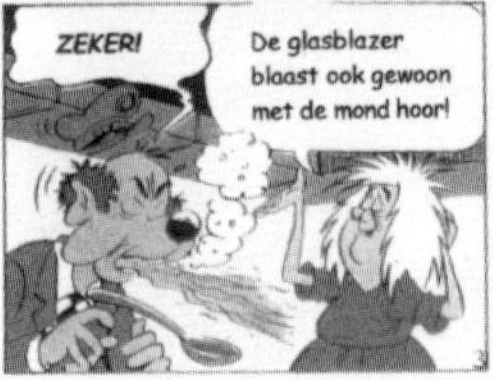

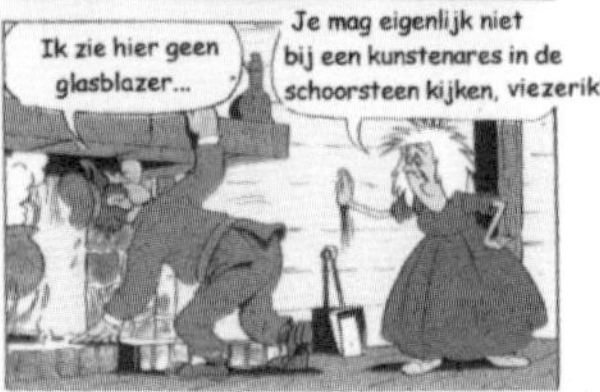

You're not supposed to look up a female artist's chimney, you dirty old man!

The glass-blower blows with his mouth too!

I don't see any glass-blower here

Before you know
it, you turn into a
statue yourself!

MA-MA-MARIA!

Why not?

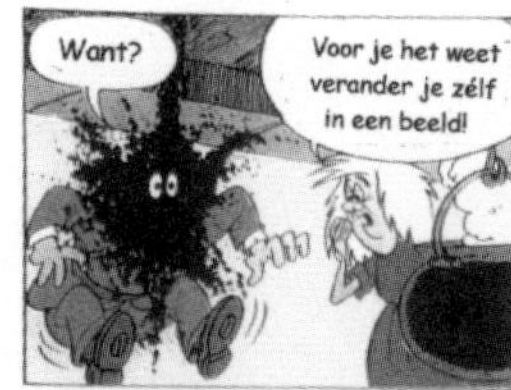

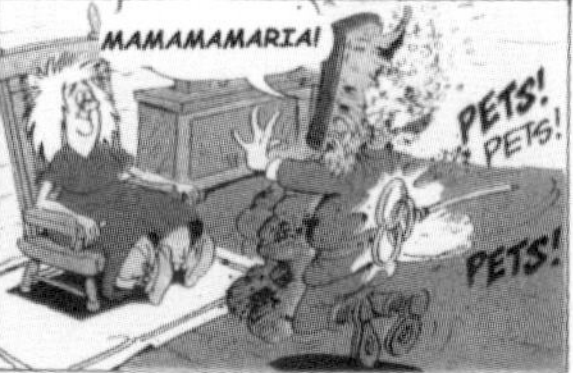

THWACK
THWACK
THWACK

That's it! I had
something ready
for Fons.

That's more like it!

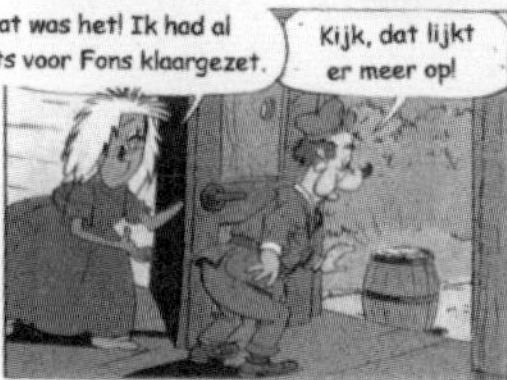

Art in the form of
a barrel containing
100,000 guilders. What
do you say
to that?

Beautiful concept!

I think this will
soon be sold!

Give my regards
to Fons.

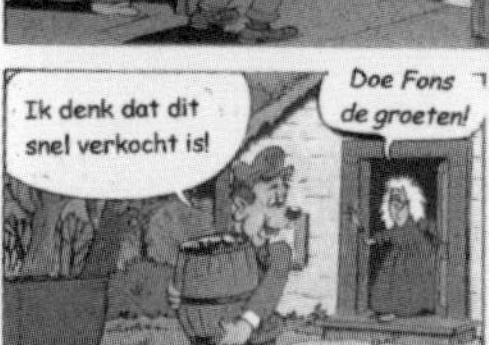
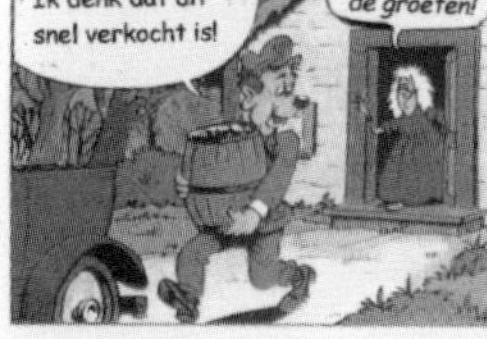

Art! Most of it's just
junk. I don't get
caught out.

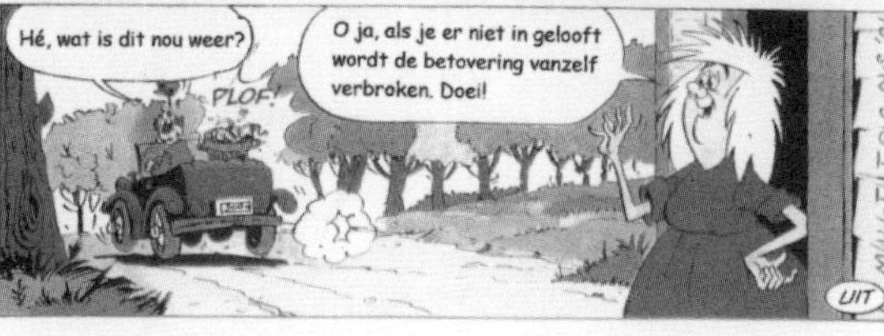

THE END

Hey, what is it this time?
CRASH!

O yes, if you don't believe
in it, the enchantment is
broken. Bye!

Maria's Hans den Hartog Jager

Het is een koude winterochtend aan het begin van maart, de dag na de grootste sneeuwbui in Nederland sinds twintig jaar. De bossen rond Arnhem zijn veranderd in een ijspaleis; de dikke laag sneeuw weerkaatst zoveel licht dat het atelier van Maria Roosen in een prachtig, hemels schijnsel baadt. Maria legt haar armen op tafel en leunt naar voren. 'In een huisje, diep in het bos woonde eens een oude bramenplukker', zegt ze. 'Hij heeft zijn hele leven nooit een mens gezien. Dan, op een dag, klopt er een verdwaalde man op zijn deur. De bramenplukker is helemaal verbaasd: "Hé je ziet er hetzelfde uit als ik!" De man lacht en zegt: "woon je hier?" "Oh ja", antwoordt de bramenplukker, "het is hier zo mooi! Ik heb velden vol met parels, zalen vol met spiegels en hele hoge gebouwen met zuilen." De man gaat snel terug naar zijn dorp en zegt: "Ik heb nu iemand ontmoet die is zo rijk, hij heeft allemaal schatten, maar hij weet er niets van." Het hele dorp trekt het bos in – maar dan blijken de parels dauwdruppels te zijn, de spiegels plassen en de zuilen bomen. Ze worden zo kwaad op de bramenplukker dat ze hem vermoorden.' Peinzend leunt ze achterover.

Is het een klassiek sprookje?
'Ik ken het van Godfried Bomans. Maar waar het in stond...'

Is het een parabel over je eigen werk?
'Nou... Ik vind het jammer dat er zo weinig ruimte voor verbeelding in de wereld is. Alles moet zo letterlijk, zo een op een. Je ziet het in de maatschappij, in de politiek, in de kunst begint *re-enactment* nu in te komen... Er is geen ruimte om mensen te laten verdwalen, er zijn geen plekken waar ze kunnen schuilen.'

Net als ik wil vragen of haar oeuvre dan zo'n vluchtwereld wil zijn, rinkelt de telefoon. Roosen maakt een gebaar van 'dat bedoel ik nou' en loopt weg – ze verwacht een transport dat niet kan wachten. Nu pas valt me op dat het atelier vol staat met Roosens eigen werk, niet in aanbouw, maar af. Op een archiefkast pronken zes glazen duiven, die ze onlangs heeft laten blazen door een Venetiaanse meesterblazer. Op de grond liggen blurbs van roze glas. Een grote zalmroze melkkan met een glazen wortel erin. Ingepakte aquarellen. En op de grond ligt een deel van de fotoreeks die ze sinds 1985 uit kranten knipt: tientallen 'overwinnaars', oftewel mensen die voor de camera hun vreugde uiten – onbekommerd, blij, euforisch. Daar zitten veel sporters bij (voetballers, schaatsers, Anky van Grunsven), Oscar-winnende acteurs, politici als Gorbatsjov en Clinton, maar ook Hendrik de Achtste, geschilderd door Hans Holbein en Matthias Grünewalds gekruisigde Christus. Ineens besef ik dat Roosens atelier eigenlijk meer een opslagplaats is dan een werkruimte, meer toonzaal dat atelier.

Als Maria weer binnenkomt, loopt ze rechtstreeks naar de tafel met afbeeldingen van haar werk. Ze pakt een foto waarop een moeder en een kind in een moestuin zijn te zien. De tuin lijkt normaal, de boerderij is op de achtergrond zichtbaar, maar daardoor vallen de wortels in de grond des te meer op – hun koppen glanzen of ze door een fee zijn aangeraakt. 'Dit bedoel ik nou met die verbeelding', zegt Roosen. 'Een paar jaar geleden werd ik gevraagd voor een project op een boerderij. Ik had net honderden glazen wortels op mijn atelier liggen, knaloranje, die eerder waren gebruikt bij een toneelstuk. Ik dacht: die laat ik planten in een moestuin, dat is vast een mooi gezicht. Bleek dat die boerderij helemaal geen moestuin had, maar ze legden er met alle plezier een aan. Dat deden ze prachtig met sla en prei en een hek tegen de konijnen – en daar heb ik die wortels tussen geplant.' Ze grijnst. 'Het bleek heel goed te werken. Er zijn heel wat van die wortels verdwenen – gejat. Zo werkt dat dus. Als je iets mooi neerzet, de verbeelding goed prikkelt, worden zelfs glazen wortels van goud.'

Waarmee we alsnog bij de kern van Roosens werk zijn aangeland. Want juist dat prikkelen van de verbeelding, soms mild, soms stekelig, is al meer dan vijftien jaar haar handelsmerk. Daarbij is ze op een vaste stijl of vaste vorm niet direct te betrappen. Roosen is, wat ze zelf noemt, een 'zoekende' kunstenaar die altijd het juiste materiaal, de juiste vorm wil vinden bij ieder idee. Begin jaren negentig werd ze bekend met een reeks kannen van roze glas, wulps en robuust. Die werden gevolgd door glazen borsten en glazen knotsen, maar daar tussendoor zwierden schijnbaar vanzelfsprekend 'losse' projecten als een paar enorme sloffen voor de 'reus van Rotterdam' en een houten babykerkje dat ze voor de manifestatie Sonsbeek 9 hing aan de Arnhemse Eusebiuskerk. Ook voorzag ze de vuurtoren van het Belgische Blankenberge van een 'pruik' van oranje scheepstouw, en liet ze onlangs nog twee enorme zonnebloemen breien, die in lange slierten door haar galerie werden gedrapeerd.

Op dit moment werkt Roosen aan een soortgelijk groot project – al valt het nauwelijks op, tussen alle werken. Voor de Triënnale van Yokohama is ze gevraagd iets te doen met de lokale vuurtoren. En dus staat daarom in een hoekje een klein model van de toren, voorlopig heeft ze de top ervan omwikkeld met felroze garen. Roosen pakt het model op, weegt het in haar handen en trekt wat aan het touw. 'Het is nog lang niet af, het kan nog totaal anders worden.'

Heb je enig idee hoe ze vanuit Yokohama bij jou terecht komen?
'Oh, dat heeft zeker te maken met het feit dat ik al een paar grote gebouwen onder handen heb gehad. De Eusebius-kerk in Arnhem, de vuurtoren van Blankenberge, dus dan denken organisatoren al snel: die doet iets met torens. Juist om die reden probeer ik zelf niet te snel op zulke verzoeken in te gaan. Ik ga eerst kijken of het gevoel goed is, of ik er iets mee kan. Als dat klopt wil ik het wel proberen.'
Wat was er goed aan Yokohama?
'Het eerste wat me beviel is dat curator Tadashi Kawamata zelf een kunstenaar is. Dat merk je meteen: hij kijkt vanuit de inhoud van het werk, en niet met het idee of het wel genoeg publiek zal trekken of zo. Hij liet me wat foto's zien, en die prikkelden me om zelf te gaan kijken. Het bleek een heel hoge toren, meer dan honderd meter, in een oude buurt. Echt zo'n *sad widow*, maar ook een typisch fallussymbool. Dus vroeg ik me al snel af of dat niet wat vrouwelijker kon.'
Is dat het eerste waar je aandenkt, de verhouding tussen mannelijk en vrouwelijk?
'Nou ja, het is een ingrediënt.'
Waar denk je dan nog meer aan?
'Mijn eerste idee was om er gewoon een ander gebouw overheen te zetten. Dat zie je tegenwoordig vaak op steigers, dat ze doeken bedrukken met een foto van het gebouw dat eronder zit – daar kun je natuurlijk ook iets heel anders voor hangen. Dat vond ik toch te reclameachtig. En ik wilde ook gebruikmaken van het uitzicht...' Ze staart naar het model. 'Ik ben er nog niet helemaal uit. Voorlopig vind ik het leuk om die enorme paal met roze touw te omkleden, dat heeft iets vrolijks en prikkelends. Maar het is nog niet genoeg.'
Als je gaat twijfelen, zoals nu, roep je dan de hulp van anderen in?
'Nee dat valt wel me... (lacht) Hoogstens van mijn vriend, want die kan goed mo-

dellen bouwen. Maar verder moet ik het toch echt helemaal zelf uitzoeken, in deze fase.'

Dat neemt niet weg dat die hulp er onvermijdelijk zal komen, al is het maar omdat samenwerken langzaam een onvervreemdbaar onderdeel van Roosens werkwijze is geworden. Het proces is eigenlijk altijd hetzelfde: Roosen bedenkt het idee, werkt het concept uit en maakt de plannen, maar ze drapeert geen touw, blaast geen glas, bouwt geen kerk en breit geen bloem – ze is er hoogstens bij als het gebeurt, als begeleider en 'inspirator'. Dat lijkt een heldere keuze, en dat maakt het des te opmerkelijker dat Roosen deze 'werkwijze' pas relatief laat vond toen Roosen haar eerste glazen kannen exposeerde, waarmee ze bekend werd, was ze al 34.

Ervaar je het zelf ook zo, dat je pas relatief laat je vorm vond?
Roosen aarzelt. 'Ja, misschien is dat wel zo. Er gaat ook wel een geschiedenis aan vooraf, maar of ik dat nu moet vertellen... Nou ja, ik ben opgeleid als tekenleraar en heb daarna de kunstacademie gedaan. In die tijd was ik nog zoekende. Toen, op mijn 27ste, overleed mijn geliefde. Dat sloeg een enorm gat in mijn leven. Ik raakte hartstikke vast, verzandde in een zwaar rouwproces, waar ik ook met therapie niet uit kwam. Op advies van mijn haptonoom ben ik toen aquarellen gaan maken. Dan ging ik achter mijn tafel zitten, met papier en aquarelverf, en probeerde vast te leggen hoe ik me voelde. Een beetje in de sfeer van: "oh vandaag voel ik me blauw" en dan tekende ik een blauwe bel.' Roosen gniffelt. 'Ja, het was echt heel ernstig.'

Had dat nog iets met professioneel kunstenaarschap te maken?
'Nou... al snel ben ik mezelf een "eis" gaan stellen: ik moest elke keer vijf tekeningen maken. Precies vijf. De eerste tekening verbeeldde dan meestal heel letterlijk mijn stemming. Bij de tweede probeerde ik de esthetiek wat toe te laten en de kern van mijn gevoel te treffen, en zo verder. Op die manier was ik meestal bij de vierde wel klaar, dan waren de emoties er uit. Maar dan moest ik nog een vijfde. Dan begon ik maar wat vrijblijvend te doen, mijn kwast leeg te maken, zeg maar. Maar het opmerkelijke was nu juist dat in die tekeningen er vaak precies uit kwam wat ik bedoelde. Blijkbaar kon ik het pas een vorm geven als de eerste emoties weg waren. Dat besef hielp me enorm om tot een essentie te komen. Tot eerlijkheid.'

Wat was er dan zo eerlijk aan die aquarellen?
'Het opmerkelijkste was dat er op het papier dingen gebeurden die ik zelf nooit had kunnen verzinnen. Ik was opgeleid als kunstenaar en dan ben je heel erg doorkneed in zaken als compositie en vorm en structuur. Dat heeft niet direct iets met het uiten van gevoelens te maken. Juist door die vorm los te laten, door intuïtiever te werken, hoefde ik me niet meer zo dwangmatig op compositie te richten. Dat werkte perfect.'

Zag je al snel dat die manier van tekenen ook goed voor je werk kon zijn?
'Het ging nog verder: ik zag al snel dat ik in het atelier vragen kon oplossen die ik in het leven niet altijd aankon. Daardoor durfde ik steeds verder te gaan.'

Hoe deed je dat? Hoe ga je 'ver' in een aquarel?
'Op allerlei manieren. Eerst werkte ik gewoon in een schetsboek, maar soms had ik dan wel tekeningen gemaakt waarvan ik dacht: die kan ik wel eens op een groter formaat proberen of uitvoeren in een ander materiaal. Soms nam ik dan een hele bak met verf en goot die uit over een vel van een paar vierkante meter. Dat werkte heel bevrijdend.'

Je bent toen al vrij snel begonnen met het maken van objecten in glas. Hoe kwam je daar op?
'Dat lag een beetje in het verlengde van dat zoeken naar grenzen. Ik maakte steeds

grotere aquarellen, en ik begon me af te vragen of ik dat vloeibare van een aquarel ook in andere materialen kon vangen. Ik had op de Academie wel eens met glas gewerkt, en dat vond ik altijd heel mooi. Toen heb ik me ingeschreven voor een cursus glasblazen. Je ging met een groep mensen naar een glasblazerij, daar kon je zien hoe het werkte en op het einde mocht je een object naar keuze laten blazen. De meeste mensen vroegen dan om de gekste dingen, met allerlei kleuren. Ik merkte juist dat ik een gewone transparante bol het allermooiste vond.'

Waarom een transparante bol?
'Het is de perfecte vorm hè? Als je in zo'n bol kijkt, zie je de hele wereld op z'n kop en tegelijk is het zo'n prachtig symbool. In Venetië heb ik eens een Christoffel met een glazen bol gezien en op een schilderij van Tintoretto staat ook een mooie – in die tijd was de transparante bol sowieso het symbool van de hele wereld. Maar goed, het grappige was dat ik die bollen dus prachtig vond, maar dat de glasblazers er niks aan vonden. Voor hen is zo'n bol de basisvorm. Als ze beginnen te werken maken ze eerst een bol en van daaruit gaan ze voorwerpen maken. Ik heb ze toen een reeks van die bollen laten blazen en daar heb ik een installatie mee ingericht, waarbij al die bollen als bellen aan de rand van een ruimte lagen.'

Voelde je op dat moment niet de
aandrang zelf glasblazen te leren?
'Nee, eigenlijk helemaal niet. Ik bedoel, ik heb het wel geprobeerd, ik heb meegewerkt in het glasatelier, deurtjes opendoen, dingen aangeven... Maar om het goed te leren, echt goed, dat kost je jaren. En het was mijn doel helemaal niet. Voor mij werkt het net zo goed, beter misschien wel, als ik het proces van blazen aanstuur, richting geef.'

Maar toch: heb je niet het gevoel dat je
werk daardoor een soort 'handschrift'
mist? Dat het te ver van je afstaat?

Of laat ik het anders vragen: maakte
je in die tijd ook werk, behalve de
aquarellen, dat je wel zelf uitvoerde?
'Oh ja hoor. Toen mijn lief was overleden heb ik een tijd heel "arbeidsintensief" werk gedaan. Het eerste wat ik daarna maakte, was een houten ketting met grote houten bollen. Daar heb ik echt maanden aan zitten hakken, alleen maar om die bollen goed rond te krijgen – dingen rond maken is heel troostend, heb ik gemerkt. Als je het verdriet oprolt, kun je weer verder leven, dan rolt het met je mee. En in dat hakken kon ik ook nog lekker mijn agressie kwijt. Later heb ik nog eens een braambol gemaakt, een grote bal van opgerolde bramentakken. Dat was hartstikke mooi. Ik had speciale handschoenen gekocht en wist precies waar de goede bramentakken groeiden. Dan ging ik er met mijn auto op uit om takken te plukken, die propte ik in de achterbak van m'n bestelwagen. Als ik dan thuis kwam knalde die deur echt open van de druk, alsof er een monster naar buiten sprong. Ik was ook hartstikke trots op die bollen, ik was echt de super-braambollenmaker.'

Dat deed je dus wel graag zelf.
'Ja, dat zou ik nooit aan iemand anders overlaten, al is het maar omdat je zelf moet uitvinden hoe het moet. Er zat ook iets van een lijdensweg in – aan het einde van de dag zat ik altijd onder de krassen. Toen werkte dat dus, ook omdat ik misschien nog meer zoekend was. Het was ook mooi hoor. Dan was ik in het bos om takken te verzamelen. Kom ik een man tegen die me wijst op allemaal gangen in de bosjes. Bleek dat hij daar tunnels en gangen aan het graven was – dat was dan zijn project. Die bol van mij heb ik later, na jaren, trouwens nog ritueel in de fik gestoken. Dat was een heel spektakel, met die bol op de grond en daarboven vlammen van wel zes meter hoog. Alsof er een meteoor was geland, zo zag dat eruit.'

*Maar bij het glas had je die behoefte
tot zelf maken niet meer.*
'Nee, vanaf dat moment is het uitbesteden eigenlijk begonnen. Dat had misschien ook wel met een soort onthechting te maken. Het is aanvankelijk ontstaan doordat ik die techniek niet genoeg beheerste, maar al snel merkte ik dat juist dat samenwerken, het deels uit handen geven voor mij heel veel toevoegt.'

*Je vindt het niet moeilijk om een deel
van de controle te verliezen?*
'Nee, want het levert juist veel op.'

*En het kost je geen moeite om het als
jouw werk te beschouwen.*
'Oh nee, want het beginidee is altijd van mij. Ik bepaal het uitgangspunt, en de uitwerking.'

*Maar toch, toen we het net over die
toren hadden, gaf je aan dat het maken
van werk voor jou een soort groeiproces is,
waarbij je telkens nieuwe ideeën
uitprobeert. In hoeverre maakt het
samenwerken het makkelijker
beslissingen te nemen? Of maakt
het dat juist moeilijker?*
Roosen aarzelt. 'Soms helpt het wel, maar dat is niet waar het om draait. Ieder werk begint bij mij altijd met een idee, maar dat idee is niet heel concreet. Het is een kwestie van voelen, associëren, verbindingen maken... Kijk een goed beeld, een goed werk moet een soort omzetting geven, net zoals eten wordt verteerd, ongeveer. Dat moet er altijd in zitten want als het te direct is, te veel een op een, vind ik er niks aan. En die omzetting ontstaat nu juist doordat ik verschillende processen bij elkaar breng. Mijn eigen ideeën en die van anderen vormen samen een soort chemische reactie die je zelf niet helemaal in de hand hebt. Daar komt uiteindelijk iets uit dat uniek is, dat ik zelf ook niet kon voorspellen, en dat me iets laat zien waar ik zelf benieuwd naar ben, waar ik iets van terugkrijg.'

*Is glas daar specifiek een geschikt
materiaal voor?*
'Nou, het heeft in ieder geval een mooie dubbelheid. Glas is gestolde materie die toch heel dicht bij het vloeibare blijft. Het is heel breekbaar, kwetsbaar, terwijl een glazen voorwerp toch vele duizenden jaren oud kan worden – er wordt nog steeds glas opgegraven uit de tijd van de Romeinen. Daarom noem ik glas ook wel gestolde energie: het kan eeuwen blijven bestaan maar ook, ineens, pats, weg zijn. Ik weet nog, de eerste keer dat een van mijn kannen brak. Een kan tikte tegen een ander en ineens pats, pats, waren er vijf kapot – vreselijk was dat. Toen leerde ik meteen dat roze glas heel gevoelig is. Dat bleek per kleur nogal te kunnen verschillen.'

*Maak je ook gebruik van die kennis?
Gaan verschillende kleuren glas
daardoor iets anders voor je betekenen?*
'Ja, dat speelt wel mee. Bij dit werk bijvoorbeeld (ze pakt een foto van haar 'Bellenrek', waarin 140 glazen "proefbelletjes" in verschillende kleuren hangen) wordt de vorm voor een belangrijk deel bepaald door de eigenschappen van het glas. Het lijken net zaadjes of spermatozoïden, maar bijvoorbeeld rood glas is heel hard en dus blijft die 'bel' heel klein, terwijl de tabakskleur, die hoefde maar een kleine zwiep te krijgen of *woesj*! daar ging hij al. Dat is dus de langste. En die roze is gebroken. Dat wil ik ook laten zien, dus die heb ik met plakband weer aan elkaar gezet en opgehangen.'

Zo worden het bijna karakters.
'Ja, ik weet nog dat ik de eerste keer bij de glasblazer kwam en zei: "Ik ga nooit iets met kleuren doen." Maar op het moment dat je er meer van weet, dat het betekenis krijgt... Zo gaat dat bij mij hè? Ik was eerst gefascineerd door dat roze en toen besloot ik er kannen van te maken. Dat bedenk ik niet van tevoren, dat komt voort uit de kleur.'

'Ik begin meestal nog steeds met een aquarel. Dan teken ik bijvoorbeeld een kan met een enorm lange tuit. Daarmee ga ik naar Bernard Heesen, de glasblazer. Voor hem is die aquarel een soort uitgangspunt. Hij begint te blazen, maar ik blijf daar wel bij, om te kijken, mee te denken, te sturen. In dat proces is trouwens wel veel veranderd. Vroeger was ik heel erg betrokken, stond ik vreselijk mee te schreeuwen en te doen. Nu heb ik geleerd wat meer afstand te nemen, om de dingen van tevoren te bespreken en tijdens het werk hoogstens nog wat opmerkingen te maken.'

'Nou ik ben wel wispelturig. Daarstraks zei ik dat ik niet van letterlijke beelden hou, maar soms wil ik dat dan ineens toch wél. Zo bedacht ik pas dat ik gewoon eens een lul en tieten en een kont van glas wilde, en die dan samen ophangen in ene netje, als een soort orgie van glas. Van die lullen had ik geen aquarel gemaakt, ik ging gewoon naar de glasblazer en zei: 'jongens, vandaag gaan we lullen maken.' Dat is natuurlijk lachen, vooral als ik zeg dat ze het naar eigen inzicht mogen doen. Dan ontstaat er meteen zo'n sfeertje dat ik leuk vind. Een soort saamhorigheid. Het zijn ook hele goeie lullen geworden.'

Roosen grijnst. 'Dat netje werkte niet. Ik kreeg die lullen hier op mijn atelier, deed ze in het netje, maar dat was niks. Dan ga ik dus dingen proberen, zoals ik eigenlijk altijd doe met dit soort werk. In dit geval dacht ik op een gegeven moment: ik hang zo'n lul eens op. Eerst hing ie hoog en toen dacht ik: nee, die moet op kruishoogte. Dat was al beter. Toen kwam dat hooitouw erbij en dat werkte mooi, maar ik wist niet zeker of het goed was. Met anderen heb ik het er nog over gehad of het geen staalkabeltjes moesten zijn, maar nee, dit werkte het beste.'

'Het komt wel allemaal uit mij voort. Maar ik ben gaan inzien wat me interesseert, hoe ik de goede vorm voor dingen vindt. En vooral... (aarzelt) ben ik beter geworden in het accepteren van dingen die ik zelf niet kan bedenken.'

Roosen lacht. 'Zo zou ik het niet willen noemen.'

Peinzend: 'Ik heb wel gedacht om het boek waarvoor we nu praten "Maria's" te noemen.'

'Het is heel Brabants, daar zeggen ze "Die is van Maria's" – meervoud dus. En Maria is toch de vrouw der vrouwen.'

'Ik heb dan toch het gevoel dat er tekortkomingen zijn.'

'Toch wel ja.'

'Ja, zeker. Maar het heeft er ook mee te maken dat ik het altijd moeilijk vind om veel van mijn werk bij elkaar te zien. Om de een of andere reden vind ik mijn werk ook altijd beter tot zijn recht komen in groepstentoonstellingen. Misschien heeft dat er weer mee te maken dat ik me graag tot andere mensen verhoud of zo...'

*Zou het ook kunnen dat je te veel
patronen herkent als je veel van je
eigen werk ziet?*
'Ja.'
Wat zijn die patronen dan?
'Het herhalen bijvoorbeeld. Neem nou die wortels waar we het straks over hadden, het feit dat ik een installatie maak die uit honderden glazen wortels bestaat…. Vroeger zou ik dat een zwaktebod hebben gevonden. Ik deed het wel, maar dan vooral met het argument dat ik verschillende kanten van een vorm of een thema wilde onderzoeken. Pas bij die wortels zag ik dat je door herhaling de losse delen ook versterkt. Al die wortels bij elkaar krijgen een enorme groeikracht. Dat vind ik dan weer mooi, groeikracht is toch de grootste kracht die er bestaat.'
Zijn er zo nog meer patronen in je werk?
Oh ja. Die grote gebaren bijvoorbeeld, die krachtmetingen, dat powerliften. Zo'n houten kerkje aan de Eusebiuskerk, of vierhonderd glazen bollen aan het plafond van het Antoni van Leeuwenhoek Ziekenhuis. Zulke gebaren zijn eigenlijk iets van de laatste jaren, ik heb daar echt iets voor moeten overwinnen. Maar voor mijn werk was het wel goed, het maakte dat ik verder kon, mijn horizon werd breder. Ik was het ook wel een beetje beu, al die schoenen en kannen. Dit gaf lucht.'
*Een rare vraag misschien, maar als we
zo praten over het uitbesteden en het
dingen bedenken: is er nou iets waarvan
je vindt dat je er zelf echt goed in bent?
Een eigen vaardigheid?*
Roosen valt stil. 'Tsjee, dat is… dat is moeilijk om van jezelf te zeggen. Ik vind in ieder geval dat ik goed kan kijken.'
Is dat alles?
'Ik kan ook goed meegaan in dingen… Maar dan vraag jij natuurlijk meteen waar ik zelf dan sta.'
*Is dat een typisch vrouwelijke eigenschap?
Of anders gezegd: je werk is, zeker in
het verleden, vaak met vrouwelijkheid*

geassocieerd. *Borsten, breekbaarheid, roze
glas. Zoek je dat op?*
'Ja, maar ik speel er ook mee. Ik hou er helemaal niet van als mijn werk als een soort pleidooi voor vrouwelijkheid wordt gezien. Dat is me te makkelijk, te plat. Ik wil juist graag de clichés over vrouwelijkheid ondervragen, die clichés een beetje uitdagen, door dingen juist heel vrouwelijk aan te pakken of juist heel tuttig of heel stoer.'
*Zien de toeschouwers die dubbele
bodem ook altijd, denk je?*
'Nee, niet altijd natuurlijk. Maar dat is ook niet erg.'
*Laat ik het anders vragen: vind jij het
belangrijk om te weten wat voor effect je
werk op de toeschouwer heeft?*
'Jan Hoet zei een keer tegen me: "Jouw werk gaat over geven." Dat vond ik heel mooi, al zou ik dat zelf nooit durven zeggen. Maar dat komt misschien ook doordat iemand ooit schreef, toen ik net wat bekender werd, dat ik in mijn werk een soort moederrol vervulde. Het verzorgen, het schenken, het aanbieden. Dat vond ik toen vreselijk.'
Waarom?
'Ach, het kwam waarschijnlijk omdat ik toen net werd opgestuwd in de vaart der volkeren. Ik werd wat bekender, deed mee aan de Biennale en ik wilde graag professioneel. Dan zit je er niet op te wachten om als een soort moeder aller moeders te worden weggezet. Nu heb ik daar geen moeite meer mee. Hoe je het ook wendt of keert: het is toch een kracht van me. Ik kan dingen laten ontstaan, laten groeien, laten opbloeien. Zeker nu ik zelf een dochter heb, besef ik dat daar niks mis mee is.'
*Is dat ook een reden waarom je die
overwinnaarfoto's steeds vaker exposeert?*
'Nee, die overwinnaars begonnen heel anders. Ik zag een keer een tentoonstelling waarop allemaal verzamelingen van kunstenaars werden geëxposeerd. Ik knipte toen af en toe al foto's uit, maar dat zag ik nooit als een verzameling. Op die tentoonstelling

stonden al die collecties bij elkaar, schoenen en miniatuurgebouwtjes, waardoor het net beelden werden. Dat vond ik zo mooi dat ik bedacht dat ik van mijn overwinnaars ook wel een verzameling kon maken.'

Het zijn eigenlijk heel verschillende foto's.
Veel klassieke winnaars, maar ook politici,
en kok Jonnie Boer. Wubbo Ockels. De David
van Michelangelo.

'Ja, nou ja, het eerste criterium waarop ik ze uitzoek is toch dat het een goede foto is. Goed beeld, zeg maar. En ze moeten iets oproepen bij mij, en dus hebben ze vaak te maken met de dingen waar ik op dat moment mee bezig ben, met mijn fascinaties. In die zin is het bijna een dagboek. Sinds mensen weten dat ik deze verzameling heb, sturen ze me wel eens overwinnaars op, maar dat werkt dus eigenlijk nooit. Daar heb ik dan te weinig mee.'

Maar waarom overwinnaars? Heeft het
iets te maken met onafhankelijkheid?
Met het boven de mensen uitstijgen,
zelfstandigheid, het gevoel hebben dat
je vrij bent?

'Nou, waar het voor mij nog meer over gaat, is dat voor die mensen de tijd lijkt stil te staan. Op zo'n belangrijk moment draait alles om hen, is er niets anders meer – en staat de tijd stil. Dat vind ik mooi, juist omdat dat je eraan herinnert waar je alles voor doet. Dat heb ik ook in mijn werk. Dat gaat soms heel moeizaam, geen zin, veel twijfels, maar als het goed gaat vergeet ik die worsteling weer. Daar krijg je dan die overwinningsmomenten voor terug, die de tijd overstijgen, net zoals dat gebeurt bij grote gebeurtenissen als geboorte en dood.'

Hoe langer ik kijk naar die foto's, hoe meer
lijnen ik eigenlijk zie naar je eigen werk.
De zonnebloemen van Van Gogh.
Het Arnolfini-portret van Van Eyck,
met daarin die beroemde 'glazen bol'...

'Daarom zit de Christus van Grünewald er ook in. Het is natuurlijk in de eerste plaats een meesterwerk, maar ik hou ook heel erg van de uitspraak van de beeldhouwer Brancusi, die ooit heeft gezegd "dat een goed beeld moet kunnen genezen". Later las ik dat psychiatrische patiënten uit de buurt van Colmar soms voor Grünewalds schilderij worden gezet, omdat ze daar rustig van worden. Ik kan me dat ook wel voorstellen, het is zo'n gedetailleerd schilderij, als je een wat verwarde geest hebt, kun je er heel veel in zien, kan het je heel veel geven.'

Wat klinkt dat vriendelijk – moederlijk,
als ik zo vrij mag zijn.

'Weet je, je vroeg me daarstraks waar ik nu echt goed in ben, wat mijn specifieke vaardigheid is. Ik geloof dat ik het antwoord weet: ik laat dingen groeien. Ik zaai het zaad en roep vervolgens de hulp van anderen in om het gewas op te kweken. Ik stuur het proces, begeleid het – eigenlijk ben ik de kunstenaar met de groene vingers. Is dat niet mooi?'

Ze is er in alle maten

Jennifer Allen

Bij Maria Roosen kunnen dingen groot worden. HEEL groot. Of klein. Piepklein. Bijvoorbeeld die glazen melkkannen: groot genoeg om er beide armen omheen te slaan en klein genoeg om in je handpalm te passen. Nadat de warme adem van de glasblazer ze gevormd heeft, worden ze gevuld met koude melk; tien liter of tien druppels. De spiegelbollen die Roosen her en der in de tuin van het Museum Boijmans Van Beuningen plaatste, weerspiegelen hun omgeving zo compact als een punt aan het eind van een zin die het hele landschap samenvat, van de grassprietjes tot en met de wolken. Gedroogde zonnebloemen, gebreid van witte en bruine wol, worden torenhoge versies van hun oorspronkelijke vorm. Dan zijn er nog de vele glazen penissen, opgeblazen tot een superformaat dat beide geslachten zullen benijden. De borsten, overdadige dubbele hangers van gekleurd spiegelglas, liggen lekker in bed gestopt of hangen in leren leunstoelen voor een tête-à-tête. En onlangs heeft Roosen haar werkterrein uitgebreid naar – en ingekrompen tot – architectuur, met parasitaire toevoegingen die niet bij hun gastheer horen, maar ook niet zonder hem kunnen. Zo voegde ze een gietijzeren wenteltrap toe aan een boom van twee verdiepingen hoog en hing ze een lange franje van oranje scheepstouw boven aan een watertoren aan een havenkade. Maquettes als het gouden huis – een schaalmodel van haar eigen huis, helemaal bedekt met bladgoud – lijken eerder uit een dwergensprookje te komen dan dat het prototypes voor gebouwen zijn. Haar verkleinde houten dubbelganger van een stenen kerk (*Mirakel,* 2001) zat aan de enorme toren van dat gebouw geplakt als een walvisjong aan z'n moeder, als een smalle schaduw wanneer de zon op z'n hoogst staat.

Uitdijend of inkrimpend, het oeuvre van Roosen vormt een unieke verzameling reuzen en miniaturen. Hoe wonderbaarlijk haar werk ook is, het gaat hier niet om goddelijke interventie. De werken bestaan in een seculiere wereld van wonderen, waarin gewone objecten – zonnebloemen of melkkannen – opeens buitengewoon worden. Roosen lijkt de zeven wereldwonderen uit te breiden met de intieme ruimtes van het lichaam, met het huiselijk domein van stoelen en trappen, met collectieve voorzieningen als geloof en water, met de natuurlijke omgeving van bos en tuin. In eerste instantie komt dit over als zowel een ouderwetse als moderne onderneming, die net zo verwant is aan de verzamelobjecten in een *renaissance-Wunderkammer* of rariteitenkabinet als aan de gebeeldhouwde monumenten voor massaconsumptie van de popart. Toch hoort Roosen in geen van beide tijdperken thuis, vanwege de manier waarop ze schaalverandering combineert met wisseling van materiaal. In de hoop een glimp op te vangen van het geheel van het goddelijk plan, zette de verzamelaar in de Renaissance zijn zinnen op natuurlijke zeldzaamheden die juist uniek waren, omdat ze bijzonder of misvormd waren (liever een zonnebloem met twee 'koppen' dan twee gebreide XL-versies). Een popartkunstenaar als Claes Oldenburg veranderde weliswaar de schaal en het materiaal van een uitgeknepen tube tandpasta, maar maakte toch een enkelvoudig monument voor een alledaags gebruiksartikel zonder de gelijkenis met het origineel uit het oog te verliezen. Roosen daarentegen is niet alleen beducht voor het reproduceren van goederen, maar bewaart in haar versies van alle-

102-103

daagse voorwerpen ook het evenwicht tussen het gelijke en het ongelijke. Haar zonnebloemen vormen een reusachtig paar en lijken wel op het origineel, maar zijn overduidelijk gebreid uit eenkleurige tinten wol – een materiaal dat ook al weinig gemeen heeft met Andy Warhols oplages van kleurrijke zeefdrukken van bloemen.

De veranderingen die Roosen schaal en materiaal laat ondergaan, houden het midden tussen realisme en verdichtsels die noch uit de natuur stammen, noch uit de fabriek voortkomen. Nogmaals, haar werk valt volledig onder het wonderbaarlijke, het Franse *merveilleux*, dat op zich weer stamt van het Latijnse *mirabilia*, een aanduiding van opmerkelijke en voortreffelijke zaken, wonderbaarlijkheden die toch vooral door God geschapen zijn. Ondanks het samenvallen van object en ontvangst is dit domein grotendeels gemeden door wereldlijke hedendaagse kunstuitingen. Eenmaal in de profane wereld gedrongen, vinden we het wonderbaarlijke vooral terug in wetenschap en literatuur, of het nu gaat om sprookjes, fictie, satire of magisch realisme. Neem bijvoorbeeld de wonderen die microscoop en telescoop hebben onthuld, naast andere wonderbaarlijke wetenschappelijke ontdekkingen en uitvindingen. Verhalen als *Alice in Wonderland* of *Gullivers reizen* moeten het hebben van overdrijvingen in schaal om een brug te slaan tussen realisme en verzinsel. De overheersende hedendaagse uiting van het wonderbaarlijke is natuurlijk de cinema en dan vooral de realistische verzinsels die in Hollywood met special effects worden bereikt; hoewel je ook kunt zeggen dat film de onverwachte verbazing over het wonderlijke heeft vervangen door de verwachting van vermaak. In haar studie over het 'merveilleux', noemt Marie-Françoise Christout een aantal kenmerken die we in het werk van Roosen terugvinden.[1] Het wonderlijke is in essentie dynamisch en behelst altijd groei, transformatie, versnelling en vertraging. Deze veranderingen worden overdreven, waardoor het mogelijk wordt om uitersten met elkaar te confronteren, of het nu reus tegenover elf is of goed tegenover kwaad. Wonderen schrikken ons op, omdat ze vertrouwde verhoudingen verstoren met geloofwaardige gelijkenissen. Aangezien de wetten van causaliteit zichtbaar blijven, is een wonder net geen illusie, zoals de bedrieglijke kunstmatigheid van een trompe l'oeil of de vingervlugheid van een goochelaar.

Roosen geeft uitdrukking aan die essentiële dynamiek van het wonderlijke door te kiezen voor organische elementen die verbonden zijn met groei, leven en metamorfose. Penissen en borsten zijn lichaamsdelen die van omvang veranderen vanwege hun rol bij de voortplanting. Zo maakt ze enorme zaadcellen van handgeblazen glas, naast grote oogballen met wisselend verwijde pupillen Roosen laat glas blazen in de lege vormen van klompen en leren broeken – organische en plooibare lichaamsbedekkingen die ook in allerlei maten voorkomen. Haar materialen komen dan ook meestal voort uit de natuur, maar worden altijd tot iets anders omgevormd als ze eenmaal aan de natuur onttrokken zijn. Glas, wol, goud, metaal en hout zijn eindeloos kneedbare materialen dic zich goed lenen voor bewerking, juist omdat ze ontelbare gedaanten en vormen kunnen aannemen, zelfs in beperkte hoeveelheden. De handwerkslieden die door Roosen worden ingeschakeld om haar werken uit te voeren, spelen een gelijkwaardige rol in deze dynamiek van het wonderlijke: de glasblazer verandert een embryonaal stuk glas vakkundig in een of ander lichaamsdeel. In Roosens overdrijvingen van zowel het miniatuurlijke als het gigantische komen meerdere uitersten samen. Door een kleine kerk aan een grote

62
1-3

3

te hangen, brengt deze kunstenaar een uitzonderlijke verschuiving in verhouding teweeg en weerspiegelt ze tegelijkertijd de terugloop van het aantal gelovigen, nu het christendom in Europa een teruggang ondergaat. De uitersten van menselijke uitwerpselen en voedsel komen samen in de wc-pot die is gedecoreerd met een overvloed aan groente of een landelijk jachttafereel. Geur treft reukloosheid in haar hangende lege parfumflesjes, ook gemaakt van glas, dat uiteraard geen geur heeft. Het leven staat tegenover de dood in de overblijvende vergeet-me-nietjes die in een minimalistisch, rechthoekig patroon op het kerkhof zijn geplant. In haar hele oeuvre, hoe dynamisch dat ook is, wordt het leven vaak in bedwang gehouden door de dood. De materialen mogen dan organisch zijn, ze beroven organische materie wel van haar vitaliteit, zoals koning Midas met zijn aanraking deed. De glazen penissen – even reukloos en leeg als de parfumflesjes – zullen nooit ejaculeren; de borsten zullen geen melk geven; de oogballen weerspiegelen, maar zien niets. Toch verschijnt deze 'dood' beslist niet als een eindbestemming, maar veeleer als een tijdelijke opschorting van het leven, als een betovering die wel is uitgesproken maar die altijd kan worden verbroken, ongedaan kan worden gemaakt door precies hetzelfde proces dat de bekoring heeft veroorzaakt. De glazen objecten zouden kunnen worden omgesmolten en opnieuw tot andere vormen worden geblazen; de zonnebloemen zouden kunnen worden uitgehaald en tot sokken, truien of wanten worden gebreid; het bladgoud zou van het miniatuurhuis kunnen worden verwijderd om de rand van een kelk of de snee van een gebonden boek te sieren.

De wonderen van Roosen scheppen niet alleen een dynamiek van uitersten, maar verstoren ook vertrouwde verhoudingen met absoluut geloofwaardige gelijkenissen. Afgezien van formaat en kleur is de kleine kerk een getrouwe weergave van het origineel. Toch moet de plotselinge verschijning ervan hoog aan de zijkant van de toren even schrikken zijn geweest voor de omwonenden, die gewend waren het bouwwerk daar 'alleen' te zien staan. *Mirakel* hoort daar, en hoort daar ook niet; de sculptuur is een kopie die z'n voorbeeld vereert (en zelfs z'n verheven hoogte imiteert) maar ook een last die z'n oorsprong bezwaart. De architecturale koppelingen van Roosen – de trap aan de boom, de franje aan de watertoren – doen een beetje denken aan de merkwaardige verbindingen in het surrealisme, maar bij Roosen passen haar toevoegingen ook functioneel bij hun gastheer. In bomen kun je klimmen: een trap vergemakkelijkt dat. Watertorens zijn hoog: franjes moeten hangen om vrijelijk te wapperen. Roosens glaswerken lijken wel op lichaamsdelen, maar zijn hun vertrouwde verband met het menselijk lichaam kwijt. De penis verschijnt niet tussen de benen van een man of zelfs maar als iets om voor te binden, maar in een serie van drie stuks die aan draadjes aan de muur hangen. De spiegelbollen weerspiegelen het landschap getrouw – inclusief de toeschouwers, die moeiteloos hun spiegelbeeld kunnen herkennen – maar nemen nauwelijks ruimte in. Wie Roosens werk niet zelf kan zien, kan toch een indruk krijgen van het opzienbarende effect ervan. Zij laat haar werken fotograferen, niet als op zichzelf staande sculpturen, maar als installaties binnen een bepaalde situatie, waarin meestal mensen voorkomen. Haar mini-kan lijkt op haar maxi-kan, maar toch kun je de twee onmogelijk verwarren op de foto's, omdat de eerste op een open hand rust en de tweede te zien is in een woonkamer, naast een vrouw die er een kabeltrui voor breit. Ook over het enorme formaat van Roosens glazen zaadcellen is geen twijfel mogelijk, omdat ze omhoog worden gehouden door wetenschappers in een laboratorium. Aangezien deze wetenschappers onderzoek doen naar voortplanting, wordt hun gebruikelijke visuele verhouding tot de zaadcel – vergroot onder een microscoop – opeens een verontrustende realiteit. Ten slotte onthullen de wonderen van Roosen de wetten van causaliteit die erachter liggen. Er gaat wel een gelijkenis maar geen illusie schuil achter de glazen lichaamsdelen, want ze zijn overduidelijk van glas. Er schuilt geen geheim, geen misleiding, in hoe de wollen zonnebloemen zijn gemaakt; het enige wat erachter steekt, is het vakmanschap van degene die ze heeft gebreid. Roosens gouden huis is geen verf die zich voordoet als het edelmetaal, maar een kleine hoeveelheid echt goud die zo dun is gemaakt dat je er een bescheiden huisje mee kunt bedekken. Als een deel van het wonderlijke in het werk van Roosen is gelegen in schaalveranderingen, dan ligt een ander deel in de zichtbare spanning tussen het rudimentaire materiaal en de uiteindelijke bewerkte vorm ervan. Goud wordt een huis, maar blijft toch koppig goud, net zoals het miniatuurhuis trouw blijft aan z'n immense oorsprong.

De schaal van het lichaam

Het menselijk lichaam blijft de toetssteen voor het gehele oeuvre van Roosen. Het piepkleine en het gigantische staan in een relatieve verhouding tot elkaar, maar in al haar overdrijvingen is het menselijk lichaam voor Roosen het referentiepunt. Niet één bepaald lichaam, en ook niet zomaar iemands lichaam, maar het lichaam van de toeschouwer. Zoals Susan Stewart opmerkt in haar studie over miniaturen en giganten, is het lichaam ons ijkpunt bij de beleving van schaal. Wij fungeren als het origineel voor de precieze symmetrie van een poppenhuis, dat ons een totaaloverzicht biedt, of voor de gro-

teske vervormingen van een reuzenfiguur, die ons overschaduwt.[2] Hoewel Roosen het lichaam expliciet figuratief weergeeft (penissen, borsten, oogballen) verwijst ze impliciet naar de kijkers, die haar overdrijvingen zullen zien in relatie tot hun eigen lichaam en beleving. Wie Roosens werk op foto's bekijkt, wordt de schaal ervan gewaar door zich te vereenzelvigen met de mensen in de achtergrond (wetenschappers, breiers) of met de omgeving zelf (een museum, een sportzaal), beide concrete verzamelplaatsen waar de tweelingborsten in hun bed waren geplaatst en gefotografeerd. Om de schaalbeleving van de toeschouwer te versterken, kiest Roosen vaak objecten die bij het menselijk lichaam passen, zoals handgrepen of huizen. De kunstenaar maakt geen complete figuur, maar impliceert het lichaam via de afwezige delen; in plaats van de gevormde voet biedt ze ons de trap of de binnenkant van een versleten schoen. De toeschouwers beleven hun eigen lichamelijkheid doordat ze zijn buitengesloten van vertrouwde ruimtes die ze normaal gesproken zelf innemen.

Roosens modelman – bestaande uit meerdere spiegelende ballen die zijn opgestapeld boven een paar stevige zwartleren schoenen – staat min of meer oog in oog tegenover de toeschouwer, afhankelijk van diens lengte. Maar ongeacht lengte ziet iedere toeschouwer zichzelf weerspiegeld als een klein vlekje in de omgeving, omdat de spiegels bolvormig zijn. Deze weerspiegeling – deels anamorfose, deels lachspiegel – doet denken aan het verrassende zelfportret van Jan van Eyck in de bolle spiegel ver op de achtergrond van het Arnolfiniportret, of aan de spiegelende oogbal van een bewakingscamera. Door dichterbij te komen wordt het lichaam van de toeschouwer wel groter, maar neemt ook de vervorming toe. Deze vervormde representatie wordt voortdurend herbevestigd, aangezien dezelfde weerspiegeling zich voordoet op het bolle oppervlak van alle spiegelende ballen die samen het gebombeerde lichaam van de man vormen. Door meerdere oogjes te houden op het totaalbeeld is deze man in staat om anderen er tenger of scheef te laten uitzien, en dat steeds weer. Onze afstand schept te veel verte; onze nabijheid brengt ons veel te dichtbij.

Alledaagse overwinnaars, sluimerende reuzen en bolhoofden

Roosens uitgebreidste werk tot op heden is haar doorlopende reeks *Overwinnaars*, van 1985 tot nu. De 190 beelden, voornamelijk uit dagbladen geknipt, vormen een wonderlijke verzameling mensen en dingen die vanwege hun uitzonderlijke karakter in het nieuws zijn gekomen. Naast allerlei sportlieden die hun overwinning vieren in verschillende sporten (van wielrennen tot voetbal) gaat het ook om voorwerpen (een enorme aardappel en een kleine microchip), rariteiten (een man met de langste baard, en het oudste vrouwelijke skelet), staatslieden (zoals Michail Gorbatsjov), bekende vrouwen (prinses Diana en Moeder Theresa), artiesten (Nick Cave en P.J. Harvey) en kunstenaars (van Jan van Eyck tot Matthew Barney). Ondanks dit schijnbaar brede overzicht kiest Roosen haar overwinnaars niet zomaar. Kennissen die haar plaatjes van bijzondere mensen toesturen, krijgen die vaak met een vriendelijk bedankje geretourneerd. Uit een overvloedig aanbod kiest Roosen alleen die figuren die op haar als overwinnaars overkomen. Het Nederlandse voetbalelftal dat het winnen van de Europese beker in 1988 viert, toont een tikje nationale trots; de aardappel – gevonden in Flevoland – is ook zo'n eerbetoon aan kost van eigen bodem. Bettine Vriesekoop en Anky van Grunsven, twee keuzes in 2004, staan voor een plaatselijke, persoonlijke geschie-

denis, verweven met geslacht. Ook het verstrijken van de tijd kan betekenisvol zijn. De man met de baard van 3,3 meter was geboren in 1826, gefotografeerd in 1904, en door Roosen opgepikt in 1987; het 7000 jaar oude skelet was van een vrouw die op 45-jarige leeftijd was overleden – even oud als Roosen zelf toen ze de foto uitkoos. Sommige overwinnaars – zoals Michael Jackson, die ze in 1996 in haar verzameling opnam – zijn inmiddels bij haar in ongenade gevallen. Anderen – zoals Nick Cave die in 1996 zei: 'De muze is geen renpaard' – hebben voor haar niets aan gezag ingeboet in de loop der jaren.

Door zich te verlaten op kant-en-klare beelden in de pers lijkt het alsof Roosen veel waarde toekent aan de manier waarop de massamedia het 'spektakel' verbreiden. Toch staat haar verzameling – door het gespecialiseerde en intieme werk dat ze eraan verricht – juist tegenover de soort nieuwsgaring van de krant, die probeert om een objectieve orde op te leggen aan actuele gebeurtenissen en pretendeert deze uitputtend te behandelen. De uitgebreidheid van *Le Monde* en de oneindigheid van *The Times* worden teruggebracht tot een draagbare omvang die je in één dag tot je kunt nemen. De krant gebruikt verkleining om een harmonieuze overgang te bewerkstelligen tussen het publieke en het private; de buitenkant (elke pagina is bedrukt, elke ruimte gevuld) komt overeen met de binnenkant (de opengeslagen pagina's omvatten de lezer, bijna als een woning). Door haar lievelingsoverwinnaars uit te knippen, bevrijdt Roosen de reus uit de begrenzing van de verkleining; te groot voor de krant, worden haar overwinnaars bevrijd uit het gewone nieuws en in een afzonderlijk toevluchtsoord geplaatst dat speciaal voor hen is gemaakt; hun beelden worden gered van de vuilnisbak om voort te bestaan als kunst en als geschiedenis. Als een halve historicus, halve redacteur vervangt Roosen de bemiddeling die de krant vervult tussen publiek en privaat door haar eigen, persoonlijke pantheon, dat een hele muur bedekt. Het formaat van de krant – de onhandige 'handgrepen' van de opengeslagen dubbele pagina – is zichtbaar met de schaar uitgeknipt, ook weer zo'n puur individuele manier waarop ze de geschiedenis vasthoudt en vormgeeft. Latere overwinnaars zijn vaak wel nog voorzien van de toenmalige context van het nieuws. Toch wordt in de gehele verzameling de illusie van compleetheid – en van objectiviteit – overschaduwd door een andere geschiedenis, die incompleet blijft omdat die verbonden is met Roosens eigen leven. Haar keuzes weerspiegelen niet alleen haar eigen voorkeuren, maar ook de biologische tijd van haar eigen lichaam, zo niet de veranderende waarden die het ouder worden op zich met zich meebrengt. Het skelet van de vrouw was zowel 7000 jaar als 45 jaar oud, was zowel het oudste skelet als het skelet van een vrouw van dezelfde leeftijd als de kunstenaar. De sporthelden worden geleidelijk verdrongen door vrouwen met een bijzonder levensverhaal – een verschuiving in belangstelling van het collectief naar de individuele ingeborene. Meegroeiend – of wegtikkend – met het leven van de kunstenaar blijft deze verzameling incompleet, niet-gesloten. Het is een organisch, levend ding dat een zekere spanning in stand houdt tussen het openbare leven van de overwinnaar en het privé-leven van de kunstenaar.

Veelzeggend in dit verband is dat Roosen het Nederlandse 'overwinnaars' in het Engels het liefst vertaald ziet als 'survivors'. Hoewel een 'survivor' ook een overwinnaar is, geeft het woord tevens aan dat haar figuren het langer volhouden dan de vluchtige kranten, en doet 'survivor' ook denken aan het Franse *survivre*, letterlijk 'over-leven'. Zo'n overdaad aan leven kleeft de overwinnaars aan – uitzonderlijke, maar sterfelijke individuen die bovenmenselijke daden verrichten die ergens tussen de aarde en de goden in liggen.[3] Toch behoort ook die overdaad aan leven in *survivre* tot de organische overdrijvingen die we aantreffen in een van Roosens vroegere werken: de pantoffels die ze liet maken voor de Rotterdamse reus. Dit werk is gebaseerd op een echte reus die in Rotterdam woonde en in de jaren 1950 overleed; toen Roosen diens schoenen had gezien in een museum, liet ze pantoffels op maat maken in een Duitse werkplaats die gespecialiseerd is in het maken van schoenen voor grote mensen over de hele wereld. De overwinnaars en de reuzen van Roosen – opgevat als een overdaad aan leven (bovenmatige prestatie en bovenmatige groei) – zijn manifestaties van een evolutie in één lichaam, als symbool van veranderingen in de collectieve ruimte. Reuzen behoren natuurlijk ook tot het eerste mensenras: ze worden al in het Oude Testament genoemd, en vereenzelvigd met extreme topografische en meteorologische verschijnselen als rotskusten en zware stormen, voor ze werden getemd als mythologische beschermheren van steden en staten.[4] Zie bijvoorbeeld de rol van Gargantua voor Mont-Saint-Michel, of die van Gog en Magog voor Londen. Roosens reuzenpantoffels – bij het bed aangetrokken en binnenshuis gedragen – verbeelden de domesticatie van de reus, zijn vlucht van het open natuurlijke landschap naar de beschutting van het gecultiveerde huis; en zijn transformatie van folklore naar verhaaltje-voor-het-slapen-gaan. Nadat de natuur geschikt is gemaakt voor een burgerbestaan, is de reus met pensioen gegaan en zie je hem alleen nog af en toe in een optocht of op een kermis. Zijn enorme omvang is niet afschrikwekkend meer, maar gewoon iets aangeborens, even onvoorzien en bizar als de enorme aardappel van Flevoland. Roosens overwinnaars – *survivors*, helden – nemen het over van de reus: we trekken ons terug uit de natuur. Hun daden van overleving komen niet voort uit de natuur, maar uit persoonlijke keuze en toewijding (ook de man met de langste baard heeft ooit het besluit genomen deze niet af te knippen); zij vormen geen rotskusten, veroorzaken geen noodweer, maar vormen wel ons medialandschap. Door onszelf de maat te nemen tegenover hun spectaculaire verrichtingen begrijpen we de grenzen, maar niet het kader, van de openbare wereld waarin we leven, zij het op kleinere schaal.

In deze historische verschuiving van reuzen naar helden is Roosens recente project een poging om ruimte te creëren voor het individu. Van oude kranten maakte ze grote papier-maché ballen en vervolgens gaf ze deze holle witte vormen aan haar vrienden met de uitdrukkelijke opdracht ze naar wens te versieren en ze over hun hoofd te zetten. Deze 'bollen' zijn tegelijk neutraal en geïndividualiseerd, het resultaat van gespecialiseerd en intiem handwerk – gecollectiviseerde arbeid die niet uit de handen van de kunstenaar komt maar voortvloeit uit haar wensen die door anderen worden uitgevoerd. Eerder hoofdtooi dan masker, verbergen deze bollen niet zozeer de individuen, maar wordt hun persoonlijkheid erdoor uitvergroot, net als hun omvang en lengte. Hoewel ze doen denken aan tekstballonnen van stripfiguren, of zelfs aan stripfiguren zelf, roepen ze ook het beeld op van kostuums bij een carnavalsoptocht. Roosen laat haar vrienden hun hoofd zelfs zo versieren dat de fijnere aspecten van hun persoonlijkheid – die je normaal gesproken alleen van dichtbij ervaart in de context van persoonlijke ontmoetingen – al van verre kunt zien. Aan deze overdrijving voegt Roosen ook nog eens mobiliteit toe, hetgeen past in onze tijd van voortdurend onderweg zijn. Toen de papieren hoofden eenmaal op persoonlijke wijze versierd waren, nam Roosen ze ook mee naar openingen van haar tentoonstellingen in galeries en musea buiten Arnhem. Aangezien haar vrienden natuurlijk niet altijd mee konden, vroeg ze andere aanwezigen om de bolhoofden tijdens zo'n opening op te zetten. Door deze overgang van de hoofden van haar vrienden naar de hoofden van nieuwe kennissen in andere steden worden de bollen draagbare dubbelgangers, levende aandenkens aan persoonlijke relaties. Hoewel hun oorsprong in het domein van het persoonlijke ligt, zijn de hoofden bestemd voor een grotere publieke ruimte. In tegenstelling tot haar gouden miniatuurhuis, dat het leed van de scheiding verzacht omdat het de afstand lijkt te verkleinen, maken Roosens bovenmaatse hoofden op een andere manier gebruik van schaal: ze doen de onbekende gasten kleiner lijken, waardoor ook hun overweldigende anonimiteit verschrompelt. Als de reuzen in een optocht of de uitvergrote gezichten van de overwinnaars in de krant, zweven deze versierde hoofden hoog boven de menigte. Het zijn bewegende bakens, die niet reizigers waarschuwen voor een rotsachtige kust, maar een zee van onbekende gezichten veranderen in een vertrouwde kring. Hier volgt Roosens gevoel voor schaal haar wens om heel dichtbij te halen wat zo ontzettend ver weg is.

1. Marie-Françoise Christout, 'Le merveilleux, catégorie esthétique', *Le merveilleux et le 'théâtre du silence' en France à partir du XVIIe siècle*, Parijs: Editions Mouton, 1965, hfdst. 21.
Hoewel ze de kenmerken van het wonderbaarlijke definieert, richt Christout zich voornamelijk op ballet.

2. Susan Stewart, *On Longing. Narratives of the Miniature, the Gigantic, the Souvenir, the Collection*, Durham/Londen: Duke University Press, 1993, xii.

3. Zie Anna Makolkin, *Name, Hero, Icon. Semiotics of Nationalism through Heroic Biography*, Berlijn/New York, Mouton de Gruyter, 1992.

4. Zie Walter Stevens, *Giants in Those Days. Folklore, Ancient History, and Nationalism*, Lincoln/London, University of Nebraska Press, 1989.

Maria's Hans den Hartog Jager

Il fait froid en ce matin du début du mois de mars. La veille, la neige est tombée en abondance sur les Pays-Bas. On n'avait pas vu une telle couche depuis vingt ans. Les bois qui entourent Arnhem se sont transformés en un véritable palais de glace. L'épaisse couche de neige renvoie tant de lumière que l'atelier de Maria Roosen baigne dans une merveilleuse clarté quasi divine. Maria pose les bras sur la table et se penche en avant. « Dans une petite maison située au fin fond de la forêt vivait autrefois un vieux cueilleur de mûres », commence-t-elle. « De toute sa vie, il n'a jamais vu aucun être humain. Et puis un jour, un homme égaré dans la forêt frappe à sa porte. Le cueilleur de mûres est tout étonné : 'Mais, tu es pareil à moi !' L'homme se met à rire et lui demande : 'C'est ici que tu habites ?' 'Oui', répond le cueilleur de mûres, 'c'est tellement beau ici ! J'ai des champs pleins de perles, des salles pleines de miroirs et de très hauts bâtiments garnis de piliers.' L'homme rentre vite dans son village et raconte autour de lui : 'Je viens de rencontrer quelqu'un de très riche, il possède d'immenses trésors, mais il ne le sait pas.' Tous les habitants du village se hâtent vers la forêt, mais très vite ils réalisent que les perles étaient des gouttes de rosée, les miroirs des étangs et les piliers des arbres. Ils en veulent tellement au cueilleur de mûres qu'ils le tuent. » Maria se penche en arrière, songeuse.

C'est un conte traditionnel ?
C'est l'écrivain néerlandais Godfried Bomans qui raconte cette histoire. Mais dans quel livre...

Est-ce une parabole de ton propre travail ?
Disons que je regrette qu'il y ait si peu de place dans le monde pour l'imagination. Il faut tout prendre au pied de la lettre, un et un font deux, point final. On le voit dans la société, dans la politique et dans l'art, la reconstitution a fait aussi son entrée... On ne laisse nulle part les gens s'égarer à leur guise, ils n'ont aucun endroit où se réfugier.

A l'instant où je vais lui demander si son œuvre se veut un refuge, le téléphone se met à sonner. Maria fait un geste signifiant « tu vois ce que je veux dire » et sort. Elle attend un transport qui ne peut attendre. C'est alors que je m'aperçois que l'atelier est rempli d'œuvres de Maria Roosen, non pas en chantier, mais achevées. Sur une armoire d'archives, six pigeons en verre se pavanent. Un maître verrier vénitien vient de les souffler à la demande de Maria Roosen. Des « blurbs » en verre rose sont posés sur le sol. Un grand pot à lait, rose saumon, une carotte en verre à l'intérieur. Des aquarelles emballées. Sur le sol est disposée également une partie des photos qu'elle découpe dans les journaux depuis 1985 : des dizaines de clichés de « vainqueurs », autrement dit des hommes et des femmes qui expriment leur joie devant l'objectif – décontractés, heureux, euphoriques. Il y a là de nombreux sportifs (des footballeurs, des patineurs, la championne d'équitation Anky van Grunsven), des acteurs lauréats d'un Oscar, des hommes politiques comme Gorbatchev et Clinton, mais aussi Henri VIII peint par Hans Holbein ou encore un Christ en croix de Matthias Grünewald. Brusquement, je réalise que l'atelier de Maria Roosen est davantage un entrepôt qu'un lieu de travail, davantage une salle d'exposition qu'un atelier.

Lorsqu'elle revient, Maria se dirige directement vers la table où sont posées des reproductions de son travail. Elle saisit une photo représentant une mère et un

120-121

70-71

153

8   enfant dans un potager. Le jardin semble tout à fait normal, on aperçoit la ferme à l'arrière-plan et, du coup, les carottes plantées dans le sol ressortent davantage – leurs têtes brillent comme si elles avaient été touchées par une fée. « Pour moi, c'est ça l'imagination », commente Maria Roosen. « Il y a quelques années, on m'a contactée pour un projet dans une ferme. Dans mon atelier, j'avais à ce moment-là des centaines de carottes en verre, d'une couleur orange vif, qui avaient servi pour une pièce de théâtre. Je me suis dit que j'allais les planter dans un potager, que ça rendrait bien. Or cette ferme n'avait pas de potager. Ils en ont alors créé un, sans problème. Ils ont très bien fait ça, c'était superbe, avec des salades, des poireaux et une clôture contre les lapins – et j'ai planté ces carottes au beau milieu de tout cela. » Elle rit. « Ça a très bien marché. Beaucoup de carottes ont disparu – chapardées. C'est ce qui se passe. Si on installe quelque chose de beau, si on excite l'imagination des spectateurs, même les carottes en verre se transforment en or. »

Ce faisant, nous revoilà au cœur du travail de Maria Roosen. Car depuis plus de quinze ans, ce qui constitue son image de marque, c'est bien cette façon de titiller l'imaginaire, parfois en douceur, parfois à rebrousse-poil. Sans toutefois que l'on puisse lui imputer un style ou une forme fixes. Maria Roosen est – selon ses propres termes – une artiste « qui cherche », et elle trouve toujours le matériau et la forme spécifiques correspondant à chacune de ses idées. Une série de pots en verre rose, sensuels et robustes, l'ont fait connaître au début des années 90. Il y eut ensuite des seins en verre et des gourdins en verre, mais au milieu de tout cela, des projets « libres » se mettaient en place comme à l'évidence : une paire de pantoufles énormes pour « le géant de Rotterdam » et une église miniature en bois accrochée à la tour de l'église St.-Eusèbe d'Arnhem lors

de l'exposition Sonsbeek 9. Maria a également doté le château d'eau de Blankenberge en Belgique d'une « perruque » faite de cordages orangés et récemment elle a imaginé deux énormes tournesols qu'elle a fait tricoter, pour les draper en longues traînes à travers sa galerie.

Actuellement, Maria Roosen travaille sur un grand projet du même genre – même s'il se remarque à peine parmi toutes les œuvres présentes dans l'atelier. On lui a demandé de réaliser une œuvre pour le phare d'Yokohama, à l'occasion de la Triennale de cette ville. Il y a donc une petite maquette de ce phare dans un coin de l'atelier. Pour l'instant, Maria a entouré le sommet de la tour de fils rose vif. Elle soulève la maquette, la soupèse et tire ici et là sur les ficelles. « C'est loin d'être terminé, le résultat définitif sera peut-être complètement différent. »

Est-ce que tu as une idée de ce qui les a amenés jusqu'à toi depuis Yokohama ?
Oh, sans doute parce que j'ai déjà travaillé sur plusieurs grands bâtiments : l'église St.-Eusèbe à Arnhem, le phare de Blankenberge. Les organisateurs ont vite fait de penser : « Maria Roosen, c'est quelqu'un qui fait des choses avec des tours ». C'est pour cette raison que j'essaie de ne pas accepter trop vite ce genre de commandes. Je vois d'abord si ça me parle et si je pense pouvoir faire quelque chose à partir de là. Si c'est bon, je veux bien essayer.

Qu'est-ce qui t'a séduite dans cette demande d'Yokohama?
D'abord le fait que le commissaire de l'exposition Tadashi Kawamata est lui-même un artiste. Ça se remarque tout de suite : il considère les choses du point de vue du contenu et non pas en s'inquiétant du nombre des visiteurs. Il m'a montré quelques photos qui m'ont donné envie d'aller voir par moi-même. En fait, il s'agit d'une tour très élevée de plus de cent mètres, située dans un vieux quartier. Vraiment une veuve triste, mais aussi un symbole

154

phallique typique. Je me suis donc demandée tout de suite comment féminiser un petit peu tout ça.

Est-ce à cela que tu penses en premier, au rapport entre le masculin et le féminin ?

Disons que c'est un ingrédient.

A quoi penses-tu par ailleurs ?

Au départ, j'avais l'idée de poser tout simplement un autre bâtiment sur la tour. On voit beaucoup ça actuellement. Pour recouvrir les échafaudages, on imprime sur une toile une photo du bâtiment caché endessous – on peut aussi évidemment accrocher quelque chose de complètement différent. Je me suis dit que cela faisait quand même trop publicité. Et je voulais aussi utiliser la vue autour...» Elle contemple la maquette. «Je ne sais pas encore. Pour l'instant, cela me plaît d'affubler cet énorme pieu de ficelles roses, cela a quelque chose de joyeux et d'émoustillant. Mais ce n'est pas encore suffisant.»

Lorsque tu hésites, comme maintenant, est-ce que tu demandes l'aide des autres ?

Non, ça va... (elle rit). Tout au plus, à mon compagnon, car il construit très bien les maquettes. Mais, pour le reste, à ce stade du travail, je dois vraiment me débrouiller toute seule.

Il n'empêche qu'à un certain moment, l'aide des autres va s'imposer, ne serait-ce que parce que la collaboration fait désormais partie intégrante de la méthode de travail de Maria Roosen. Le processus est toujours le même : Maria Roosen conçoit une idée, la développe et fait les plans, mais elle n'enroule pas de cordes, ne souffle pas de verre, ne construit pas d'église et ne tricote pas de fleurs. Elle est tout au plus présente lors de l'exécution, en tant qu'accompagnatrice et en tant qu'«inspiratrice». Ce choix semble tellement lumineux qu'on s'étonne que Maria Roosen n'ait trouvé cette «méthode» qu'assez tardivement. Lorsque l'artiste a exposé les premiers pots en verre qui l'ont rendue célèbre, elle avait déjà 34 ans.

Est-ce que toi aussi tu estimes n'avoir trouvé ta forme qu'assez tardivement ?

Maria Roosen hésite.

Oui, c'est peut-être vrai. Pourtant, cela n'est pas venu comme ça, il y a eu une histoire avant, mais en parler maintenant je ne sais pas. Bon, j'ai suivi une formation de prof de dessin et ensuite j'ai fait l'académie des Beaux-Arts. A cette époque, je me cherchais encore beaucoup. Et puis, l'homme que j'aimais est mort. J'avais 27 ans. Cet événement a créé un vide énorme dans ma vie. Je me suis retrouvée complètement bloquée. J'ai sombré dans un deuil dont je n'arrivais pas à sortir, même avec une thérapie. Sur les conseils de mon haptonome, j'ai alors commencé à faire des aquarelles. Je m'asseyais à ma table avec papier et aquarelle, et j'essayais de consigner mes sentiments. C'était du genre «aujourd'hui, je me sens bleue», et je dessinais alors une bulle bleue.

Maria Roosen pouffe de rire.

C'était très, très sérieux.

Est-ce que cela avait encore quelque chose à voir avec ton métier d'artiste ?

Eh bien... j'ai commencé très vite à m'imposer des «contraintes» : à chaque fois je devais réaliser cinq dessins. Cinq exactement. En général, dans le premier, je représentais mon humeur de manière très littérale. Dans le second, j'essayais de donner plus de marge à l'aspect esthétique et d'arriver à l'essentiel de ce que je ressentais, etc. En travaillant de cette façon-là, au quatrième, j'avais souvent terminé, les émotions étaient exprimées. Mais je devais encore en faire un cinquième. Alors, je me mettais à faire un peu n'importe quoi, à vider mon pinceau, disons. Et bizarrement, c'était dans ce dessin que l'expression était la plus juste. Apparemment, je n'arrivais à la forme qu'une fois débarrassée de mes premières émotions. Cette connaissance m'a beaucoup aidée pour arriver à l'essentiel. A la sincérité.

Sur le papier il se passait des choses que je n'aurais jamais pu imaginer moi-même. C'était ça le plus étonnant. J'avais eu une formation d'artiste et donc, on est très au fait des questions de composition, de forme, de structure. Cela n'a pas grand chose à voir avec l'expression des sentiments. Or, en laissant tomber cette façon de faire, en travaillant de manière plus intuitive, je n'étais plus complètement obsédée par la composition. Ça a très bien marché.

Tu as vite compris que cette manière de dessiner pouvait aussi être bonne pour ton travail ?
Et ce n'est pas tout. J'ai très vite compris que je pouvais résoudre dans l'atelier des problèmes que je n'arrivais pas toujours à surmonter dans la vie. J'osais aller plus loin à chaque fois.

Comment t'y prenais-tu ? Comment va-t-on « plus loin » dans une aquarelle ?
De multiples façons. Au début, j'utilisais simplement un carnet de croquis, mais pour certains dessins je me disais parfois qu'il serait bon de les reprendre en grand format ou en utilisant un autre matériau. Il m'est arrivé de prendre une cuvette remplie de peinture et d'en verser le contenu sur une feuille de plusieurs mètres carrés. C'était très libérateur.

Peu de temps après, tu as commencé à faire des objets en verre. Comment en es-tu arrivée là ?
C'était un peu dans le prolongement de ma recherche sur la transgression des limites. Je faisais des aquarelles de plus en plus grandes et je commençais à m'interroger sur la façon de capter la fluidité de l'aquarelle dans d'autres matériaux. A l'académie, il m'était arrivé de travailler sur le verre, et je trouvais toujours cela très beau. Je me suis alors inscrite à un cours sur le soufflage du verre. On allait visiter en groupe une fabrique de soufflage, on assistait à la fabrication du verre et, à la fin, on pouvait se faire souffler un objet de son choix. La plupart des gens demandaient alors des objets complètement extravagants, très colorés. Je me suis rendue compte que ce que moi je préférais, c'était au contraire une simple boule transparente.

Pourquoi une boule transparente ?
C'est la forme parfaite, n'est-ce pas ? Lorsqu'on regarde dans une boule transparente, on voit le monde à l'envers et, en même temps, c'est un symbole tellement magnifique. Une fois, à Venise, j'ai vu un saint Christophe portant une boule en verre. Il y en a aussi une très belle sur un tableau du Tintoret – à l'époque, la boule transparente était de toute façon le symbole de l'univers. Bon, le plus drôle était que je trouvais donc ces boules magnifiques, alors que les souffleurs de verre trouvaient ça complètement inintéressant. Pour eux, la boule est une forme de base. Lorsqu'ils commencent à travailler, ils soufflent d'abord une boule et c'est à partir de là qu'ils créent des objets. Je leur ai demandé alors de souffler une série de boules et j'en ai fait une installation en les posant comme des bulles au bord d'un espace.

N'as-tu pas eu envie à ce moment-là d'apprendre toi-même à souffler le verre ?
Non, pas du tout. C'est-à-dire, j'ai bien essayé, j'ai travaillé dans un atelier de verre. J'ouvrais les portes, je passais les choses Mais pour bien apprendre, vraiment bien, cela prend des années. Ce n'était pas du tout mon objectif. Pour moi, cette façon de procéder marche aussi bien, et peut-être même mieux. Je dirige le processus, j'indique la direction à suivre.

Tout de même, ne crois-tu pas qu'en procédant ainsi, il manque à ton travail une certaine « écriture personnelle » ? Qu'une distance se crée ? Ou, en disant les choses autrement : à cette époque, en plus des aquarelles, tu faisais aussi des œuvres que tu réalisais toi-même ?
Oui, aussi. Après la mort de l'homme que

9

j'aimais, j'ai fait pendant un certain temps des œuvres «qui exigeaient un travail intensif», comme on dit. La première chose que j'ai réalisée après sa mort, c'est un collier en bois composé de grosses boules. J'ai taillé pendant des mois entiers, uniquement pour arriver à obtenir des boules rondes – j'ai remarqué que créer des objets ronds est très réconfortant. Lorsqu'on met son chagrin en boule, on peut ensuite continuer à vivre, il se met à rouler avec soi. Et en taillant allégrement le bois de ces boules, je me débarrassais aussi de mon agressivité. Plus tard, j'ai fait encore une boule de mûrier, une grosse balle formée de branches de mûrier enroulées. C'était drôlement beau. J'avais acheté des gants spéciaux et je savais exactement où poussaient les bonnes ronces. Je partais en voiture chercher les branches que j'entassais dans le coffre de ma camionnette. Lorsque j'arrivais chez moi, la portière s'ouvrait d'un bond tant la pression était forte, comme un monstre qui surgit de sa boîte. J'étais drôlement fière de ces boules, j'étais vraiment le super-fabricant-de-boule-de-mûrier !

Ça, tu aimais bien le faire toi-même.

Oui, je n'aurais jamais pu confier cela à quelqu'un d'autre. D'abord, parce qu'il faut trouver soi-même la façon de le réaliser. Ce processus avait aussi un côté chemin de croix. A la fin de la journée, j'étais à chaque fois couverte d'égratignures. A l'époque, ça marchait, sans doute aussi parce que j'étais peut-être encore plus en recherche. Mais c'était beau aussi, vraiment. Un jour, j'étais dans les bois à chercher des branches. Je tombe sur un homme qui me fait voir toutes sortes de galeries percées dans les buissons. En fait, c'était lui qui creusait ces tunnels et ces galeries. C'était son projet. La boule que j'ai faite, je l'ai d'ailleurs brûlée par la suite, des années plus tard, au cours d'un rituel. C'était un vrai spectacle, cette boule par terre et les flammes qui s'élevaient à six mètres de hauteur au moins. On aurait dit qu'un météore venait d'atterrir.

Mais pour le verre, tu n'éprouvais plus ce besoin de fabriquer toi-même.

Non. En fait c'est à partir de ce moment-là que j'ai commencé à confier l'exécution à d'autres. Peut-être que cela correspondait aussi à une sorte de détachement. Au départ, c'est venu de mon manque de maîtrise de la technique, mais très vite j'ai compris que le fait de travailler ensemble, de me reposer en partie sur d'autres personnes, m'apporte énormément.

Ne trouves-tu pas difficile de ne pas tout contrôler ?

Non, parce que cela m'apporte beaucoup.

Et considérer le résultat comme ton travail ne te pose pas problème ?

Pas du tout, car l'idée de départ est toujours la mienne. C'est moi qui détermine le point de départ et l'élaboration.

Tout de même, lorsque nous parlions de la tour il y a quelques instants, tu disais que pour toi le « faire » est une sorte de processus qui te permet d'essayer à chaque fois de nouvelles idées. Jusqu'à quel point le fait de travailler ensemble facilite la prise de décision ou au contraire rend cette décision plus difficile ?

Maria Roosen hésite.

Cela aide parfois, mais ce n'est pas ce qui importe. Chez moi, au départ, il y a toujours une idée, mais ce n'est pas une idée concrète. Il s'agit alors de sentir, d'associer, d'établir des liens... Une bonne sculpture, une bonne œuvre doit amener une sorte de transmutation, un peu à la façon dont les aliments sont digérés. Il faut toujours qu'il y ait cela, car si c'est trop direct, trop «un et un font deux», cela ne m'intéresse pas. Cette transmutation a lieu parce que je combine différents processus. L'union de mes propres idées et de celles des autres amène une sorte de réaction chimique que l'on ne contrôle pas complètement. De là surgit finalement quelque chose d'unique que je ne pouvais pas non plus prévoir moi-même et que je suis curieuse de découvrir moi aussi, qui m'apporte quelque chose en retour.

Et le verre convient tout spécialement ?
Il possède en tout cas une belle dualité. Le verre est un matériau solidifié qui reste pourtant tout près de l'élément liquide. Il est très fragile, vulnérable. En même temps, un objet en verre peut se conserver des milliers d'années. Aujourd'hui, on trouve encore du verre datant de l'époque romaine. C'est pour cette raison que je qualifie aussi le verre d'énergie solidifiée : il peut exister pendant des siècles, mais il peut aussi disparaître d'un coup, crac. Je me rappelle la première fois que j'ai cassé un de mes pots. L'un d'entre eux a heurté un autre et crac, crac, il y a eu cinq de cassé – c'était affreux. J'ai appris du même coup que le verre rose est très fragile. Entre les couleurs, les différences sont grandes.

Est-ce que tu te sers de ce savoir ? Les différentes couleurs de verre ont-elles une autre signification pour toi parce que tu sais cela ?
Oui, j'en tiens compte. Dans cette œuvre par exemple, (elle prend une photo de son œuvre *Étagères de bulles* où 140 « bulles-éprouvettes » en verre de différentes couleurs sont accrochées à des planches), le caractère spécifique du verre détermine en grand partie la forme des bulles. On dirait des graines ou des spermatozoïdes, mais comme le verre rouge est très dur, la « bulle » est restée très petite. Le verre couleur tabac au contraire, à la moindre poussée, hop ! il démarre. C'est donc le plus long. Et le rose est cassé. Je veux aussi montrer ça, c'est pourquoi je l'ai recollé avec du papier adhésif et je l'ai accroché.

De cette façon-là, ils deviennent presque des personnages.
La première fois que je suis allée chez le souffleur de verre, je me rappelle, j'ai dit que je ne travaillerais jamais avec les couleurs. Mais dès qu'on en sait davantage, que cela acquiert une certaine significa-

tion... C'est comme ça que je fonctionne, n'est-ce pas. J'ai d'abord été fascinée par ce rose, et j'ai alors décidé de faire des pots. Je ne conçois pas ce genre de choses à l'avance, elles découlent de la couleur.

Lorsque tu parles de collaboration, jusqu'à quel point délimites-tu ce qui est à toi et quelle marge laisses-tu à l'autre ?
Aujourd'hui encore, je commence la plupart du temps par une aquarelle. Je dessine par exemple un pot pourvu d'un bec immense. J'emporte ce dessin chez Bernard Heesen, le souffleur de verre. Pour lui, l'aquarelle est le point de départ. Il commence à souffler le verre, mais je reste à côté de lui, pour regarder, pour réfléchir avec lui, diriger. Dans ce processus, les choses ont d'ailleurs beaucoup changé. Autrefois, je m'impliquais énormément, je criais et je me démenais terriblement. Maintenant, j'ai appris à garder une certaine distance, à discuter à l'avance et, pendant le travail, à me borner à quelques remarques au plus.

Cela se passe-t-il toujours de cette façon-là ?
Je reste assez imprévisible. Tout à l'heure, j'ai dit que je n'aimais pas les images trop littérales, mais parfois, il me prend quand même l'envie d'en faire brusquement. Ainsi, il n'y a pas longtemps, j'ai eu envie d'une bite, de seins et d'un cul en verre pour les accrocher ensemble dans un filet, comme une sorte d'orgie en verre. Je n'avais pas fait d'aquarelles de ces bites, je suis allée simplement chez le souffleur de verre et je lui ai dit : « aujourd'hui, on fait des bites ». Alors on a beaucoup ri bien sûr, surtout quand je leur ai dit qu'ils pouvaient les faire à leur goût. J'aime bien l'atmosphère qui se met en place à ce moment-là. Une sorte de complicité. Et les bites sont superbes !

Finalement, tu ne les as pas accrochées dans un filet, mais très méchamment à une corde de foin orange, raide et tranchante.
Maria Roosen rit.
Le filet, cela ne fonctionnait pas. On m'a

apporté ces bites ici dans mon atelier, je les ai mises dans le filet, mais c'était vraiment rien du tout. Dans ce genre de situation, je me mets comme d'habitude à essayer d'autres trucs. Ici, à un certain moment, je me suis dit : j'accroche une des bites pour voir. Je l'ai d'abord accrochée en hauteur, puis j'ai pensé : « non, il faut la mettre à hauteur d'entrejambe ». C'était déjà mieux. Ensuite, j'ai ajouté cette corde de foin et cela faisait bel effet, mais je n'étais pas sûre que c'était bien. J'en ai discuté avec d'autres personnes pour voir si des câbles en métal ne seraient pas préférables, mais non, c'est cela qui marchait le mieux.

Pourtant, lorsque tu décris ainsi ta façon de procéder, je me demande jusqu'à quel point ton travail actuel a encore à voir avec cette canalisation des émotions de l'époque de tes aquarelles « thérapeutiques ».

Toutes ces œuvres sont issues de ma propre expérience. Mais j'ai commencé à prendre conscience de ce qui m'intéressait, à comprendre comment je trouvais la forme adéquate. Et surtout... (elle hésite) aujourd'hui j'accepte mieux des choses que je ne peux pas concevoir moi-même.

En ce sens, tu t'es surpassée ?

Roosen rit.

Je n'utiliserais pas ce terme-là.

Je formule ma question différemment : si tu réunissais dans un grand espace la totalité de ton œuvre, tous ces objets et les vases et les fleurs, aurait-on un juste reflet de ta personne, de ton être ? Ou serait-ce au contraire quelque chose de moindre ?

Elle réfléchit.

J'ai pensé intituler le livre qui nous occupe maintenant : *Maria's*.

Ah bon ?

Dans le Brabant, les gens ont l'habitude de dire : « Celui-ci est de Maria's » – on utilise donc le pluriel. Et Marie est quand même « la femme entre toutes les femmes ».

En ce sens, est-ce qu'on peut dire que ton œuvre est un reflet de ta personnalité ?

Pourtant, j'ai l'impression qu'il y a des manques.

Le travail est moindre ?

Oui quand même.

Est-ce parce que dans ton esprit l'œuvre est toujours mieux que dans la réalité ?

Oui, certainement. Mais aussi parce que je trouve toujours difficile de voir un grand nombre de mes œuvres réunies dans un même lieu. D'une façon ou d'une autre, je considère que, dans les expositions de groupe, mon travail est davantage mis en valeur. Peut-être à nouveau parce que j'aime bien me mettre en rapport avec les autres ou un truc comme ça...

Serait-ce aussi qu'en voyant tes œuvres réunies, tu reconnais trop les mêmes motifs ?

Oui.

Quels sont ces motifs ?

La répétition par exemple. Prenons les carottes dont on parlait tout à l'heure, cette installation qui consiste en des centaines de carottes en verre... Autrefois, j'aurais considéré cela comme un signe de faiblesse. Je l'ai quand même réalisée, mais surtout en me donnant à moi-même le prétexte de vouloir étudier les différents aspects d'une forme ou d'un thème. Avec ces carottes, j'ai vu que la répétition renforce aussi les parties séparées. C'était nouveau pour moi. Toutes ces carottes réunies dégagent une énorme impression de croissance, de force végétative. Et je trouve ça beau. La force végétative, c'est quand même la plus grande force qui existe.

Y a-t-il d'autres motifs dans ton travail ?

Oh oui ! Les grand gestes par exemple, ces épreuves de force. La petite église en bois à l'extérieur de l'église St.-Eusèbe ou les quatre cent boules en verre accrochées au plafond de l'hôpital Antoni van Leeuwenhoek. Ces expressions datent en fait des dernières années. Pour y arriver, il m'a fallu vraiment surmonter certaines choses. Mais pour mon travail, le résultat a été positif, cela m'a permis d'aller plus loin, mon horizon s'est élargi. Et puis, j'en avais un peu marre, toutes ces chaussures et tous ces pots. Ça donnait de l'air.

*Une question peut-être un peu bizarre, mais
on parlait du fait de confier l'exécution de
certaines choses à d'autres ou de concevoir
soi-même les choses : y a-t-il quelque chose
en quoi tu es vraiment bonne ? Une aptitude
qui à ton avis est vraiment la tienne ?*

Maria Roosen se tait.

Pff, c'est... c'est difficile de porter un tel
jugement sur soi-même. En tout cas, j'estime que je sais bien regarder.

C'est tout ?

Je suis aussi quelqu'un qui accepte facilement ce qui se présente, ce que les autres
proposent... Bien entendu tu vas me demander où je reste, moi ?

*Est-ce un trait de caractère typiquement
féminin ? Je pose ma question autrement :
ton travail, surtout autrefois, a souvent été
associé à la féminité. Des seins, des objets
fragiles, le verre rose. Est-ce que tu
recherches cela ?*

Oui, mais je joue aussi avec. Je n'aime pas
du tout que mon travail soit considéré
comme une sorte de plaidoyer en faveur de
la féminité. C'est trop facile, c'est une lapalissade. Je veux au contraire questionner
les clichés sur la féminité, provoquer un
peu ces clichés, par exemple en traitant les
choses de manière très féminine, ou au
contraire très « à l'eau de rose » ou très
rude.

*Est-ce que tu penses que les spectateurs
voient toujours l'idée qui est derrière ?*

Non, pas toujours bien sûr. Mais cela ne
fait rien.

*Je formule ma question différemment : est-ce
important pour toi de savoir quel effet ton
travail peut avoir sur le spectateur ?*

Jan Hoet m'a dit une fois : « Le sujet de ton
travail, c'est le don. » J'ai trouvé ça très
beau, même si je n'aurais jamais osé le dire
moi-même. Peut-être aussi parce qu'au
moment où je commençais à être connue,
quelqu'un a écrit que, dans mon travail,
j'accomplissais une sorte de tâche maternelle. Soigner, se donner, se dévouer.

A l'époque, je trouvais ça horrible.

Pourquoi ?

Sans doute parce qu'à ce moment-là, je
venais d'être propulsée sur les devants de
la scène. Je commençais à être connue, je
participais à la Biennale de Venise et je
voulais être une professionnelle. A ce
moment-là, on n'a vraiment pas envie de
se retrouver cataloguée « mère entre
toutes les mères ». Aujourd'hui, cela ne me
gêne plus. On peut tourner les choses dans
tous les sens, il n'en reste pas moins que
c'est ma force. Je sais faire surgir des
choses, les faire grandir, les faire s'épanouir. D'autant plus maintenant que j'ai
moi-même une fille, je me rends compte
qu'il n'y a pas de mal à ça.

*Est-ce la raison pour laquelle tu exposes
de plus en plus souvent ces photos de
« vainqueurs » ?*

Non, l'histoire des photos de « vainqueurs » a commencé autrement. J'avais
vu une exposition consacrée à des collections d'artistes. A l'époque, il m'arrivait
déjà de découper des photos, mais pour
moi, cela n'avait rien à voir avec une collection. Dans l'exposition dont je parle,
toutes les collections - des chaussures, des
édifices miniatures - étaient présentées de
telle sorte qu'elles devenaient de véritables
sculptures. J'ai trouvé ça tellement beau
que j'ai pensé constituer aussi une collection avec mes photos de « vainqueurs ».

*Ces photos sont de toutes sortes. Beaucoup
de « vainqueurs » classiques, mais aussi
des hommes politiques et un cuisinier
néerlandais comme Jonnie Boer. Ou encore
l'astronaute Wubbo Ockels ou le David
de Michel-Ange.*

Oui, enfin, mon premier critère, c'est
quand même que la photo est bonne. Que
ce soit, disons, une bonne image. Elles doivent aussi m'évoquer quelque chose. Elles
rejoignent donc mes préoccupations du
moment, mes fascinations. En ce sens,
c'est presque un journal intime. Depuis
que l'on sait que j'ai cette collection, on

m'envoie des photos de « vainqueurs »,
mais en fait ça ne marche jamais. Ces pho-
tos-là ne sont pas assez proches de moi.

Mais pourquoi des « vainqueurs » ? Est-ce à
cause du sentiment d'autonomie ? de cette
façon de se placer au-dessus des autres ? de
leur indépendance ? du sentiment d'être libre ?
Pour moi, ce que je vois surtout, c'est que
pour toutes ces personnes, le temps a l'air
de s'arrêter. En cet instant terriblement
important, elles sont le centre de tout, il
n'y a rien d'autre – et le temps s'arrête.
Je trouve ça beau, aussi parce que ça me
rappelle pourquoi on fait tout cela. J'ai la
même chose dans mon travail. C'est parfois très pénible, je n'ai pas envie, je doute
beaucoup, mais lorsque ça marche, les dif-
ficultés sont à nouveau oubliées. On reçoit
alors en retour ces moments de victoire
qui abolissent le temps. Comme lors des
grands événements de la vie, telle que la
naissance et la mort.

Plus je regarde les photos et plus j'y vois des
liens avec ton propre travail. Les tournesols
de Van Gogh. Le portrait des Arnolfini de
Van Eyck avec la célèbre « boule en verre »...

C'est pour cela que le Christ de Grünewald
est là aussi. D'abord, bien entendu, parce
que c'est un chef-d'œuvre, mais j'aime
aussi énormément cette phrase du sculp-
teur Brancusi qui dit « qu'une bonne
sculpture doit pouvoir guérir ». Par la
suite, j'ai lu quelque part que, dans les
environs de Colmar, on installe parfois des
malades psychiatriques devant le tableau
de Grünewald parce que ça les apaise. Je le
conçois très bien. Ce tableau est tellement
détaillé ! Si on a l'esprit un peu confus, on
peut y voir des tas de choses, cela peut
apporter énormément.

Des propos bien altruistes ! – maternels,
si je peux me permettre.
Tu m'as demandé tout à l'heure en quoi je
suis vraiment bonne, quelle était mon
aptitude spécifique. Je crois que j'ai maintenant la réponse : je fais pousser des
choses. Je sème une graine et ensuite je
fais appel à d'autres pour cultiver la plan-
te. Je dirige le processus, je l'accompagne –
en fait je suis « l'artiste aux mains vertes ».
C'est beau, non ?

Elle existe en toutes tailles

Jennifer Allen

Maria Roosen fait parfois les choses en grand. TRÈS grand. Ou petit. Tout petit. Comme ces pots à lait en verre : ils sont assez grands pour qu'on les entoure des deux bras et assez petits pour tenir dans le creux de la main. Une fois que la chaude haleine du souffleur de verre leur a donné forme, ils sont remplis de lait froid, dix litres ou dix gouttes. Les miroirs sphériques que Maria Roosen a éparpillés dans le jardin du Musée Boijmans Van Beuningen, reflètent leurs alentours avec la compacité d'un point à la fin d'une phrase qui résume tout le paysage depuis les brins d'herbe jusqu'aux nuages. Des tournesols séchés, tricotés avec de la laine blanche et marron, se métamorphosent en versions démesurées de leur forme originelle. Il y a aussi les nombreux phallus en verre, enflés jusqu'à en devenir surdimensionnés et exciter l'envie de personnes des deux sexes. Les seins, plantureux pendants en verre étamé de couleur, sont bordés dans des lits ou se prélassent dans des fauteuils en cuir pour un tête à tête. Récemment, Maria Roosen a élargi son domaine d'activité – et l'a réduit – à l'architecture, avec des ajouts parasites qui n'appartiennent pas à leurs hôtes mais ne pourraient pourtant pas exister sans eux. Elle a ajouté un escalier à vis en fonte à un arbre haut de deux étages dans une forêt et elle a accroché une longue frange de cordage orange au sommet d'un château d'eau qui se dresse sur le quai d'un port. Ses maquettes, comme la maison dorée – un modèle réduit de sa propre demeure entièrement revêtue d'une feuille d'or – ressemblent davantage à des objets nains d'un conte de fées qu'à des prototypes de bâtiments. Sa minuscule réplique en bois d'une église en pierre (*Mirakel,* 2001) était plaquée sur l'immense tour de cet édifice

comme un baleineau cramponné à sa mère, ou comme une ombre étroite sous le soleil de midi.

Qu'elle se dilate ou qu'elle rétrécisse, l'œuvre de Maria Roosen constitue une collection unique de géants et de miniatures. Certes, elle tient du prodige, mais elle ne doit rien à l'intervention divine. Son œuvre appartient à un monde séculier plein de merveilles où des objets ordinaires – tournesols ou pots à lait – deviennent soudain extraordinaires. Maria Roosen semble accroître les Sept Merveilles du monde en y ajoutant les espaces intimes du corps, l'univers domestique peuplé de chaises et d'escaliers, des équipements collectifs comme la foi et l'eau, les sites naturels de la forêt et du jardin. De prime abord, son projet paraît à la fois suranné et moderne, proche des objets de collection d'un *Wunderkammer* – ou cabinet de curiosités – de la Renaissance ainsi que des monuments sculptés pour la consommation de masse que nous a légués le Pop Art. Néanmoins, la combinaison d'une modification de l'échelle et de l'emploi de matériaux différents exclurait Maria Roosen de ces deux périodes. Dans l'espoir d'entrevoir la totalité des desseins divins, le collectionneur de la Renaissance recherchait des raretés naturelles, précisément uniques car elles étaient exceptionnelles ou difformes (un tournesol à deux têtes aurait été préférable à deux versions XL tricotées). Un artiste du Pop comme Claes Oldenburg modifiait effectivement l'échelle et le matériau d'un tube de dentifrice écrasé, mais il réalisait pourtant un monument simple pour un article d'usage courant tout en visant à la ressemblance avec l'original. En revanche, non seulement Maria Roosen répugne à reproduire des produits, mais elle conserve également l'équilibre entre la ressemblance et la dissemblance dans son interprétation d'objets courants. Ses tournesols forment un couple gigantesque semblable à l'original, mais ils sont manifestement tricotés avec de la laine de couleur monochrome – une matière qui n'a déjà pas grand-chose de commun avec les sérigraphies multicolores de fleurs d'Andy Warhol.

Les modifications que Maria Roosen apporte à l'échelle et aux matériaux équilibrent le réalisme et une création qui ne provient ni de la nature ni d'une usine. Une fois de plus, son œuvre relève entièrement du surnaturel, du merveilleux, qui dérive lui-même du mot latin *mirabilia*, qui décrit des choses étonnantes et admirables, le plus souvent créées par Dieu. Malgré la coïncidence de l'objet avec sa réception, ce domaine a largement échappé aux créations séculières de l'art contemporain. Une fois qu'il a pénétré dans le monde profane, le merveilleux est plus courant en science et en littérature, que ce soit sous la forme de contes de fées, de fiction, de satire ou de réalisme magique. Songez à cet égard aux miracles révélés par le microscope et le télescope, de même qu'à d'autres découvertes et inventions scientifiques prodigieuses. Des récits tels qu'*Alice au pays des merveilles* ou *Les voyages de Gulliver* reposent sur des exagérations à l'échelle pour maintenir un pont entre réalisme et fiction. La principale expression contemporaine du merveilleux se manifeste évidemment au cinéma, et tout particulièrement dans les fictions réalistes obtenues à Hollywood grâce à l'emploi d'effets spéciaux. On pourrait naturellement affirmer que le cinéma a remplacé l'ébahissement inattendu du miracle par l'attente du divertissement. Dans son étude sur le merveilleux, Marie-Françoise Christout mentionne plusieurs caractéristiques que l'on retrouve dans l'oeuvre de Maria Roosen.[1] Le merveilleux est essentiellement dynamique et implique toujours une croissance, une transformation, des accélérations et des ralentissements. Ces changements sont outrés, ce qui permet de confronter les extrêmes, qu'il s'agisse d'un géant et d'un elfe ou du bien et du mal. Les miracles nous stupéfient parce qu'ils perturbent des rapports familiers au moyen de ressemblances crédibles. Étant donné que les lois de causalité restent visibles, le miracle ne constitue donc pas exactement une illusion, que ce soit l'artifice du trompe-l'œil ou la dextérité du prestidigitateur.

Maria Roosen exprime la dynamique essentielle au miracle en privilégiant les éléments organiques liés à la croissance, la vie et la métamorphose. Les phallus et les seins sont des organes qui changent de taille du fait de leur rôle dans la reproduction. Elle réalise aussi des spermatozoïdes géants en verre soufflé, ainsi que de gros globes oculaires aux pupilles dilatées variables. Maria Roosen fait souffler du verre dans les formes évidées de sabots et dans des pantalons en cuir – enveloppes organiques et souples du corps qui existent aussi dans de nombreuses tailles. D'ailleurs, les matériaux qu'elle emploie proviennent généralement de la nature, mais ils subissent immanquablement une transformation une fois qu'ils en ont été extraits. Le verre, la laine, l'or, le métal et le bois sont des matières infiniment malléables qui se prêtent bien à l'ouvrage, précisément parce qu'elles peuvent adopter d'innombrables formes et aspects, même en quantités limitées. Les artisans que Maria Roosen engage pour exécuter ses œuvres jouent un rôle équivalent au sien dans la dynamique du miracle : le souffleur de verre transforme de façon experte une masse embryonnaire de verre en un organe quelconque. Dans les exagérations de Maria Roosen, depuis la miniature jusqu'au gigantisme, plusieurs extrêmes se touchent. En accrochant une petite église à une grande, l'artiste opère une modification exceptionnelle des proportions tout en mettant en évidence le recul du nombre de croyants, maintenant que le christianisme est sur le déclin en Europe. Les extrêmes des déjections et nourritures humaines se rencontrent dans une cuvette de W.-C. décorée d'une foison de légumes ou de tableaux de chasse champêtres. L'odeur rejoint l'absence d'odeur dans ses flacons de parfum vides suspendus, également en verre, c'est-à-dire en un matériau évidemment inodore. La vie affronte la mort avec les myosotis vivaces, plantés sur un rectangle minimaliste dans un cimetière. Dans l'ensemble de son œuvre, pourtant extrêmement dynamique, la vie est souvent bridée par la mort. Les matériaux ont beau être organiques, ils n'en ôtent pas moins toute vitalité aux matières organiques, comme le roi Midas qui changeait tout en or. Les phallus en verre – aussi inodores et vides que les flacons de parfum – n'éjaculeront jamais ; les seins n'allaiteront jamais ; les globes oculaires réfléchissent les images mais ne voient rien. Cependant, cette « mort » n'apparaît certainement pas comme une destination finale. C'est plutôt un ajournement passager de la vie, tel un charme qui a été jeté mais pourrait toujours être rompu, annulé par le processus même qui a provoqué l'enchantement. Les objets en verre pourraient être refondus pour adopter d'autres formes ; les tournesols pourraient être défaits et la laine servir à tricoter des chaussettes, des chandails ou des moufles ; l'or en feuilles pourrait être détaché de la maison miniature pour couvrir le rebord d'une coupe ou les tranches d'un livre relié.

Les miracles de Maria Roosen ne se contentent pas de créer une dynamique des extrêmes, ils perturbent aussi les rapports familiers par des ressemblances parfaitement crédibles. En dehors de sa taille et de sa couleur, la petite église est une reproduction exacte de l'original. Néanmoins, son apparition soudaine, à un point élevé du flanc de la tour, a sans doute donné un choc aux habitants du quartier habitués à voir un édifice solitaire. *Mirakel* en fait partie sans en faire vraiment partie. La sculpture est une copie qui révère son modèle (au point d'imiter son éminente élévation) mais aussi un fardeau qui accable son origine. Les accouplements architecturaux de Maria Roosen – l'escalier ajouté à l'arbre, la frange au château d'eau – rappellent un peu les curieux assemblages du surréalisme, à cette différence près que les ajouts de cette artiste remplissent une fonction auprès de leurs hôtes. On peut grimper dans les arbres : un escalier facilite la tâche. Les châteaux d'eau sont élevés : une frange doit être accrochée pour qu'elle volette librement au vent. Les œuvres en verre de Maria Roosen ressemblent à des organes, mais elles ont pourtant perdu leur rapport familier avec le corps humain. Le phallus n'apparaît pas entre les cuisses d'un homme ni même comme un godemiché, mais existe en série de trois, pendus à des fils sur un mur. Les miroirs sphériques réfléchissent fidèlement le paysage – y compris les visiteurs qui peuvent aisément reconnaître leur reflet – tout en occupant un espace minime. Ceux qui n'ont pas la possibilité de voir les œuvres de Maria Roosen de leurs propres yeux pourront malgré tout se faire une idée de la stupéfaction qu'elles provoquent. Elle les fait photographier, non pas comme des sculptures isolées, mais comme des installations présentées dans un cadre particulier où apparaissent généralement des personnes. Son mini pichet ressemble à son maxi pichet, mais on ne saurait les confondre sur les photographies car le premier est posé sur la paume d'une main tandis que l'autre est montré dans une salle de séjour, à côté d'une femme qui lui tricote un pull-over à torsades. Il n'y a aussi aucun doute possible sur le gigantisme des spermatozoïdes en verre de Maria Roosen, car ils sont tenus en l'air par des chercheurs dans un laboratoire. Vu que ces chercheurs étudient le phénomène de la reproduction, leur rapport visuel habituel avec le spermatozoïde – grossi sous un microscope – se transforme soudain en une réalité inquiétante. Enfin, les miracles de Maria Roosen révèlent les lois de causalité dont ils émanent. Les organes en verre offrent une ressemblance mais non pas une illusion, car ils sont manifestement réalisés en verre. Il n'y a ni secret ni tromperie sur la fabrication des tournesols en laine ; il y a uniquement l'habileté de la personne qui les a tricotés. La maison dorée de Maria Roosen n'est pas faite de peinture qui se fait passer pour le métal précieux, mais d'une petite quantité d'or véritable étiré au point d'en revêtir une modeste maison. Si une partie du miracle de l'œuvre de Maria Roosen réside dans les modifications de l'échelle, une autre partie provient de la tension visible entre le matériau rudimentaire et sa forme façonnée finale. L'or se transforme en maison tout en restant obstinément de l'or, tout comme le modèle réduit de la maison reste fidèle à son immense origine.

L'échelle du corps

Le corps humain reste la pierre de touche de toute l'œuvre de Maria Roosen. La miniature et le gigantisme existent l'une par rapport à l'autre, mais le corps humain constitue le point de référence de toutes ses exagérations. Non pas un corps spécifique, ni un corps quelconque, mais le corps du spectateur. Comme le remarque Susan Stewart dans son étude sur les miniatures et les géants, notre corps est l'étalon de notre perception de l'échelle. Nous nous substituons à l'original pour la symétrie précise d'une maison de poupée qui nous offre une vue synoptique, ou pour les déformations grotesques d'un colosse qui nous fait de l'ombre.[2] Bien que Maria Roosen donne une représentation explicitement figurative du corps (phallus, seins, globes oculaires), elle s'adresse implicitement aux spectateurs, qui appréhenderont ses exagérations en relation avec leur propre corps et leurs expériences personnelles. Ceux qui regardent les œuvres de Maria Roosen en photographies prennent conscience de leur échelle en s'identifiant soit avec les personnages représentés dans le décor – chercheurs ou tricoteuses – soit avec le cadre même, comme le musée et le gymnase, c'est-à-dire des lieux de rassemblement concrets où ont été installés et photographiés les seins jumeaux qui se prélassent au lit. Pour sensibiliser le spectateur à l'échelle, Maria Roosen choisit aussi des objets adaptés au corps humain, comme des poignées ou des maisons. L'artiste ne crée pas une forme complète, mais elle suggère le corps par le truchement des organes absents ; au lieu d'un pied sculpté, elle nous offre l'escalier ou l'intérieur d'une chaussure usée. Les spectateurs prennent conscience de leur propre corps par leur exclusion d'espaces familiers qu'ils occuperaient normalement.

L'homme modèle de Maria Roosen – composé de plusieurs miroirs sphériques empilés sur une paire de grosses chaussures en cuir noir – regarde le spectateur plus ou moins dans les yeux, selon la taille de celui-ci. Cependant, indépendamment de sa taille, chaque spectateur y voit son reflet comme un point minuscule dans le décor, étant donné que les miroirs sont sphériques. Cette image réfléchie – en partie anamorphose et en partie miroir déformant de fête foraine – rappelle l'étonnant autoportrait de Jan van Eyck dans le miroir convexe, tout au fond du tableau du

Couple Arnolfini, ou bien l'œil spéculaire d'une caméra de surveillance. Si le spectateur se rapproche, son corps augmentera de taille, certes, mais la déformation de l'image s'accentuera également. Cette représentation déformée est constamment réaffirmée car la même réflexion se produit sur la surface ronde de tous les miroirs sphériques qui composent ensemble le corps bulbeux de l'homme. Comme il observe de tous ses yeux l'ensemble de la situation, cet homme est en mesure de donner aux autres une apparence frêle ou tordue, à maintes reprises. Notre distance crée un éloignement bien trop important ; notre proximité nous rapproche beaucoup trop.

Vainqueurs quotidiens, géants assoupis et bulles de tête

70-71 La série en devenir, intitulée *Overwinnaars* en néerlandais (Vainqueurs), qui s'étend de 1985 à aujourd'hui, constitue l'œuvre la plus vaste de Maria Roosen jusqu'ici. Les 190 images, pour la plupart découpées dans des quotidiens, forment une curieuse collection d'individus et de choses dont on a parlé dans les journaux du fait de leur caractère exceptionnel. Outre une multitude de sportifs célébrant leur victoire dans des disciplines diverses (de la course cycliste au football), on y voit aussi des objets (une pomme de terre gigantesque et une puce électronique minuscule), des curiosités (l'homme qui a la plus longue barbe et le plus vieux squelette de femme), des hommes d'État (par exemple Mikhaïl Gorbatchev), des femmes célèbres (Lady Di et Mère Térésa), des musiciens (Nick Cave et P. J. Harvey), des artistes (de Jan van Eyck à Matthew Barney). Malgré l'ampleur apparente de son tour d'horizon, Maria Roosen ne choisit pas ses vainqueurs au hasard. Elle a tendance à retourner poliment les coupures de presse représentant des personnes exceptionnelles que lui

envoient certains amis. Parmi une offre surabondante, Maria Roosen sélectionne exclusivement les personnages qu'elle considère personnellement comme des vainqueurs. L'équipe de football néerlandaise qui fête sa victoire en coupe d'Europe en 1988 dévoile une note de fierté nationale ; la pomme de terre – trouvée dans le Flevoland – est un autre hommage aux nourritures du pays. Le choix de Bettine Vriesekoop et Anky van Grunsven, en 2004, exprime une histoire locale, personnelle, entremêlée de condition féminine. L'écoulement du temps peut être chargé de sens. L'homme à la barbe de 3,3 mètres est né en 1826, sa photo date de 1904 et Maria Roosen l'a ajouté à sa collection en 1987 ; le squelette âgé de 7000 ans appartenait à une femme morte lorsqu'elle avait 45 ans – c'est-à-dire au même âge que l'artiste à l'époque. Certains vainqueurs – comme Michael Jackson qui a rejoint sa collection en 1996 – sont depuis tombés en disgrâce. D'autres – tel que Nick Cage qui déclara en 1996 que « la muse n'est pas un cheval de course » n'ont encore rien perdu de leur autorité au fil des ans.

Comme elle s'en remet à des images de presse toutes faites, Maria Roosen semble valoriser la diffusion du « spectacle » par les médias. Pourtant, vu la spécificité et l'intimité du travail qu'elle accomplit, sa collection contraste avec la collecte d'informations journalistiques qui s'efforce d'imposer un ordre objectif aux événements actuels et prétend les traiter exhaustivement. L'ampleur du *Monde* et l'immensité du *Times* sont réduites à un format maniable dont le contenu peut être absorbé en une seule journée. Le quotidien utilise la réduction pour effectuer une transition harmonieuse de l'espace public à la sphère privée ; l'extérieur (chaque page est imprimée, chaque espace rempli) correspond à l'intérieur (les pages ouvertes enclosent le lecteur, pour ne pas dire qu'elles l'abritent). En découpant ses vainqueurs favoris, Maria Roosen délivre le géant des limites de la réduction ; ses vainqueurs, trop grands pour le journal, sont libérés des nouvelles ordinaires et accueillis dans un refuge distinct, construit spécialement pour eux ; leurs images sont repêchées dans la poubelle pour subsister à titre d'art et de fait historique. Mi historienne, mi rédactrice, Maria Roosen remplace le rôle intermédiaire que le journal joue entre le domaine public et le domaine privé par son panthéon personnel qui couvre un mur entier. Le format du journal – les « poignées » incommodes de l'annonce double page – a manifestement été découpé avec des ciseaux, un autre exemple de sa manière purement individuelle de retenir et de modeler l'histoire. Les vainqueurs plus récents sont souvent encore dans le contexte journalistique qui les environnait au départ. Néanmoins, dans l'ensemble de sa collection, l'illusion d'intégralité – et d'objectivité – du journal est éclipsée par une autre histoire qui reste incomplète parce qu'elle est liée à la vie personnelle de Maria Roosen. Ses choix ne reflètent pas uniquement ses goûts personnels, mais aussi le temps biologique de son propre corps, et peut-être même l'évolution des valeurs qui advient avec l'âge. Le squelette de femme avait à la fois 7000 et 45 ans, c'était le plus vieux squelette mais aussi le squelette d'une femme du même âge que l'artiste. Peu à peu, les vainqueurs sportifs sont supplantés par des femmes ayant vécu une vie exceptionnelle – un déplacement d'intérêt du collectif au natif individuel. Cette collection, qui s'accroît parallèlement à la vie de l'artiste – ou à son rythme – reste incomplète, ouverte. C'est une chose organique, vivante, qui entretient une certaine tension entre la vie publique du vainqueur et la vie privée de l'artiste.

À cet égard, il est révélateur que Maria Roosen choisisse de traduire le titre néerlandais « overwinnaars » par le mot « survivors » en anglais. Quoiqu'un « survivor » soit aussi un vainqueur, un battant, le mot indique également que ses personnages résistent plus longtemps qu'une publication éphémère, tout en faisant penser au mot français « survivre ». Une telle rage de vivre, un tel excès de vie est inhérent aux vainqueurs – des êtres d'exception, mais mortels, dont les exploits surhumains se situent entre la terre et les dieux.[3] Cependant, cet excès de vie contenu dans *survivre* fait également partie des exagérations organiques que nous trouvons dans une des œuvres antérieures de Maria Roosen : les pantoufles qu'elle a fait fabriquer pour le géant de Rotterdam. Cette œuvre fait allusion à un vrai géant qui a vécu dans cette ville et y est mort dans les années 1950 ; après avoir vu ses chaussures dans un musée, elle a fait confectionner des pantoufles sur-mesure par un bottier allemand spécialisé dans la fabrication de chaussures pour les personnes de grande taille du monde entier. Les vainqueurs et les géants de Maria Roosen – pris au sens d'un excès de vie (performance excessive et croissance excessive) – sont des manifestations d'une évolution qui se produit dans un corps unique et qui symbolise les mutations au sein de l'espace collectif.

Bien entendu, les géants appartiennent à la première espèce humaine : l'Ancien Testament mentionne déjà leur existence et les associe à des phénomènes topographiques et météorologiques extrêmes comme les falaises et les fortes tempêtes, avant qu'ils soient domptés et servent de protecteurs mythologiques de villes et d'États.[4] Pensez par exemple au rôle de Gargantua pour le Mont-Saint-Michel ou à celui de Gog et Magog pour Londres. Les pantoufles géantes de Maria Roosen –

enfilées au saut du lit et portées à la maison – expriment la domestication du géant, sa fuite du paysage naturel, découvert, jusqu'à la maison, abri cultivé ; mais aussi son évolution, du folklore jusqu'aux contes de fées racontés aux enfants à l'heure du coucher. Après que la nature a été adaptée à la vie civile, le géant a pris sa retraite et il ne fait que de rares apparitions, dans un défilé ou une fête foraine. Sa taille démesurée ne provoque plus l'épouvante, c'est une simple anomalie congénitale, tout aussi fortuite et bizarre que la pomme de terre gigantesque du Flevoland. Les *overwinnaars* de Maria Roosen – vainqueurs, *survivors*, héros – prennent le relais du géant et reflètent notre propre retrait de la nature. Leurs exploits pour survivre ne proviennent pas de la nature, mais d'un choix et d'un zèle personnes (même l'homme qui a la plus longue barbe a décidé un jour de ne pas la couper) ; ils ne créent pas de falaises, ne provoquent pas de violentes tempêtes, mais en revanche, ils modèlent notre paysage médiatique. Lorsque nous nous comparons à leurs réussites spectaculaires, nous comprenons les limites, mais non pas le cadre, de l'univers public dans lequel nous vivons, quoiqu'à une plus petite échelle.

Dans ce glissement historique des géants aux héros, le récent projet de Maria Roosen tente de créer un espace pour l'individu. Elle s'est servie de vieux journaux pour fabriquer des grosses boules en papier mâché. Ensuite, elle a donné ces formes creuses à ses amis en leur demandant expressément de les décorer à leur guise et de se les mettre sur la tête. Ces « bulles » qui sont en même temps génériques et individualisées, résultent d'un travail artisanal spécialisé et intime – un travail collectivisé qui ne provient pas des mains de l'artiste mais de ses désirs, réalisés par d'autres. Ces bulles, qui tiennent

davantage de l'ornement de tête que du masque, ne dissimulent pas tant les individus qu'elles n'exagèrent leurs personnalités tout comme leur volume et leur hauteur. Bien qu'elles fassent penser aux bulles qui contiennent le texte des personnages de bandes dessinées, ou même à ces personnages eux-mêmes, elles évoquent aussi les déguisements d'un cortège de carnaval. Maria Roosen accorde même à ses amis la liberté de décorer leur tête de telle façon que les traits les plus subtils de leur personnalité – que l'on ne remarque en temps normal que de près, dans le contexte des contacts personnels – sont visibles de loin. Maria Roosen ajoute encore à cette exagération la mobilité, propre à notre époque de déplacements incessants. Après que les têtes en papier mâché avaient été customisées, Maria Roosen les a emmenées avec elle aux vernissages de ses expositions dans des galeries et des musées à l'extérieur d'Arnhem. Étant donné que ses amis ne pouvaient pas toujours l'accompagner, elle a demandé à d'autres invités de se coiffer d'une bulle lors des vernissages. Par ce passage des têtes de ses amis dans leur intimité aux têtes de nouvelles connaissances dans d'autres villes, les bulles se transforment en doubles portatifs, souvenirs vivants de ses relations personnelles. Bien qu'elles aient leur origine dans le domaine personnel, les têtes sont destinées à un espace public plus vaste. Contrairement à sa maison miniature dorée, qui apaise la souffrance de la séparation parce qu'elle semble réduire la distance, les têtes démesurées de Maria Roosen utilisent l'échelle de façon différente : pour rapetisser les invités inconnus et réduire leur écrasant anonymat. Ces têtes décorées planent bien au-dessus de la foule, comme les géants dans un défilé ou les visages agrandis des vainqueurs dans les journaux. Ce sont des balises mouvantes, qui n'avertissent pas

les voyageurs de la proximité d'une falai-
se mais métamorphosent une mer de
visages inconnus en entourage familier.
Ici, le sens de l'échelle de Maria Roosen
suit son désir d'amener tout près ce qui
est extrêmement loin.

1. Marie-Françoise Christout,
« Le merveilleux, catégorie
esthétique », *Le merveilleux et le
« théâtre du silence » en France à partir du XVIIe siècle*, Paris :
Éditions Mouton, 1965,
chap. 21.

Quoiqu'elle définisse les caractéristiques du merveilleux,
Christout se concentre surtout
sur le ballet.

2. Susan Stewart, *On Longing.
Narratives of the Miniature, the
Gigantic, the Souvenir, the Collec-
tion*, Durham & London : Duke
University Press,
1993, xii.

3. Voir Anna Makolkin, *Name,
Hero, Icon. Semiotics of Nationalism
through Heroic Biography*,

Berlin/New York, Mouton de
Gruyter, 1992.

4. Voir Walter Stevens, *Giants in
Those Days. Folklore, Ancient
History, and Nationalism*,
Lincoln & London, University of
Nebraska Press, 1989.

Maria Roosen

Oisterwijk 1957
Lives and works in Arnhem

Education

1976–1981 Moller Instituut, Tilburg
1981–1983 Academie voor Beeldende Kunsten, Arnhem

Solo exhibitions

1986
Maria Roosen. Beelden en Tekeningen, Hooghuis, Arnhem

1988
Maria Roosen. Recent Werk, Virtu I.B.K., Nijmegen

1994
Spring!, Gemeentemuseum Helmond, Helmond
De cilinder, as a part of 'Zomerbeelden', Culturele Raad Goes, Goes (cat.)

1996
jeuk, Galerie Fons Welters, Amsterdam

1997
Maria Roosen. Nieuw Werk, Vleeshal, Middelburg

1998
On the occasion of the presentation of the book *Ziezo*, Art book, Amsterdam

1999
Home is where the heart is, Kunstvereniging Diepenheim, Diepenheim

2001
Maria Roosen in Himmelblau, Groninger Museum, Groningen

2002
ooo... spiegelbeeld... ooo, Museum Dhondt-Dhaenens, Deurle
Presentation on the occasion of the performance of 'Wortel van glas', HETPALEIS, Antwerp, with Josse de Pauw and Stefan Perceval

2004
Met, Galerie Fons Welters, Amsterdam

Group exhibitions

1987
Twee jaar Oceaan, Oceaan, Arnhem (cat.)

1990
Te gast, Gemeentemuseum Arnhem, Arnhem (cat.)

1991
Dr. Brewster & Co, former passengers terminal Holland-Amerika Lijn, Rotterdam (cat.)
The pleasure of being involved..., Stichting Kaus Australis, Rotterdam (cat.)

1992
Project 381 B, Stichting Still, Rotterdam (cat.)

1992–1993
Peiling 92, Museum Boymans-van Beuningen, Rotterdam (cat.)

1993
Zonder Titel. Fünf Positionen aktueller Kunst aus den Niederlanden und Flandern, Frankfurter Kunstverein Steinernes Haus am Römerberg, Frankfurt am Main (cat.)

1994
WATT, Witte de With, center for contemporary art, Rotterdam (cat.)
Slow Whoop Siren, Galerie Fons Welters, Amsterdam
This is the show and the show is many things, Museum van Hedendaagse Kunst, Ghent (cat.)
EN SUITE, Vereniging voor het Museum van Hedendaagse Kunst, Ghent
Videotapes, Casco, Utrecht

1995
Zomers Zolder, Kasteel van Rhoon, Rhoon
XLVI *Esposizione Internazionale d'Arte, Biennale di Venezia. Dumas, Roosen, Van Warmerdam*, Dutch Pavilion, Venice (cat.)
Beeld in Zicht, Museum voor Moderne Kunst Arnhem, Arnhem

Art Cologne, Fons Welters
  stand, Cologne (cat.)

1995–1996
Glasobjecten, De Nederlandse
  Bank, Amsterdam
Time, Galerie Fons Welters,
  Amsterdam

1996
Telefoonstraat twintig,
  Telefoonstraat 20, Tilburg
Kunst Moet Moet Kunst,
  Province of Gelderland,
  Van Reekum Museum,
  Apeldoorn (cat.)
*De Muze als Motor. Brabant 200
  jaar*, De Beyerd, Breda (cat.)
Exchanging Interiors, Museum
  Van Loon, Amsterdam (cat.)

1997
The Beauty and the Beast,
  Gallery Unlimited, Athene
*Het Drinkglas. Internationale
  glasmanifestatie Leerdam en
  omstreken*, Fort Asperen
STAD(*t*)T-ART – *Kunst in 56
  homöopatischen Dosen*,
  Kunstverein Schwerte,
  Schwerte (cat.)
ELP, Niggendijker, Groningen

1998
7 jaar kunstprijs Mama Cash,
  Arti et Amicitae,
  Amsterdam (cat.)
*Magritte en de hedendaagse
  kunst*, Museum voor
  Moderne Kunst,
  Oostende (cat.)
Liste, Basel
Sugar Moutain, Galerie van den
  Berge, Goes
*Rob Birza, Tom Claassen, Maria
  Roosen*, Galerie Fons Welters,
  Amsterdam
*A-BOERDERIJ, the ecstatic life of
  artists*, stichting i-buro,
  Tilburg
*Going up the country. Kunste-
  naars uit de Galerie Fons
  Welters*, De Paviljoens,
  Almere (cat.)

*Copy Culture. 40 jaar Amster-
  dams Grafisch Atelier*, Arti et
  Amicitae, Amsterdam (cat.)
Werk in oplage, Minerva 200,
  Groningen
Colliers. Claartje Keur's collectie,
  Museum voor Moderne
  Kunst, Arnhem (cat.)
Art Cologne, Galerie Fons
  Welters stand, Cologne

1999
Avoiding Objects, Apex Art,
  New York
*Merijn Bolink, Job Koelewijn,
  Matthew Monahan, Maria
  Roosen, Berend Strik, frontroom,
  Carlos Amorales*, Galerie Fons
  Welters, Amsterdam
Delta Ceramic, Het Princesse-
  hof, Leeuwarden (cat.)
*Serendipity (The borders of
  Europe)*, Watou (cat.)
De soep en de wolken, Berg en
  Bos parc, Apeldoorn (cat.)
Tekeningen, Galerie Fons
  Welters, Amsterdam

2000
BolinkClaassenRoosenStrik,
  Galerie Fons Welters,
  Amsterdam
Het gekke huis, De Gelderse
  Roos, Wolfheze (cat.)
Everything needs time, Honiton
  Festival, Honiton (cat.)
  Spacex Gallery, Exeter
Inkeer, Oude Stefanuskerk,
  Borne (cat.)
*Ontmoetingen Hemelrijkseweg
  10*, Hemelrijkseweg 10,
  Deurne
Red de kabouter (compiled by
  Sven Lütticken, Reinout
  Rutte), Galerie Fons Welters,
  Amsterdam

2001
*Artline 5, Interaktionen – Natur &
  Architektur*, Borken (cat.)
Sonsbeek 9. Locus/Focus,
  Arnhem (cat.)
OIKIA (bags project), Almere

2002
Kunstenaars van de galerie,
  Galerie Fons Welters,
  Amsterdam
A Haunted House of Art (com-
  piled by Gabriël Lester),
  Outline, Amsterdam
Een raadsel voor Zoersel,
  Zoersel (cat.)

2003
Groupshow, Galerie Fons
  Welters, Amsterdam
SHINE, Museum Boijmans Van
  Beuningen, Rotterdam (cat.)
Kunst op de Boerderij,
  Frederiksoord
*Armour: de fortificatie van de
  mens*, Fort Asperen,
  Asperen (cat.)
*2003 Beaufort. Triënnale voor
  hedendaagse kunst aan zee*,
  Blankenberge (cat.)
*Comme des Garçons: 40 views of
  an icon, 40 countries* (cat.)

2004
Art Rotterdam, Galerie Fons
  Welters stand, Rotterdam
Epifyten, Hortus Botanicus,
  Amsterdam (cat.)
Lustwarande 04, Tilburg

2005
Nous le passage, 25ste
  Poëziezomer, Watou (cat.)
De Paleistuin, Den Haag
  Sculptuur, The Hague (cat.)
*Art Circus, Jumping from the
  Ordinary*, International
  Triennale of Contemporary
  Art, Yokohama

Commissions (realized)

1992
Arnhemse Milieuprijs,
commissioned by the City
of Arnhem

1997
Kunsttoepassingen Zorg-
voorziening Zuidwester,
Oud-Beijerland, with the
Mondriaan Foundation

1998
Sketch proposal, Dorpstraat,
City of Zoetermeer

1999
Gift for Heads of State, City of
Amsterdam
Sketch proposal, Provincial
Government Building
's-Hertogenbosch, Province
of Noord-Brabant
(realization 2000)
Sketch proposal, City of
Apeldoorn
Sketch proposal, Akzo,
Organon, Oss
(realization 1999–2000)
Sketch proposal, Het Oosten
housing corporation, Am-
sterdam (realization 2000)

2000
Art commission, *Vitrine 2000*,
Rabobank, Oisterwijk

Ogen voor het Oosten,
Sarphatistraat 410, Het
Oosten housing corpora-
tion, Amsterdam
Art commission, Akzo Nobel
Art Foundation, CQ-gebouw
Organon, Oss
Art commission, perfume
bottle, Rabobank Nederland
Art commission, *Glassubject*,
jubilee gift for VARA broad-
casting corporation

2002
Art commission, *1+1=3*,
Alem traffic circle, City of
Maasdriel, Kerkdriel
Art commission,
Wortel van glas, HETPALEIS,
Antwerp, with Josse de
Pauw and Stefan Perceval

2003
Art commission,
Centraalbeweging, WRA,
Diemen
Sketch proposal, sculpture
Aelbert Cuyp, Dordrecht
Sketch proposal, Madurodam
Sketch proposal, ABN–AMRO
bank, Amsterdam
Art commission, 'Hoogte-
punten' Rijksgebouwen,
Keuringsdienst van Waren,
Woensel

2004
Sketch proposal, Loenshof,
Enschede
Sketch proposal, Farwest,
Amsterdam
Art commission, *Regenboog*,
Antoni van Leeuwenhoek
Ziekenhuis, Amsterdam
Art commission, *Toiletten*,
Rabo Theater, Hengelo
Sketch proposal, VGZ, Tilburg
Sketch proposal, De Brugse-
poort library, Gent
Sketch proposal, Rabobank,
Vorden
Sketch proposal, Provincial
Government Building
's-Hertogenbosch, Province
of Noord-Brabant

2005
Art commission,
Madonna van Enschede,
Loenshof, Enschede
Art commission,
sculpture Aelbert Cuyp,
City of Dordrecht

Publications by the artist

1986
Roosens onderzoek in Hooghuis,
Belvedere, Stichting
Plaatsmaken, Arnhem

1992
'De wereld in de wereld uit',
Metropolis M, no. 5, pp. 7-8

1994
'Imaginaire Tentoonstelling
(III)', *Metropolis M*, no. 3,
pp. 32-33
'Imaginaire Tentoonstelling',
Metropolis M, index vol. 15,
pp. 4-5

1998
Ziezo. Maria Roosen,
Galerie Fons Welters,
Amsterdam
(Dutch/English)

Catalogues

1987
Trace, werk en werkplaatsen van jonge kunstenaars, exhib. cat. De Gele Rijder, Arnhem
Twee jaar Oceaan, exhib. cat. Oceaan, Arnhem

1990
10 jaar De Gele Rijder, exhib. cat. De Gele Rijder, Arnhem

1991
Dr Brewster & Co, exhib. cat. Centrum Beeldende Kunst, Rotterdam
The pleasure of being involved..., exhib. cat. Stichting Kaus Australis with Let Geerling, Rotterdam

1992
Act Local, Think Global/project 381 B, exhib. cat. Stichting Still, Rotterdam
Peiling 92, negen jonge kunstenaars, exhib. cat. Museum Boymans-van Beuningen, Rotterdam
Tentoonstellingen 1992, exhib. cat. De Gele Rijder, Arnhem

1993
Zonder Titel. Fünf Positionen aktueller Kunst aus der Niederlanden und Flandern. Philip Akkerman, Patrick Van Caekenbergh, Franky DS, Maria Roosen, Lydia Schouten, exhib. cat. Frankfurter Kunstverein Steinernes Haus am Römerberg, Frankfurt am Main

1994
Cahier # 2 june 1994, exhib. cat. Witte de With, center for contemporary art, Rotterdam
This is the show and the show is many things, exhib. cat. Museum van Hedendaagse Kunst, Ghent
Zomerbeelden. De Cilinder, exhib. cat. Culturele Raad Goes, Goes

1995
46e. Biennale di Venezia, Dumas, Roosen, Van Warmerdam, exhib. cat., Venice
Kunst Moet Moet Kunst, Province of Gelderland, exhib. cat. Van Reekum Museum, Apeldoorn

1996
Art Cologne Internationaler Kunstmarkt, exhib. cat., Cologne
De Muze als Motor. Brabant 200 jaar, exhib. cat. De Beyerd, Breda
Exchanging Interiors, exhib. cat. Museum Van Loon, Amsterdam

1997
STAD(*t*)T-ART – *kunst in 56 homöopatischen Dosen*, exhib. cat. Kunstverein Schwerte, Schwerte

1998
7 jaar kunstprijs Mama Cash, exhib. cat. Mama Cash Cultuurfonds, Amsterdam
Magritte en de Hedendaagse Kunst, exhib. cat. Museum voor Moderne Kunst, Oostende
Almere cahier 2, kunstenaars uit de Galerie Fons Welters, exhib. cat. De Paviljoens, Almere
Copy Culture, exhib. cat. Amsterdams Grafisch Atelier, Amsterdam
Colliers, exhib. cat. Museum voor Moderne Kunst, Arnhem

1999
Soep in de wolken, exhib. cat. Berg en Bos parc, Apeldoorn
Toolpub, dutch mountains, (edited and designed by Roelof Mulder), Amsterdam
Serendipiteit, exhib. cat. 'Poeziëzomer', Watou

2000
Het gekke huis, exhib. cat. De Gelderse Roos, Wolfheze
everything needs time.../alles heeft tijd nodig..., exhib. cat. Honiton Festival, Honiton
Inkeer, Stichting Collage, Kortenhoef
Retour peilen. Presentatie en verantwoording beeldende kunst en vormgeving provincie Gelderland 1996–1997–1998–1999, Province of Gelderland
Richard Fernhout, Colin Huizing, *Het Nederlandse Kunstboek. 500 Nederlandse kunstenaars, 500 afbeeldingen, 500 jaar Nederlandse kunst*, Uitgeverij Waanders, Zwolle

2001
artline 5, interaktionen–Natur & Architektur, exhib. cat. Stadt Borken/S.M.A.K., Gent
D. Roelstraete (red.), *Sonsbeek 9. Locus Focus*, Stichting Sonsbeek, Arnhem
Nieuwe Kunst/New Art in Amsterdam. A Public Space Odyssey, Amsterdams Fonds voor de Kunst, Amsterdam, p. 24
M. van Schijndel, V. Klaassen (red.), *Unlocked No (1)*, Kunstcollectie Rabobank, Utrecht, pp. 96, 97, 205, 210

2002
Een collectie. Een keuze uit de verzameling van de ABN–AMRO *Bank*, p. 29

2003
Proof of Principle, Akzo Nobel Art Foundation, pp. 282, 284-286, 290-293
SHINE, exhib. cat. Museum Boijmans Van Beuningen, Rotterdam, p. 20

Karin van Munster,
Beelden in de Berm. Vijf-en-tachtig kunstobjecten vanuit de auto, ANWB, The Hague, p. 84
2003 Beaufort. Triënnale voor Hedendaagse kunst aan zee, exhib. cat. PMMK, Museum voor Moderne Kunst, Oostende

2004
40 views of an icon, exhib. cat. Comme des Garçons perfumes team, Barcelona
Epifyten, exhib. cat. Stichting Epifyt, Amsterdam

2005
Crysalis, Teoria dell'Evoluzione, exhib. cat., Castello Svevo, Trani
Nous le passage, exhib. cat., Watou
De Paleistuin, Den Haag Sculptuur, exhib. cat., The Hague
Unlocked # 2, Kunstcollectie Rabobank, Eindhoven

Articles

1992
'Milieuprijs Gemeente Arnhem', *Het Blad, driemaandelijks tijdschrift over de beeldende Kunst in Gelderland*, p. 27

1993
Wim van Mulders, 'Peiling '92. Is men in staat te worden wie men denkt te zijn', *Kunst en Museumjournaal*, vol. 4, no. 5, pp. 62-65

1994
Wim van Mulders, 'Maria Roosen', *Ruimte*, vol. 11, no. 1, p. 45
Rutger Pontzen, 'Jonge kunst is keukentafelkunst, zes nieuwe Nederlandse kunstenaars', *Vrij Nederland*, no. 8, pp. 49-51

1995
Mariska van der Berg, 'La Bella Figura. Over schaalvergroting en verschuivingen in Venetië', *Ruimte*, vol. 12, no. 2, pp. 10-15
Rutger Pontzen, 'Maria, Marlene en Marijke: Nederland in Venetië', *Vrij Nederland*, no. 14, pp. 46-49
Wolfgang Träger, 'Biennale-Venedig. Ein Foto-Rundgang', *Kunstforum*, no. 131 (August/October), pp. 112-115

1996
'Glas en Erotiek. Maria Roosen', *Indruk, Bouwfonds Nederlandse Gemeenten*, vol. 24, no. 4, pp. 12-14
Pietje Tegenbosch, 'Onderste uit de kan', in: *Akzo Nobel Art Foundation. Collection 1*, vol. 17

1997
Arie Korteweg, Jan Tromp, 'De tijd van de grote scheppers ligt achter ons', *de Volkskrant*, 24 December 1997 (*Perspectief* supplement)

1998
Paul Depondt, 'Maria Roosen: denken met het gefragmenteerde lichaam', *Ons Erfdeel*, vol. 41, no. 1, pp. 53-58
Sven Lütticken, 'Tom Claassen & Maria Roosen', *De Witte Raaf*, vol. 12, no. 74, pp. 36-37
Let Geerling, 'Rozentuin', *Metropolis M*, vol. 19, no. 4, p. 57
Nicoline Baartman, Marijn van der Jagt, 'De sekse van kunst', *de Volkskrant* ('Kunst op komst' *Magazine*)
Elly Stegeman, 'Maria Roosen', in: *Hedendaagse beeldhouwers in Nederland en Vlaanderen*, Stichting Ons Erfdeel, Rekkem, pp. 38-41

1999
Peter Nijmeijer, 'Gedichten als nagedachten', *Vrij Nederland*, no. 28, pp. 54-56
Peter van Vleken 'Poezie in de "koeienkerker" in Watou',

Brabants Dagblad
Karin Veraart, 'In de hitte gonzen gedichten', *de Volkskrant* ('Kunst & Cultuur' supplement)
Wilma Sütö, 'Een huiselijk en hartverwarmend feest', *de Volkskrant* ('Kunst & Cultuur' supplement)
Wim van der Beek, 'Doorlopend verhaal van Maria Roosen', *De Telegraaf*
Sandra Smallenburg, 'Flaneren in het park en soms een kunstwerk zien', *NRC Handelsblad*
'De soep in de wolken', illustrations in: *BK informatie*, no. 5, p. 27
Henk van der Meulen, 'Opgebaarde hond en keramische penisobjecten', *Leeuwarder Courant*
'Amen', 'Furious', *Dutch # 23*, p. 50

2000
'Toiletpot (sphinx)', *The dummy speaks*, no. 3
Harald Schole, 'Werk zonder woorden', *kM*, no. 33, pp. 29-30
'Bloemen te koop!', *Villa d'Arte*, no. 2, p. 64
Sandra Smallenburg, 'Maria Roosen, "Ik heb ze zelf leven ingeblazen"', *VARA tv magazine*, no. 45, pp. 108-109

2004
Marina de Vries,
 'Overlever Roosen laat
 onrust achterwege',
 de Volkskrant, 4 June 2004

'Kampioen?',
 NRC Handelsblad,
 12 June 2004

Tineke Reijnders,
 'Bubbels met een glimlach',
 AMC *Magazine*, nummer 9,
 november 2004

Activities

1992–1994
Co-founder of Still
Foundation, Rotterdam

1992–2001
Sculpture teacher, Academie
Minerva, Groningen

1994
Lecture on her work on the
occasion of the exhibition
'First show without Maria...',
Rotterdam

1995
Guest teacher post-graduate
course, AKI, Enschede

1996
Guest teacher, Hogeschool
voor de Kunsten, Arnhem
Guest teacher, Jan van Eyck
Academy, Maastricht
Lecture 'Er staat een paard in
de gang', Lectures series,
Hogeschool,
's-Hertogenbosch
Lecture on her work, Acade-
mie Minerva, Groningen
External examiner, Gerrit
Rietveld Academie,
Amsterdam

External examiner,
Constantijn Huygens Chris-
telijke Hogeschool voor de
Kunsten, Kampen

1997
Guest teacher post-graduate
course, AKI, Enschede
External examiner AKI,
Enschede

1998
Lecture 'Over de noodzake-
lijkheid en/of ongevraagde
adviezen', Atelier Guda
Koster/Harmen de Hoop,
Amsterdam
Guest teacher post-graduate
course, Academie Minerva,
Groningen
Discussion on 'the rules of
art', De Badcuyp,
Amsterdam

1999
Lecture on her work, 'The
Spectacle', Constantijn
Huygens Christelijke
Hogeschool voor de
Kunsten, Kampen
External examiner AKI,
Enschede

Guest at *RadioUit*
(NPS Cultuur), presented by
Kenneth van Zijl,
16 July 1999

2000
'Wat is mooi', interview on
the beautiful in the arts,
with Cornel Bierens

2002
External examiner,
Hogeschool voor de
Kunsten, Arnhem

2004
Advisor lerarenopleiding
Willem de Kooning
Academie, Rotterdam
De Avonden (VPRO), radio
interview by Hans den
Hartog Jager, 9 July 2004

Jennifer Allen is a Canadian critic who has been based in Berlin since 1995. She publishes frequently in *Artforum* (New York), *De Witte Raaf* (Brussels) and *SITE* (Stockholm). Allen has written many critical essays in art books and catalogues (LA Raeven, Omer Fast, Martin Kippenberger, Jens Haaning, *Parasite Paradise*, Madeleine Berkhemer, Atelier van Lieshout, Hester Oerlemans).

Wigger Bierma (1958) has been a freelance graphic designer since 1985. He has taught typography in Arnhem (Werkplaats Typografie) and Amsterdam (Rietveld Academy). His preferred projects at the moment are those in which the design of a book has an intrinsic relation with the content.

Hans den Hartog Jager (1968) is a writer and an art critic for *NRC Handelsblad* and other media. His first novel, *Zelf God worden* [Becoming God yourself] was published in 2003. His *Verf, hedendaagse Nederlandse schilders over hun werk* [Paint, contemporary Dutch painters on their work] appeared in 2004.

Liedeke Kruk (1959) is an artist, film director and photographer. She makes portraits and film installations of artists, friends and events.

Wiebo van Mulligen (1958) is an artist. He works with various media, including cartoons, text, photography, stuffed animals and popcorn.

Astrid Vorstermans (1960) is an art historian, editor and publisher. She set up Valiz in 2003 to initiate, compile and publish books on contemporary art and culture and to organise (research) projects.

Jennifer Allen is een Canadese criticus, sinds 1995 werkt zij vanuit Berlijn. Zij publiceert regelmatig in *Artforum* (New York), *De Witte Raaf* (Brussel) en *SITE* (Stockholm). Allen schreef meerdere kritische essays voor kunstboeken en -catalogi (o.a. over LA Raeven, Omer Fast, Martin Kippenberger, Jens Haaning, *Parasite Paradise*, Madeleine Berkhemer, Atelier van Lieshout, Hester Oerlemans).

Wigger Bierma (1958) is sinds 1985 zelfstandig grafisch ontwerper. Bierma was docent typografie in Arnhem (Werkplaats Typografie) en Amsterdam (Rietveld Acade-mie) en richt zich momenteel bij voorkeur op het ontwerpen van boeken waarbij de vormgeving op een zinnige manier moet rijmen met de inhoud.

Hans den Hartog Jager (1968) is kunstcriticus voor onder andere *NRC Handelsblad* en schrijver. In 2003 debuteerde hij met de roman *Zelf God worden* en in 2004 verscheen *Verf, hedendaagse Nederlandse schilders over hun werk*.

Liedeke Kruk (1959) is kunstenaar, filmmaker en fotograaf. Zij maakt portretten en film-installaties van kunstenaars, vrienden en gebeurtenissen.

Wiebo van Mulligen (1958) is kunstenaar. Hij werkt met verschillende middelen, inclusief cartoons, tekst, fotografie, opgezette dieren en popcorn.

Astrid Vorstermans (1960) is kunsthistoricus, redacteur en uitgever. In 2003 startte zij Valiz, voor het initiëren, samenstellen en uitgeven van boeken over hedendaagse kunst en cultuur en het organiseren van (onderzoeks)projecten.

Jennifer Allen est critique d'art. Canadienne installée à Berlin depuis 1995, elle publie régulièrement des articles dans *Artforum* (New York), *De Witte Raaf* (Bruxelles) et *SITE* (Stockholm). Jennifer Allen est l'auteur de nombreux essais critiques pour livres d'art et catalogues (LA Raeven, Omer Fast, Martin Kippenberger, Jens Haaning, *Parasite Paradise*, Madeleine Berkhemer, Atelier van Lieshout, Hester Oerlemans).

Wigger Bierma (1958) a son propre bureau de designer graphique depuis 1985. Après avoir enseigné la typographie à Arnhem (Werkplaats Typografie) et à Amsterdam (Rietveld Academie), il se consacre actuellement à la création de livres qui concilient présentation et contenu de manière satisfaisante et sensée.

Hans den Hartog Jager (1968) est critique d'art et écrivain. Il travaille notamment pour le quotidien néerlandais *NRC Handelsblad*. Son premier roman *Zelf God worden* [Devenir Dieu] est paru en 2003. En 2004, il a publié le livre *Verf, hedendaagse Nederlandse schilders over hun werk* [De la peinture. Des peintres néerlandais d'aujourd'hui parlent de leur travail].

Liedeke Kruk (1959) est artiste plasticienne, cinéaste et photographe. Elle réalise des portraits et des films-installations sur des artistes, des proches et des événements.

Wiebo van Mulligen (1958) est artiste plasticien. Dans son travail, il utilise les moyens les plus divers, par exemple des cartoons, des textes, des photos, des animaux empaillés ou encore du pop-corn.

Astrid Vorstermans (1960) est historienne d'art, rédactrice et éditeur. En 2003, elle crée Valiz afin d'initier, de rédiger et d'éditer des livres sur la culture et l'art contemporains, et d'organiser des projets (de recherche).

Colophon

Authors: Jennifer Allen,
Hans den Hartog Jager
Compilation: Maria Roosen,
Liedeke Kruk, Wigger
Bierma, Astrid Vorstermans
Photography: Liedeke Kruk;
except: pp. 8, 42-43, 56, 93,
102-103 Jan Broekstra; pp. 46,
92 Christa van Kolfschoten;
p. 77 Ella Nijstadt; p. 119 Dirk
Pauwels; pp. 1, 33, 39, 44-45,
66-67, 72, 90, 96-97, 108-109,
112-113 Maria Roosen; pp. 34-
35 (spread), 64-65, 118
Gert Jan van Rooij
Cartoon (pp. 114-117): Wiebo van
Mulligen
Graphic design: Wigger Bierma
Assistance graphic design:
Joyce Limburg
Assistance artist:
Steven Vinkenoog
Translation: Annette Eskénazi
(E-F, text Allen), Marie-Luc
Grall (D-F, text Den Hartog
Jager); Peter Mason (D-E,
text Den Hartog Jager);
Leo Reijnen (E-D, text Allen)
Copy editing: Els Brinkman,
Astrid Vorstermans
Lithography and printing:
Drukkerij Lecturis bv,
Eindhoven
Publisher: Valiz, book and
cultural projects, Amsterdam
www.valiz.nl

*Maria Roosen's wishes to thank /
Maria Roosen bedankt:*
Jan Broekstra, Liedeke Kruk,
Wiebo van Mulligen, Juliana
van Mulligen, Fons Welters,
Astrid Vorstermans, Wigger
Bierma, Carolien & Yvonne
Evers, Nanda Janssen, Linda
Nieuwstad, Vincent de Boer,
HETPALEIS, Glasblazerij
Ajeto, Pino Signoretto,
De Oude Horn, Bernard
Heesen, Art Front Gallery,
Stichting De Ocaan, bridal
couple
her friends / haar vrienden;
Loes Bonekamp, Jan
Broekstra, Ciel van Dooren,
Jeroen & Mischa
Doorenweerd, moeder Do,
Anneke van der Eerden, Flip
Kwakkel, Marianne Hasel-
hoff, Jacqueline & Texas van
Leeuwenstein, Hester Oerle-
mans, Marry Overtoom, Elly
Stegeman, Steven Vinkenoog

Available in the Netherlands,
Belgium and Luxemburg
through Centraal Boekhuis,
Culemborg; Scholtens,
Sittard and Coen Sligting
Bookimport, Amsterdam, NL,
sligting@xs4all.nl,
fax +31-(0)20-6640047
Available in Europe (except
Benelux, UK and Ireland),
Asia and Australia through
Idea Books, Amsterdam, NL,
idea@ideabooks.nl,
fax +31-20-6209299,
www.ideabooks.nl
Available in the United King-
dom and Ireland through
Art Data, London, UK,
orders@artdata.co.uk,
fax +44-208-742 2319
Available in the USA: DAP,
New York, dap@dapinc.com,
fax (+1) 212-6279484,
www.artbook.com

This publication was made
possible, in part, by the
Netherlands Foundation for
Visual Arts, Design and
Architecture, Amsterdam in
cooperation with the
Mondriaan Foundation,
Amsterdam; Harten Fonds
Foundation, Rotterdam;
De Gijselaar-Hintzenfonds
Foundation, Amsterdam;
the Prince Bernhard Culture
Foundation, Amsterdam;
the Province of Gelderland

www.valiz.nl

NUR: 642, 640
ISBN 90-808185-6-9
Printed and bound in the
Netherlands

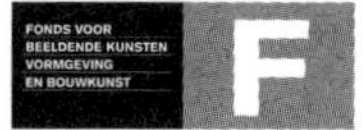

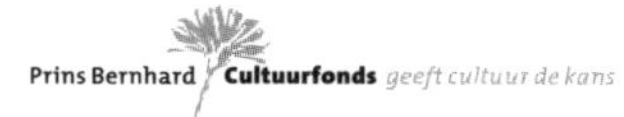

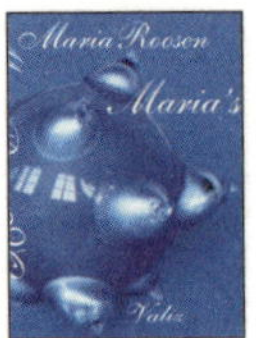

cover

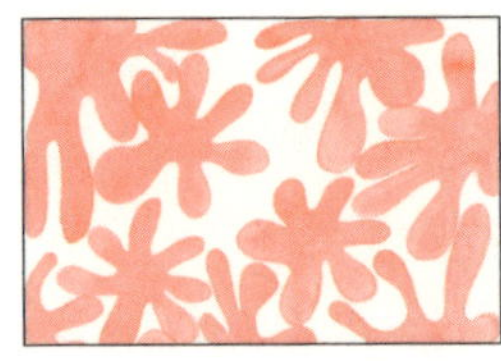

endpapers

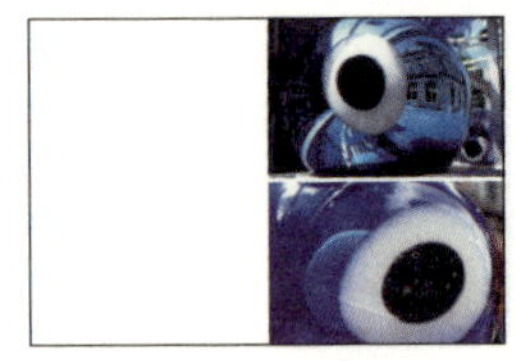

1

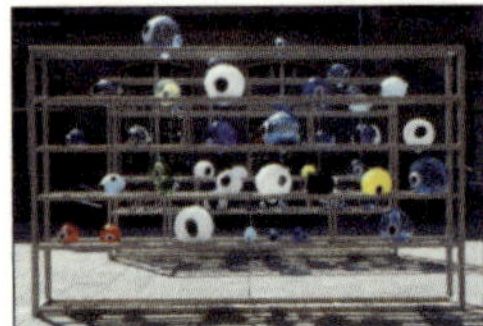

2 3

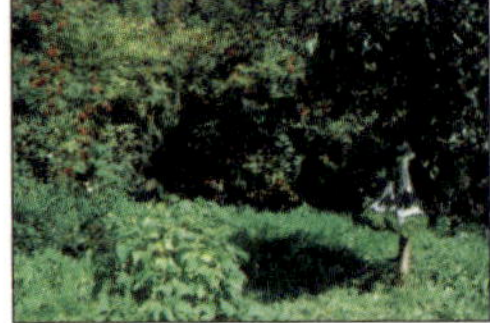

4 5

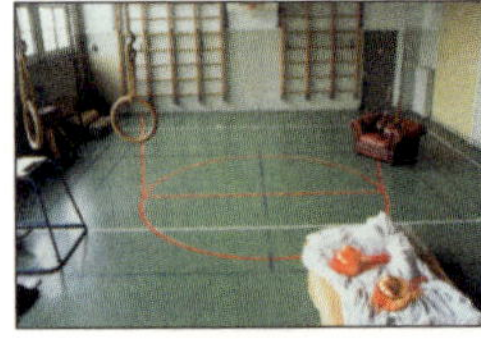

6 7

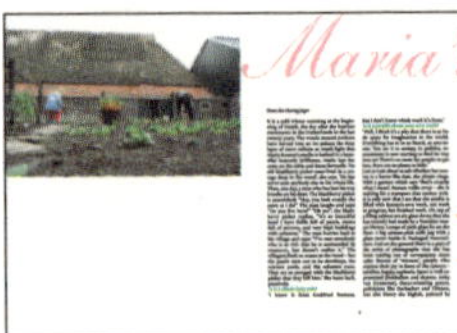

8 9

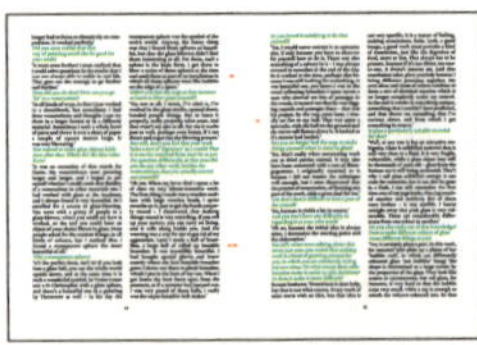

10 11 12 13

Cover
Goedendag (Mace) 1995
glass, mirror, Ø 74 cm

Endpapers
Aquarel [Water colour] 2001
24 x 32 cm

1
Ogen voor het Oosten
(details) 2000
glass, metal,
245 x 40 x 400 cm
location/collection: Woning-
bouwvereniging Het Oosten,
Amsterdam (NL)

2/3
Ogen voor het Oosten 2000
glass, metal,
245 x 40 x 400 cm
location/collection: Woning-
bouwvereniging Het Oosten,
Amsterdam (NL)

4/5
Spiegelborsten aan de boom
[Mirror breasts on the tree]
1993
glass, mirror, plum-tree,
Ø 60 cm each
collection: Museum voor
Moderne Kunst, Arnhem (NL)

6/7
Studio view 1995
Chesterfield 1995
Chesterfield chair, glass,
130 x 90 x 10 cm
Bed 1994
glass, cloth, wood,
60 x 200 x 120 cm

8
Z.T. 2003
Manifestation 'Jaar van de
boerderij'
['Year of the farm'] 2003,
Frederiksoord (NL)
glass, vegetable garden,
11 x 6 m

9
Hans den Hartog Jager
Maria's

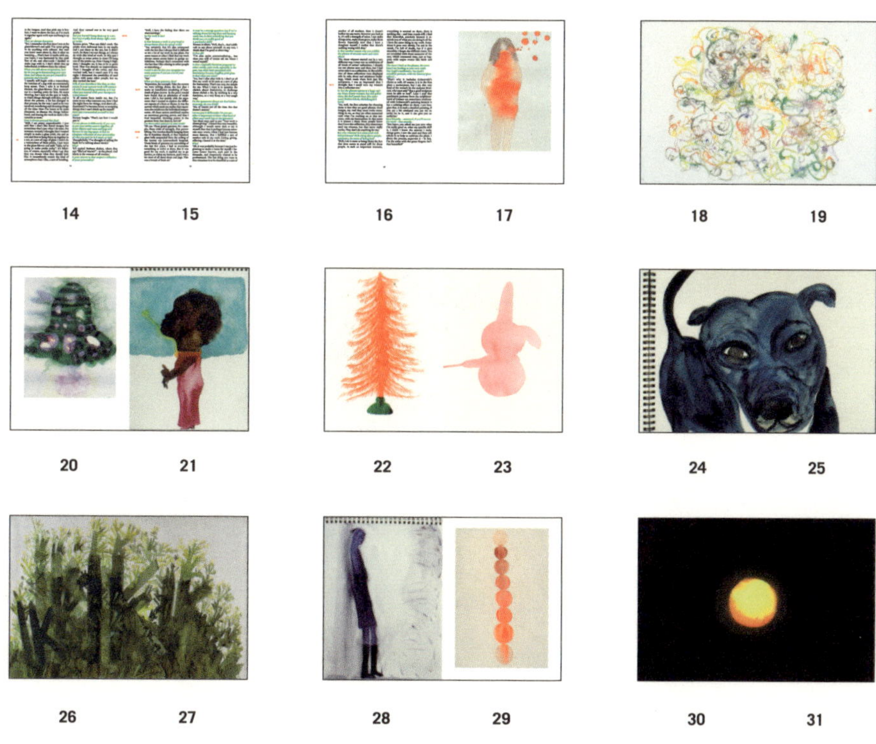

17
Zelfportret [Self-portrait] 2004
water colour, 32 x 24 cm
private collection

18/19
Z.T. 2000
water colour, 152 x 225 cm
collection: Akzo Nobel Art
Foundation (NL)

20/21
Paddestoel [Mushroom] 1999
water colour, 152 x 118 cm

22/23
Rode kerstboom
[Red Christmas-tree] 1995
water colour, 32 x 24 cm
Lullenpot [Pot of pricks] 1998
water colour, 32 x 24 cm

24/25
Zora 1998
water colour, 24 x 32 cm

26/27
Ikken [I's] 1999
water colour, 116 x 155 cm
collection: ABN AMRO (NL)

28/29
Gary Hill 1999
water colour, ballpoint,
24 x 32 cm
Paren [Pairs, pairing] 2002
water colour, 120 x 84 cm
collection: ABN AMRO (NL)

30/31
Oven 1993
water colour, 24 x 32 cm

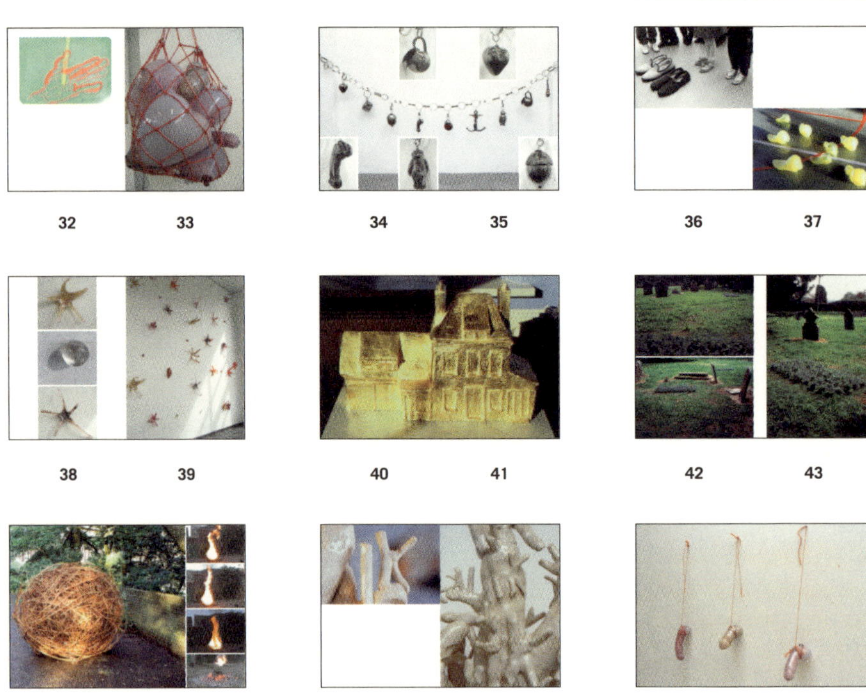

32   33

34   35

36   37

38   39

40   41

42   43

44   45

46   47

48   49

32/33
Hand 1994
water colour, 24 x 32 cm
Orgie [Orgy] 2005
glass, net, 100 x 40 x 60 cm

34/35
Home is where the heart is/ Bedel-ketting [Charm bracelet] 1998
charm bracelet, glass, metal,
360 cm long + details of
bangles, Ø 20-30 cm

36/37
Pantoffels voor de Reus van Rotterdam [Slippers for the
Giant of Rotterdam] 1992
fabric for slippers, sheepskin,
European size 63
collection: Shell, Nederland;
on loan to Museum Boijmans
Van Beuningen, Rotterdam
Gele Muilen
[Yellow Muzzles] 1994
molten glass blown into

wooden shoes, 15 x 30 x 15 cm,
14 x 28 x 14 cm

38/39
*Muurbloempjes
(Centraalbeweging)*
[Wallflowers (Central
movement)] 2003
glass, Ø 8-60 cm
installation, 6 x 8 m
WRA, Diemen (NL)

40/41
Gouden huis
[Golden house] 2001
ceramics, gold leaf,
32 x 47 x 21 cm
collection: Akzo Nobel Art
Foundation (NL)

42/43
Forget-me-nots 2000
5 flower beds of
forget-me-not, 180 x 90 cm
Honiton Festival,
Graveyard Honiton (GB)

44/45
Doornenbol
[Bramble-ball] 1998
rolled bramble-branches,
Ø 160 cm
Vuurbol (Verbranden van de doornenbol) [Fireball, burning of
the bramble-ball] 2000

46/47
Ikken [I's] (details) 1999
ceramics, 36 x 27 x 42 cm

48/49
Jean, Pierre et Claude 2004
glass, rope,
175 x 198 x 30 cm
private collection

50/51
Kan met kleintje [Jug with
small one] (detail) 2001
glass, 40 cm x Ø 35 cm
private collection

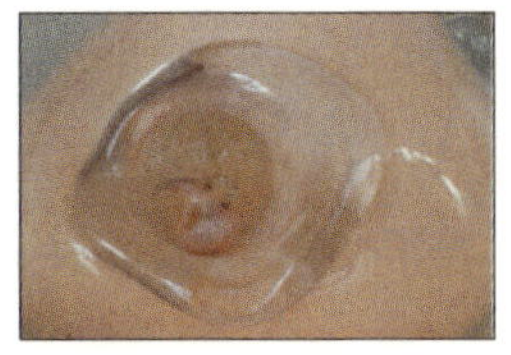
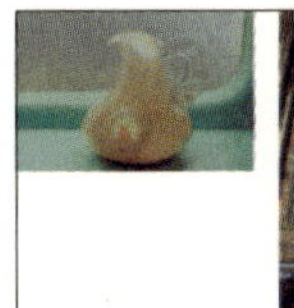
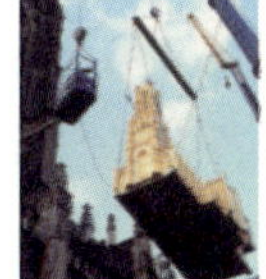

50   51   52   53   54   55

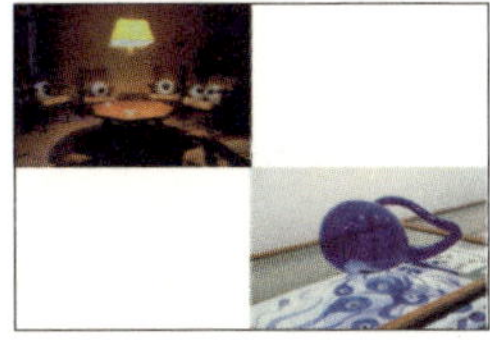
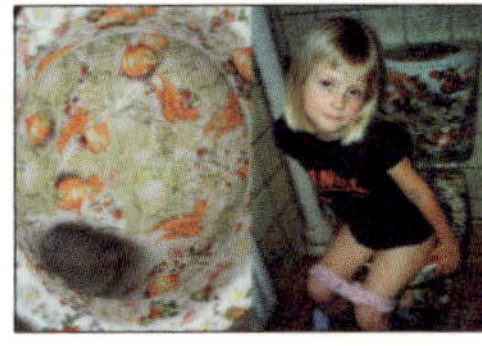
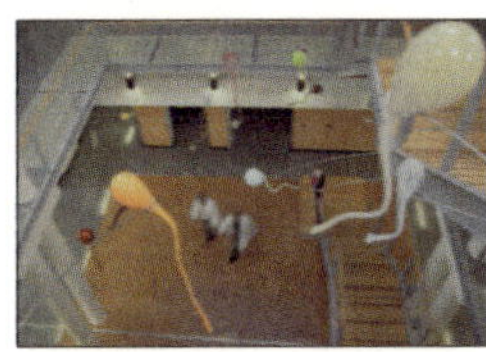

56   57   58   59   60   61

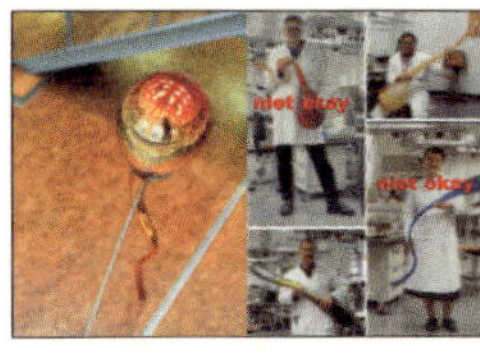
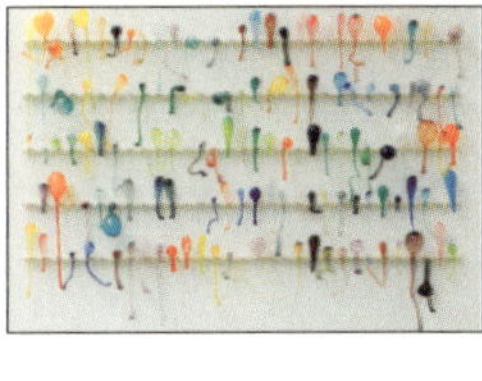
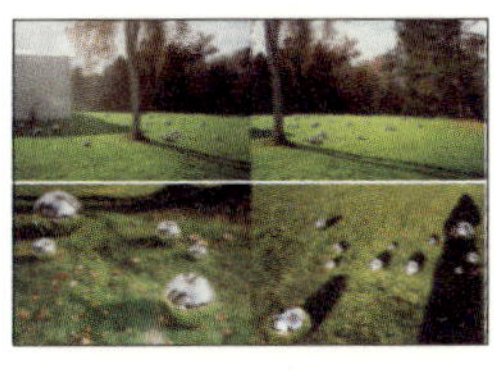

62   63   64   65   66   67

52/53
Kan met kleintje [Jug with small one] 2001
glass, 40 cm x Ø 35 cm
private collection
Mirakel [Miracle] 2001
exhibition 'Sonsbeek 9', 2001,
St. Eusebius church,
Arnhem (NL)
wood, linseed oil,
860 x 700 x 760 cm, 5000 kg,
hangs 30 m high

54/55
Mirakel [Miracle] 2001
exhibition 'Sonsbeek 9', 2001,
St. Eusebius church,
Arnhem (NL)
wood, linseed oil,
860 x 700 x 760 cm, 5000 kg,
hangs 30 m high

56/57
Ogen [Eyes] 2000
exhibition 'Het gekke huis'
[The crazy house],

Wolfheze (NL)
glass, Ø 35 cm
Oog op vitrine
[Eye on show-case]
(detail) 2002
glass, water colours,
40 x 88 x 67 cm

58/59
Toiletpot (Sphinx) [Toilet bowl
(Sphinx)] 1998 (detail)
porcelain with ceramic
transfers, 80 x 40 x 70 cm
collection: Kunstvereniging
Diepenheim (NL)
Toiletpot (Sphinx, jachttaferelen)
[Toilet bowl (Sphinx,
hunting scenes)] 2004
porcelain with ceramic
transfers, 80 x 40 x 70 cm
location: Galerie Fons
Welters, Amsterdam (NL)

60/61
Z.T. 2000
installation in atrium,

CQ-building Organon
glass, stainless steel
collection: Organon, Oss (NL)

62/63
Z.T. (detail) 2000
installation in atrium,
CQ-building Organon
glass, stainless steel
collection: Organon, Oss (NL)
*Laboratory workers at Organon
with parts of Z.T.*
collection: Organon, Oss (NL)

64/65
*Glass colour bubbles nr. 2
(Happy sperm)* 1998
glass, wood, metal,
160 x 180 x 20 cm
private collection

66/67
oooSpiegelbeeldooo
[oooMirror imageooo]
(detail) 2002-2003
128 mirror-glass balls

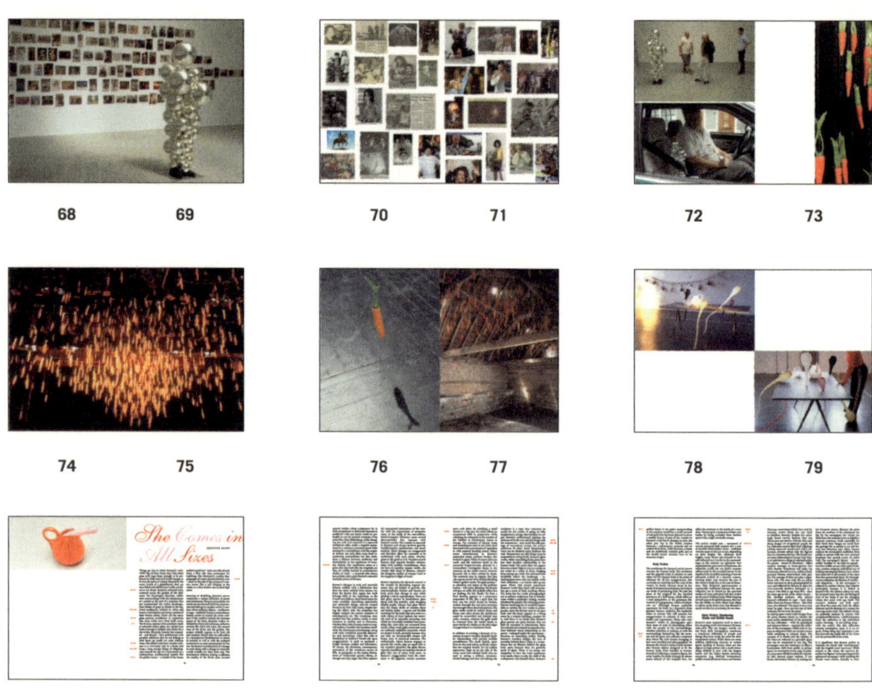

68 69 70 71 72 73

74 75 76 77 78 79

80 81 82 83 84 85

installation in garden
Museum Dhondt-Dhaenens,
Deurle (B)
collection: Museum
Boijmans Van Beuningen,
Rotterdam (NL)

68/69
Spiegelbollenfiguur [Figure of
mirror-glass balls] 2004
exhibition 'Met',
Galerie Fons Welters, 2004
glass, metal, Van Bommel
shoes, 180 cm high
collection: ABN AMRO (NL)
at the background:
Overwinnaars [Survivors]
1985-2005

70/71
Overwinnaars [Survivors] (a
selection) 1985-2005,
work in progress
newspaper clippings,
various sizes, postcards
(see page 128/131)

72/73
Spiegelbollenfiguur [Figure of
mirror-glass balls] 2004
exhibition 'Met',
Galerie Fons Welters, 2004
glass, metal, Van Bommel
shoes, 180 cm high
collection: ABN AMRO (NL)
Spiegelbollenfiguur
[Figure of mirror-glass balls]
model 2003, study for
sculpture Aelbert Cuyp,
Dordrecht (NL)
Christmas-balls, 34 cm high
Wortelregen [Rain of Carrots]
detail 2002
theatre play 'Wortel van glas'
['Carrot of Glass'], in cooperation with Josse De Pauw,
Stefan Perceval
HETPALEIS, Antwerp
glass, nylon, 9 x 7 x 7 m

74/75
Wortelregen
see page 73

76/77
Wortelregen
[Rain of Carrots] (detail) 2002
HETPALEIS, Antwerp
see page 73
Wortel van glas
[Carrot of Glass] 2005
exhibition 25th Poëziezomer
Watou, 'Nous le passage',
Watou (B), 2005
1000 glass carrots, life-size

78/79
Tafel [Table] 1998
wood, glass, metal,
160 x 176 x 150 cm
at the background: *Home is
where the heart is/ Bedelketting*
[Charm bracelet] 1998
charm bracelet, glass, metal,
360 cm long

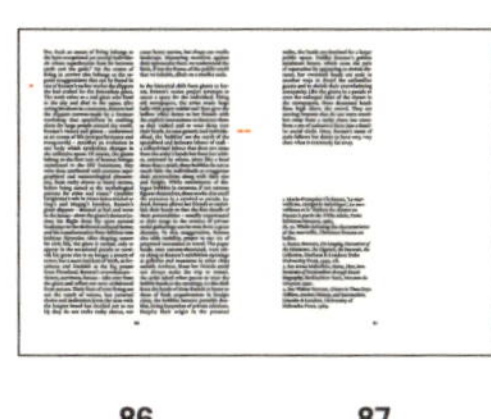
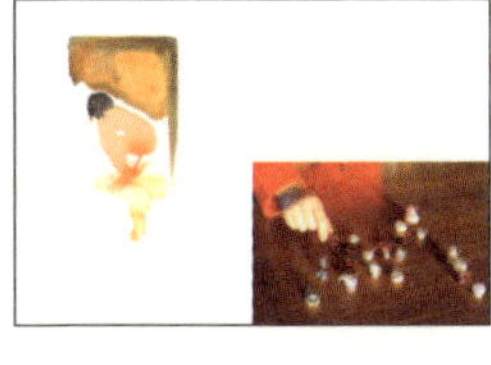
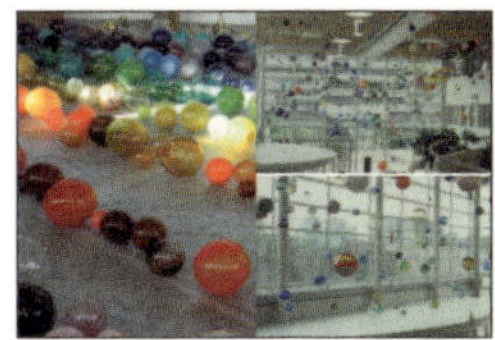

86 87   88 89   90 91

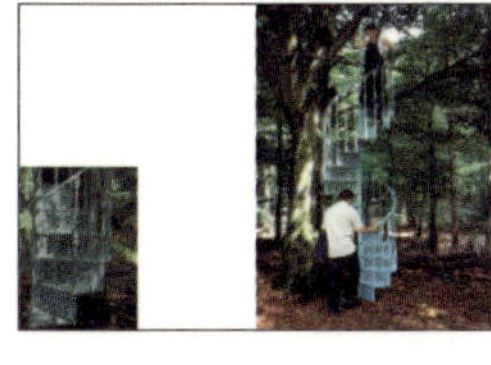
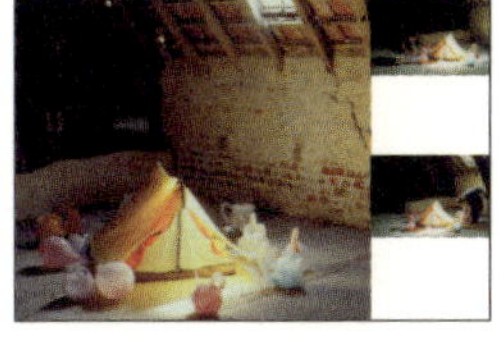

92 93   94 95   96 97

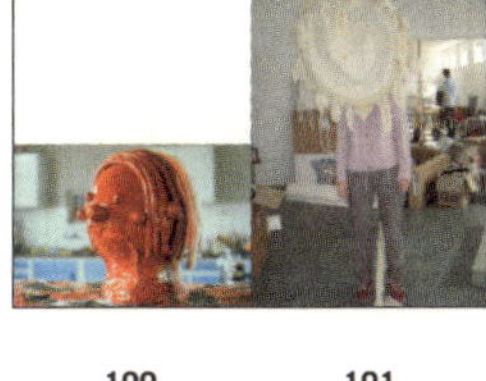
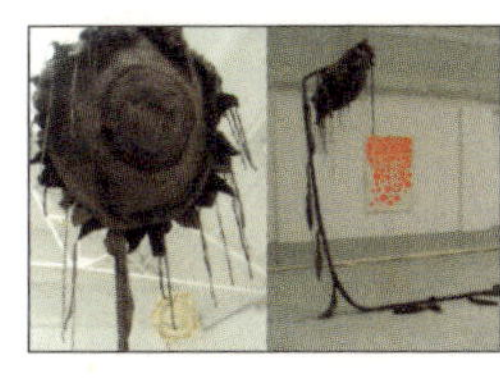

98 99   100 101   102 103

80
Rode kan met tong
[Red jug with tongue] 2001
glass, Ø 40 cm
private collection

81
Jennifer Allen
She Comes in All Sizes

88/89
Pissing woman 1994
water colour, transferred to an
offset print, 31,5 x 23,5 cm
edition by De Vereniging voor
het Museum voor Heden-
daagse Kunst, Ghent
water colour: private
collection
Roze kannetjes
[Pink little jugs] 2000
15 pieces, glass, Ø 2 cm

90/91
Regenboog [Rainbow] 2004
400 glass balls, aluminium
bangles, gold leaf

Antoni van Leeuwenhoek
Hospital, Amsterdam (NL)

92/93
Trap [Staircase] 1999
exhibition 'De soep en de
wolken' ['The soup and the
clouds'], Berg en Bos,
Apeldoorn (NL)
Spanish cast-iron spiral staircase, 370 cm high

94/95
Tentje [Small tent] 1998
exhibition Poëziezomer
Watou, 'Serendipity, The
Borders of Europe',
Watou (B) 1999
canvas, glass, 70 x 150 x 125 cm

96/97
Tros spiegelborsten [Bunch of
mirror breasts] 1996–1999
mirror-glass, wood, rope,
Ø 160 cm collection: Noord-
Brabants Museum,
's-Hertogenbosch (NL)

98/99
Zonnebloemen [Sun flowers]
exhibition 'Home is where
the heart is', Kunstvereniging
Diepenheim, (NL) 1999

100/101
Zelfportret
[Self-portrait] 2000
ceramics, 25 x 25 x 28 cm
Zonnebloem [Sun flower] in
studio 2004
knitted black sheep's wool,
Ø 150 x 900 cm (length)
collection: Nederlands
Textielmuseum, Tilburg (NL)

102/103
Zonnebloem [Sun flower]
detail 2004
knitted black sheep's wool,
exhibition 'Met',
Galerie Fons Welters, 2004
Ø 150 x 900 cm (length)
collection: Nederlands
Textielmuseum, Tilburg (NL)

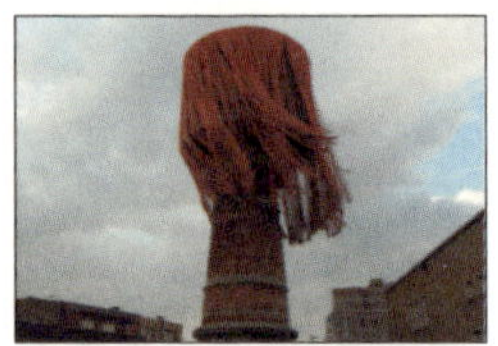
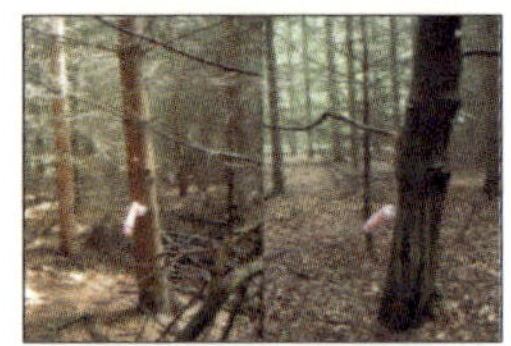
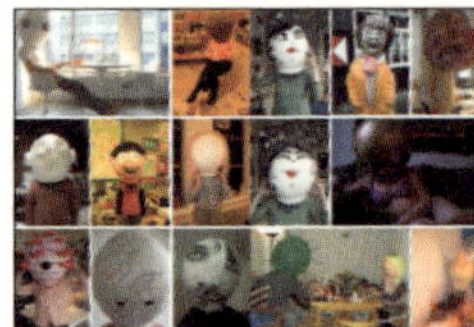

104 105 106 107 108 109

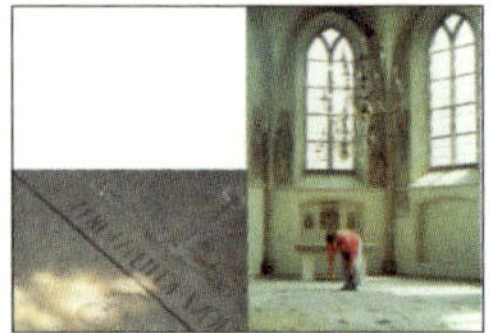
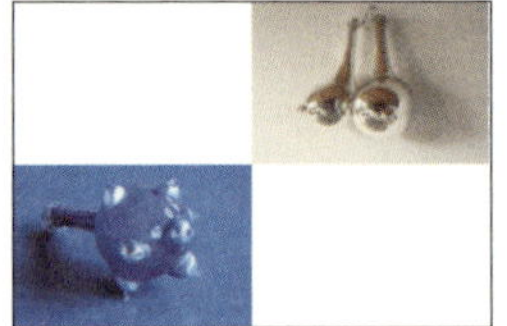
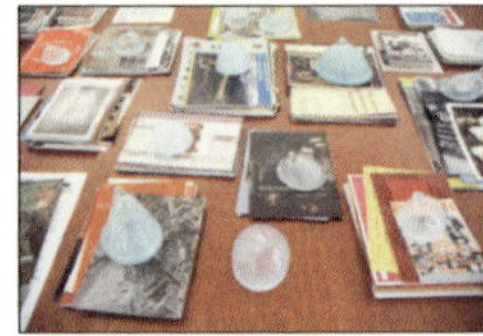

110 111 112 113 114 115

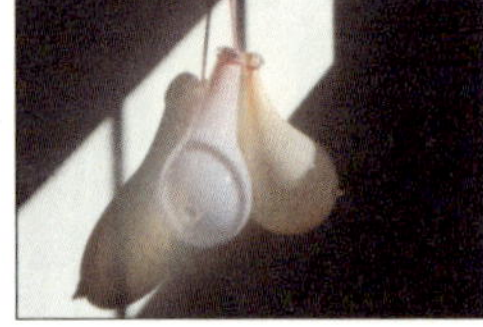
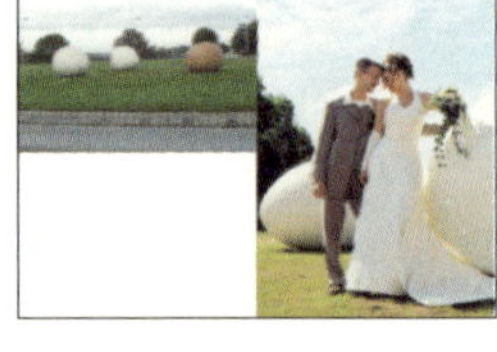
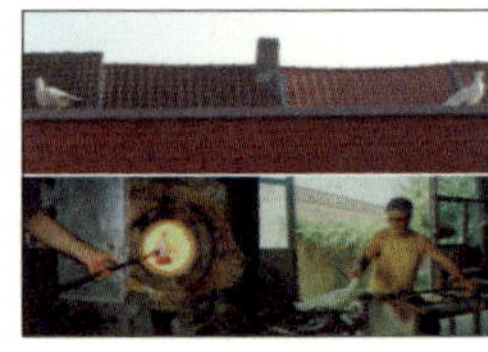

116 117 118 119 120 121

at the background:
Bubbels [Bubbles]
water colour, 155 x 106 cm
collection: AMC,
Amsterdam (NL)

104/105
Pruikentoren [Wig's tower]
2003
exhibition '2003 Beaufort',
coast Belgium
watertower Blankenberge (B),
128 km rope, 40 m high

106/107
*Jean, Pierre et Claude dans le
fôret* [Jean, Piere and Claude
in the woods] 2004
exhibition 'Lustwarande',
Tilburg (NL) 2004
glass, rope, 30 cm

108/109
Friends (Masks) 2005
papier-maché, paint and/or
collage, 55 x Ø 50 cm

110/111
Borne 2000
glass, various sizes

112/113
Goedendag [Mace] 1995
glass, mirror, Ø 74 cm
Spiegelborsten
[Mirror breasts] 1993-2001
mirror-glass, Ø 60 cm
private collection

114/115
Presse-Papiers 1999
glass, invitations for art
events, 5-12 cm
multiple Kunstvereniging
Diepenheim (NL)
private collection

116/117
Z.T. 2003
glass, Ø 60 cm
private collection

118/119
Één plus één is drie (1+1=3) 2002
coloured concrete, Ø 175 cm,
Ø 225 cm, total outline 15 m
roundabout N322, Alem,
west of Zaltbommel (NL)
Één plus één is drie (1+1=3)
detail 2002
coloured concrete, Ø 175 cm,
Ø 225 cm, total outline 15 m
roundabout N322, Alem,
west of Zaltbommel (NL)

120/121
top: *Duiven* [Pigeons] 2005
glass, life-size
Library, De Brugse Poort,
Ghent (Be)
bottom: *Duiven, work in
progress* [Pigeons, work in
progress] 2004
studio Pino Signoretto,
Murano (I)
October 2004

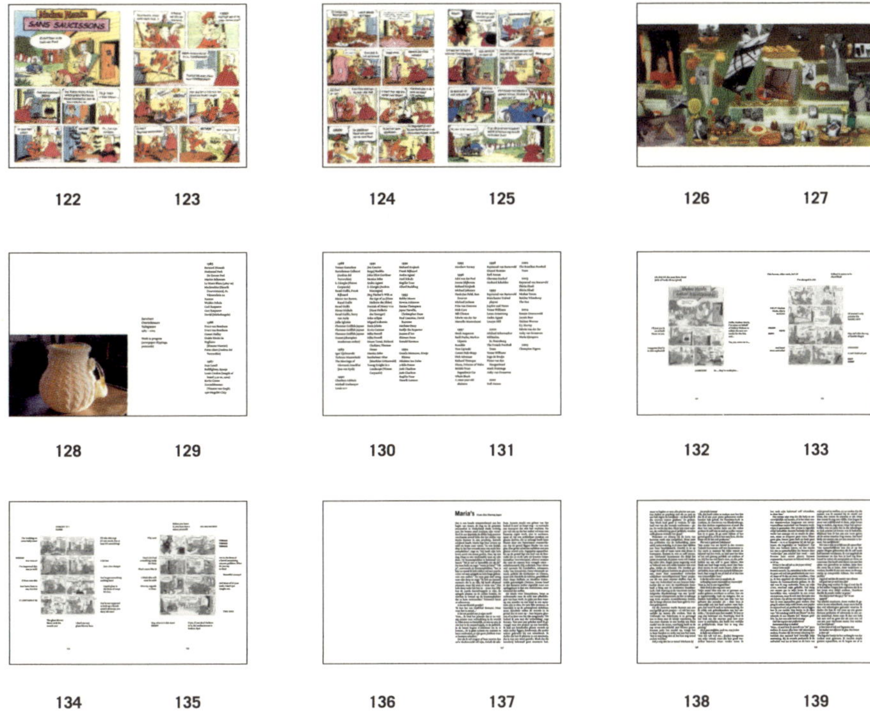

122   123   124   125   126   127

128   129   130   131   132   133

134   135   136   137   138   139

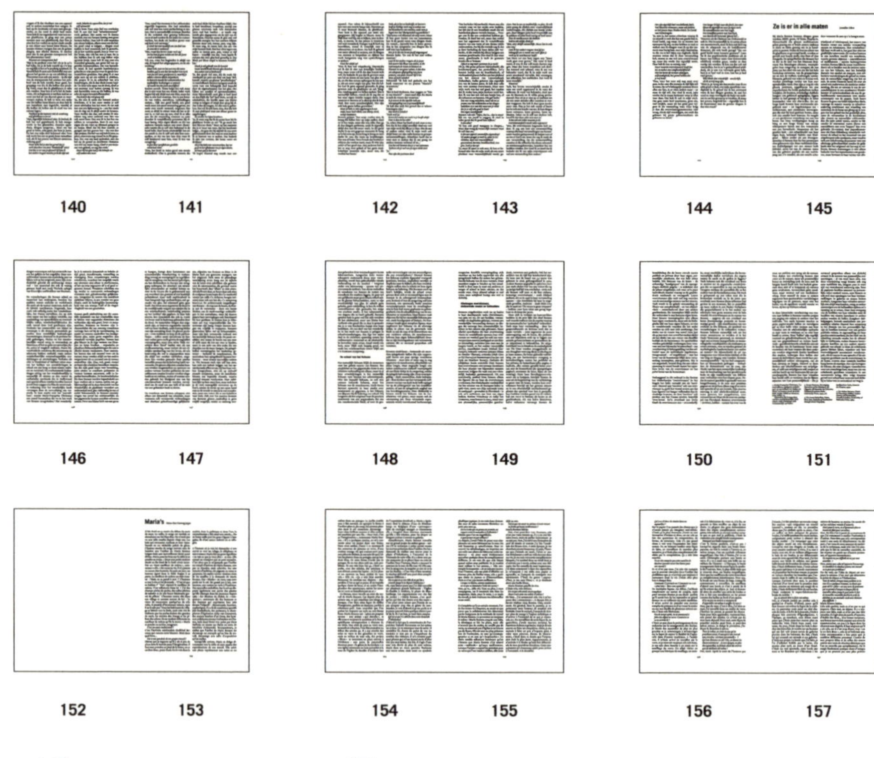

Endpapers
Aquarel [Water colour] 2001
24 x 32 cm

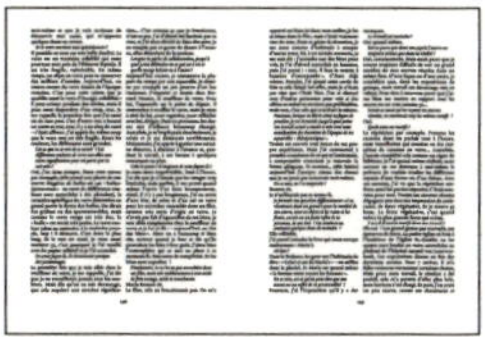

158 159

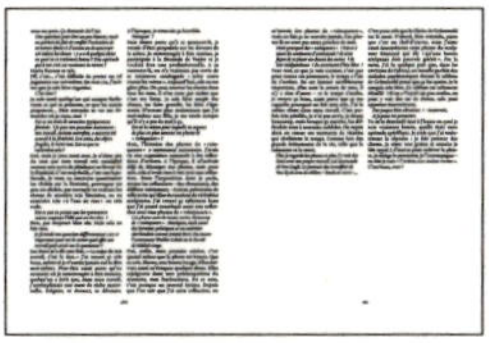

160 161

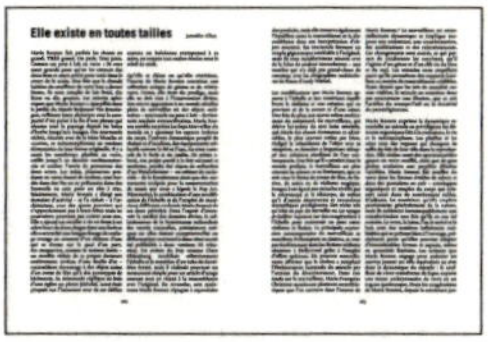

162 163

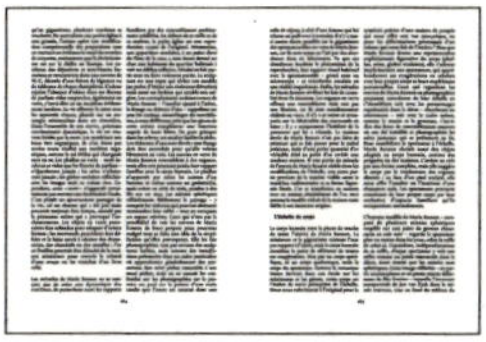

164 165

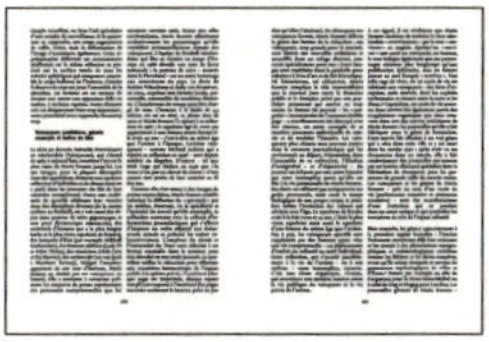

166 167

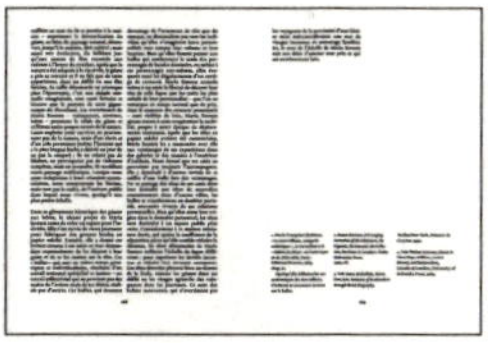

168 169

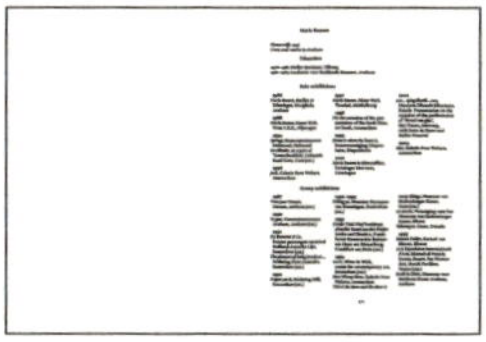

170 171

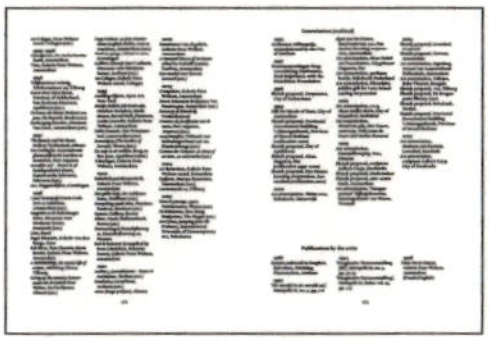

172 173

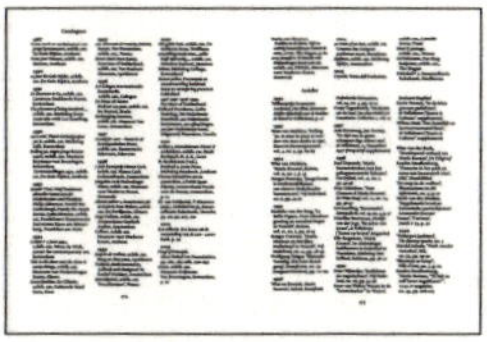

174 175

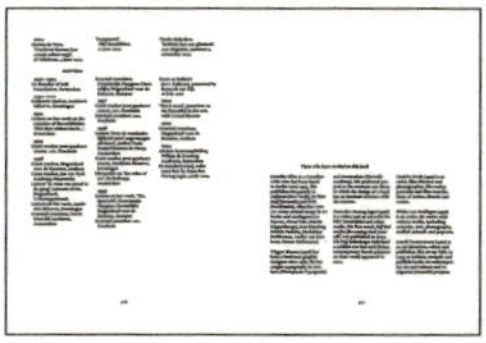

176 177

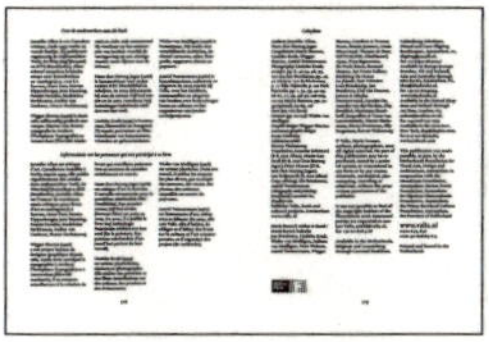

178 179

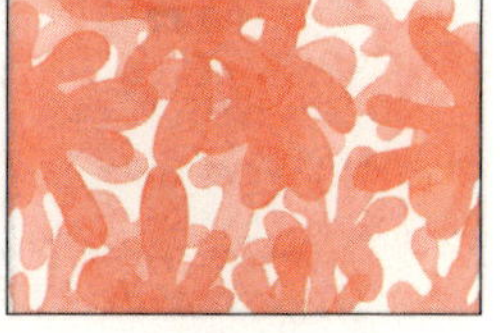

Endpapers

Maria

Maria

Roosen

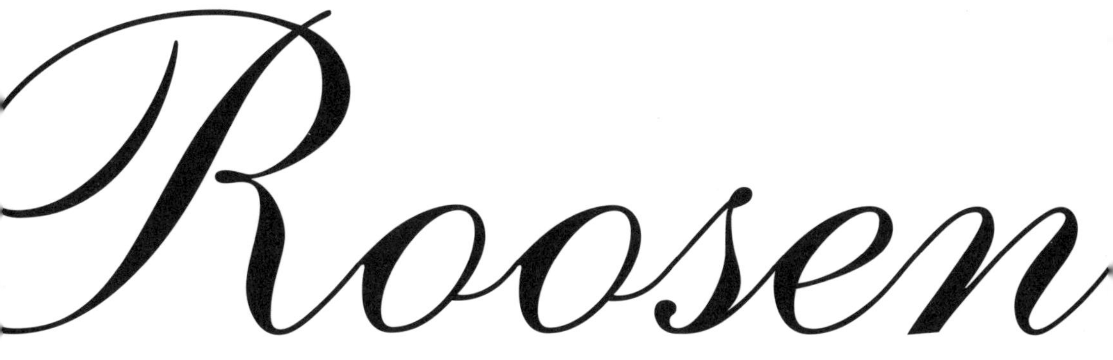

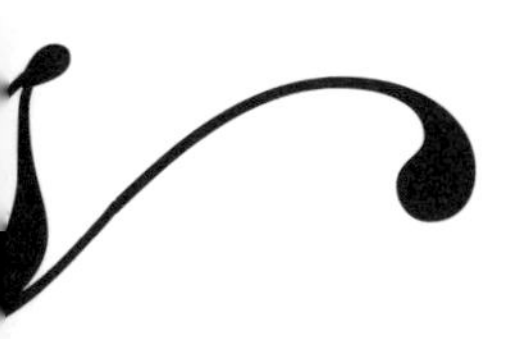

Jennifer Allen

Hans den Hartog Jager

Liedeke Kruk

Wiebo van Mulligen

Valiz, Amsterdam

Voor Tjeu en Do

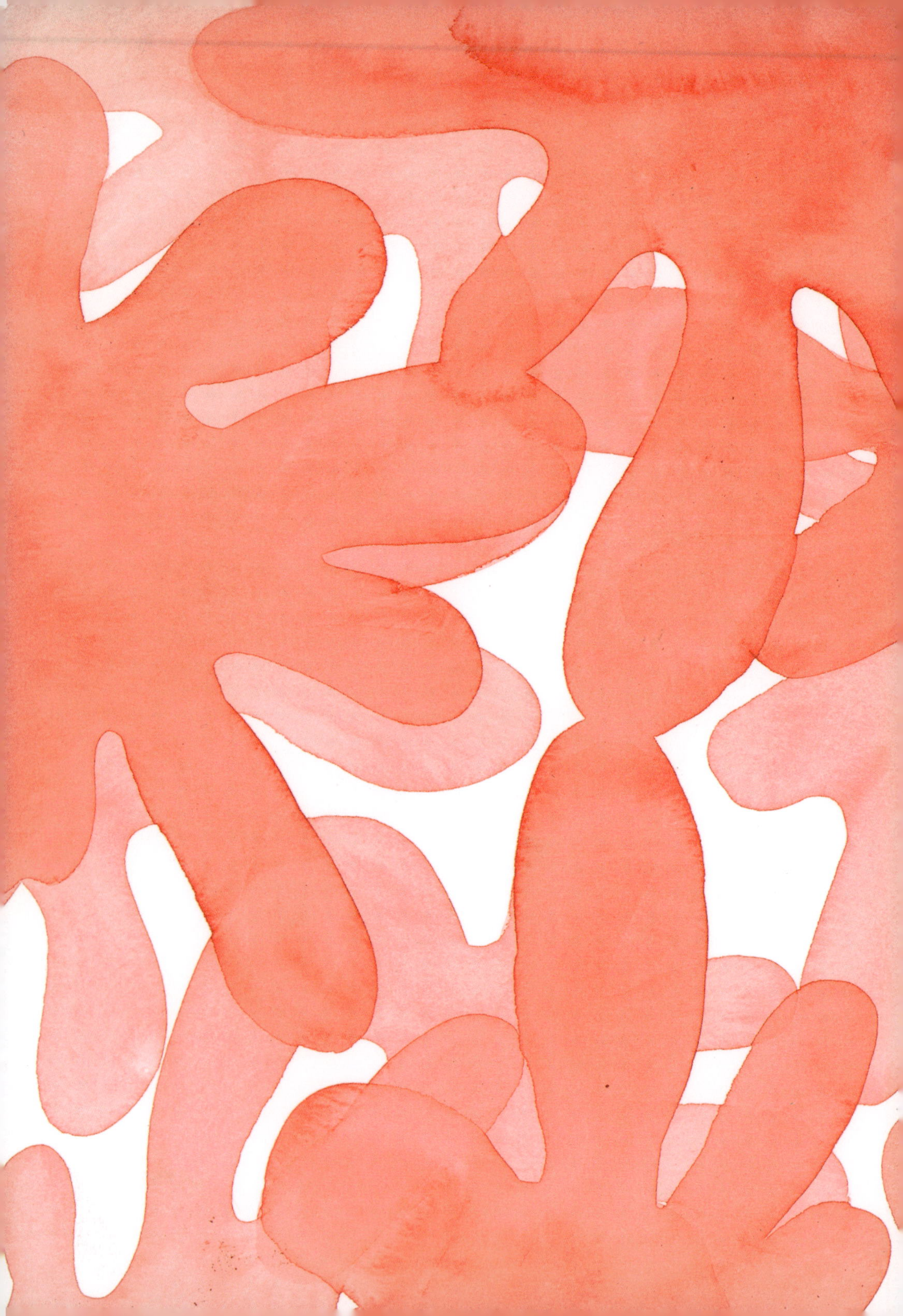